THE

GREEN DICTIONARY

KEY WORDS, IDEAS AND RELATIONSHIPS
FOR THE FUTURE

Compiled by Colin Johnson

An OPTIMA book

First published in 1991 by
Macdonald Optima, a division of
Macdonald & Co. (Publishers) Ltd

A member of Maxwell Macmillan Pergamon Publishing Corporation

British Library Cataloguing in Publication Data

Johnson, Colin
   Green dictionary.
   I. Title
   333.703

   ISBN 0-356-19568-6

Macdonald & Co. (Publishers) Ltd
Orbit House
1 New Fetter Lane
London EC1A 1AR

Typeset in Times Roman by Leaper & Gard Ltd, Bristol

Printed and bound in Great Britain by
The Guernsey Press Co. Ltd, Guernsey, Channel Islands.

Colin Johnson is an author, philosopher and organic farmer. He had a varied career as a design engineer and consultant before commiting himself to a green way of life. He now lives in a housing co-operative on an organically farmed small holding in Wales, producing Soil Association standard food for sale as well as food and fuel for the co-operative.

Colin Johnson is author of many books on health and the environment, and articles on politics, economics and social issues.

CONTENTS

ACKNOWLEDGMENTS

Compiling a dictionary is the modern equivalent of the entrance exam for the ancient Chinese civil service, where there was only one question for applicants: 'Tell us everything you know.' Some are believed to have spent their lives in the examination room. Fortunately the labours of others were available to me in this particular examination of green words and ideas for the future.

Everyone who attempts a dictionary owes much to all those who by their earlier labours have made the task easier. In compiling this green dictionary I acknowledge the contribution made by those touchstones of the present culture, *The Concise Oxford Dictionary*, *Chambers Dictionary*, and the magnificent *Encyclopedia Britannica.* Also, as the frequent references in the text will indicate, I owe much to the work in matters green of John Button. The contribution of all those whose work has been assembled into what I believe will prove a directly accessible reference work to green thoughts and ideas, is, I believe, acknowledged in the references to each entry. Inevitably this belief will prove false, and I must ask those who are omitted to accept that this is due to ignorance rather than intent, and to include themselves in the spirit of the work, over which I hold no copyright and make no claim.

My labours have born fruit with the indispensable help of Arabella Melville, companion on many journeys beyond the front edge, whose qualities have illuminated many areas where mine were lacking. I must also acknowledge the supportive and encouraging role of my agent, David Grossman, and the constructive input of Harriet Griffey and her colleagues at Macdonald Optima. I am aware that my thanks are an inadequate reward to you all.

INTRODUCTION

Humanity has provoked a global crisis that may only be solved by actions in every area of human activity, which, while encompassing everything from the most mundane and everyday to the most esoteric and long-term, will together amount to a collective act of directed evolution for the future.

Diverting current 'progress' from its terminal course and directing our evolution towards a sustainable future springs from what happens in our minds. It involves not so much what we think, although that is obviously important, but rather the ways in which we think. The evolution of new ways of thought for the future will require the evolution of language – the primary means we use to express and communicate our thoughts.

Language evolves naturally and continually. Few could cope today with *The Canterbury Tales* in Chaucer's original 14th-century form, yet finding a point of change which affected the whole language is practically impossible. Words and meanings are continually changing, with slow and lasting tides marked by waves and ripples constantly in motion, reflecting the many uses human societies find for language. New forms and meanings bubble and blend continuously in the form of slang or jargon, some to become permanent in the mainstream, most to disappear once their exclusivity is lost. Ancient and archaic forms are retained for their magic and mystery; they add to the authority of solemn or legal usage, and may also reveal intentions and mechanisms which, although still active, have been lost under more recent veneers of use and assumption.

In modern society language is a multi-faceted medium. Each area of life develops or retains its own 'speak'. Individuals living in almost any part of Britain may have to speak many different sorts of English: the local dialect at home, the nouveau with children, the jargon of job or career, and so on. As a reflection of the reductionist philosophy which dominates Western culture, our many 'speaks' within a parent language tend to separate and isolate each area of society, rather than unite the whole. To update Winston Churchill, we are people isolated by our common languages.

It may be an exaggeration to claim that the fragmentation of language has created barriers to communication, for language, as the outer expression of inner processes, may be only a symptom of

the malaise from which we suffer. Beneath the divisions and frag-
mentations which mark our use of words, our common communication has gone underground, it has slipped below the outposts of
cliché, headline and catchphrase, into the realm of assumption.
Thus the charlatan can say 'I am sure we all know what we mean
by ...' And he is right except, in the absence of any statement of
what is actually meant, the assumption, which may be different for
each of us, is accepted as common to us all. In the most complex
and fast-moving culture humanity has produced, meaning has been
reduced to shared emotion and prejudice. The charlatan's trick is
most often used by defenders of the status quo, or other reaction-
aries. 'We all know what we mean by right and proper, green,
nuclear power, pornography, freedom, reasonable, etc., etc.' The
danger is that the more we rely on assumptions, those deeply
implanted cultural values, the less we are able to address the reality
of issues before us.

Even with words and ideas upfront in open communication,
greens have problems. Our present shared linguistic repertoire
contains comparatively little, in words or concepts, which
addresses the needs of the future. Thus the symbiosis between
language and culture tends to act against change for the future;
they form parts of a self-sustaining system which, as a whole, is
unsustainable.

Economics brings all these problems together. Economics must
be one of the most commonly addressed socio-political topics, yet
few have any understanding or education relevant to the subject.
The words used – inflation, GNP, trading deficit, and so on – are
all traded on the basis of assumption. Any underlying reality for
the human creation we know as economics, such as the bearing
capacity of the earth, finite resources, and so on, is ignored. Thus,
within the grey terminal system, there can be a 'green' economic
proposition based upon the notion that natural resources and
global dynamics can be priced to fit them into the present market
model of economic activity. In the absence of any other language
or ideas of economics, the terminal grey culture can subvert green
aspiration and deny or pervert its ideals. The unsatisfactory past is
carried forward to predetermine the future because we don't know
what we are talking about.

The Green Dictionary is intended to be a part of the process
which seeks to serve the needs of the future. It addresses the need
for a common global culture. That does not mean that we should
all become the same, living as parts of a uniform monolithic whole.

Rather, the need is for a common foundation, based upon the reality of life on earth, its limits and possibilities and the terms within which life may be indefinitely sustainable; or, if you prefer, for a thin cultural umbrella under which diversity among humanity may shelter and all life fulfil its potential. Whichever analogy you choose – perhaps a combination of both, forming a structure within which all life is held – words and ideas are needed to describe the requirements and dynamics of the processes essential to the creation of such a desirable reality. These words and ideas are the necessary tools, both for conscious evolution and for the broad single purpose of the creation of sustainable life on earth.

At times of great change in the tide of human history, new words emerge and old ones extend or take on new meanings as communication chases the evolution of new ideas. The last decade of the 20th century is such a time; it is a truism that those of us alive in this decade confront choices which will direct the fate of the world and most of its life stock for aeons to come. We have a vital need to communicate new ideas, new perceptions, new models of ways of living which are compatible with the totality of life on earth.

With humanity speaking around six major, thirty secondary, and countless tertiary languages, each subject to an infinity of dialects and variations, the words themselves must become secondary to the ideas they represent. Humanity needs to share a clear understanding of these ideas, an understanding which can transcend individual languages. For it is only by this means that we will create the foundation of our vital global culture. Words, in whatever language, are keys which unlock particular concepts.

In times of change, both keys and concepts are subject to change. This book should not be seen as an authoritative final source, but as a guide to essential territory which is undergoing rapid and unpredictable change. We all run the risk faced by the publishers of the 1990 tourist guide to Berlin ('the divided city'), which unfortunately went to press in September 1989. While any errors caused by change are unlikely to be of that magnitude, nevertheless if this work does contain such errors, because things have evolved or changed for the better towards the just and sustainable future we all desire, they should be welcomed. Indeed, I hope that by using this book as a guide each reader will become a factor in the changes that will help to make it obsolete. If, instead of detailing key words, ideas and relationships for the future, the book were to become a historical record of part of the means by which humanity secured the future of life on earth, it could be shelved to gather quiet dust in a forgotten corner while life fulfils its potential for the celebration of heaven on earth.

For now, however, new dictionaries need to transmit the ideas which we all need to share for the future. Without such common perception the forces which are generated by our division will destroy us and much else in the world. Within a consciously created unity there can be infinite diversity – of language, form, culture and ways of life. *The Green Dictionary* is intended to contribute to the creation of the human cultural umbrella under which all peoples and all life may shelter. We share one earth and one destiny; to survive and sustain we must share one minimal vital culture.

NOTES ON FORM AND USE

Wherever possible entries have been given a standard format.

ENTRY, entries (aka – also known as – **door**) Will be explained in the simplest current form first. The 'grey' meaning will be given first: as a means of controlling or regulating access; followed by the green or extended new meaning: an open point of access, inclusivity and choice.

Secondary meanings or compounds will follow, first by 'suffix':

ENTRY POINT

And then by 'prefix':

SIDE ENTRY

Other related meanings or uses of 'entry', such as 'double entry', will be referred on to the most appropriate heading, as:

DOUBLE ENTRY see **accounts**.

Within the entry, other *words* or *ideas* which appear in the dictionary will be given in *italics* to indicate the relationships of the *words* and *ideas*.

Also authors and quotations will be referenced numerically.[1]

At the end of the entry, there will be three further sections:

Relationships Will cross-refer the principal concepts related to this entry to other entries, such as **fence, wall, gate**.
See also Will give secondary or opposing relationships in other entries, as **closed, shut, access**.
References
1 My use of 'references', while usually referring to the source of a particular thing, has been extended to cover notes and the development of ancillary matters. Its meaning should not be interpreted in the strict academic sense.

Use *The Green Dictionary* as any other dictionary, with one important difference: follow through the relationships. Everything is connected to everything else. Part of our conscious evolution requires that we begin to think in terms of the relationships between things, rather than simply of things themselves.

If you have no particular word in mind, the following may get you into the possibilities of the networks of meaning which may be constructed from the relationships within the dictionary:

Grey terminal culture teaches us to see things in terms of simple single issues, of *linear* arrangements of cause and effect *structured* in *hierarchies* of interest, dominance or *power*. This view of *reality* is as *unbalanced* as the effects it is *projecting* into the world. The *green* understanding is that this way of thinking amounts to a form of mental imprisonment; things just aren't like that.

Green sustainable culture will be based on the understanding that everything is more complex than it may appear; that the *processes* of *nature* are *cyclic* rather than *linear*; that ultimately everything is connected with everything else and that connected things tend to have *synergistic relationships*. Most things in *nature* are arranged in *matrices*, from which suitable *networks* are structured which express the *interrelationships* of their *existence*. It is these patterns which we have to understand; indeed our ways of thought must reflect this understanding, *shifting* from the *hierarchy* to the *matrix*. In doing this our ways of thinking will have *evolved*, so that their pattern more closely matches the working pattern of our brains.

In a *universe* alive with its own logic, pursuing *infinite cycles* in *time* and space, the affairs of a minor planet may lack significance. For each of us, experiencing our brief once-in-eternity existence, those affairs must become our principal concerns. The human *objective* should be nothing less than the *creation* of heaven on this *earth* – heaven that allows for all and for the circumstances of each age, heaven that will endure until true Armageddon when our *sustaining* star becomes unstable and the molecules of *life* are once more scattered from their temporary planetary home, scattered to chance in space and *time*. The *green objective* is this *creation*; for our journey from here to eternity nothing less will do. To reject the challenge, to *sink* passively into *grey terminality*, would amount to a denial of our humanity; to succeed may be the ultimate fulfilment of our *potential*.

ACID RAIN (first recorded use 1872, Robert Angus Smith, in *Air and Rain: The Beginnings of a Chemical Climatology*) Rain or other atmospheric precipitation which is more than normally acid.[1] Normal rain is a very weak acid. Small amounts of various naturally occurring oxides mix with atmospheric water to form weak acid solutions, e.g. carbon dioxide produces weak carbonic acid. Normal rain slowly etches rocks and minerals, releasing small amounts of chemicals. In this way the planetary water cycle contributes to the circulation of the many substances necessary to *life* processes.

Acid rain is caused by increased concentrations of some oxides in the atmosphere produced by burning *fossil fuels,* such as coal in power stations and petrol in cars. The exhaust gases produced contain concentrated chemical oxides, including those of sulphur and nitrogen. Sulphur dioxide (SO_2) mixes with water (H_2O) to form sulphuric acid (H_2SO_4), while nitrous oxides form nitric acids.

Acid rain is excessively corrosive; it dissolves chemicals out of soil, which normal rain does not – for example aluminium which poisons people and lakes – and damages forests. Damp acid air damages *trees,* causes measurable increases in respiratory diseases and attacks the fabric of buildings. Illness is also caused by drinking acid water that may contain excesses of dissolved metals.

Acid rain is the primary example of human action distorting a natural planetary cycle and tipping it into a catastrophic imbalance. The destruction of forests will add to climatic distortion, and changing rainfall patterns could spread the effects of acid rain, further distorting the climate, thus adding to the overall greenhouse effect.

<u>Relationships</u>   **greenhouse effect, economic growth, energy, expectations.**

<u>See also</u>   **waldsterben, fossil fuels, pollution, trees.**

<u>References</u>

1 Acidity and alkalinity are measured by reference to the pH scale. A pH of 7 is neutral, pH 6 and below is acid.

2 See Fred Pearce, 1987, *Acid Rain: What is It, and What is It Doing to Us?* Penguin Books, London.

ACTIONS   Things people do – 'Watch what they do, rather than what they say.'
Relationships   **honesty.**

AD HOC (Latin = for this particular purpose)   Principle of temporary organisation around a declared objective – 'Let ad hocery rule!'[1]
A means of organising which avoids bureaucratic or institutional forms while achieving desired ends. The focus of an ad hoc group is on *function* rather than the social standing or position of its members; on purpose rather than prestige or power. Ad hoc groups are open to anyone interested in their purpose.
Relationships   **affinity group, consensus, inclusive.**
See also   **agenda.**
References
1 Peter Cadogan, trying to reorganise the Aldermaston March to take advantage of the 'Species for Peace' revelations.

ADAPT   Change, make suitable or fit for different use, purpose, or circumstances.
ADAPTATION   (see **anticipation**) Process of, or capacity for, adapting, originally used primarily in biology, subsequently in *ecology.*
Part of the *evolutionary dynamic* where *life* processes interact with the *environment,* either by adjusting to the *environment* or by adjusting the *environment* to *needs.*
Since humanity settled to agriculture, some 20,000 years ago, our *progress* has amounted to the increasing adaptation of the *environment* to suit our *needs.* Science and *technology* have vastly increased our ability to alter the *environment.* The *global predicament* is the result of unforeseen effects of the *processes* and scale involved (see **limits**).
In non-human *evolution* adaptation may enable a species to maintain its relative *position* in the *web of life,* in response either to *environmental changes* or to *evolutionary* adaptation by other species, or it may be a *change* which may give one species an apparent advantage in relation to others. Within the total *biosphere* there is continual *change* as the physical *environment evolves* and *life* adapts to new circumstances. However *life* also acts and adapts

to stabilise the *global environment*[1], so overall *change* tends to be very slow, the whole experienced at any point in time as *dynamic stability.* If one species adapts in a way which causes local *imbalance,* usually by excessive *numbers,* the web adjusts by a combination of *means,* such as disease, *limits* to *food* supplies, or increases in predators, to restore *balance.*

Human adaptation has had the effect of removing the *natural* constraints on our *position* within the *biosphere.* The result is the population explosion which is overwhelming the planet. *Numbers,* combined with *technology,* are both *consuming* the planet and destroying its ability to restore *balance.* Some see this as a *Gaian* adaptation to the human threat; the planet will adapt, making *life* impossible for humans, and possibly for all large mammalian *life* forms.

In the green view adaptation to *sustainable* ways of *living* requires that humans accept the *inherent limits* of *nature* and the *environment,* and seek *fulfilment* within them.

Relationships   **anticipation, balance, limits, cycle of life.**

See also   **Gaia, evolution, morphology, numbers.**

References

1 See J.E. Lovelock, 1979, *Gaia: A New Look at Life on Earth,* Oxford University Press, Oxford, England; 1989, *The Ages of Gaia: a Biology of Our Living Earth,* Oxford University Press, Oxford, England.

AFFINITY GROUP   Modern origin in the *non-violent direct action* peace and civil rights groups during the 1960s and 1970s in America. During preparations for the march on Montgomery, Alabama, participants enrolled in schools of non-violence, where as well as practising dealing with racist provocation and violence, bonds were formed between the demonstrators; also for the action in Nashville, Tennessee, to desegregate the lunch counters, buses and public toilets. First specifically defined as such at the Seabrook anti-nuclear action, USA, 1977.

An *ad hoc* group formed for a common purpose. Members of the group get to know and trust each other, reach decisions by *consensus,* develop mutual understanding to the point where any one may speak for all, generally seeking to *create* bonds which allow them to act as one, blending and sharing their emotional, physical and intellectual strengths. Such affinity groups provide support and *motivation structures,* developing *synergy* around the purpose for which they were formed.

Such groups tend to form where small numbers reject oppression. People gather in groups, hold hands, touch hearts, feel/share the affinity of the cause, and channel energy, focusing love. At many points in history people have faced death under such circumstances; it is something people will do as an expression of the strength of their beliefs.

Relationships   **attunement, synergy, morphology**.

See also   **ad hoc, consensus**.

AGE OF AQUARIUS   see **Aquarius**.

AGENDA   Things to be done; usually a list of items of business for discussion and decision.

HIDDEN AGENDA   Origin believed to be in medical sociology, the hidden agenda of medical schools, where it was observed that paramedics could be trained to general practitioner level in two years, whereas it takes seven to nine years to train a doctor. The extra time was required by the hidden agenda, learning to fulfil the *socio-cultural position* of a doctor, as opposed to the medical *function*. Part of this *socio-cultural* fulfilment is the *symbiosis* between individual medical students and medical *institutions*.

A hidden agenda comprises the undeclared aims or things done, hidden effects or purposes, within the *dynamic* of various *processes*. Because they are hidden, such agenda may only be revealed by observation or experience of the *process* involved. *Trees* may be seen as plants whose agenda is the common simple one of all *life* – to *grow* and reproduce. Their hidden agenda may be seen as their contribution to climatic stabilisation for the benefit of all *life*, and habitat provision for many species.

In human affairs the *existence* of hidden agenda are most apparent in *institutional forms* of organisation. The declared purpose becomes perverted by the hidden agenda; governments never keep their promises, the revolution is always betrayed. The *needs* of the *institution* take precedence over the *needs* of people. The importance of the *institutional* hidden agenda lies in its capacity for *environmental* destruction; when combined with the effects of the hidden agenda of the *genetic* imperative to increase population, the *global predicament* may be seen as the fulfilment of the hidden agenda of Western industrial *culture*.

Relationships   **institution, life, power**.

See also   **culture**.

AGRIBUSINESS   see **chemiculture.**

AGRICIDE (see **chemiculture**)   Term used by organic farmers to describe the effects of conventional agriculture.

The inevitable destruction of the ability of the *land* to support *life* by *grey* farming practices, mainly by the use of *biocides* and intensive *mono-culture*. As industrial *intensive* farming reduces the living content of vital top-soil, it becomes unable to resist normal (sic) weathering and is washed away by rain, such soil loss being an increasing phenomenon around the world.

The historical process whereby over-use and pressure of *numbers* turn fertile soil to desert. North Africa was the corn basket of the Roman empire; the vast unmeasured *diversity* of the Amazon rainforest is reduced to sterile sand in a matter of years via the chainsaw and beefburger ranching.

<u>Relationships</u>   **chemiculture, biocide, food,** total **toxic** overload.
<u>See also</u>   **organic, land.**

ALTERNATIVES   Choice of things which are mutually exclusive; one thing available in place of another.

Alternative has come to be used to define anything which is different from the mainstream *choice* within *culture*. Since such differences remain part of the *culture* which defines them, alternative predominantly means one thing in place of another, rather than a thing which *excludes* another. Thus *alternative* medicine subscribes to the conventional medical *ethic* of curing disease, rather than the true alternative of *creating health*. Such alternatives are partial substitutes only, marked by *change* at one level with conformity at many others; that is, superficial practical change while the underlying mainstream ideology (the source of the problem) is maintained.

A true alternative would have a different frame of reference to the accepted *choice*. The threat of alternatives to the status quo is defused by containing their ultimate *objectives* within the frame of reference of current *culture*.

Green alternatives are those things which *exclude* the conventional *grey option* by differences in their *structural* reference. True alternatives are necessary if a break with *terminality* is to be effected and a *sustainable culture created*. However, it would be preferable if the distinction of 'alternative' were dropped; things are either *green* and *sustainable*, or not. Within *green culture* a series of equally valid *options* could be *created*. *Options* within *sustainable* parameters should be seen as one thing in place of another. For the present it is the unsatisfactory *cultural* context which provokes the search for alternatives.

Relationships   **philosophy**.

See also   **sustainability**.

ALTRUISM   Regard for others as a principle of action.

A *life-positive value* which should be *extended* and *amplified*.

Greens believe regard for others should be *extended* progressively, in the *form* of *rights*, to all *life*. The same may also be true for its *environment*, in the planetary and cosmic context. All things are connected; all *life* within the planetary web constantly interacts with its *environment* in the *Gaian whole*; *values* applicable to one must be applicable to all.

Relationships   **perspective, rights**.

See also   **ethics, spirituality**.

AMPLIFIED MAN   The concept originated by George Girodias[1] to summarise modern man, extended by access to technology and energy, given speed to shrink and degrade the world.

> Taken in its entirety, the increase in mankind's strength has brought about a decisive, many-sided shift in the balance of strength between man and earth. Nature, once a harsh and feared master, now lies in subjection, and needs protection against man's powers. Yet because man, no matter what intellectual and technical heights he may scale, remains embedded in nature, the balance has shifted against him, too, and the threat that he poses to the earth is a threat to him as well.[2]

Relationships   **terminal culture, extension**.

See also   **nature, Gaia**.

References

1 George Girodias, 1990, *Being Fair to Posterity*, paper given to The Academic Inn/Council for Posterity, 24 Abercorn Place, London NW8 9XP, England.

2 Jonathan Schell, 1982, *The Fate of the Earth*, Picador, London.

ANARCHY   Absence of government in a society.

More properly the absence of imposed, authoritarian, government in society.

Positively, the belief that people can manage their affairs without such government.

ANARCHISM

How would you feel if you discovered that the society in which you would really like to live was already here, apart from a few little local difficulties like exploitation, war, dictatorship and starvation? An anarchist society, a society which organises itself without authority, is always in existence, buried beneath the snow, buried under the weight of the state and its bureaucracy, capitalism and its waste, privilege and its injustices, nationalism and its suicidal loyalties, religious differences and their super-stitious separatism.[1]

ANARCHIST   One who believes that all government should be abolished.

In the *grey* world it is assumed that the absence of government – that is, of a *system* of imposed authority in society – automatically brings disorder. It is also assumed that anarchy is synonymous with *chaos.*

For many *greens* anarchy means *freedom* and individual *responsibility.* It is the basis of *green social structures.* As a *political philosophy* anarchism centres on the belief that no individual should have authority over another, unless that authority is freely given and accepted and may be freely revoked or denied. ('Anarchism, if it means anything at all, is trying to remove coercive authority from human relationships': Alan Albon).

Under its universal banner of *freedom,* anarchism has inspired many lines of thought and expression. Its scope ranges from the romantic, egotistical and highly individual, to various, not always compatible, social blends of anarcho-syndicalism, communism and pacifism. Although there may be as many sorts of anarchism as there are anarchists, and specific references to authoritative sources are rarely possible, there are classics and biographies which give the sources of various areas of anarchist thought.[2] The best known contributor to current green/anarchist thought is Murray Bookchin.[3]

The increasing *power* of the *institutional* nation state in the 20th century, wherein each individual may be disposed as required by the state and the *structure of life* is prescribed by compatible institutions, the rules and demands of which the individual must observe, has caused anarchists to concentrate their *opposition* to authority in its most ubiquitous manifestation, the nation state and its *structure* of government. For most people, nurtured in close *symbiosis* with authoritarian *culture,* it is easy to overlook the fact that the *structures* which direct our lives are human constructions, and not immutable parts of some *natural* order.

The logic of the *political principles* of anarchy become more attractive as the *terminal nature* of the current *culture* emerges. It is bitterly opposed by the vested interests of the status quo, since it involves the devolution of *power* to the individual, and reformation of the *economic order.*

Contrary to the belief propagated by the status quo, anarchism is not, indeed cannot be, coercive. My *freedom* ends where another's begins. Anarchists should not be violent, unless reacting to violence, and they cannot force their views on others, since that would be a denial of the *freedom* to believe otherwise. Anarchy therefore has to accept the paradoxes of compromise in all human affairs (although at times the *process* may be protracted and vociferous).

'Whether or not it is called anarchism, a belief in individual freedom and responsibility and the right not to be coerced by arbitrary authority is central to green thinking.'[4]

Relationships   **freedom, responsibility, community, rainbow alliance, structure, matrix.**

See also   **authority, hierarchy, rights, institutions.**

References

1 Colin Ward, 1989, quoted in a *Freedom* supplement, Freedom Press, Angel Alley, 84b Whitechapel High Street, London E1 7QX.

2 Anarchist classics are mainly of historical interest since in general they share the assumptions of pre-green culture, if differing from that culture on fundamental issues such as the question of authority (principally in the relationship of person to state) and the organisation of industry and the economy. Nevertheless they represent the work of thinkers who stood against main features of the predominant culture around them. See:

George Woodcock, 1956, *Pierre-Joseph Proudhon, a Biography*, Routledge & Kegan Paul, London.

Vernon Richards, 1965, *Errico Malatesta: His Life and Ideas*, Freedom Press, London.

Prince Petr (Peter) Kropotkin, 1902, *Mutual Aid: A Factor in Evolution*, undated edition by Extending Horizon Books, Boston, USA. (A view of evolution which proposes that co-operation was more important than competition in evolution. An alternative to the Darwinian view and its religious opposition) 1899, *Fields, Factories and Workshops Tomorrow*; 1974 edition, George Allen & Unwin, London.

3 Murray Bookchin, 1974, *Post-Scarcity Anarchism*, Wildwood House, London.

4 John Button, 1988, *A Dictionary of Green Ideas: Vocabulary for a Sane and Sustainable Future*, Routledge & Kegan Paul, London.

In 1886 Petr Kropotkin, with others, founded Freedom Press to publish anarchist propaganda. The press and bookshop survive, as does the journal *Freedom*. All may be found in Angel Alley, 84b Whitechapel High Street, London E1 7QX. In 1986,

Freedom: A Hundred Years was published, a representative collection of anarchist thought at that time – a good introduction.

ANIMAL RIGHTS   see **rights**.

ANTICIPATE   Discuss, consider, use, spend; prepare for, expect, before the due or natural time.

ANTICIPATION   In the green use of anticipation the concept of the natural time of an *event* or *process* is fundamental. It is also essential to the concept of balance (see **balance**).

> To everything there is a season, and a time to every purpose under the heaven.
>
> A time to be born, and a time to die; a time to plant, and a time to pluck up that which is planted.[1]

Our *awareness* of *time* and mortality is part of our ability to anticipate *events*. Combined with our *awareness* of the *processes* of other *life forms*, it has allowed us to exploit the *potential* of plants and animals as *food*. Without this ability we would not have settled to agriculture and laid the foundations for complex human *cultures*.

The ability to anticipate is central to *survival*. However there is little point in being able to anticipate circumstances without *potential*, either to avoid disaster and/or to *create* more desirable *alternatives*.

Anticipation is also bound up with *expectation*. If our *expectations* are fulfilled – that is, our *assumptions* are confirmed – things will proceed as we think they should. If, however, our anticipation is disrupted things will be perceived as going wrong.

In human *structures* such as *institutions*, it is important that the anticipation of the system be fulfilled. If it is disrupted to any significant degree the organisation may cease to *function*.[2]

In the unfolding *morphology* of *nature* most anticipation amounts to the fulfilment of *inherent potential* in response to changing circumstances, either in the *environment*, the species or individual being. When that *potential* is exhausted the entity will not be able to adapt to changes and will fail.

If there is a qualitative difference between human and other *forms* of *life* it may be in our greater ability to anticipate consciously. To over-simplify – for this is only a matter of degree – whereas other *life* experiences 'now', combined with memories of past events, as its *perceptive* repertoire, humans can imagine *future events* and anticipate the *processes* which may be relevant to them, like beavers adjusting dams to cope with coming floods, or squirrels hoarding nuts for winter. In humans, imagination, or anticipatory vision, enables us to *create*, to construct our *future* actively.

ANTICIPATORY ADAPTATION   The *green* argument for changes in the ways we live, away from *terminality* towards *sustainability*, is based upon the belief that we can, indeed must, anticipate the disastrous effects of our present ways and act to avoid the disaster we have initiated. If we wait until the disease is confirmed, rather than act on the symptoms, it will be too late. We have both to anticipate the *potential* of the disaster, and to find the best means of *adapting* to avoid it.

Relationships   **adaptation, potential, morphic field.**
See also   **evolution, inherent, philosophy.**
References

1 The Christian *Holy Bible*, Ecclesiastes 3:1.
2 See Colin Johnson, 1991, *The Green Bible: Creating Sustainable Life on Earth*, Thorsons, London.

ANTHROPOCENTRIC, ANTHROPOCENTRISM (from the Greek anthropo = human, mankind; kentron = centred)   The *grey* view, particularly of Western Judeo-Christian *cultures*, with regards humans as the central fact of the *universe* and of *life*.

ANTHROPOMORPHISM (from the Greek anthropo = human, mankind; morphe = form)   Attribution of human form or personality to gods, animals etc.

To anthropomorphise is to attribute qualities which are believed to be exclusively human (see **anthropocentric**) to other *life* forms or entities; term used by *grey culture* as a means of derogation, usually because it is felt to be unscientific.

Green belief, based on the *holistic nature of life*, is that all *life* shares more in common than those features which separate it. In many ways humanity may be regarded as the summary of *life*, in some ways the best fulfilment of its *potential*, but in other ways its worst.

Life functions *symbiotically*, each form and species intimately interdependent on the others. Life on earth is an inclusive phenomenon; it is as unrealistic to attempt to erect absolute barriers between forms as it is to merge them totally. What we share may be enough to validate our expressions of anthropomorphism (see **life**).

Relationships   **Gaia, holism, morphology.**
See also   **symbiosis, synergy.**

ANTHROPOSOPHY   see **biodynamics**.

APPROPRIATE TECHNOLOGY   see **technology**.

AQUARIUS   Sign of the zodiac, the water-bearer, so called because its annual appearance coincides with the flooding of the Lower Nile; person born under this sign, 21 January–19 February or thereabouts.
AQUARIAN   Aquarians were a sect in the early Christian church which insisted on the use of water instead of wine in the Lord's supper.
AQUARIAN AGE   (see **new age**) A millennium of love and light, of new awareness and consciousness, popularised by the song, 'Aquarius' ('This is the dawning of the age of Aquarius ...') from the musical *Hair*.

> I was drawn to the symbolic power of the pervasive dream in our popular culture: that after a dark, violent age, the Piscean, we are entering a millennium of love and light – in the words of the popular song, 'The Age of Aquarius' (sic), the time of 'the mind's true liberation.' Whether or not it was written in the stars, a different age seems to be upon us; and Aquarius, the water-bearer in the ancient zodiac, symbolising flow and the quenching of an ancient thirst, is an appropriate symbol.[1]

References
1 Marilyn Ferguson, 1981, *The Aquarian Conspiracy*; quoted in John Button, 1988, *A Dictionary of Green Ideas, Vocabulary for a Sane and Sustainable Future*, Routledge, London.

ARCHETYPE (from the Greek, arkhetypon = a first stamp or impression)   Subsequently to mean an original model or proto-type. In psychology, meaning a primordial mental image inherited by all.
More recently to mean a pervasive idea, symbol or image which forms part of our collective *sub-conscious*. The idea was popular-ised by Swiss psychiatrist Carl Jung[1] in his development of the concept of an impersonal substratum underlying the 'personal unconscious' consisting of many inherited archetypes.
The problem of creating a *sustainable future* is one of extending ourselves beyond the limits of our collective archetypes to a new phase of consciously directed *evolution*. To achieve this we need to

understand both the nature of the inner self-regulating system and how it may be manipulated to create our own archetypes.

Relationships   **mind, autopilot.**

See also   **evolution, consciousness, morphology.**

References

1 Carl Gustav Jung (1875–1961). Jung also produced the idea of the psyche as a self-regulating system.

ARK   A chest or box; term used to denote age or antiquity – 'Must have come out of the ark'; generally implied to be Noah's ark, a ship in which Noah and his family, together with two of every creature, were saved from the flood.[1]

GREEN ARK   By analogy ark has come to mean both the earth in danger, and also a means of salvation. Green arks are being assembled in a *grey* world. This modern usage was consolidated by John and Nancy Todd of the New Alchemy Institute,[2] an alternative biotechnology research institution.

A green ark can be anything which protects or *extends* the *natural environment*, from a window box to a *bio-region*.

References

1 The Christian *Holy Bible* Genesis 5–9.

2 Eds Nancy and Jack Todd, 1977, *The Book of the New Alchemists*, E.P. Dutton, New York.

    The New Alchemy Institute, PO Box 432, Woods Hole, Massachusetts 02543, USA.

    Ark has also been used in the green sense by Dennis Pirage and Paul Ehrlich, 1974, in *Ark II: Social Response to Environmental Imperatives*, Freeman, San Francisco, USA; by Norman Myers, 1979, in *The Sinking Ark*, Pergamon Press; by Lee Durrell, 1986, in *The State of the Ark*, The Bodley Head, London; and others.

ARTIFICIAL   Made by art, not natural.

As artefact, a product of human art and workmanship. More usually artificial things, particularly substances, are described as man-made.

Artificial substances are a major concern for *greens*. This is because they are usually products of chemical industries, where one thing may be substituted for its *natural* counterpart, or, more significantly, where entirely unnatural substances are created. The latter are the result of compounding natural substances in ways which are unlikely to occur in *nature*, to produce a variety of novel molecular shapes.

These artificial molecules may be used for an almost endless variety of things, anything from drugs or *biocides* to *food* flavourings or shampoo. The *process* of compounding reaches its peak in polymer chemistry, where a compound is made from a molecule which is formed from a number of repeated (polymerised) units of more simple compounds (monomers). This *process* is central to the plastics industry. Compounds are usually joined together by taking advantage of the agreeably *cohesive nature* of the carbon atom, a process which is at the heart of all the molecules involved in *life*; hence this branch of chemistry is described as 'organic'.

It is the *organic life-nature* of the chemical feedstock used to produce artificial substances that causes problems. Some substances, such as *biocides*, rely on their affinity with *life* forms and *cycles* for their ability to disrupt them fatally. Others, like plastics, take life-molecules and lock them outside *life cycles* so that these substances spend a short time as usable artefacts and an infinity as *polluting waste*.

Artificial substances cause *environmental problems* because they take life-molecules and use them to produce substances which do not occur in *nature*; *nature* therefore cannot deal with them by re-assimilation into other *life cycles*. Worse, these substances can have entirely unpredictable effects. PCBs (polychlorinated biphenols), primarily used in electrical equipment because of their thermal stability, but with many other uses, including at one time in high-gloss wet-look lipstick, are now found to cause sterility in aquatic mammals and damage to their immune *systems*. Nobody could foresee, when throwing them away, that they would accumulate in the surface waters of the oceans and produce this effect. Similarly, who would have predicted that CFCs (chlorofluorocarbons), used in refrigerators and aerosols, would destroy the *ozone* layer? More importantly, nobody ever considered it necessary to look for such effects.

All artificial chemicals are 'safe' when new. Even those acknowledged as poisons are sold as safe, 'providing they are used in accordance with the manufacturers' instructions'. *Problems* only emerge later when, because of the very *nature* of the substances, it is frequently too late to do anything about them. Compounding the *problem* is the *linear* view of science, that there will only be one *effect* (the one intended) caused by the substance. Thus the *problems* of pesticide residues in food, or those caused by drug metabolities, were denied for many years, as was the possibility that such *problems* could even arise.

Precise figures are not available, but over 5 million artificial substances have been *created* and it is estimated that between 40 and 50,000 are in everyday use.

Ultimately the problem with artificial substances is one of *philosophy*. *Grey culture* believes that playing molecular (Russian) roulette with *life* and the *environment* is a legitimate commercial enterprise. *Green philosophy*[1] rejects anything which takes *life*-materials outside the *great cycle of life*, unless the artefacts produced have indefinite *utility*.

Relationships **pollution, waste**, total **toxic** overload, great **cycle of life**.

See also **balance, environment**.

References

1 Colin Johnson, 1991, *The Green Bible: Creating Sustainable Life on Earth*, Thorsons, London.

See also, Rachael Louise Carson (1907–1964), 1965, *Silent Spring*, Penguin Books, London; and Murray Bookchin, (under the pseudonym Lewis Herber, 1962), 1974, *Our Synthetic Environment*, Harper & Row, New York.

ASSERT Vindicate claim or give effect to rights or opinions.

ASSERTIVENESS The art of maintaining *rights* or expressing opinions without being either submissive or unnecessarily aggressive. A quality which may require dogmatic insistence blended with patient reason. The ability to respond clearly and appropriately.

Being assertive in any cause requires *valuing* and taking yourself seriously (seriousness should not be confused with solemnity). It also demands that you learn to communicate effectively using all the means available within your *culture*, or, better still, invent new ways.

Relationships **rights, responsibility**.

See also **community, perception**.

ASSUME Take as being true, for argument or action.

ASSUMPTION That which is taken as being true, usually in the absence of conscious thought or reasoning, or on the basis of incomplete knowledge.

Much of our day-to-day action is based upon assumptions. Indeed, the complexity of our *culture* is such that we could not manage in any other way. We take most of what we find around us for granted, trusting others to fulfil their part in the *cultural dynamic*, as they trust us to fulfil ours.

Our assumptive base, that body of unquestioned belief which directs our lives, is formed in *symbiosis* with our *culture*. Most people are happy to live within the *culture* of their birth; few question the assumptive base they inherit. This may be fine if the *culture* is *healthy* and *sustainable*; when it is not there is little option other than to begin the painful *process* of questioning.

Greens assume that it is essential to *change* our *culture* from *terminality* to *sustainability*. Changing *culture* begins by changing individuals, and individual *change* begins by questioning the assumptions upon which the *culture* is based.

Relationships   **mind, nurture, culture, philosophy**.
See also   **awareness, autonomy, autopilot**.

ATTUNE   To bring into musical accord.

ATTUNEMENT   The process of getting in touch with yourself, of interpreting and responding appropriately to inner messages of need, as well as of reacting in the same way in groups of people and other *life* and *environmental* situations. Also used in spiritual context. In the group context

> Attunement is like 'tuning up' an orchestra, so that each individual's sound will complement and harmonise with the others. Here, balance is sought between the interests, needs and talents of all members of the group. Most attunement processes engage all workers in the opportunity either verbally (through various consensus methods) or intuitively (through visualisation or meditation) to express their unique viewpoints about how the group should achieve its goals and about their desired role in the group.[1]

From the *green perspective* it is important that the individual and group be self-attuning. Consideration of a directed message, or inspiration from outside, may be the purpose of attunement, but it should not direct the *process*.

The *process* of attunement is not *inherently green*. The goal to which the group or individual is attuned may be totally unacceptable to *greens*, e.g. the attunement of fascists at the Nuremburg rallies or that of Zen warriors.

Relationships   **morphology, affinity group, ad hoc, autopilot, autonomy**.
See also   **function, dynamic**.
References
1 Susan Campbell, 1983, in *Earth Community*.

AUTHORITY   The power or right to enforce obedience; delegated power to achieve purpose or objective; an individual or body having authority; also source, personal or published, of recognised expertise or opinion.

For *greens* the question of authority concerns its source. If authority is freely given for a specific purpose, and anyone with authority is accountable to those over whom or in whose name it is exercised and those individuals may withdraw that authority, then it may be acceptable. What is completely unacceptable is the idea of *inherent* authority, that is authority *assumed* or taken by an individual or body by usurpation, by birth or by *position*, usually in a corporate or *institutional body*.

Relationships   **freedom, responsibility, power.**
See also   **hierarchy, structure, function, position.**

AUTONOMY   Right   of   self-government;   personal   freedom; freedom of the will.

For greens personal autonomy is essential. This is difficult because our *cultural* nurture encourages us to define ourselves in terms of a variety of prescribed roles and stereotypes. The exploration of *self*, and self-definition in terms of the requirements of the *future*, rather than acceptance of the inheritance of the *past*, is a necessary step towards self-directed *evolution*. Yet at the same time we must accept that 'No man is an Island, entire of itself; every man is a piece of the Continent, a part of the main',[1] and be *aware* of our dependence and contribution to others of our species and to *life* as a *whole*.

Autonomy in social affairs is desirable, but depends upon the *structure* of the social group. Living in autonomous *communities*, *federated* by common interest or purpose is the ideal on which most *greens* agree, and towards which we should work. The autonomous *institutional* nation state denies personal autonomy, as does life or work within corporate *institutions*.

Relationships   **community, structure, morphology.**
See also   **culture, anarchy, federation, co-operation.**
References
1 John Donne (1571–1631), *Devotions XVII*.

AUTOPILOT   Automatic pilot; device which maintains preset course, correcting any deviation.

Within any entity, whether animate or otherwise, there are *agenda* which dictate *form* and *behaviour* in relation to a variety of variables, both internal and external.[1] For example, water exists in various forms, as liquid, ice or steam, depending upon its heat *en-*

ergy level, purity and the pressure of its *environment.* Its state is an *inherent* property of the molecular entity, water. The *form* in which it *exists* depends upon the orientation and movement of the collective of molecules. The *nature* of this *inherent* organisation, which always produces the same result, may be thought of as the shared autopilot of those molecules (see **morphology**).

In life *processes* the *nature* of the autopilot is immeasurably more complex. We are familiar with the *genetic process* which governs our lives; the unfolding of the *genetic* script is best thought of as the expression of *potential,* of a series of options which are fulfilled within *limits,* e.g. if we are well nourished we will grow to our maximum size, if we are active we will be muscular, and so on. The maximum and minimum *limits* of these options are set by the inherent autopilot.

The autopilot also operates in complex *social structures.* In this area much of the resulting behaviour is described as instinctive (*instinct* is an innate propensity to certain seemingly rational acts performed without conscious intention; or innate, usually fixed, patterns of behaviour, especially in response to certain stimuli). Such behaviour is usually ascribed to animals, e.g. the herd instinct, but it also applies to humans and their *socio-cultural extensions.*

Autopilots *exist* within all human *structures,* from groups to entire *cultures.* They produce both *synergistic* and stabilising effects on such formations. Hence people in groups behave in ways which are at times unthinkable to individuals, and *cultures* become highly resistant to change.

We build autopilots into the group *structures* we *create* without conscious intention; they are factors with which we have yet to come to terms, as are the seemingly irrevocable embedded commands (in computerese) they carry.

Relationships   **agenda, morphology, potential**.
See also   **synergy, evolution**.
References
1 David Bohm, 1980, *Wholeness and the Implicate Order,* Routledge & Kegan Paul, London; Rupert Sheldrake, 1981, *A New Science of Life,* Blond & Briggs, London.

AWARE   Conscious of; not ignorant; having knowledge of.
AWARENESS   Conscious of, or having knowledge of, things.

For *greens* awareness of *process,* of the *dynamics* of *life* within the *Gaian whole,* is important. Ultimately *sustainable life,* which includes humanity, will depend upon our awareness of *processes* and our ability to live in ways which are compatible with them.

Try to be a person upon whom nothing is lost. An open mind behind open eyes, with senses *attuned* to the *needs* of the planet.

In *institutional society* awareness is a property of the heretic.

SELF-AWARENESS   A state of maximum consciousness of your inner processes and their outward expression, and awareness of such expression on others, your immediate surroundings and the global environment.

Relationships   **creativity, spontaneity, limits**.

See also   **process, Gaia**.

AWAY (see **infinite away**)   A central *myth* of *grey culture*; it is essential to believe that 'away' *exists*, somewhere else. Unfortunately there is no such place.

B

BALANCE Equilibrium, steady state; balance of nature, constancy of conditions resulting from interaction of living things; harmony of design and proportion; steady state, as keeping things in balance; power to decide, as in hold the balance.

The *grey* concept of balance in things is conditioned by *linear* thinking; balance is seen in terms of the original meaning of two things hung from a beam to compare their weight, the mechanism used being described as a balance. *Grey* balance is essentially static around some common features. Thus the concept can be used to perpetuate inequalities, or maintain extreme opposites or unacceptable contradictions (see **thematic compatibility**).

Holding the balance usually means maintaining the *status quo,* as in media balance, where powerful establishment views are offered against trivial *alternatives,* or the *assertion* is made that 'There is no alternative',[1] so there is never a debate of basics, such as the concept of *power,* or the *structure* of society; there is a 'balance of power'[2] and that is *assumed* to be satisfactory. Such a balance is characterised by arms races, terror and, ultimately, destruction.

For *greens* balance is essentially *dynamic.* The balance of *nature* is seen as the property of a complex *matrix* with a constantly moving *centre* which *shifts* within the *whole,* reflecting the changing interactions within the *web of life.* Each component of the web, from the molecular to the *Gaian whole,* has its own local *centre* of balance which contributes to the state of the whole. In all senses balance is a summary of properties at a particular point in time.

While the *centre* of balance is contained within certain *limits* (the property of *homoeostasis,* whereby relatively *stable* equilibrium is maintained between the interdependent elements of a *system,* especially in physiological *processes* in living beings), the *system* will maintain its integrity, the being will remain viable.

Human activity has unbalanced many of the *systems* which maintain the overall balance of the *biosphere.* Whether we have pushed them so far off-centre that they may not recover is a question which remains to be answered.

The ideal state of balance would be where all *forms* of *life* could fulfil their *potential*, providing that in so doing they did not inhibit the fulfilment of others.

To re-establish a *sustainable* balance in the *biosphere* we must reduce or stop those activities which contribute to effects such as *acid rain*, *ozone* depletion and the *greenhouse effect*. We must eliminate *pollution* and re-establish those parts of *life* which have been diminished by it. We must stop activities which cause *genocide*, and we must bring human *numbers* within the *carrying capacity* of the *biosphere*. For *sustainable life* in the *future* we need to map the *web of life*, to describe the interactions of the *morphology* of its many components and understand the effects of their interactions. Then we may act as minimally intrusive stewards of the balance of the *future*.

Balance is essential to most things; any blessing overdone rapidly becomes a curse.

Relationships   **Gaia, limits, holism, morphology**.
See also   **nature, evolution**.
References
1 A frequent saying of Margaret Thatcher, British Prime Minister 1979–90.
2 A phrase first coined by Sir Robert Walpole, British First Lord of the Treasury, in a speech in the House of Commons, 13 February 1741.

BARTER ECONOMY   see **economy**.

BASIC NEEDS   see **needs**.

BEING   State of existence, usually of living thing; in creation, to bring artefact into being.

Also as the opposite of 'doing'; being in a *position*, instead of fulfilling a *function*. And as the 'poseur' syndrome of *grey culture* where people 'be' something else as an escape from their normal reality; first observed as the weekend ravers of the late 1950s, where the grey-suited would dress as beats (later beatniks) and attend jazz festivals; now seen as the dedicated followers of instant fashion. People who spend their time being are usually not very good at doing things.

In the *spiritual* sense being is used to *connect* the individual with aspects of the *environment*, as in earthing, or meditative *processes* which are intended to unite the individual with *nature*, etc.

Erich Fromm contrasts 'having' and 'being' modes of human

existence, where being 'means aliveness and authentic relatedness to the world'. Having denotes possession, reflecting the desire to make everything into one's property which lies at the root of consumerism. A shift from having to being in this sense is a profound and essential psychological change.[1]

A *quality* which implies respect. Any being contributes to the whole of *life*. In the *green* sense being means being an *aware* part of the totality of *life*, living within the *natural limits* of the *whole* in ways which enhance that totality. A Council for All Beings[2] has been formed to give a voice to the considerations of all beings in human directed affairs.

Relationships   **life, spirit**.
See also   **limits, potential**.
References
1 Erich Fromm, 1978, *To Have or To be?*, Jonathan Cape, London.
2 Council for Posterity, 24 Abercorn Place, London NW8 9XP.

BICYCLE   Two-wheeled person-powered vehicle. Using minimal resources and capable of lasting indefinitely, easy to repair (parts may be recycled). The ultimate *green* machine so far.

Relationships   **transport, health**.
See also   **finite resources, appropriate technology**.
References
See Richard Ballantyne, 1983, *Richard's Bicycle Book*, Pan Books, London. In my edition of this otherwise excellent book the epicyclic hub gear (Sturmey-Archer three, four or five speed) is omitted as too complex for the average rider to deal with. Not so (in my opinion); the hub gear is a fascinating mechanism which hardly ever needs maintenance; if yours does, do not be put off.

BIO-   (from the Greek bios = (course of) human life.) Usually of life in general.

This prefix has limitless applications; only those words of particular relevance to specific *green* issues have been included.

BIO-ASSIMILABILITY   Property of substance which may be readily and beneficially absorbed by living organisms.

Bio-assimilability should be a feature in the design of degradable products so that they will *enhance* the *life forms* and *cycles* which *recycle* the material from which they are made. Human artefacts would thus become beneficial parts of the *life-cycles* of the planet.

Relationships   **biodegradable, organic**, great **cycle** of **life**.
See also   **limits, pollution**.

BIOCENTRIC, BIOCENTRISM   Life-centred.

Desirable *quality* of *green culture*, focus of *green philosophy*[1].
System of belief which gives precedence to *life* and *life needs*.

Most present cultures are *death*-centred, in that many *systems*
of belief and *dogma* upon which they rely stress that *life* on earth is
only a path to a state after *death* where rewards, perfection, peace
and other desirable things denied on earth may be found.

Relationships   **life, death**.

See also   **Gaia, ecology**.

References

1 Colin Johnson, 1991, *The Green Bible: Creating Sustainable Life on Earth*,
Thorsons, London.

BIOCENTRIC EQUALITY   see **rights**.

BIOCIDE (1947, Greek, bios + Latin caedere = life-destroying)
Usually *artificial* (although not necessarily) chemical used to
eradicate unwanted *life* forms, particularly in modern farming.

Biocides, many of them persistent, are used in millions of tonnes
annually. 'Can anyone believe it is possible to lay down such a barrage
of poisons on the surface of the earth without making it unfit for all
life?'[1]

Greens reject the use of all *artificial* biocides, and seek ways to
eliminate the necessity for such drastic interference with the
balance of *nature* (see **organic**).

Relationships   **artificial, chemiculture**, total **toxic** overload.

See also   **pollution, limits**.

References

1 Rachel Louise Carson (1907–1964), 1965, *Silent Spring*, Penguin Books,
London.

See also, Richard Body, 1987, *Red or Green for Farmers (And the Rest of Us)*,
Broad Leys Publishing, Saffron Waldon, Essex, England.

BIODEGRADABLE   Substance capable of being decomposed by
the action of living organisms, usually by bacteria or fungi.

Biodegradability is a *life* property; all living things are biodegradable when they die. The materials of one *form* of *life* are
released and re-used in new *forms*. This is the nature of the *great
cycle of life*.

Human activity removes many substances from *natural* planetary and *life cycles*. The effects are resource depletion and global
systems overload via *pollution*. *Artificial* substances, particularly
plastics, are rarely biodegradable. For the *future*, *artefacts* made

from non-biodegradable substances should be designed to have indefinite *life* (see **finite resources**).

Biodegradability should not be seen as the answer to every *waste* problem. It is a part of the *natural process* of *life cycles*, but only *functions* effectively when those *cycles* are in *balance*. To rely on biodegradability as the means of cleaning-up the results of human activity is like treating the rest of *life* as our dustbin. Biodegradability should be a guiding *principle*, but we should aim for *bio-assimilability* – that is, the design of degradable products which will *enhance* the *life cycles* which use them next.

Relationships   great **cycle** of **life, balance, pollution.**
See also   **waste, artificial, recycling.**

BIODYNAMICS   A method of gardening initiated by Rudolf Steiner,[1] in which *organic* practice is carried out in phase with seasonal, planetary and lunar cycles. By this means biodynamic gardening hopes to augment the advantageous properties of desirable plants while inhibiting the activities of predators.

Also a branch of biology dealing with the *energy* production of organisms (see *bioenergetics*).

Also name given to various methods of psychotherapy.

Relationships   **organic, food.**
See also   **energy.**

References
1 Rudolf Steiner (1861–1925); Austrian social philosopher, devised a new philosophy called anthroposophy, a synthesis of 19th-century philosophical ideas and theosophical material. Described as a 'spiritual science', anthroposophy explains life in terms of humanity's spiritual nature and teaches that people have faculties for spiritual comprehension that can be developed through pure thought.

See also his autobiography, 1925 (English translation 1951) 1986, *The Course of My Life*, Anthroposophic Press, USA.

BIOENERGETIC(S)   The study of *energy* production and flow within and between organisms, being extended to the study of *energy* levels in social groups (see **biodynamics**).

Also a body-based *therapy* developed from the work of Wilhelm Reich[1] by Alexander Lowen, which concentrates on the importance of grounding yourself in your body and its *relationship* to the earth.

Relationships   **being, affinity.**
See also   **therapy, health.**

References
1 Wilhelm Reich (1897–1957), Austrian psychiatrist, an associate of psychoanalyst Sigmund Freud in Vienna during the 1920s, wrote *The Function of the Orgasm*,

1927, English translation 1942, in which he stated that the discharge of sexual energy is necessary for individual health, and that sexual repression is an integral part of all authoritarian societies.

BIOREGION   A *natural* region, exhibiting diversity and stability, defined by its ecological coherence:

> There is a distinct resonance among living things and the factors which influence them that occurs specifically within each separate place on the planet. Discovering and describing that resonance is a way to describe a bioregion.[1]

> The earth presents itself to us not as a uniform global reality, but as a complex of highly differentiated regions caught up in the comprehensive unity of the planet itself. There are arctic and tropical, coastal and inland regions, mountains and plains, river valleys and deserts. Each of these has its distinctive geological formation, climatic conditions, and living forms. Together these constitute the wide variety of life communities that may be referred to as bioregions. Each is coherent within itself and intimately related to the others. Together they express the wonder of this garden planet of the universe.[2]

BIOREGIONALISM   The proposition that human ways of *life* should be compatible with the requirements of the *diversity* of bioregional communities of the planet.

> Such a bioregional community is self-propagating, self-nourishing, self-healing and self-fulfilling. Each of the component life systems must integrate their own functioning within this community functioning to survive in any effective way.[2]

> The most fully developed bioregional organisation is probably the Ozark Area Community Congress (OACC), founded in 1976 and based on the principle of 'political economy', by which the Congress means that political consciousness must be bioregionally orientated and must operate as an extension of natural or ecological laws. The Congress, which considers itself an alternative representative body for the Ozarks, is committed to achieving regional self-reliance and sustainable economics by using renewable resources and respecting the integrity of the environment.[3]

> Bioregionalism begins by acting responsibly at home. Welcome home![4]

Relationships   **community, ecology, balance, numbers**.
See also   **diversity, stability, evolution**.
References

1 Peter Berg, 1978, *Reinhabiting a Separate Country*, Planet Drum, USA.
2 Thomas Berry, 1990, 'Bioregions: The Context for Reinhabiting the Earth', in *Fourth World Review*, Number 40/41, 1990, 24 Abercorn Place, London NW8 9XP.
3 Charlene Spretnak & Fritzjof Capra, 1986, *Green Politics*, Grafton, London.
4 Kirkpatrick Sale, 1985, *Dwellers in the Land: The Bioregional Vision*, Sierra Club Books, San Francisco, USA.

BIOSPHERE   Regions of earth's crust and atmosphere in which living matter is found.

The concept has been *extended* by the *Gaia* hypothesis[1] and the implications of *holism* to include the planet and its physical *environment*.
Relationships   **life, Gaia, holism**.
See also   **environment**.
References

1 James Lovelock, 1979, *Gaia: A New Look at Life on Earth*, Oxford University Press, Oxford, England.

BLACK ECONOMY   see **economy**.

BLUEPRINT   Reproduction of architectural, engineering or other drawing, so called because early processes reproduced in blue. Now used in the wider sense for plan or strategy, or mental *model* or *paradigm*.
BLUEPRINT FOR SURVIVAL   Generic term for *green* and conservation proposals for the *future*.

The classic blueprint for survival was published by *The Ecologist*[1] magazine and subsequently as a book.[2]
Relationships   **model, paradigm, policy**.
See also   **community, politics**.
References

1 *The Ecologist*, Worthyvale Manor, Camelford, Cornwall PL32 9TT, England.
2 Edward Goldsmith, Robert Allen, Michael Allaby, John Davoll and Sam Lawrence, 1972, *Blueprint for Survival*, Penguin Books, London.

BRIARPATCH   Concept derived from the Brer Rabbit folk tales of Uncle Remus, where the rabbit was protected by the thorny nature of his environment.
BRIARPATCH NETWORK   USA originally, now also in Canada, Sweden, Finland and Japan; system of small business *organisation*

and *ethics* based on simplicity, openness and *honesty*, with the emphasis on service rather than profit. Briarpatch businesses only engage in activities which have minimum impact on the *environment*, preserve *resources*, and involve enjoyable *work*. The belief is that by operating in this way the businesses and their members will avoid the ills of larger society.

Relationships   **organisation, work, co-operation, human scale.**
See also   **community, economics, provision.**

BUREAUCRACY   Government by central administration, officials of such government being bureaucrats; *system* of administration characterised by rigidity, lack of imagination, inertia. A *system* highly resistant to *change* or innovation. Usually organised as a hierarchy, wherein position will take precedence over *function*. Remote and inefficient, bureaucracies rapidly develop their own *agenda*.

Bureaucracies are the essential organs of *terminal culture*.

Relationships   **hierarchy, institutions, position, function, status quo.**
See also   **structure, ad hoc.**

C

CARRYING CAPACITY Ecological term, the amount of *life*, either *number* of a particular species or *number* of species, which a region or *system*, such as a river or river valley, can support indefinitely.

The concept takes no account of the *quality* of *life* which may be supported as it is restricted to assessing *quantities*.

For *greens* the *quality* of *life* is paramount. The *balance* within a *bioregion* or *system* of such a region is the important factor; optimum *balance* is achieved when the *quality* of all *life* is maximised.

<u>Relationships</u>   **ecology, bioregion, balance.**
<u>See also</u>   **quality, numbers.**

CARTESIANISM (aka **reductionism**) After French rationalist philosopher and mathematician Réné Déscartes (Latinised to Cartesius, hence Cartesian) 1596–1650. Known as 'the father of modern philosophy' – hence his frequent pillorying as a, if not the, root of the modern predicament.

In an age dominated by clerics and conflicting theological *dogma*, Déscartes sought the certainty of knowledge in the explanation of *natural* phenomena by the application of reason via the *extension* of the logic of mathematics to every question. This led him (in the steps of St Augustine) to the proposition 'Cogito ergo sum' (I think, therefore I am, I exist). The claim to truth of the proposition was based upon its clarity and distinction, and the infallibility of god from whom all *knowledge* was ultimately derived.

His most practical contribution was the discovery and formulation of co-ordinate geometry (1637), the placing of a point by reference to intersecting straight (datum) lines.

CARTESIAN DUALISM   The source of our dominant *cultural* attitudes to *life*. It is based upon the notion that the *mind* and the *body* are separate entities with mutually exclusive properties. In deference to religion Déscartes proposed that the soul, another separate entity, resided in the pineal gland. This tricky point settled, it was further held that the separate parts can only be united, as in man, by the intervention of god. Animals, lacking the possibility of a rational soul, are regarded as mere automata. This, augmented by religious views of *homocentricity*, allowed humanity to dispose of the *natural world* as it wished.

Modern rationalism is mainly a critical development of Cartesian metaphysics and (British) empiricism. The mechanistic world view it projects gives rise to the *analytical* approach of modern science and the *linear* view of cause and *effect*. It is also the cause of our disastrous divorce from *nature*.

Green philosophy rejects dualism and the *mechanistic* approach in favour of *holism* and belief in the *coherence* of all *life* and the *connectedness* of all things. As with much upon which *grey terminal culture* relies, the *assertion* of Déscartes, 'I think, therefore I am', should be reversed – 'I am, therefore I think'. This allows for the sentience of all beings, and the proposition of a wider concept of *life* in a *universe* alive with its own logic.

Relationships   **mechanism, terminal culture, philosophy**.

See also   **analysis, synthesis, holism**.

CASUALTY   Result of accident, mishap, disaster; person killed or injured in war.

CASUALTY PATTERN, CASUALTY PROBLEM   Despite the many advances of civilisation the present human *way of life* produces high casualty rates; we have not moved away from the general proposition of high losses characteristic of all *life*. Globally 25 per cent starve and an increasing proportion are *malnourished*. In the *first world* high casualty living, with premature *death* and chronic disease, is the norm. We have a series of established *cultural* casualty patterns. If things continue as at present these patterns will be maintained, with higher *death*/disease rates as *environmental deterioration* continues.

However, human advances have had the effect of increasing gross *numbers*, so, paradoxically the greatest threat now comes from population pressure (see **compression**). We have so filled every nook and niche of the planet that the globe cannot go through its normal repertoire of *change*, e.g. with volcanic or weather events, without killing large *numbers*.

While things must *change* if we are to have a *future*, any *change* will alter the casualty pattern; there is no way we can avoid this. The best we can hope for is to minimise the casualty rate (see **cul-de-sac**).

If *sustainable green* options were to be initiated tomorrow, the trauma of *change*, of separation from the *terminal* past, would still be subject to the momentum of the old trying to drag everything down. The proposition of universal admission that so much was wrong, and the emergence of the will to *change*, is unlikely. Perhaps the best that may be hoped for is a minimal crash of the old *terminal* order, with the *chaos* of *change* and *restoration* spread over one or two centuries.

Things may have to get a lot worse before they get better.

Relationships   **numbers, compression, terminal culture.**

See also   **needs, economics.**

CATASTROPHE   Sudden or widespread disaster; event subverting system of things; disastrous end; ruin.

Also theory of *change* in *nature*, originally concerned with geology, subsequently extended to all natural processes. A mathematical model of sudden *change*, based on calculus[1] (see **shift**).

Greens see catastrophe, in the sense of disastrous end, as the destination of current *culture* and, in the sense of *events* which may subvert the present *system* of things, may welcome *events* which will *disrupt progress* to that destination (see **anticipation**).

Any *change* may be seen as catastrophic if those affected are content with the status quo. In human affairs catastrophe may be seen as a relative evaluation – one person's catastrophe may be another's sunny afternoon.

In the sense of *natural change*, catastrophe is an imprecise description of the *change* from one state to another, of a *morphic shift* (see *morphology*).

Relationships   **change, evolution, morphology.**

See also   **terminality, progress.**

References

1 Alexander Woodcock and Monte Davis, 1978, *Catastrophe Theory*, E.P. Dutton, New York.

CAUSATION   see **morphology.**

CELEBRATION   The observation of a special event or occasion with festivities and/or ritual.

Celebrations are events which reinforce behaviour and belief, mark particular points of *life* or seasons, create and maintain social cohesion.

For the *future* we need to *create* more celebrations, to *shift* the emphasis of *life* from struggle, toil, conflict, etc. – the *values* of *grey culture* – towards the enjoyment of *being*. *Life* is its own celebration; *green progress* involves discovering the ecstasy of *ecology*, and building it into our *ways of living*.

Relationships   **being, living, art of**
See also   **life**, **ecology**.

CENSOR   Person expressing views or opinions on the morals or behaviour of others; official with the power to enforce suppression of the expression of opinions, description of behaviour, or their pictorial representation, usually on grounds of obscenity or sedition.

Also, in psychology, the power by which unconscious ideas and/or memories of particular events are denied by the conscious mind.

A censor is someone who can say, do, or experience something a million times so that you may not do so once.

CENSORSHIP   Act of censoring.

Greens reject the *principle* of censorship. It is contrary to the requirements of *freedom* and *responsibility*. It is also a denial of *reality*. That is not to say that the *right* of a person to express views or *opinions* on the *morals* or behaviour of others is rejected (for that would be censorship), but the *power* to enforce those views is denied.

Censorship derives from two concerns: the wish to impose control over thoughts and behaviour which may threaten the status quo, usually by restricting various forms of communication; and the wish to control socially unacceptable behaviour, usually by the same means. The dividing line between the two is fine, and frequently lost, and the whole question is frequently fraught with confusion; for whereas the former is totally unacceptable, the objective of the latter may be valid, even necessary.

Censorship by governments usually centres on *sexuality*. It is notable that *sexual* repression is an integral part of most authoritarian societies, although in recent years some have swung to the opposite extreme, using the circus of witless pornography as a diversion from *political* or *economic reality*. The question is ultimately one of *cultural values*; in the West (as a generalisation) murder is a crime, but its graphic depiction is not; sex is not a crime, but its depiction is. One can go further: videos showing women terminally penetrated by entertaining psychopaths with chainsaws are socially acceptable, but those showing natural, even loving, penile penetration are banned or at least suppressed.

Nevertheless, starting from the rejection of imposed censorship by unaccountable *authority*, *greens* accept the need for *communities* to agree their own *social values*. Thus a *diversity* of behavioural patterns and relative *freedoms* of expression would be available.

The *principles* which should guide the acceptability of behaviour or expression are that they should not involve enforced *participation*, nor should the concept of victimless crime be allowed to stand.

For the *future* we need to think the *unthinkable*, to go into those closed self-censored areas of the human *mind*. It may well be that all that we discover should not be loosed upon our fellows or the world, that we need to devise ways of insulating our self-exploration and its results until our *philosophy* can guide judgments about use and validity of expression. Perhaps this is the way our universities should develop.

Relationships   **power, sex, freedom, authority**.
See also   **community, change, rights**.

CENTRE   Position at the summary of distances (or forces) from the boundary (or within) of a space (or body). Position at which properties are assumed to act. The place where everything important seems to be happening, as in centre of government.

Also the position within a person reached at times of heightened awareness, extreme stress, etc.

There are many alternative and life-enhancing centres, devoted to various pursuits, such as the Centre for Alternative Technology.[1] If you are interested in a particular thing check a good local resource guide[2] for a suitable centre.

There is an *intuitive* worry about centres. They inevitably become sources of *power* as well as of *resources*. Centres can lead to centralisation, and become fixed as an *institution*; the original purpose gets lost in the machinery of its provision.

Greens prefer a multitude of centres, forming a *matrix* or *network*, shifting according to *need* and *purpose*, rising and fading with changing *energy* levels – a pattern of *life structure* analogous to that of the functioning of the mind itself.

Relationships   **matrix, structure, dynamic, focus**.
See also   **mind, life structure**.
References
1 Centre for Alternative Technology, Llwyngwern Quarry, Machynlleth, Powys, Wales.

2 See, compiled by John Button, 1990, *New Green Pages: A Directory of Natural Products, Services, Resources and Ideas*, Macdonald Optima, London; or, Michael Barker, 1984, *Directory for the Environment*, Routledge & Kegan Paul.

CFC   Chlorofluorocarbons. *Artificial* substances used in the electronics industry as a cleaner,[1] in aerosols as a propellant, in refrigeration, and in the production of plastic foams, destroying *ozone* layer and assisting *greenhouse effect* (see **artificial**).

CFCs are classified by numbers: CFC-10 is used in aerosols; CFC-11 is used in making plastic foam; CFC-12 is the cleaning substance used in the electronics industry. When CFCs are released into the atmosphere, they rise slowly taking about seven years to reach the stratosphere. But once they are there, under the influence of the sun's ultraviolet light they break down into chlorine atoms which destroy the ozone layer. This allows harmful UV radiation to pass through to the earth's surface. Because it takes so long for the CFCs to reach the stratosphere, any reduction in their use on earth does not have an immediate effect on the concentrations in the stratosphere. Replacements for CFCs are being developed, which should reduce the problem eventually. It is a pity that CFCs have this unfortunate effect on the ozone layer, since in other ways they are ideal gases, being stable and non-toxic.[2]

<u>See also</u>   **symptom, problem, pollution**.
<u>References</u>
1 The electronics industry accounts for around 45 per cent of CFC use; it is used to clean circuit boards.
2 Peter Hodgson Collin, 1988, *Dictionary of Ecology and the Environment*, P.H. Collin Publishing, Teddington, Middlesex, England.

CHANGE   Become different, often by comparison.
Things are always changing. Even when circumstances are perceived as *stable*, the *reality* is the *relativity* of continuous constant change. We become aware of change when the rate at which it occurs alters.

Change in human affairs is called *progress*. This allows a rationalisation, of inevitability and desirability, to be linked to whatever is done or proposed. *Greens* believe that the direction of current change is *unsustainable*, and that humanity *consciously* needs to direct its *progress* towards *sustainability*. This requires fundamental change in ourselves, our species and our ways of *living*.

The following quotation is a good summary of the *green* desire for the *nature* of change:

> After a time of decay comes the turning point. The powerful light that has been banished returns. There is movement, but it is not brought about by force ... The movement is natural, arising spontaneously. For this reason the transformation of the old becomes easy. The old is discarded and the new is introduced. Both measures accord with the time; therefore no harm results.[1]

Intuitively we know that desirable change will not be that easy. Opposition to the status quo has the effect of refining and reinforcing it; the opposites merge into *thematic compatability* (the Tweedledum and Tweedledee of pluralist *politics*). Nor are traditional ideas of *revolutionary* change applicable; *revolutions* are not about changing fundamental *structures*, rather they are about who controls the *structure*: 'we need change, but change so fundamental and far-reaching that even the concepts of revolution and freedom must be expanded beyond all earlier horizons'.[2]

The changes necessary for a *sustainable future* are many. Most fundamental is the need for *self-directed evolutionary* change among the human species; next the need for *ways of living* which are compatible with *life* rather than antagonistic to it. 'We either learn to live within the great cycle of life, or perish without.'[3]

<u>Relationships</u>   **anticipation, potential, morphology, evolution, sustainability**.

<u>See also</u>   **catastrophe, progress, terminal culture, chaos**.

<u>References</u>

1 *I Ching*, quoted in Fritjof Capra, 1982, *The Turning Point: Science, Society, and the Rising Culture*, Simon & Schuster, New York, USA.

2 Murray Bookchin, 1981, *The Ecology of Freedom: The Emergence and Dissolution of Hierarchy*, Cheshire Books, Palo Alto, California, USA.

3 Colin Johnson, 1991, *The Green Bible: Creating Sustainable Life on Earth*, Thorsons, London.

CHAOS   Formless primordial matter; utter confusion; a lack of perceptible order.

Chaos is the *perception* of a state of *change*; it is feared because *change* is feared, and because the outcome is likely to be unpredictable. *Nature* is chaotic, producing endless *change* within a greater *stability*.

<u>Relationships</u>   **change, morphology, anticipation**.

<u>See also</u>   **evolution, purpose**.

CHEMICAL   Substance made of natural molecules, either found or produced by refining, mixing or compounding, these processes described as chemistry (see **artificial**).

CHEMICULTURE (chemical + agriculture)   Also known as agri-business, intensive farming.

Chemiculture – agriculture and farming which has become totally reliant upon basic chemical inputs, particularly *biocides*, soluble fertilisers and drugs, usually in intensive mono-crop systems.[1]

Agribusiness – farming dominated by industrial methods and annual balance sheet accounting. It shares with chemiculture a lack of consideration for the health of the *land*, the *environment*, animals, or the *quality* of the *food* it produces, which is thought of as 'product', a part of the denial of its *life-nature* and *needs*.

Intensive farming – the practice of getting as much 'product' from *land* or other facilities as possible. In the process *nature* is distorted and destroyed by whatever means necessary; geological features are removed, *ecological diversity* banished, *plants* and animals selectively bred and *genetically engineered*. Fields become *green deserts* of *mono-culture*, farms become factories, and animals are subjected to abuse and torture which will horrify any future ages and should bring shame to the present. The whole process depends on high levels of *chemical* inputs – chemiculture.

How have things got into this *unsustainable* and potentially *terminal* position? Traditional farming is hard and demanding; the farmer has to be both physically strong and healthy, and intelligent (a rare combination in cities); his skills developed over a lifetime and passed on through successive generations. Some of this rare breed survive in farming in industrialised societies. However, *technology* and *chemistry* offer an apparent way out; an easier life for the competent and the possibility that any fool could farm. In short, the products of the chemical industry were substitutes for good husbandry.[2] But, as with many apparently easy options, farmers found they had exchanged one treadmill for another; they have become caught on the chemical treadmill and are kept there by an *economic* machine which progressively reduces the farm-gate price of their output. To stay in farming they had little choice – but that little, in the form of *organic farming*, is being taken up by an increasing number as the impossibility of chemiculture becomes apparent.

The pressures on farmers and their stock have been intensified by *consumers*, who have only been concerned with the price of *food* rather than its real cost. *Consumers* have also ignored the *quality* of what they have eaten – if it was on the shelf, it was assumed to be OK. Although the real nature of meat has been disguised by sterile *plastic* packs, and by other forms of processing, awareness of the basic importance of a sound and *sustainable food* supply is spreading – the increase in *organic food* output is largely *consumer* led.

Farming is not a natural act, and the excesses of chemiculture may be seen as the logical end of a *food* production *ethic* which seeks to dominate *nature* rather than work with it. The final end of this *grey culture* process is that we eat *chemicals* and cut out all the middle men and *life forms*, a trend on the increase in the 'food' end of the *chemical* industry.[3]

Relationships   **food, health, terminal, consumer, philosophy.**
See also   **life contract, pollution.**
References

1 Orville Schell, 1978, *Modern Meat: Antibiotics, Hormones, and the Pharmaceutical Farm*, Random House, New York, USA.
2 Sedley Sweeney, 1985, *The Challenge of Smallholding*, Oxford University Press, Oxford, England.
3 See Eric Millstone, 1986, *Food Additives: Taking the Lid off What We Really Eat*, Penguin Books, London.

CHERNOBYL   Synonym for nuclear disaster.

The chances are that sometime, somewhere, a nuclear reactor and its containment structure will be breached by an explosion; or that a sealed tank full of seething radioactive waste to be entombed far below man's dwelling places will get ruptured. The consequences in either case could be a radioactive cloud several hundreds of times more lethal than that which settled upon Hiroshima or Nagasaki.[1]

Although a complete core melt down has never yet occurred, there have been numerous partial 'accidents' which have released amounts of radioactive material into the *environment*, from the world's first source of nuclear electricity in the USA, EBR-1 in 1955, to one of the latest at Chernobyl in Russia in 1986.

Relationships   **terminal.**
See also   **energy.**
References

1 Peter Bunyard, 1970, 'Is There a Peaceful Atom', in *The Ecologist*, Volume 1, Number 1, The Ecologist, Worthyvale Manor, Camelford, Cornwall, England.

CHI From Chinese; flow or flux of force or *energy*; a *spiritual perception* of the *organisation* of *energy*.

The understanding derived from the insights of chi have led to practical developments in China such as acupuncture, the understanding of magnetism and the compass, gunpowder and chemical warfare.

Chi may be seen as a soft push at the door of *knowledge*, as a reciprocal process with a door that is ready to open.

Relationships   **energy, Tao, holism.**

CHINA SYNDROME   Synonym for nuclear disaster. See **Chernobyl.**

CHOICE   Access to options, being able to select from *alternatives* or a range of things, actions, etc.

The *global predicament* is generated by the myriad of choices we each make as part of our normal everyday lives. The world is being destroyed by the ordinary actions of millions of us going about our affairs. Like raindrops falling to create a flood, each of us contributes to the gathering tides of disaster which rise higher as *viability* sinks.

The choices made by those people alive in the last decade of the 20th century are directing the course of *life* on the *planet* for decades into the *future*, in some instances for *eternity*. For that reason it is crucial that we examine the details of our 'normal' everyday lives, every action we consider as ordinary.

For the *future*, there are only two valid questions to govern choice. Is it (whatever is proposed) *sustainable*? If yes, proceed to question two; if no, reject and think again. Does it (whatever it is) *enhance life* (all *life*)? If yes, proceed; if no, reject and think again.

For the present, it is important to realise that every choice we make is important. No one is so distant from, or so powerless in relation to, the *global predicament* that they cannot have some influence. 'The front is long' make the best choices where you are, and things will *change*.

Overall there really is no choice; either we go *green*, totally and without exception, or we go nowhere.

Relationships   **alternative, perception, sustainable, philosophy.**
See also   **consumer, process, Impossible Party.**

CITY   *Green* thinking is ambiguous about the concept of the city.[1]
Modern humanity has a strong urban, if not urbane, streak; we like

the possibilities, the novelty, *energy* and excitement generated by the *compression* and anonymity of the traditional city.[2] Yet present city *structures* are *unsustainable*. 'As the cities become bigger, the sum total of practical ecological sensitivity in the population diminishes, until we are at last asking what is economically impossible of the planet.'[3]

Cities depend upon their *power* to command the vast range of inputs necessary to maintain their populations. Around the world ever greater *numbers* are pulled into vast megacities where deprived people believe they may find satisfaction for *needs* or *wants*. To feed itself the city has to command more *resources*; more people outside are deprived, and move to the city to find satisfaction...

Cities have their own self-sustaining *dynamic*; they provide the feedstock for *corporate/institutional* endeavour. The majority of people in cities are dependent for their livelihood upon such *structures* because they evolved precisely to command *resources* for the city. By strengthening these *corporate structures*, people increase their dependence, so ensuring the maintenance of *corporate/institutional* feedstock. In short, to maintain itself, the city develops a *dynamic* which *distorts* the world outside and people within. In many ways cities are about degeneracy.

Cities for the *future* should be designed with their *unsustainability* in mind; as plug-together modules which may be *re-used* in progressively smaller aggregates; as self-contained *structures* in acknowledgment of their essentially alien, out of *human scale, nature*.

The *green alternative* focuses on life in *community*, on *local satisfaction* in the provision of *need*, of life within *human scale*.[4] The objective is a different *life dynamic* to that projected by the city; one that, while encompassing as many of the advantages as possible, avoids the problems generated by mass humanity, and that is also *sustainable*.

Relationships   **scale, community, culture, institutions**.

See also   **centre, Impossible Party, local satisfaction, housing**.

References

1 See Leopold Kohr, 1989, *The Inner City: From Mud to Marble*, Y Lolfa, Talybont, Dyfed, Wales.
2 See Lewis Mumford, 1938, *The Culture of Cities*, 1961; *The City in History*, Penguin Books, London.
3 Theodore Roszak, 1981, *Person/Planet: The Creative Disintegration of Industrial Society*, Paladin, London.
4 Kirkpatrick Sale, 1980, *Human Scale*, Secker & Warburg, London.

See also *Fourth World Review*, a publication 'for small nations, small communities and the human spirit', SAE to 24 Abercorn Place, London NW8 9XP.

CIVIL DISOBEDIENCE see **non-violent direct action**.

CIVIL LIBERTIES, CIVIL RIGHTS see **rights**.

CIVILISATION A difficult concept to define, even in *grey* terminology. It implies living in a state of enlightenment, with an educated and refined population. Also a highly developed *society*, with a rich *culture*. All the terms used to describe civilisation are *relative*; there is no absolute state of civilisation, and one *culture's* civilisation may be another's unthinkable barbarism. 'As civilisation advances, poetry almost necessarily declines.'[1] Our feelings about civilisation are ambiguous, for there is a cost, only partly recognised when incurred, for its advantages.

It is convenient to think of *ways of life* with particular characteristics, and which endured for some time, as civilisations, e.g. the Roman, Greek, etc. Our present civilisation is distinguished by its *dependence* upon the consumption of *finite* resources; if only for this reason it is *unsustainable*, bound for failure as certainly, if more *catastrophically*, as those of the past. One characteristic all civilisations have shared is the unshakable belief in their *power* to endure indefinitely.

Greens seek a different civilisation, one characterised by *sustainability* within the *limits* of the *biosphere* and planetary resources; by *balance* in all expressions of *life*; by *diversity* of *human cultures* under a thin *green cultural umbrella*; by *freedom* to fulfil *potential*, combined with *responsibility* in the *choice* of *possibilities*. 'True civilisation may be looked at as a positive-sum game between human beings and the rest of nature in which both emerge as winners.'[2]

Relationships **culture, philosophy**.
See also **terminality, catastrophe, change**.
References
1 Thomas Babington Macaulay (1800–59) *Literary Essays: Milton*.
2 Ignacy Sachs, in *Resurgence Magazine*, Ford House, Hartland, Bideford, Devon, England, May 1983.

CLIMATE Conditions of temperature, winds, humidity, rainfall, etc.; expression of average conditions of weather for area, region or season. Characteristic of planetary zone, as in tropical, temperate, arctic, etc.

CLIMATIC CHANGE (aka CLIMATIC SHIFT) A natural pheno-menon produced by the interaction of many influences. Among these are: the solar system *environment* of the planet; and the radiation and particle emissions from the sun, which vary, princi-pally with the 11-year sun-spot cycle, but also with the distance of the earth from the sun; *changes* in planetary inclination to the path of its solar orbit; variations in planetary geography and chemical composition; and *changes* in the composition of the *biosphere*.

Human activity has recently become a factor in climatic change. We are changing the composition of the atmosphere; generating *waste* heat, and degrading the *biosphere* on a massive scale. The effects are largely unpredictable, but they are not likely to be benign.

Relationships **pollution, economics, technology.**
See also **greenhouse effect, ozone.**
References
See John Gribben, 1989, *Hothouse Earth: The Greenhouse Effect and Gaia*, Bantam Press, London.

CLINICAL ECOLOGY Study of allergy and food/chemical intol-erance in relation to *chemical pollution* of food and the *environ-ment.* Therapeutic system based on *pollution* reduction and control of body reactions to substances which precipitate *symptoms* in susceptible individuals by the use of minute doses of the substances which are believed to provoke reactions (see **symptoms**).

Analysis of illness and proposals for *health* based on the propo-sition that you cannot have healthy people in an unhealthy *envi-ronment*, that 'the needs of the planet are the needs of the person, and vice versa'.[1]

Many *grey* doctors, including most allergists, do not agree with clinical ecologists about causes, *symptoms* or appropriate treat-ment of allergic disorders. According to clinical ecologists,[2] but not conventional allergists, allergy can be masked so that reactions are not readily apparent. These masked allergies are believed to cause illnesses ranging from migraine through abdominal problems and aches to schizophrenia.

Relationships **health, ecology.**
See also **environment, pollution.**
References
1 Theodore Rozak, 1979, *Person/Planet: The Creative Disintegration of Industrial Society*, Gollancz, London.
2 British Society for Clinical Ecology, Dr Michael Radcliffe, Hythe Medical Centre, Hythe, Hampshire, England.

CLOTHING One of the basic necessities in most parts of the world.

An *extension* of the skin which, beyond practicality, may be frequently changed as a means of display and communication.

The majority of clothing is made from *artificial* substances. For the *future* we need to *change* to *natural* substances like wool, linen and cotton.

Relationships   **needs, sustainability.**

See also   **artificial, pollution.**

CLUB OF ROME An informal association concerned with the present and future predicament of man. Formed in 1968 by Italian economist and industrial manager, Dr Aurelio Peccei, a group of 30 individuals from 10 countries first met at the Accademia dei Linci in Rome – hence the name.

The purposes of the Club of Rome were to foster understanding of the interacting components, *economic, political, natural* and *social,* that contribute to the global *human dynamic,* with the objective of influencing the public and policy makers on *future decisions.*

Their most influential work so far has been the publication of *The Limits to Growth.*[1] Based on interactive computer *modelling* of various aspects of *growth,* population, industrial output, *food, resource depletion,* and *pollution,* they concluded that there are *limits* to *growth.*

Although time and awareness have made their conclusion obvious, the importance of this aspect of the work of the Club of Rome is in the methods they used. *Modelling* the interaction of aspects of the *biosphere,* mapping the *web of life* and its *dynamic,* is an essential future task for our understanding and *stewardship* of the planet, and the complete understanding of the *limits* within which we have to *live.*

Relationships   **models, limits, morph mapping, web of life.**

See also   **economics, pollution, Gaia.**

References

1 Donella H. Meadows, Dennis L. Meadows, Jorgen Randers, William W. Behrens, 1972, *The Limits to Growth: A Report for the Club of Rome's project on the Predicament of Mankind,* Pan Books, London.

CO-EVOLUTION (see **evolution**) The evolution of things together; things which evolve together. First used in ecology to describe reciprocal evolutionary relationships.

The most important aspect of co-evolution is that between

humans and their *culture*. From within this *symbiosis* we project *institutional extensions* into the *global environment* where they develop a de facto *life* of their own. The implications of this product of co-evolution are profound (see **institutions**).

Relationships   **ecology, evolution, culture, institution.**
See also   **symbiosis, synergy.**

COHERE, COHERENCE, COHERENT   Of parts or whole; sticking together, united, consistent, compatible.

Important property of parts of *system*, essential for integrity of *whole*. *Life* forms a coherent planetary *whole*, except for its present human dimension.

Relationships   **holism, system, structure.**
See also   **anticipation.**

COLLECTIVE   see **commune, co-operative, community.**
COLLECTIVE SUBCONSCIOUS   see **subconscious.**

COMMON OWNERSHIP (see **briarpatch, co-operative**)   A business or enterprise in which all those engaged own the capital resources and share products and profits.

'The third way in industry' (Ernest Bader, founder of the Scott Bader Commonwealth), avoiding the conflict of interests between labour and capital.

COMMUNE   Group of people living together intentionally and sharing accommodation, goods, etc.

An idealistic solution to many of the problems and absurdities of living in *grey culture*. However, it is not an easy option. The axiom that hell is other people can be too easily verified, possibly because although humans are essentially tribal animals, returning to close proximity living is both against recent *evolutionary* trends and involves more subtle *forces* in our *nature* than we presently recognise.

There are many communes around the world, each different, reflecting the interests and intentions of their members. Communes tend to organise in *networks*.

Relationships   **community, network, co-operative.**
See also   **housing, life style.**
References

If you would like to know more, SAE to: Communes Network, c/o Some People in Leicester, 89 Evington Road, Leicester, England; or, International Communes Network, Communiad, Box 15128, 10465 Stockholm, Sweden.

COMMUNITY Organised political, social or municipal body; body of people living in same locality, or having same religion or profession. Also group practising community of goods (see **commune**). A community is the basic cell of the body social. 'A community is a social unit in which the personal relationships of its members are the dominant influence determining its character.'[1]

Community is central to *green* ideas of *social/economic* organisation for the *future. Green* interpretation of community concentrates on concepts of *human scale,* identity and mutality. It is a positive idea, concerned primarily with the *quality of life.* A *social* community may be any group where everyone is known to the others, where privacy is possible and isolation avoidable, where all may speak and every voice be heard. The direction of *life* in the *future* is seen in *self-reliant* communities of compatible individuals/families, controlling every aspect of their lives, organised into *federal networks* of *need* or interest.

Human scale in community can be seen as a global *network* of a million communities of around a thousand people, where *diversity* among communities will provide a variety of *socio-cultural* options for individuals.

Life in community could re-connect people with the realities of the land, the *carrying capacity* of the *bio-region,* the *limits* of the *natural systems* within which we have to *live,* while simultaneously making the riches of human ability and experience available.

Living in small community therefore makes every kind of sense to me; living closer to other people, living more lightly on the land, using less, wasting less, becoming more attuned to the earth's rhythms, learning to be less dependent on the dominant society's economic institutions and so less attached by necessity to its values and demands – all these things taken together begin to form a picture for me of what life is supposed to be all about.[2]

Life in community should be an agreeable way of expressing the flow of *life,* of allowing for personal idiosyncrasy within shared aspirations and for *freedom* with *responsibility.*

Relationships   **culture, bioregion, life structure, diversity**.

See also   **human scale, limits, anarchy**.

References

1 John Papworth, in *Fourth World Review,* Number 38, 1990, 24 Abercorn Place, London NW8 9XP.
2 George Clark, in *Communities* magazine, March/April, 1971.

COMPETENCE   see **efficiency, system**.

COMPETITION (see **rules**)   Ethic or value of present *culture*, whereby the vast majority lose, or things are chosen on the basis of exclusive qualities.

The dominance of competition as a *socio-economic principle* is rejected by *greens* in favour of *co-operation*, where everyone may share the rewards, objectives may be achieved with minimal *waste*, and things may be selected by consideration of all their qualities.

Competition should be removed from areas of *vital need*, precisely those areas where it is currently so disastrously present.

Relationships   **exclusion, waste, hierarchy**.
See also   **evolution, balance**.

COMPLEMENTARY MEDICINE

The range of healing practices which can be distinguished from mainstream medicine by their belief in the vital importance of the self-healing capabilities of the human body, and their general (although not universal) belief in the importance of a holistic approach to health.[1]

Relationships   **health, anticipation, holism, homoeostasis**.
See also   **alternative, thematic compatibility**.
References

1 John Button, 1988, *A Dictionary of Green Ideas: Vocabulary for a Sane and Sustainable Future*, Routledge & Kegan Paul, London.

COMPOST   Mixed manure of *organic* origin; loam soil or other medium with added *organic* matter.

COMPOST HEAP   Structure of layers of *organic* matter, left and allowed to rot down to produce compost; added to soil to improve/maintain soil fertility.

Much of what we currently *waste* is *organic* material; that is, it was recently alive or consists of *life* molecules. These substances are the planet's most valuable *resource*. All such *life* matter should be returned to the *cycle of life* at the highest *energy* level (greatest molecular complexity) possible. For these reasons all *organic* material should be composted, or left for the best use by *life*, e.g. by not burning cleared brush but leaving it to shelter other *life* forms as it slowly decays and its substance is re-absorbed by many levels of the *biosphere*.

The compost heap is not so much *recycling* as a means of completing the *cycle of life*.

Relationships   **organic, biodynamic**.

See also   **waste, away, recycle**.

References

See Lawrence D. Hills, 1977, *Organic Gardening*, Penguin Books, London.

COMPRESS   Squeeze together, bring into small space.

COMPRESSION, SOCIAL COMPRESSION   The effect of crowding, where population *numbers* are increasing rapidly; state before fundamental *change* caused by *numbers*. The same effect may be created or exacerbated by the same *numbers* moving faster in the same space.

Part of the *evolutionary* mechanism (see **evolution**). *Life* converts its *environment* into replicas of itself. Compression is generated by increasing *numbers*; they will either exhaust the *environment* and *sink*, or *shift* to a successive *evolutionary* form.

The point about compression by population *numbers* is that it distorts *natural* patterns of *living, changes* behaviour among those subjected to it, and *changes* the *nature* of subject individuals, groups and species. The distorted species may then *change* the *balance of nature* in the *environment* around it (see **morphology**).

Much of the endemic stress in *grey culture* is caused by compression; the resulting disease statistics are *symptomatic* indicators of the underlying *socio-cultural* malaise. Part of the *problem* is that crowding and compression (and stress itself) are exciting – they get the adrenaline flowing. The combination of crowded sedentary living which at the same time excites can not only be prematurely fatal for individuals, but it tends to *create* a self-perpetuating *socio-cultural cycle* which may prove globally fatal.

Much aberrant behaviour may be ascribed to living in a state of compression (see **sink**). This may be seen in relative terms, since one of the effects of compression is to stimulate *changes* which may lead to a breakout into a new *evolutionary paradigm* (see **shift**). The more usual outcome is a *catastrophic sink*.

It is probable that those subjected to compression by their own behaviour are unaware of the *process* and its effects.

Relationships   **anticipation, evolution, sink, shift**.

See also   **change, catastrophe, terminal culture**.

CONFRONTATION   see **opposition, non-violent direct action**.

CONNECTEDNESS   see **holism**.

CONSCIOUS   Aware of, self and/or external circumstances, knowing (see **mindset**).
CONSCIOUSNESS   Totality of person's perceived thoughts and feelings, perception of existence or parts thereof.

> Consciousness is always consciousness *of* something, it is a whole divisible only falsely into an independent subject and object. In consequence everything in consciousness is meaningful, it being the function of consciousness to synthesize the flow of human experience into intelligible structures.[1]

Greens think in terms of the necessity for changing human consciousness; of developing a unified consciousness, based on *green philosophy* and understanding of the *needs* of the *biosphere*; of *life structures* which are sustainable while allowing for different levels of consciousness or degrees of *awareness* (see **structure**).

The ability to influence, to make *choices*, within the unfolding of the *potential* of all things (see **Tao**, **morphology**).
CONSCIOUSNESS-RAISING   Process of increasing awareness of particular issues, of personal growth.

Intentional consciousness raising is usually a group activity, where *knowledge* and experience are exchanged, and ideally a *synergistic dynamic* occurs which brings new insight or understanding to all participants.

Public consciousness-raising is generally by way of demonstration, or specific media activity (as *Greenpeace* actions, or writing books), or other campaign.

Relationships   **mindset, perception, evolution, growth.**
See also   **assumption, expectations, change.**
References
1   John Sturrock, 1986, *Structuralism*, Paladin, London.

CONSENSUS   Agreement on matter or action; majority view.

Greens reject the adequacy of the majority view in consensus. Its meaning is taken as a *decision* supported by all those involved or affected. All *decisions* of *principle* should be by consensus, whereas those of *detail*, subsequent to *principle*, may be taken by *democratic* majority (see **democracy**).
Relationships   **affinity group, community, decision.**
See also   **democracy, rights.**

CONSERVATION Preservation, especially of *natural resources*, environment, etc. 'The briefest definition runs; Conservation is wise use, but this implies acceptance of the sophisticated assumption that non-use may be an acceptable type of use.'[1]

There are several applications of conservation, some valid, some dubious. Conservation of *finite resources*, or things made from them, is obviously essential. Conservation of buildings, etc., which are noteworthy or part of a *culture's* heritage is desirable. Having to conserve *natural* habitats, species, elements of the *biosphere* is an admission of the failure of humanity to recognise the *realities* of *life*. From where we now find ourselves it may be the only option, essential if parts of the *web of life* are to *survive*, but too often it is regarded as enough, as an end rather than a means for a new beginning.

Conservation is necessarily retrospective, since things are rarely in a state of preservation in *nature*. *Nature* should not require it, and unless the *human activity* which makes it necessary is also addressed, half the equation is missing. 'It will take a few more years for our societies to understand that environmental protection, improvement, and all these other fine words serve simply as ornamental paving stones to hell.'[2]

<u>Relationships</u>   **restoration, wilderness, web of life, Gaia.**
<u>See also</u>   **rights, life.**
<u>References</u>
1 Max Nicholson, 1969, *The Environmental Revolution: A Guide to the New Masters of the World,* Hodder, London.
2 Rudolf Bahro, quoted in *Fourth World Review,* Number 34/35, 1989, 24 Abercorn Place, London NW8 9XP.

CONSERVER SOCIETY Means of transition from *consumer society* to *sustainable future*: living in simple sophistication, without *waste* or pointless affluence and primitive status display; reducing *transport* needs, especially the *waste* of international trade (see **economy**); moving towards *stable self-reliance* and *community self-sufficiency*; using *appropriate technology*; seeking *ways of life* which re-integrate *human scale* activity within the *bioregion*.

<u>Relationships</u>   **choice, potential, change.**
<u>See also</u>   **consumer, Impossible Party, limits.**

CONSUME Destroy, use up, eat or drink, spend, waste; (passive) entirely preoccupied with.

CONSUMER   One who consumes.

Person who buys goods or services; everyone is to some degree a consumer. Over the years the *balance* in *society* and among individuals between being a consumer or a producer has changed, mirroring the *shift* first from an agrarian society to an *industrial economy*, and now to a concentration on services and *institutional* manipulation. While the *First World* still consumes each other's washing machines and drives each other's cars, increasingly material goods and necessities are fed into service *economies* from a production base which has moved elsewhere. Commanding wealth to maintain consumption is part of the unbalanced *dynamic* of the present global *economic system*.

The imbalance in the way of life of individuals in consumer societies is reflected in the fact that a significant proportion of such populations report 'shopping' as their principle leisure activity.

The *future* will require a *restoration* of *balance* within a different *economic system*. While we may trade and consume the products of others, the *dynamic* must be based on mutality and equity, rather than privilege and exploitation – 'they [prisoners] are degraded to the status of mere consumers'.[1]

CONSUMERISM   The protection of the interests of consumers.

The dominant ethic of consumerism is 'more but better please – and preferably cheaper.' The focus is on value for money from the *perspective* of the purchaser. The concept is a reflection of the *expectations* of populations divorced from the *reality* of *resources*, industry, agriculture and *food*. Increasingly, the consumer's contract with the world is to push buttons; pushing the ultimate button will consume everything.

CONSUMER SOCIETY   One existing in a state of institutional dependence. Superstore, car, freeway, TV, little house (nice kids), lost in present, isolated amid all the others, running on credit, fast-forward, going nowhere.

EXCESSIVE CONSUMPTION   A requirement for the *health* of the *terminal economy* and its belief in perpetual *growth*.

GREEN CONSUMERISM   The belief that by informed consumption, industry and agriculture may be reformed, *pollution* diminished, and the *environment* saved. A conceptual contradiction (see **system**).

While providing a useful entrée to awareness of the multitude of considerations involved in the consumer society, it is at best a way of slowing world degradation, a means of buying a little more *time*. However, we must all start where we find ourselves, and in the *unsustainable terminal culture* for the majority, that is as consumers.

That consumer is best who consumes least. 'The most subverse act in a consumer society is the refusal to consume; it is also one of the safest.'[2]

Relationships **Impossible Party, economy, utility, community**.

See also **conservation, pollution**.

References

1 Ivan Illich, 1973, *Tools for Conviviality*, Marian Boyars, London.

See John Elkington and Julia Hailes, 1988, *The Green Consumer Guide: From Shampoo to Champagne, High Street Shopping for a Better Environment*, Gollancz, London.

2 Derek Wall, 1990, *Getting There: Steps Towards a Green Society*, Green Print, London.

CO-OPERATE Work together for a purpose; concur in producing an effect.

CO-OPERATION Act (perhaps, more properly, art) of working, living, sharing, together for agreed purposes or ends.

The co-operative *principle* is dominant in *green* affairs. In this sense it is the *opposite* of *competition*; co-operation allows ends to be achieved for all with the minimum of *waste* and maximum *utility* of *resources*.

Co-operation implies selection on a wide qualitative basis; many attributes, talents, properties may be included.

CO-OPERATIVE A form of organisation; a group enterprise or project operated for the benefit of the members of the group.

There are two strands to the co-operative movement in Britain. Traditionally co-operatives were organised to benefit *consumers*, originally to supply sound produce at reasonable prices to members. Such co-operative societies have developed into massive retail chains and specialist suppliers, e.g. farming supply co-operative societies.

More recently producer co-operatives have become more numerous. In the mid 1960s there were five producer co-operatives in Britain, organised as Demintry (the Society for Democratic Integration in Industry), and some years ago a woman's magazine supplement listed 3,500 women's co-operatives.

The essence of producer co-operatives is that those who *work* in them have equal status and exercise control over all affairs of the enterprise, although *authority* may be delegated for day-to-day matters. Sometimes co-operatives are referred to as co-ownerships, workers' control enterprises or syndicates. A good traditional test of the degree of co-operation and equity is 'do you decide your own wages?'

The growth of co-operative enterprises in Britain owes much to the formation of ICOM[1] (Industrial Common Ownership Movement) and ICOF[2] (Industrial Common Ownership Finance). It was also helped by the founding, via an Act of Parliament in 1978, of the Co-operative Development Agency (CDA). The central agency is quite properly withering away, but nearly every local authority has a local CDA to assist those wishing to start a co-operative enterprise.

The next stage for such co-operatives is for the enterprise to become related directly to *community* needs in a *system* of *mutual* response and *dynamic stability*.

CO-OPERATIVE LIVING (see **community**)   Ways of living where as much as possible is shared, from housing to goods and work. Ranging from *communes* to *common ownerships*, the underlying ethic is that of co-operation. Does it make sense for ten houses each to have two cars, two TVs, two fridges, a freezer, washing machine, vacuum cleaner, etc.? It does for General Products Inc., but not for people or the earth.

HOUSING   (or other specific) CO-OPERATIVE A group organised on a co-operative basis to provide access to shared facilities for its members.[3]

Relationships   **common ownership, community, economy, ego, inclusivity, potential, synergy**.

See also   **competition, consumer**.

References

1 Industrial Common Ownership Movement, Vassilli House, 20 Central Road, Leeds, England.

2 Industrial Common Ownership Finance, 4 St Giles Street, Northampton, England; or the Scottish Co-operatives Development Committee, Templeton Business Centre, Bridgeton, Glasgow, Scotland.

3 National Federation of Housing Co-operatives, 88 Old Street, London, EC1V 9AX; or Scottish Homes, Roseberry House, Haymarket, Edinburgh, Scotland.

CO-OWNERSHIP   see **co-operative**.

COUNTER-   In the opposite direction; running counter to; act contrary to.

Although counter- has elements of *opposition*, in that it is a *reaction* to something *established*, it is intended to mean something more distinct, in that it offers a radical difference rather than a simple *opposition* which has the danger of forming a *thematically compatible whole* with that which is *opposed.* Counter- implies different *ends*, although the *means* may be similar.

Thus whereas *grey society* believes in *competition*, *greens* believe that *co-operation* is more rational. Although the *ends* achieved may appear the same, this is only because the real costs of *competition* are ignored and the benefits of *co-operation* discounted.

COUNTER-ACTION   Action which involves different solutions to those adopted by *grey society.*

COUNTER-CULTURE (see **culture**)   *Culture* based on a different *philosophy* to that of the mainstream, living by different *principles* which will generate other practices.

COUNTER-ECONOMY   A general term covering all the activities, e.g. *co-operatives*, black, voluntary, *alternatives* such as appropriate *technology*, involving new approaches to various aspects of the *economic system.*

Relationships   opposition, alternative, change.

See also   culture, economy, creativity.

References

1 Theodore Roszak, 1971, *The Making of a Counter Culture*, Faber & Faber, London.

CREATE   Bring into *existence.*

CREATION   Beginning of *existence.*

The implication of 'bring' in create is that *existence* is brought about by or through something. The totality of creation is usually ascribed to various deities; in their absence it may be thought of as the *nature* of things to be and to come into *being.*

CREATIVITY   The expression of potency (see **power**). In the expression of a creative act, it is usually assumed that an improvement occurs.

Humans find essential pleasure in creativity. It can involve every level of our *being*, from the most ancient residues of our *evolutionary* past to our furthest reach into the *future* of which we are capable. Yet creation is a paradoxical act. The creation of something inevitably involves the destruction of something else; the new replaces the old. Perhaps recognition of this creativity has become compartmentalised in *grey culture* and classified into means of legitimate expression, e.g. art, literature, design, advertising, PR, and so on. Eventually it slides into ways which serve the *culture* which legitimises it. Creativity ultimately disappears in the maintenance of *stability.* The most basic expression of the *need* to create may be found in the desire to create order.

Creativity has a *cyclic quality*, reflecting that of *life* itself, and probably that of the cosmic arena in which it is set. Periods of *stability*, of *uniformity* of expression, are *disrupted* by something new coming into *existence*. So there is inevitable conflict – creation versus *stability* (better the devil you know?). Creativity is the exception in *nature* rather than the norm, yet everything that exists is the result of creativity, and the *future* depends upon *viable creation*.

Human creativity has *extended* our influence to every part of the biosphere and far beyond into space and *time*. As we are slowly learning, to our cost, many creations have entirely unpredictable effects – 'I exist therefore I think' (see **Cartesianism**). That which is created tends to develop a *life* of its own.

Creativity has a *spiritual* dimension. The act itself, whether of genetic *change* in the form of *life*, in expressions of the human *spirit*, in perception brought from the edge of sanity or the *future*, or in the birth of a galaxy, may be the sign of a restless *spirit*.

Creativity is also bound inextricably with *ego*: 'The primary imagination I hold to be the living power and prime agent of all human perception, and as a repetition in the finite mind of the eternal act of creation in the infinite I AM.'[1] Paradoxically, it is also the means chosen to extinguish the pain of awareness; we seek to create beyond ourselves to deny the proposition of *mortality*.

Relationships **morphology, change, being, purpose, existence, spirit**.

See also **synthesis, formative causation, extension**.

References

1 Samuel Taylor Coleridge (1772–1834), *Biographia Literaria*, Ch. 13.

CRISIS *Turning point*, especially of disease; time of danger.

A decisive point in *time* or *process*, the culmination of *events* from which *change* must ensue. Hence *environmental* crisis, population crisis, etc.

The crisis of capitalism hypothesis of Marxist–Leninists is based upon false *assumptions*; generally, that capitalism will face a catastrophic crisis because of its nature. However, crises are the essential lifeblood of the *system*; if markets remain static they fail, fluctuations are essential. Profits can be made from both shortages and gluts.

Relationships **anticipation, change, shift**.

See also **catastrophe, evolution, numbers**.

CUL-DE-SAC (from the French = literally bottom of a bag) Usually a blocked path or way with only one means of access.

A *model* of the *global predicament* inspired by Western *industrial culture*. As we see termination at the end of the cul-de-sac, more of the world's population wish to pack into the same *predicament*; they cannot yet see the blank wall. How do we get out? That is the problem that the *green* movement addresses.

Relationships **casualty, problem, culture, change**.

See also **shift, sink, compression, numbers**.

CULTURE That which is cultivated.

The concept of *human* culture is a complex one, but as with many complex things there is an underlying simplicity; culture is that which is repeated. The *form* of repetition does not matter; unique things of a *culture*, like the Mona Lisa, may be copied or simply repeated in the mind at the mention of the words. Thus our inner *awareness* of culture may consist of many things of which we have no direct knowledge, but of which we have learned through a variety of communications. And, as Marshall McLuhan[1] pointed out, the means of communication themselves have a modifying influence on the culture they propagate. In cultural terms nothing is value-free, nothing is culturally neutral; there are no innocent bystanders, everything has some effect; the more it is repeated the greater the effect is likely to be.

Dominant aspects of *life style* and *values* of members of a culture are frequently summarised as a description of the culture; thus 'Western industrial culture', 'Christian culture', 'Coca-cola culture' etc. Of course cultures are never that simple, and modern cultures are complexes of many overlapping and interacting subcultures. This interaction, of subcultures and *individuals*, produces the *dynamic* of the culture.

Individuals interact *symbiotically* with their *culture*, both forming and being formed by it. The culture into which people are born is the dominant factor in shaping their lives, their *assumptions, expectations* and beliefs. And in turn they contribute to that culture helping to maintain its direction and *sustain* its *dynamic*.

The origin of culture is in the beliefs of people; these cause them to behave in particular ways which are repeated if they are satisfactory. What people believe in this sense is their *philosophy*. Culture is the projection of *philosophy* via beliefs, *principles* and *assumptions* derived from that *philosophy*. As with communication, *philosophy* interacts with culture in *symbiosis*.

All current major cultures, whatever their founding *philosophies*, share one common characteristic: they are *unsustainable*; their *philosophical* foundation is flawed. Generically they are termed *grey* or *terminal* cultures because they are based on *ways of life* which are destroying the *planet* and are dependent on *finite resources*.

Culture is a product of combined human consciousness, the sum of our beliefs, attitudes, thoughts and creativity. It determines how we cope with the world, how we react to everything that happens to us; it determines our relationships and the way we think. Our culture is dominated by male assumptions, male priorities; technology and economics, the priorities of business, have created a world ecological crisis which can only be met with a resurgence of feminine values.[2]

Greens seek to create a *sustainable* culture. To achieve this, *green philosophy*[3] attempts to define the *needs* for *creating sustainable* human *ways of life*, ways which are complementary to the *biosphere*. The primary *need* is for the propagation of a *global green* cultural umbrella under which a *diversity* of human subcultures may shelter indefinitely.

Since culture is that which is repeated, by spreading *green* ideas and beliefs that culture will be created.

GREY CULTURE   see **terminal**.

TERMINAL CULTURE   see **terminal**.

Relationships   **philosophy, symbiosis, sustainability, mindset, meme**.

See also   **diversity, limits**.

References

1 Marshall McLuhan and Quention Fiore, 1967, *The Medium is the Massage*, Penguin Books, London.
2 Arabella Melville, 1990, *Natural Hormone Health: Drug-free Ways to Manage Your Life*, Thorsons, London.
3 Colin Johnson, 1991, *The Green Bible: Creating Sustainable Life on Earth*, Thorsons, London.

CYCLES   Recurring series of events, operations, or states. Also wheeled vehicle, as bicycle, tricycle, etc.

CYCLIC   Recurring in cycles, belonging to a cycle.

For *greens*, cyclic, in the sense of belonging to a cycle, is a *principle* which should govern all human *processes*. In *grey culture* most *processes* are *linear*, reflecting the predominance of analytical thought and the belief in simple cause and effect *relationships*.

Thus *linear* accounting ignores the irreplaceable *nature* of *finite resources* and how to cost (or how to ensure) the final disposal (sic) of products and waste. Cyclic accounting would show the true cost of things by taking the complete cycle into account. This would reveal the impossible direction of current *progress*.

Greens believe that human activity should be compatible with the *needs* of *nature*. Thus everything we produce should either last indefinitely, or be designed to integrate with other parts of *self-sustaining natural* cycles. Only in this way can *waste* and *pollution* be eliminated.

CYCLE OF LIFE   Everything in *nature* is cyclic.[1] If we journey in from space, the *universe* itself is probably cyclic; like most others, our local galaxy spins; on one of its outer arms our solar *system* spins around the sun. Our planet turns on its axis as it follows its annual path around the sun. Because the axis of the *earth* leans in relation to its path, we have the annual cycle of seasons. And because *earth* has a satellite, the moon, we have another cycle of ocean tides and weather influences. These cyclic phenomena produce effects on our planet which stimulate and govern its *life*. The effects of the cyclic revolutions of moon and planet in relation to the sun act as the interweaving eternal heartbeats of all *life*, the eternal cycles of heaven on earth.

Within the planetary whole there are many interacting cycles, from those of the *life* stock of carbon-based molecules, endlessly cycling through different levels of *energy* and forms of *life*, to the very fabric of the geosphere, as continents arise and subside, carried around the molten core by the motion of tectonic plates. Every aspect of the *Gaian whole* is involved in cyclic *processes*. All such *processes* are interconnected, all contributing simultaneously to the renewal and *stability* of the whole; *life* is *sustained* under the sum of the influences to which it contributes.[2]

The *global predicament* arises because human activity has broken or damaged many of the cycles which *sustain planetary life*. We do not know if, or to what degree, they may recover. For the *future* we must change our ways of doing things if there is to be any chance of *recovery*.

GREAT CYCLE OF LIFE   Description of planetary *life* as a whole, from inception to present; process of *Gaian whole*.[3]

The progressive divorce of *humanity* from *nature* under *mechanistic philosophy* has led us ever further out of the great cycle of life by encouraging us to believe that we can live without the *sustaining* activities of the *natural* world. This may be the greatest *illusion* of *terminal culture*; it leads to the proposition of trying to live as aliens on our home planet. The reality is that we either learn to live within or we perish without.

<u>Relationships</u>   **Gaia, morphology**.

<u>See also</u>   **creativity, synergy, symbiosis**.

<u>References</u>

1 See **energy**. For practically all purposes, energy cannot be regarded as cyclic; it is a one-way flux, a flow. The second law of thermodynamics (see **entropy**) holds until theoretical macro universal cycles are considered, and also, paradoxically, the minutiae of quantum effects. Part of the search in theoretical physics for a unifying theory seeks to reconcile these extremes.

2 James Lovelock, 1979, *Gaia: A New Look at Life on Earth*, Oxford University Press, Oxford, England.

3 James Lovelock, 1989, *The Ages of Gaia: A Biology of Our Living Planet*, Oxford University Press, Oxford, England.

DE- The problem with many de- words is that, at best, they simply imply the opposite of that upon which they depend; they usually do not define adequately or positively that which is desired. (See **opposition, thematic compatibility**.) Independent words and unambiguous meanings, which do not relate to those which they oppose, are therefore preferable.

DEATH Cessation of vital functions; event that marks the termination of *life*.

The end of one form, when its life-molecules are once more released to the *biosphere* to form new arrangements of *life*, or are directly absorbed by another as *food*. Something dies all the time so that others may live; the essence of the *great cycle of life* is the constant exchange of *energy* from one *life force* to others in the cumulative *processes* of *evolution*.

We all participate briefly in *life*, experiencing an individual interval in *eternity* during which our *form* grows from conception, to fulfil its *potential* as best it can, before returning with our death to the reservoir of *life*.

Being re-absorbed by the biosphere can be problematic; many people are so *polluted* with preservatives, *biocides* and drug residues, emulsifiers, stabilisers, etc., from *food*, plus the loading of *chemicals* they receive from the *industrial environment*, that a corpse can be an environmental hazard.[1] High temperature incineration may solve that problem, but add to the *greenhouse effect*. If we could clean ourselves up, old fashioned burial might be the best option. Or you could be eaten by a loved one; if I have to go, let me live on in essence as part of you, or let me run with the dogs and fly with the birds. . .

Relationships   **life, purpose**.

See also   **great cycle of life, holism**, total **toxic** overload.

References

1 The problem is widespread; whale corpses washed up on the east coast of America fit the US definition of toxic waste.

DECENTRALISATION   see **diffusion**.

DECISION (see **choice**)   Formal judgment; considered *choice*, making up one's mind, means of resolution.

Most of the decisions we make are *culturally* conditioned; that is they rely upon a complex of *assumptions* and *expectations* derived from our *culture*. For the *future* we need to be aware of our situation (see **global predicament**) and take *conscious* decisions.

Two parameters govern decisions for the *future*. Is it *sustainable*? Does it enhance *life*? If whatever is proposed does not meet these criteria we should decide against it and think again.

Relationships   **autopilot, perspective, responsibility, philosophy**.
See also   **assumption, expectation, hidden agenda**.

DEEP ECOLOGY   The development of *ecology*, a branch of biology concerned with organisms' relationships to one another and their surroundings, from a descriptive minor science (now referred to as shallow ecology) to the science of the relationships of all *life* and its context. 'The essence of deep ecology is to ask deeper questions. The adjective "deep" stresses that we ask why and how, whereas others do not.'[1]

Definitions of deep ecology vary; as the scientific part of *holistic* belief, it may also defy comprehensive definition. As a science it is in its infancy; however as a new world view, the *perspectives* of deep ecology, and of deep ecologists, are making major contributions to *green philosophy*.

[It] is emerging as a way of developing a new balance and harmony between individuals, communities and all of Nature. It can potentially satisfy our deepest yearnings; faith and trust in our most basic intuitions; courage to take direct action; joyous confidence to dance with the sensuous harmonies discovered through spontaneous, playful intercourse with the rhythms of our bodies, the rhythms of flowing water, changes in the weather and seasons, and the overall processes of life on Earth.[2]

Deep ecology is 'simple in means, rich in ends.'[1]
Relationships   **life, holism, Gaia**.
See also   **philosophy**.
References
1 Arne Naess, Norwegian philosopher, 'father' of deep ecology, quoted in 2.
2 Bill Devall and George Sessions, 1985, *Deep Ecology: Living as if Nature Mattered*, Peregrine Smith Books, Salt Lake City, Utah, USA.

DEMOCRACY   Form of government by all the people, either directly or by representative; form of society without hereditary, class, or other distinctions; tolerant of minority views.

Democracy is a flexible, fragile concept; it is also very rare. At its best it could give a direct and equal say to all those who are affected by *decisions*; at its worst it involves façades for the repression of minorities and the exercise of privilege. Passive representative democracy too easily becomes rule by *institutionalised* and unaccountable *bureaucracy.*

As a means of expressing the will of a body of people (a *community*) by voting, democracy is valid if: the voting basis is equal; the *process* is active; the *agenda* is open; and the *process* is *direct* and open to all those affected. Majority vote *decisions* should concern details, whereas matters of *principle* should be decided by *consensus*. Additionally, the *process* should facilitate whatever debate is necessary without limits (see **consensus**).

<u>Relationships</u>   **community, co-operative, ad hoc, politics.**
<u>See also</u>   **institution, agenda, choice.**

DEVELOPMENT   Gradual unfolding, fuller realisation of *potential, growth, evolution*; product, a more elaborate form.

In *grey culture* development usually means maximising *exploitation*; as in the undeveloped *(Third) World,* or urban, regional, industrial, etc., development. In the more general senses of fuller realisation, or more elaborate *forms*, the word has many applications.

Greens generally focus on the *exploitive* meaning. And there is the *problem*; most of us live in the developed world, where we accept all the advantages of our situation while at the same time seeing the impossibility of everyone in the undeveloped world doing the same. Resolving the contradiction is at the core of the search for *green economic* theories, which will offer *fulfilment* of *need* and *satisfaction* beyond basics, self/personal-development without destroying – developing to *death* – the *earth.*[1]

The most reasonable concept to emerge so far is *sustainable* development.[2]

SUSTAINABLE DEVELOPMENT   That is, *living* in ways which are *sustainable*; developing *natural resources* so that, while improving people's living standards, the source of that improvement is not exhausted.

Sustainable development is, at best, an unsatisfactory half-way house concept. Between the interests of *grey* and the *needs* of *green*, it may mean gardening wild rainforest in the name of conservation, or *exploiting* fragile *ecosystems* and endangered species in the name of *need*. It remains a *homocentric* concept, coupled to the ideas of *flow economics*. In short, it remains beset with unresolved contradictions.

However, sustainable development is not the same as *economic growth*, and the key to the development of sustainable development is *land reform*, no matter where in the world it is to be applied.

If valid, the concept demands that, at the same time that the *third world* engages in sustainable development, the *first* (over-developed) *world* should un-develop – another concept for which we lack a suitable word. The essence of what is required is that we should *live* in *sustainable* ways (see **sustainable, restoration, retrospective innovation**).

PERSONAL DEVELOPMENT (see **personal growth**)   We must go head first into the future.

Whatever an individual's circumstances, expanding self-*awareness*, combined with *global* awareness, is a priority. This may seem a mockery to the 25 per cent who starve, to those who suffer armed conflict as an everyday fact of *life* and *death*, to those who are deprived of the basic necessities of *life*. However it remains true (see *casualty problem*). Unless we change ourselves, our species, our *ways of life*, there will be no *future* (see **choice**). Part of the *first world dynamic* of un-development should be to assist the rest of the human family purposefully with the wealth and *resources* we will no longer *need*.[3]

Relationships   **morphology, growth, Impossible Party, economics, numbers, sustainable**.

See also   **sustainable, energy, consumption**.

References

1 See Ronald Banks (ed.), 1989, *Costing the Earth*, Shepeard-Walwyn, London; Mary Inglis and Sandra Kramer (eds), 1985, *The New Economic Agenda*, The Findhorn Press, Forres, Scotland, (especially the excellent contribution by José Lutzenberger); Guy Dauncey, 1988, *After the Crash: The Emergence of the Rainbow Economy*, Green Print, London.

2 Michael Redclift, 1987, *Sustainable Development: Exploring the Contradictions*, Methuen, London.

3 See Teresa Hayter, 1989, *Exploited Earth: Britain's Aid and the Environment*, Friends of the Earth, London.

DEVOLUTION, DEVOLVE   These are de- words for which there is no apposite alternative. Re-evolution would be correct, but revolution means something else.

Descent, fall, through a series of *changes*, as with property, by succession; deputing, delegating of *power* to lower responsible bodies, as in political devolution. The negative implications of descent, of failure, mar the concept.

For *greens* there are two areas of application for devolution. First in the political sense, where the devolution of *power* to progressively smaller units, eventually to the *community*, is seen as an essential requisite of a *sustainable future* (see **diffusion**). In *grey* usage this generally means the containment (retention) of *power* by passing it from one *institution* to another.

Second, in the re-evolutionary sense, where to halt our *terminal progress* we need to unravel our historical *socio-cultural evolution*, step back, and find a new direction towards a *sustainable future* (see **evolution**). This requires *conscious choice* of the options remaining to us, rather than reliance on blind *progress*.

Relationships   **diffusion, community, change**.
See also   **evolution, culture**.

DIFFUSE   Spread out, not concentrated; not concise.
DIFFUSION, DIFFUSING   Interpenetration of substances by natural movements of their particles; spread of elements of one *culture*, region or people to another.

The spread of *power* and control away from centralised *hierarchical structures* to progressively smaller social units, wherein individuals may take *responsibility* for their lives and the provision of *needs*. Diffusion is essential for the *creation* of different, *sustainable forms* of *social structure* and *organisation*.

Also, for this to happen the human population has to become less concentrated, or alternatively to remain concentrated but in fewer centres.

Relationships   **power, responsibility, community, federation**.
See also   **matrix, network, bioregion**.

DIGGER   (see **Leveller**) Colloquial. Australian or New Zealander, especially soldier; member of 17th-century English fundamentalist group who cultivated common land. More recently, hippie (sic) believing in universal common property.

From a sub-group of the Levellers, calling themselves the Diggers, who, under the leadership of Gerard Winstanley,[1] cultivated common land in Surrey and built houses before being driven off by the local establishment.

References
1 See Christopher Hill (ed.), 1973, *Winstanley: The Law of Freedom, and Other Writings*, Pelican Classics, Penguin Books, London.

DIRECT Straight, to the point, without intermediaries, unambiguous.
DIRECT ACTION   Exertion of pressure on *community* or body by action for declared end, as strike or non-compliance; action seeking immediate effect.

Society has many *structures – institutional*, habitual, *bureaucratic*, legal, etc. – designed to protect the status quo or *changes* the establishment wishes to impose. Direct action is a means of penetrating these *structures* to confront the issues and people directly involved. Also used as a means of bringing issues to the attention of a wider audience via the media, as with *Greenpeace* actions. The essence of direct action is that it is undertaken by individuals directly, rather than through intermediaries, such as politicians, or processes, such as filling in forms or petitions. Hence it is also referred to derogatively as 'extra-parliamentary' or 'outside recognised channels' by those who disagree with it, and as 'people power' by those in favour.

DIRECT KNOWING, DIRECT KNOWLEDGE   see **intuition**.
Relationships   **responsibility, freedom**.
See also   **change, hidden agenda, community**.

DIVERSE Various, different, unlike in nature, appearance of qualities. qualities.
DIVERSITY   Being diverse.

It is a *green* axiom that in *nature* diversity is strength. It is a requirement for the *future* in human affairs; we must seek *unity* in diversity (and vice versa).

The essence of the belief in the necessity for diversity in *natural* and human affairs is that it provides an *anticipatory* safeguard against the unseen hazards of the *future* and is an expression of the *potential* of things.

Diversity increases the capacity of *balance* within the *dynamics* of *evolution*; the greater the diversity, the greater the *stability* of the *whole*.

For the *future greens* see human *communities* as diverse *cultural* expressions within the *unity* of a *green philosophy*. However, it is important to avoid pressures for 'green conformity'; the front is long, there must be room for all, now and in the future.

Of the problems we have generated, it is the loss of biological and *environmental* diversity that humanity has inspired that may prove the most serious, and in the long term the most disastrous. We may have lost so many elements of the *web of life* that crucial parts of what remains may also fail.

Relationships   **synergy, symbiosis, community, culture**.

See also   **balance, evolution, morphology**.

DREAM   Series of random but connected perceptions in mind, usually during sleep.

Possibly our *conscious* experience of the inner *life* of our *minds*; the interaction between *consciousness* and the rest, of which we become *aware* during our most unconscious states. Dreams can contain the most extreme possibilities from within, for which we may or may not be ready (see *morphic resonance*).

DREAMTIME   Australian natural people's expression, roughly meaning connectedness.

That state of near *consciousness*, a timeless state when *past* and *future* merge, when self-*awareness* dissolves into *awareness* of everything that has contributed to the present experience of self, and things that may come beyond the present individual experience.

Relationships   **intuition, morphology, holism**.

See also   **Tao**.

DUALISM   see **Cartesianism**.

DYNAMIC(S)   Of motive force, as opposed to static; of force in operation.

Motion, flow of *energy* within a *system*; the result of *energy* flow.

The expression of the force or *energy* generated between things, or the expression of such a *potential*; as in population dynamics, the effects caused by certain *numbers*. The expression may be *stable*, or *changing*, as in the power output of an engine at various revolutions per minute.

For *greens* the most important idea of dynamics is in the inter-action of various expressions of *life*, particularly in that produced between humans and their *socio-cultural extensions*. Thus we wish to *change* the *socio-cultural* dynamic of *grey culture* from *termi-nality* or, *alternatively*, to *create* a *sustainable* dynamic, a *way of life* which may continue indefinitely.

The dynamics of a *sustainable future* would be *cyclic*; everything would be part of the continuous *process* of *life*, contained within its *great cycle*, yet allowing *change* and the *fulfilment* of *potential*. This is the essence of the dynamic *balance* we have to achieve.

All *systems* have dynamic properties, from the smallest elementary particle to the *universe*, most of them *cyclic* in *nature*. The more complex the *system* the wider its range of dynamic expressions is likely to be (it has greater *potential*). For this reason much of what we do, of *processes* we initiate, has unpredictable effects. We simply do not know enough about the dynamic *potential* of things. Who would have thought hairsprays could destroy the *ozone layer*?

Relationships   **energy, synergy, potential, critical mass, symbiosis, vitality**.

See also   **structure, system, synthesis, life**.

EARTH Dry land, soil ground; the old English name for our home planet. 'We are part of the earth and it is part of us ... The earth does not belong to man; man belongs to the earth. This we know. All things are connected, like the blood which unites one family.'[1]

Our concept of earth as planet has been changed by the *Gaia hypothesis*,[2] which describes the planet as a total *living system*, almost analogous to a mega-cell.[3]

EARTH COMMUNITY A conceptual description, used to emphasise the fact that humanity is a part of the total community of planetary *life*.

EARTH DAYS Celebrations of *life*, the earth, the universe and everything, originated in 1969 by Americans Gaylor Nelson and Dennis Hayes. First happened in America in 1970; by 1990 the idea had spread around the world and involved millions. Usually celebrated on 22 April (see **celebration**).

Relationships **Gaia**, **life**, **sustainable**.

References

1 Chief Seattle, 1855.
2 James Lovelock, 1979. *Gaia: A New Look at Life on Earth*, Oxford University Press, Oxford, England; James Lovelock, 1989. *The Ages of Gaia: A Biology of Our Living Earth*, Oxford University Press, Oxford, England.
3 Lewis Thomas, 1980. *The Lives of a Cell*, Allen Lane, London.

EARTH FIRST! An organisation and newspaper[1] based in Arizona, USA, committed to 'any creative means of effective defence against the forces of industrial totalitarianism'. Their logo consists of a crossed tomahawk and monkeywrench.[2]

Ecomilitancy (see **eco-**) raises many questions for *greens*. How far should we go to save the world; under what circumstances, if any, is destruction, of artefacts or people, justified? It is the old question: 'Do the ends justify the means?', and the even older question: 'What shall it profit a man, if he shall gain the whole world, and lose his own soul?'[3] Where does acceptable ecomilitancy slide into unacceptable ecofascism?

We each have to decide these questions for ourselves. Personally I believe means must not only be compatible with ends, but must become ends in themselves; expediency, rationalisation, or any other means which dilutes this proposition rapidly turns into a slippery slope to other ends.[4] It is a matter of personal *philosophy* – if we cannot maintain philosophical integrity on the brink of *terminality* we are lost, whatever we do.

Relationships   **morality, change**.

References

1 *Earth First!*, PO Box 5871, Tuscon, Arizona 85703, USA. In an article. 'Outlaws of Nature', published in *20/20*, January 1990, by Time Out Publications, London. *Earth First!* followers were characterised as 'wilderness warriors', and it was reported that the FBI regarded them as a terrorist conspiracy.

2 See Dave Forman (ed.), 1987, *Ecodefense: A Field Guide to Monkeywrenching*, Ned Ludd Books, Tuscon, Arizona.

3 The Christian *Holy Bible* St Mark, 8:36.

4 See Colin Johnson, 1991, *The Green Bible: Creating Sustainable Life on Earth*, Thorsons, London.

ECO- (from the Greek, *oikos* = home)   Prefix, as in *ecology* and *economics*.

Over the 1970s and 1980s this prefix has rapidly gained popularity, both as an accurate component of descriptive terminology and as a convenient shielding umbrella or fashion accessory.

John Button, in his all-embracing *Dictionary of Green Ideas*, lists no fewer than 104 eco-words. These range appropriately from ecoaccident to ecowisdom, and include the predictable ecobore, ecoculture; the tasty ecolate; the intriguing ecoparty, ecopornography; and the questionable ecoguerrilla, ecoheretic, although not ecocapitalism (unless this is covered by ecocatastrophe); and skipping from ecomarxism to ecomuseum (no ecomilitants? – see **Earth First!**). John would welcome further sightings of this burgeoning genre – postcards please, giving word and details of source to John Button, c/o Routledge, 11 New Fetter Lane, London EC4 4EE, or Routledge, Chapman & Hall Inc., 29 West 34th Street, New York, NY 10001.

As I am endeavouring to limit this dictionary to key words, ideas and their relationships for the future, eco- entries will reflect this purpose.

ECOHOLISM   The inherent coherence of relationships within a particular environment; the dynamics of the *web of life*.

Greens believe it is vitally important to maintain the *integrity* of

environments and the *diversity* and *coherence* of their *life* stock. Our scientific endeavour should be directed to the appreciation of the *forms*, connections and *dynamics* involved (see **morphology**).
Relationships   **deep ecology, stewardship, responsibility.**
See also   **Gaia, integrity.**

ECOLOGY   Originally a branch of biology concerned with organisms' relationships to one another and their surroundings.

> When in the 1850s the German zoologist Ernst Haeckel[1] was wondering what to call the new science of living things with their environmental context, he chose the word *ökologie*, which was rapidly taken into English as 'ecology'. The term derives from the Greek words *oikos* and *logos*, meaning 'the study of homes'.[2]

Ecology has *evolved* into the *green* science of *life*. In so doing it has crossed the *philosophical* boundary from its original concern with *linear simple relationships* characteristic of *grey mechanistic reductionism* to considering the *interconnectedness* of all *life* and its *dynamic* interactions within a *holistic* concept of *existence* (see **deep ecology**).[3]

> Although ecology may be treated as a science, its greater and overriding wisdom is universal. That wisdom can be approached mathematically, chemically, or it can be danced or told as a myth ... It is manifest, for example, among pre-Classical Greeks, in Navajo religion and social orientation, in romantic poetry of the eighteenth and nineteenth centuries, in Chinese landscape painting of the eleventh century, in current Whiteheadian philosophy, in Zen Buddhism, in the worldview of the cult of the Cretan great Mother, in the ceremonials of Bushman hunters, and in the medieval Christian metaphysics of light. What is common among all of them is a deep sense of engagement with the landscape, with profound connections to surroundings and to natural processes central to all life.[4]

Part of human *evolution* into *sustainable ways of living* within the *limits* of *life* is to discover the *ecstasy* of ecology, the joy of appreciation as part of the *whole*.
Relationships   **holism, morphology, Gaia.**
See also   **integrity, coherence.**
References

1 Ernst Heinrich Haeckel (1834–1919). One of the first to sketch the genealogical tree of animals, Haeckel also explained that the life history of the individual is a

recapitulation of its historic evolution (see **evolution**). Haeckel recognised the importance of sexual selection before Darwin produced his evolutionary model.
2 John Button, 1990, *New Green Pages*, Macdonald Optima, London.
3 For the on-going development of ecology in its diverse manifestations, see *The Ecologist*, Subscription Dept., Worthyvale Manor, Camelford, Cornwall PL32 9TT, England, or MIT Press Journals, 55 Hayward Street, Cambridge, MA 02132, USA.
4 Paul Sheppard, 1969, 'The Subversive Science', quoted in Bill Devall and George Sessions, 1985, *Deep Ecology*, Gibbs Smith, Layton, Utah, USA.

ECONOMICS   Practical and theoretical science of the production and distribution of *wealth*; application to a particular thing, as in the economics of authorship.

Known as the dismal science[1] (a general description, not specific to its application to authorship). 'Conventional economics is a form of brain damage.'[2] 'Modern economists are not so much scientists as jugglers who endeavour to keep many balls in the air without ever touching reality.'[3]

Modern economics is about the command of *resources*, whether by individuals or *institutions*. The use of *resources* is unrelated to *needs*; usually it is concerned with the acquisition of other or more *resources*. Other effects, beyond the production of *wealth* (a measure of *resource*), such as the distribution of *wealth*, are incidental and only accepted where unavoidable. The economic *process* has its declared *agenda* and its *hidden agenda* (see **institution**).

From a *global perspective* it is clear that modern economic *systems* are incapable of *fulfilling* human *needs*, especially if the elementary requirement of *sustainability* is added; indeed, such fulfilment is not part of the *system*'s purpose. Modern *industrial* economies are indulging in an *Impossible Party* of plunder and *consumption*, with no thought, other than to keep the party going, before collapsing exhausted over the edge of possibility (see **Impossible Party**).

While recognising this, *greens* face the usual dilemma: is it possible to *reform* the present *system*, or must we junk it and start again? *Reformists*[4] propose that, by adding '*environmental* costs', the current *system* may become *green* and continue. Such *reform* fails on obvious ground: how do you value the priceless, or that which you do not know *exists*? *Reform* also maintains the *homocentric* view of *existence*; it is the addicted party-goer turning the stereo down a little while continuing to wreck the house around him (see **market**).

To create a sustainable economic *system*, we can pick valid pieces from the old *system* and build them into a new *system* based upon *green philosophical values*.[3] But many of these *values* are in direct and irreconcilable opposition to those of *grey culture* in general and its economic *system* in particular.

Greens reject the presumptions of *exploitation*, *growth*, oppressions, *power* and privilege, and the very mechanism of *institutional* provision and deprivation, the foundations upon which *grey* economics depend (see **subversion**).

The economic model we seek is founded upon *practices* compatible with equity, *mutuality*, *rights*, *sustainability*, the *rights* and *enhancement* of *life*, *stability* or *less*, *self-reliance* and *community* control.

It would be over-optimistic to expect to point to one unified *green* economic theory at this time. The problem is appreciated, and solutions are being discussed.[5] For now each of us can only do whatever is in our *power* to *consume less*, to *consume* wisely, to make the most of *finite resources*, using the least amounts of *energy* possible. Things have to *change*; if you are serious about the *future* you will contribute whatever you can to *change*, most usefully by altering the way you maintain your *life*.

Present economic *systems* grew in an unconscious or crude way, motivated by greed, *power* and selfish opportunism. Our new *system* must be part of a wider *evolutionary paradigm*, purposefully designed for *sustainability*.

ECONOMY (FLOW and STOCK)   Organised system, or result of the application, of economics.

Together with *politics* and *religion*, the economy makes up the trinity upon which the modern *state* is built, and from which Western *culture* is *projected* into the world.

For all the distinctions made between major economic *systems* of the world, of East/West, between *market*/command, capitalist/communist, all *industrial* economies amount to the same thing as far as the *environment* is concerned. They are all based on flow.

The modern economy can be seen as a giant vacuum cleaner; it sucks the *environment* in at one end and pumps out *waste* at the other. Depending on where you are in *relation* to the economic machine, you may be impoverished by it, fed by the flow, enjoy the party in the control room, or be destroyed by its output. Most people experience a blend of all of these; the purpose of individual economic activity is to make the blend as personally advantageous as possible. Because of its inherent dependence on *growth*, the system must suck up *more* each year and *process* it faster.[6] The *system consumes* the *future* as well as the *environment* (see **GNP**).

The modern *industrial* economy is the means by which we conduct our *war* against the planet, againt *nature*, *life*, and ultimately against ourselves. The *system* is clearly *terminal.*

A *green* economy will be based on stock.[7] The *principles* of a stock economy are straightforward. Human need fulfilment must be contained indefinitely within the *finite material* and *renewable natural resources* of the planet. The basic requirements are for *maximum utility* of *materials* and *minimum consumption* of *energy.* This means that things which are made must be designed to last indefinitely, to be capable of *re-use, repair* and, finally, *recycling* at the highest possible *energy* level. Our present economic *system* depends upon *consumption* of *fossil energy*; all sources are *finite*, and their *consumption* is causing *climatic change* and other *pollution* effects. We have to plan for the use of *ambient energies –* solar, geothermal, tidal* and *biological.*

For a *green* economy we need a common *global* currency, a *system* of money, whether of tokens, plastic or electronic, which will operate in the form of time-based credit which cannot be hoarded or accumulated, only used. This would allow common pricing, reward and provision, and dispense with all the activities which currently make money out of money (see **universal credit economy UCE**).

Against this background, the *evolution* of a green economy depends on open *agenda* which enable us to clarify our *needs*, redefine *wealth*, question all *wants* and devise other *means* of fulfilment. The way we live our lives should incorporate as directly as possible the ways we fulfill our *needs.*

As Maynard Keynes (1833–1946), father of the modern demand-led market economy and the international monetary system, foresaw:

> the point may soon be reached, much sooner than we are all of us aware, when needs are satisfied in the sense that we prefer to devote further energies to non-economic purposes. This means that the economic problem is *not –* if we look into the future – *the permanent problem of the human race.*[8]

True, we have transferred the *problem* to the world at large.

BLACK ECONOMY   Economic activity which is 'unofficial'; that is, not declared to government or tax authorities. Those participating are either dishonest cheats or brave commercial guerrillas, depending on your point of view. The concept is only marginally relevant to the *future*.

BUDDHIST ECONOMY   A concept from Fritz Schumacher's *Small is Beautiful*,[9] where he revives Mahatma Gandhi's idea of the economics of permanence. Precursor of the *stock* economy (see **right livelihood**).

GIFT ECONOMY   *Community*-based mechanism where surplus or unwanted things are given to others, seen as capable of *extension* into *community*-based labour credit schemes and, eventually, of meeting the money economy through local banking *systems*.

INFORMAL ECONOMY   A term that is only relevant by comparison to the 'proper' or formal economy. Usually it means unpaid work, either by desire or as a means of subsidising the inadequacies of the formal economy (see **thematic compatibility**).

MARKET ECONOMY (see **market**)   The economic *religion* of the west. The *market* is *assumed* to be a *process* with *inherent natural qualities* of *wisdom*, direction and *knowledge*. 'You can't buck the market' simply means you conform or fail. The *market* has its own *dynamic*, yet it is all a human *creation* and as such may be *changed* or dispensed with. In *markets*, money speaks, people without are not heard, and *life* is destroyed in silence.

MONEY ECONOMY   Money is basically a form of *information*. Traditionally related to rare and enduring substances, such as metals and stones, it was used as a common language of exchange. Today those rare forms have become so common that their value has to be preserved artificially by price fixing and hoarding. Because of our inability to adapt, the *earth* is still torn apart for things which are then buried in vaults.

The *reality* of money as *information* is apparent in the operation of modern exchange activities, which are predominantly electronic streams in or between computer chips. The form of money does not really matter, as long as its value at a point of transformation is agreed.

NATURAL ECONOMY   Once it was all free.[10] Everything on earth lived as part of the *energy*/matter exchange *system* of the *great cycle of life*. The imposition of a human economy on to the natural economy has enabled many things to happen; principally a vast increase in human *numbers*, but at the cost of the *earth*. We have lost sight of the fact that whatever we do, ultimately we rely on the natural economy to maintain the basics of *life*. Whatever shape the human economy takes, unless it is contained within the capacity of the natural economy, it is either *consuming* the *future* or *life* itself.

<u>Relationships</u>   **institutions, war, progress, assumptions, expectations, needs.**

<u>See also</u>   **development, growth, waste, pollution, numbers, balance.**

<u>References</u>

1 From Thomas Carlyle (1795–1881), 'Respectable Professors of the Dismal Science', *Latter Day Pamphlets*, 1, 'The Present Time'.

2 Hazel Henderson, quoted in John Elkington and Tom Burke, 1987, *The Green Capitalists: How to Make Money – and Protect the Environment*, Gollancz, London.

3 Colin Johnson, 1991, *The Green Bible: Creating Sustainable Life on Earth*, Thorsons, London.

4 See David Pearce, Anil Markandya, Edward B. Barker, 1989, *Blueprint for a Green Economy*, Earthscan, London. Tries to fit the environment into economics, instead of vice versa, and continues the assumption that man can live without nature – it is only necessary as a resource. Oh dear.

5 See Mary Inglis and Sandra Kramer (ed.), 1985, *The New Economic Agenda*, Findhorn Press, Forres, Scotland; Stuart McBurney, 1990, *Ecology into Economics Won't Go, or Life is Not a Concept*, Green Books, Hartland, Bideford, Devon, England; Guy Dauncey, 1988, *After the Crash: The Emergence of the Rainbow Economy*, Green Print, London.

6 See Donella H. Meadows, Dennis L. Meadows, Jorgen Randers, William W. Behrens, 1972, *The Limits to Growth: A Report for The Club of Rome's Project on the Predicament of Mankind*, Pan Books, London.

7 The Ecologist, 1972, *A Blueprint for Survival*, Penguin Books, London.

8 John Maynard Keynes (1883–1946), 'Economic Possibilities for Our Grandchildren', published in *Essays in Persuasion*, 1984, Macmillan, London. I am grateful to Peter Cadogan for drawing this to my attention.

9 Fritz Schumacher, 1974, *Small is Beautiful*, Abacus, London.

10 See Ken Smith, 1988, *Free is Cheaper*, The John Ball Press, Gloucester, England.

ECOSPHERE   see **biosphere**.

ECOSYSTEM (see **bioregion**)   The complex of interacting *life* and *environment* in a particular place or region. The sum of planetary ecosystems is referred to as the *biosphere* or simply as *Gaia*.

<u>Relationships</u>   **life, environment, morphology.**

<u>See also</u>   **synergy, symbiosis, ecology.**

ECO-TOPIA   see **utopia**.

ECSTASY   Exalted state of feeling, rapture, extreme delight. We have to discover the ecstasy of ecology (see **ecology**). Timeless, a fleeting moment, a continuing state (see **balance**).

<u>Relationships</u>   **life, love, being.**

<u>See also</u>   **holism, spirituality.**

EDUCATE Give intellectual and moral training, pass on knowledge, experience, etc.

EDUCATION Systematic course of instruction or training. 'It is impossible to give a soldier a good education without making him a deserter.'[1]

In *grey culture* there is a widening division between education, which has become an *institutional*, historic *process*, and what people learn, by way of the necessities to meet the requirements of *life* in their particular circumstances. The two are the same or continuous for a small minority only.

Institutional education is subject to the *hidden agenda* of *cultural* continuity, conformity, of acceptance of that which is taught; it is a means of fitting people into a socio-cultural context. Education in this sense is part of the *global predicament*; people are not encouraged to think and act as *free* individuals with a sense of *responsibility*, matured by the experience of their senses, including the lessons of their mistakes, in *co-operation* with others. Rather, children are taken away from *life* and locked into various *cultural paradigms*. This encourages *cultural continuity*, the unquestioned acceptance of *assumptions* and *expectations*, of life on *autopilot*.

The concept of education, of a *process* separate from everyday life with a formal *agenda*, is difficult to reconcile with the *needs* of the *future*. Our *life structure* should incorporate *growth*, discovery, learning and teaching as *natural* parts of the *whole* experience. To halt our *terminal progress* we need to turn off the feedstock of people contributing to the *terminal* process.

The most immediate *need* is to separate *future* education from the prejudices of the past, from its disastrous entanglement with *political*, *economic* and *religious* dogma; to end the '*natural*' *continuity* of the present *system*; to *free* children from the prejudices and beliefs of their parents. To create a *green culture*, the *cultural paradigms* of the past have to be dissolved.

Yet 'no education' is not a realistic substitute; people have to be taught basic skills, literacy, numeracy, as well as knowledge of self and the *life-context* (in much of which the present *system* is marked by its failure, particularly in Britain). Thereafter it is a matter of facilitating individual exploration and *growth*, of sources of uncontaminated *information*, and a *community* context in which the results may be expressed. *Life* in *self-reliant communities* will demand many skills, many areas of competence. The *future* is for multi-dimensional people: one-dimensional people have had their day.

Education in the *future* must be open, no longer a box into which the passive can put *responsibilities*, but an active continuing mutual part of everyone's *life*, related to the needs and activities of *life* in *community*, yet plugged into global facilities and ideas. We each have to be individuals on whom nothing is lost, who may fulfil all of our *potential* and express all that is acceptable in *co-operation* with others for the benefit of the *global community*. 'Men are born ignorant, not stupid; they are made stupid by education.'[2]

Relationships   **mindset, hidden agenda, culture, institution, art of living.**

See also   **anarchy, morality, potential.**

References

1 Henry David Thoreau (1817–1862), 1985, *Walden, a Corcordance*, Macmillan, London. See also Ivan Illich, 1971, *De-schooling Society*, Penguin Books, London..
2 Bertrand Russell (1872–1970), 1946, *History of Western Philosophy*, George Allen & Unwin, London.

EFFICIENCY   Ratio of useful work done in relation to *energy* expended.

The present use of efficiency, as business efficiency, *economic* efficiency, *industrial* efficiency, etc., is an example of *extension* of meaning within *grey culture* which has disastrous results.

People degrade systems to the level of their own competence and understanding. This applies to everything, from work to electric toasters and the planet.

The only valid use of efficiency as a determining concept is in the use of *energy*. Other applications, whereby *processes* are altered, usually without regard for their total effects, amount to cutting corners; too often it is these corners which support *life*, maintain *diversity* and *coherence* within the *whole*.[1] The application of efficiency to *processes* other than *energy* use is the product of *linear* thinking.

Relationships   **energy, entropy, cyclic, existence.**

See also   **waste, pollution.**

References

1 See José Lutzenberger 'Gaian Economics', in Mary Inglis and Sandra Kramer (eds), 1984, *The New Economic Agenda*, Findhorn Press, Forres, Scotland, where the example of a process change in a factory which destroys a community and much of the local ecological infrastructure is given.

EGO   Part of mind that reacts to reality and has sense of individuality.

EGOISM   Ethical theory that treats self-interest as foundation of morality; systematic selfishness; being self-opinionated.

For the future, the *needs* of individual ego need to be subsumed by the *needs* of the planet. A new concept of *balance* between 'I want' and *Gaia needs* must to be struck.

Relationships   **consciousness, awareness, perspective**.

See also   **morphic resonance, change**.

ELITE   The best.

The term depends upon relative values and the competitive ethic.

ELITISM   Advocacy or reliance upon leadership; acceptance of domination by select or specialist group.

Arising from the *natural* differences between people and their interests, the dominance of elites is a *function* of the *structure* of *society*.

There will always be people who are at the forefront of developments; but this need not provide a mechanism for the *exploitation* of others. A *green social structure* would aim to spread *responsibility* so that no person achieves a *social function* where they cannot be replaced by another. The *dynamics* should maintain *coherence* without blunting its *emerging* or *adaptive* edge (see **creativity**).

Relationships   **function, position, structure, meme**.

See also   **power, morphology**.

EMERGE   Come out, become known, come into being.

EMERGENCE   The point at which the *future* becomes now. *Process* running its course; as in the emergence of characteristics under the influence of the *genetic process. Changing forms* of *existence* with varying *energy* levels, as ice from water.

The *future* unfolds; the *process* may be accepted passively, or *anticipated* with *purpose*. The shape of the *future*, the *morphology* of human *existence*, may be *changed* within the *limits* of the interaction between its *potential* and ours. It is an illusion that we have no influence; we *create* the *future* now. The *green* debate is about the *nature* of that *future*.

Relationships   **anticipation, meme, future, morphology, evolution**.

See also   **potential, growth, change**.

ENERGY   'Energy is eternal delight!'[1]

It is also force, the ability to do work; kinetic energy, ability to do work by virtue of motion; mass (or rest) energy, ability to do work by properties of matter; potential energy, ability to do work by virtue of position, or inherent properties, such as stress, reactions, etc. – properties defined by physical science within the mechanistic tradition and derived from the first law of thermo-dynamics. Work in this sense generally means a transformation of state or position or any complex of interactions of the two. The First Law bases its definition on the propositions of *stability* and displacement.

There are also the universal energies, usually described as forces – gravitational, electro-magnetic, weak nuclear and strong nuclear.

> In the case of a universe that is approximately uniform in space, one can show that this negative gravitational energy (the energy expended in separating bodies against the force of gravity) exactly cancels the positive energy represented by the matter. So the total energy of the universe is zero.[2]

The more local law of the conservation of energy states that energy (or its equivalent in mass) can neither be *created* nor destroyed. The point about energy from an earthly point of view is that it is a *flux*, a one-way *flow*; energy will dissipate from higher levels to lower. Energy seeks *entropy*; it can only be used, not *recycled* (see **entropy**).

We have created a *way of life* which depends upon energy; any hiccup at the oil wells shakes the house of cards. We are all *ampli-fied* and *extended* by our use of *fossil fuel* energy; the excess of human *numbers* depends upon the *sustainable flow* of energy through *economic* and agricultural *systems* which the coal-fired *In-dustrial Revolution* made possible. Most major *forms* of planetary energy involve the release of heat. It is the carbon atoms from earlier *forms of life* and their combination with oxygen through burning that releases carbon dioxide, causes the *greenhouse effect*,[3] climate modification and *pollution* (see **acid rain**).

For a *sustainable future* we *need* to live within a *sustainable energy/pollution equation*. The sources of *sustainable energy* are known; their *limits* are not.

ENERGY ACCOUNTING Energy accounting has to become the primary measure of efficiency in any *process* or product. Reducing the *consumption* of energy may be helped by energy labelling products, but the benefits will be lost without a *change* in the *struc-ture* of human *life* so that we live within ambient energy sources and the capacity of the *environment* to cope with *wastes* produced. Only on these terms may we experience the eternal delights of energy.

AMBIENT (RENEWABLE, SOFT) ENERGY (ambient, from French/ Latin = surrounding, on both sides, to go around)   Energy drawn from the surroundings; all *sustainable* energy sources are ambient, that is they may be drawn upon indefinitely.

BIOLOGICAL, BIOMASS ENERGY   Generally taken as the energy which may be drawn from plant material, as in fermentation for alcohol, the extraction of oil or methane gas, although the most traditional forms, as peat, wood or fibrous vegetation for burning, still remain crucial in many parts of the world. Use involves burning and the production of CO_2, etc.

GEOTHERMAL ENERGY   Energy which may be drawn from the molten layers of the *earth*; for example in Iceland, where volcanic activity is near the surface. Also by drilling and circulating water, using heat exchangers. A clean source requiring further development. Presently the drawbacks are the relatively low temperatures and the conversion losses involved.

HYDRO (WATER, WAVE) ENERGY   Hydro-electric energy is also known as white coal.

Energy from water has great *potential*, as it is drawn from the *natural cycles* of the planet and converted directly into electricity, a *process* involving *minimal pollution*. The questionable area of hydro energy is that involving *environmental* destruction by building dams to create containment lakes.[4]

LIFE ENERGY   The energy of *living* matter. The traditional distinction between animate and inanimate has become blurred by the understanding that all *life*-molecules are star-stuff,[5] and the implications of the *Gaia hypothesis*.[6] May be seen as a *spiritual* or divine property, or as the expression of the *potential* of certain complex molecular *forms* when arranged in particular ways (see **life**).

LIVE (ANIMAL, HUMAN) ENERGY   The most traditional source of energy – metabolic/muscle power, of people, and in combination with other animals. It can be convincingly argued that our increasing use of *fossil fuels* and decreasing use of our bodies is related to the increase in intractable chronic disease. Whatever the connection, it cannot be denied that all animals are intended to be active, and that human energy is one source which has declined in contemporary society under a variety of *pressures* and faulty *assumptions*. It is an indication of the *inherently* unhealthy *nature* of the present *social structure* that, when individuals realise the need for physical activity, it has to be *artificially* added in the form of exercise.

A *healthy* and *sustainable way of life* would maximise the (pleasurable) use of muscle power as a *natural* component of the *lifestyle*. In turning up the inner metabolic fires not only would the illness care and its attendant *waste* be minimised, but the use of *fossil fuels* for *transport* and *heating* could be greatly reduced.

SOLAR ENERGY   The sun is the only significant source of planetary energy input.

If we could capture and convert the merest fraction of 1 per cent of the solar energy that bathes the planet, it would provide for our *needs* until eternity. We need to concentrate development effort on this reality; current problems involve conversion factors and climatic variability. Redirected human ingenuity, where are you?

WIND ENERGY   Probably the oldest form of energy used by man, or more likely woman, to clear husk from seeds and nuts.

Wind energy has served *humanity* well; the windmill has been developed to pump, generate, grind, pulp and saw. It is a useful, if not entirely reliable, source of energy. And because the cost (both financial and in terms of energy) of the conversion machinery is relatively low, wind power remains a high *efficiency* option.

Beyond the ambient sources of energy are those which generate the majority of our energy, *fossil fuels* and nuclear reactions:

FOSSIL ENERGY   Mainly coal and oil, also gas. These fuels are the remains of previous *life forms* which have been modified by inclusion in the earth's crust. In addition to fuel, they also provide the feedstock for the 'organic' chemical industries (see **artificial**).

These substances are burned to convert their *potential* energy via heat to motion, electricity, or industrial force. The Western *way of life* depends upon the conversion of vast *quantities* of fossil energy. In conversion *pollution* is released into the atmosphere; carbon atoms from earlier *forms of life* are combined with oxygen to produce carbon dioxide and *pollutants* which harm *health*, modify climates, and produce *acid rain* and photo-chemical smogs (see total **toxic** overload).

Our dependence on *fossil fuels* is not *sustainable*. Not only are these fuels a *finite resource* which could be better used in other ways, but their use is destroying the *environment*. There may be techno-fixes for the worst problems, but these are only short-term measures which may buy a little time while *sustainable* sources are adopted.

NUCLEAR (FISSION) ENERGY   Energy produced when uranium atomic nuclei break down, producing other radioactive particles, heat, and releasing free neutrons; these neutrons bombard other atomic nuclei and cause them to break down. This is the nature of the nuclear (chain) reaction. It is initiated by refining uranium ore so that it contains sufficient refined uranium to produce enough neutrons by natural decay to sustain the reaction if enough of the material is gathered in a critical mass. It is controlled by inserting carbon rods into the uranium mass to absorb free neutrons and thus limit the reaction. 'The fission process releases a tremendous amount of heat that is used to boil water. The resulting steam drives a turbine that generates electricity. A nuclear reactor, then, is a highly sophisticated, expensive, and extremely dangerous device for boiling water.'[7]

As with many vast *institutional* endeavours, nuclear energy has a *hidden agenda.* It is about the production of weapons-grade uranium for bombs. The two processes are practically inseparable, and in conventional economic terms the expense of nuclear electricity can only be justified by the weapons subsidy (see **nuclear power**).

The insoluble problem with nuclear fission reactions is radioactive *waste.* Every reactor produces tons of *waste* directly each year, but from mining and refining, to reprocessing and final decommissioning of the facility, the whole process is marked by the release of radioactive *pollution* into the *environment.* Most dangerous of the radioactive byproducts is plutonium, the most toxic and most long-lived of all the isotopes (Pu-239), which has a half-life[8] of 24,000 years. This means that *toxic* quantities will be around for longer than we can imagine, at least 500,000 years. The practical implications are a measure of nuclear insanity; plutonium has to be safely isolated from the *environment* for a longer *time* into the *future* than humanity and its *evolutionary* precursors go back into the past.

There is no such thing as a totally safe nuclear *process,* or a safe radiation level. The inevitable past and *future* leaks leave a needless trail of *death* and suffering, mainly from cancers, as the most enduring achievement of nuclear energy. In a few short decades *terminal man* and his *culture* have *created* an inheritance for the *future* which will leave them eternally cursed.

Proponents of 'green' nuclear energy argue that it does not produce greenhouse gases. Not directly, but:

Though the carbon dioxide emissions from the fossil fuels consumed in nuclear power construction and fuel cycle operation are relatively small at the present, if nuclear power is expanded, in any serious attempt to stop global warming, these emissions will grow as poorer quality uranium sources are used. Eventually, at very low ore grades, even a technically advanced nuclear fuel cycle will produce as much carbon dioxide as an equivalent coal-fired power station.[9]

Whatever *form* of energy is used, most involve the problems of conversion.

CONVERTED (CONVERSION) ENERGY   Most energy has to be converted, either to express the *potential* of the source material, as by burning, or to change its *form*, as from heat to motion, to electricity, to sound, etc.

At every stage of conversion there are losses: petrol engines are between 12 and 20 per cent efficient at the flywheel; electricity loses around 80 per cent in conversion and transmission. Energy is very leaky stuff (see **entropy**). Obviously the more direct the source in relation to use the better: hence the attraction of photoelectric cells, designed to convert solar energy to electricity directly. Conversion is subject to the law of conservation (see **energy**) and most energy ends up as *waste* heat, some of which can be re-converted and *re-used*, although only from large sources. Combined heat and power (or heat, light and power), CHP, generating stations use this technique to minimise direct *waste*.

PERSPECTIVE OF ENERGY USE   Energy use has to be reduced, energy dependence avoided wherever possible. *Grey culture* refuses to take the problem seriously; ambient sources are dismissed with dinosaur smugness, *communities* are *structured* to run on oil, the *flow* of the energy-dependent *economy* is encouraged. Houses are not designed to be energy efficient; *waste* and inefficiency is rewarded. It does not have to be like this; *change* is essential (see **choice**).

Relationships   **economy, politics, environment, chi**.

See also   hidden **agenda, pollution**.

References

1 William Blake (1757–1827), *The Voice of the Devil.*
2 Stephen W. Hawkins, 1988, *A Brief History of Time: From the Big Bang to Black Holes*, Bantam Press, London.
3 Fred Pearce, 1989, *Turning Up the Heat: Our Perilous Future in the Global Greenhouse*, The Bodley Head, London.
4 See (at the library – cost £120 in 1990), Edward Goldsmith and Nicholas

Hildyard, *The Social and Environmental Effects of Large Dams* (three volumes), Ecosystems Ltd, Worthyvale Manor Farm, Camelford, Cornwall, PL32 9TT, England.
5 Carl Sagan, 1983, *Cosmos*, Random House, New York, USA.
6 James Lovelock, 1979, *Gaia: A New Look at Life on Earth*, Oxford University Press, Oxford, England.
7 Fritjof Capra, 1982, *The Turning Point: Science, Society, and the Rising Culture*, Simon & Schuster, New York, USA.
8 The half-life of a radioactive substance, that is one subject to spontaneous decay by the emission of particles or energy, is the period of time during which half of the material will have decayed.
9 Dr Nigel Mortimer, quoted in *Green Line*, Number 82, October 1990, page 20. *Green Line*, 34 Cowley Road, Oxford, England.

ENTROPY The loss of *energy* (or *information*) within a *system* due to its circumstances; measure of the degradation or disorganisation of a *system*. Usually equated with disorder. The concept of entropy derives from the second law of thermodynamics, and can be summarised thus: 'The entropy of a *system* always increases with time.'

To get to grips with the concept, we need to dissect the terminology; loss within a *system* is straightforward enough, but disorganisation and degradation (unless simply numerical) are *value*-laden terms. When the idea of disorder is equated with entropy the short-sightedness of the underlying *philosophy* becomes apparent: what greater order could there be than the total entropy of nothing?

Entropy is best thought of in terms used to derive it in the second law, of *stable* equilibrium states and the special *processes* which connect one such state with another. In these terms entropy is the equalisation of states, the flow of *energy* from a 'higher' (more energetic) state to a 'lower' state. This is more *holistic* than *homocentric* notions of disorder.

Thus in *changing* things from one state to another, whether materials or *energy*, there will always be losses. In practical terms there is no such thing as a completely closed loss-free *system*: everything is connected to everything else; *energy flows*, materials are dissipated.

To return to humans and disorder, whenever we *create* what we see as order, say by making a complex building from sand, clay, iron ore, and so on, the result is disorder in the form of holes in the ground from which the materials were extracted and *pollution* from the *energy* expended in their conversion. Which is order and which is entropy? The *values* are relative, the effects obvious.

Entropy is the factor which dictates that we must live within the *self-sustaining cycles* of the planet and the *limits* of its *resources*. But can we have faith in the *cycles of life* – are they not subject to entropy? Yes – and no. Yes, in that we all decline and die. No, in that *life* goes on and is subject to *synergy*, the opposite of entropy.

It is the purpose/motivation of *life processes* to overcome entropy, to increase in complexity with *time (evolution)* rather than *devolve* to greater simplicity. Human *creations* cause problems in the *environment* because we assume they contribute to, or are a natural part of, the *life conspiracy*, or at least are passive to its current context. Entropy ensures they are not. Most of *existence* has other motivation; *energy* is a *flux* which seeks the most dispersed *form*, to *flow* to its lowest level of expression; matter seeks *stability* in *form*. For both, entropy is the mechanism which achieves these objectives. A *green way of life* would understand this fundamental difference, and take account of it in its *relationship* with other *life*, the *environment* and the way *needs* were *fulfilled*.

Only *life* opposes entropy – that may be its unique *quality*.

Relationships   **energy, life, synergy, existence**.

See also   **finite resources, sustainability, symbiosis**.

References

See Jeremy Rifkin with Ted Howard, 1985, *Entropy: A New World View*, Paladin, London.

ENVIRONMENT   Surroundings; the physical and biological *system* supporting *life*[1]; the place where you live; here and now.

The stage within which the *dynamics* of *life* occur. For *greens* the key fact about the environment is that it is one; we share one world, one destiny. There are no isolated environmental niches; things affect the total environment. As the *Gaian hypothesis*[2] elegantly explains, *life* cannot be considered in isolation; in many senses *life* is the environment.

ENVIRONMENTAL DISRUPTION   Anything which reduces the capacity or diversity of *life*. We are accustomed to think in terms of 'force majeur', but the most dangerous environmental disruptors are likely to be the persistent chemicals and *pollutants* we release into the *biosphere* (see **artificial**). The *health* of any *system* is reduced by disrupting the *anticipation* of that *system*; much human activity is beyond the *anticipatory* capacity of the *natural environment* (see total **toxic** overload).

ENVIRONMENTALISM   Concern with the environment, usually centred on isolated issues, e.g. 'wildlife', particular habitats or species, or urban improvements, such as *tree* planting or anti-litter campaigns.

Reformist, cosmetic, of limited use, because the *assumption* is that if we care for particular aspects of the environment, i.e. address particular problems we are causing, everything else is or will be OK. Environmentalism in this sense avoids/hides the underlying issues.

Concern for the environment is frequently equated with being *green*, but *green* concerns embrace far more than limited environmentalism. Being *green* is not the same as environmentalism. The *stability* derived from equating the two is part of the *grey cultural paradigm*. Environmentalism can be seen as an attempt to work within the *existing socio-cultural* framework as a means of alleviating or mitigating the worst *symptoms* of that *culture*. It is a reaction, always several steps behind the *problem*, usually focused on short-term policy issues of resource allocation. That is not to say that environmentalism should be discouraged; rather that its limits and context must be recognised.

ENVIRONMENTAL IMPACT ASSESSMENT (EIA)   *Green*speak from the *grey* world. First made a requirement of large building developments in the USA, the idea has spread, encouraged by a combination of good, if *homocentric*, intentions and PR value. The concept embodies the arrogance of *grey science*: that we have comprehensive *knowledge* and can actually carry out such an assessment. It also implies that the 'correct' action will be taken in the light of such an assessment.

MAN-MADE ENVIRONMENT   Somewhere else, *artificial*.

As *pollution* effects build up, the rich are likely to transfer the effects by attempting to live like aliens in entirely *artificial* environments, in the belief that this may be a route to salvation (see **institutions**).

Relationships   **Gaia, holism, morphology, evolution**.

See also   **deep ecology, matrix, cycle of life, finite resources**.

References

1 For comprehensive news on problems and related action and research see the excellent *The Environment Digest*. Environmental Publications Ltd, Panther House, 38 Mount Pleasant, London WC1X 0AP.

2 James Lovelock, 1979, *Gaia: A New Look at Life on Earth*, Oxford University Press, Oxford. See also *The Ecologist*, Worthyvale Manor Farm, Camelford, Cornwall PL32 9TT, England; and John Barr (ed.), 1971, *The Environmental Handbook*, Ballantine/Friends of the Earth.

EQUALITY   see **rights**.

ETHICAL INVESTMENT   see **investment**.

ETHICS   Of morals and morality, correct, honourable; a system of ethics, code of behaviour; the science of morals, *principles, values* guiding conduct. 'The primary ethical teaching of all times and places is "cause no unnecessary harm".'[1]

With the increasing polarisation of religion into indifference or fundamentalism and the realpolitik acceptance that might is right, ethics has become unfashionable in *grey culture*. The underlying reason is that ethical questions demand a questioning of the *values* and *assumptions*, the very direction, of the *status quo*; a proposition which provokes unacceptable anxiety since the likely answers are predictable and equally unacceptable.

The *green* view of ethics has been eloquently expressed by Murray Bookchin:

> The reinstatement of an ethical stance becomes central to the recovery of a meaningful society and a sense of selfhood, a realism that is in closer touch with reality than the opportunism, lesser-evil strategies, and benefit-versus-risk calculations claimed by the practical wisdom of our time. Action from principle can no longer be separated from a mature, serious, and concerted attempt to resolve our social and private problems. The highest realism can be attained only by looking beyond the given state of affairs to vision of what *should* be, not only of what *is*.[2]

The response to the *global predicament* has been to question the current *cultural* ethic and seek new *values*; regrettably the *process* has been dominated by the mechanics of *reductionist philosophy* and has thus been fragmented, as land, environmental, social, etc., ethics, rather than as part of a unified *philosophical whole* more in keeping with fundamental *green* beliefs and the *needs* of our situation. Nevertheless the need is appreciated – 'What we must now face up to is the fact that human ethics cannot be separated from a realistic understanding of ecology in the broadest sense'[4] – and attempts at comprehensive *synthesis* have been made.

<u>Relationships</u>   **philosophy, morality, spirituality**.

<u>See also</u>   **mind, assumptions, culture**.

<u>References</u>

1 Gary Snyder, 1983, on 'Song of the Taste', 1970, in Bill Devall and George Sessions, 1985, *Deep Ecology*, Peregrine Smith Books, Salt Lake City, Utah, USA.
2 Murray Bookchin, 1986, *The Modern Crisis*, Black Rose Books, Montréal, Canada.

3 Van Rensselear Potter, 1971, *Bioethics: Bridge to the Future.*
4 See Colin Johnson, 1991, *The Green Bible: Creating Sustainable Life on Earth*, Thorsons, London.

EUTROPHY   To fill up with nutrients.

EUTROPHIC   Of a body of water. Imbalance of *life* caused by excessive basic nutrients for plants, which kill animal *life* by oxygen deprivation.

EUTROPHICATION   Catastrophic imbalance usually caused by addition of sewage or chemical fertiliser run-off into body of water.

Relationships   **environment, chemiculture, waste**.

See also   **economics, pollution**.

EVENT   Result, outcome, of process; fact of a thing's happening.

Life in *grey culture* focuses on events in preference to the *processes* that generate them. Thus other effects of *process*, the discounted costs of *systems*, the *hidden agenda* of *structures*, are all largely ignored (see **global predicament**).

Relationships   **process**.

See also   **celebration**.

EVOLUTION   Opening out, unfolding, developing; development of organism, process, organisation, society, cosmos; emergence from simpler forms; derivation rather than of special creation.

Expression of *inherent potential* under particular circumstances. The *dynamic* expression of *holism*.

EVOLUTIONARY MECHANISM   Classically, *life* forms evolve to fill *environmental niches*; they adapt to circumstances. In *changing* circumstances the most adaptable survive; in *stable* circumstances the fittest thrive. All *life* seeks to convert as much of the *environment* into replicas of itself as possible; *numbers* are the safeguard against the unforeseen hazards of the *future*. The combination of changing circumstances and pressure of *numbers*, with *changes* in the organism itself, produces a variety of stresses, summarised as *compression*.

As *compression* builds up within a species, group or environment, there are three options for the *life* forms involved: to *adapt*; to *shift* to another *form*; or to *sink* (to reach a peak of development and then fall back or degenerate to a residual *form*, or fail altogether) (see **genetic shift, shift, sink**).

EVOLUTIONARY MODEL   Traditional models are characterised by *linear* discrete relationships; one form ends and its successor begins. Since evolution is the expression of *inherent potential*, and

terms; that evolution is complex, amounting to specific expressions within a *coherent whole* of *inherent potential* under particular circumstances. The expression may only be one of many possible *forms*, and will depend upon the circumstances or *changes* which initiate it.

HUMAN EVOLUTION (CONSCIOUS, SOCIAL, CULTURAL)   The trail of human *biological* evolution has been well mapped, and details are being continuously revised. What has been missing until comparatively recently is a description of our social evolution, the *dynamics of life* between our emergence as *Homo sapiens* and recorded history – roughly the last million years.

Human prehistory is a matter of conjecture, but the story so far seems to fit the results.[9] The salient features are of *changing* emphasis; while human physiology has remained more or less stable, our brain size has progressively increased. At the same time our personal social *structures* have changed, from tribal to extended families, to nuclear families and to contemporary singles, while our socio-cultural evolution has produced a global complex of nurturing forces and successive influences.

We find ourselves today with static (if over-evolved) bodies, the mental *processes* of tribal gatherer hunters, brains that have generated their own evolutionary *dynamic*, and the proposition of trying to catch up with the socio-cultural evolution we have projected into the world. The enigma of the human brain amounts to this: if it cannot adapt to cope with the circumstances it has produced, it may turn out to have been one of the most disastrous examples of over-specialisation in the evolutionary story.

We are in a state of increasing *compression*, and we are *projecting* it on to the entire *biosphere*. Humans have subjected themselves to accelerating evolutionary stresses over the last two million years. For most of this time we lived as gatherer hunters. Twenty thousand years ago we settled to agriculture, 200 years ago we initiated the *fossil* fuel-based *Industrial Revolution* and around 20 years ago the cybernetic age of electronic *information* took over. We do not yet realise where, apart from *terminality*, this *compressive* trend is leading. We hang in the balance, at a *time* when a *sink* of *catastrophic*, even *terminal*, dimensions is foreseeable, yet the *dynamics* of the *processes* we have unleashed appear to have passed beyond individual control. Is the *nature* of this passage an evolutionary factor we have so far failed to appreciate, but one with which we will have to come to terms if human salvation is to be possible (see **institutions**)?

Our *future need* is for a collective act of self-directed conscious evolution. We have been influencing evolution since we settled to agriculture some 2,000 years ago; we have been disrupting it under the banner of blind *progress* since the *Industrial Revolution*. Our *adaptation* for the *future* requires that we subject ourselves to the *processes* we have been inflicting on the world at large, that we take control of the *processes* in which we are involved. 'As H.D. Thoreau said, "we front up to the facts and determine to live our lives deliberately, or not at all".'[10]

We must go head first into the *future*. This requires that we *change* not only what we think, but the actual *processes* of thought, the way we think. To put it crudely, we think in *linear* terms, forming conceptual *hierarchies* and *processes* which are a reflection of primal social (genetic) relationships. For the *future* our ways of thought need to reflect more closely the patterns of the organ of thought itself – the brain/mind. We need to see things in terms of complex inter-relationships, of *matrices* with *networks* of *relevance*, of *functional* influences and inner *consensus*.

The *questions* we confront are: Can we perform a most unnatural act of evolution? Can we step back from the edge of *terminality* and find a new direction forward to *sustainability*? Can we extract ourselves from the *cultural/institutional structures* which carry us towards the edge? Can we evolve new *ways of life* in human terms which are compatible with our *global environment*?

Relationships   **existence, life, genetics, morphology, creation, institution.**

See also   **change, stability, sink, shift.**

References

1 See Rupert Sheldrake, 1981, *A New Science of Life*, Blond & Briggs, London.

2 Charles Darwin (1809–82), 1982, *Origin of Species*, Penguin Books, London. (Originally published by Odhams Press, London in 1859.)

3 Jean Baptiste Pierre Antoine de Monet, Chevalier de Lamarck (1744–1829). Lamarck was the first man whose conclusions on the subject excited much attention. This justly-celebrated naturalist first published his views in 1801; he much enlarged them in 1809 in his *Philosophie Zoologique*, and subsequently, in 1815 in the introduction to his *Hist. Nat. des Animaux sans Vertébres*. In these works he upholds the doctrine that species, including man, are descended from other species. He first did the eminent service of arousing attention to the probability of all change in the organic, as well as in the inorganic world, being the result of law, and not of miraculous interposition (Charles Darwin, in *An Historic Sketch*, previously to the publication of the first edition of *The Origin of Species*)

4 Prince Petr (Peter) Kropotkin (1842–1921), aka The Anarchist Prince, 1988, *Mutual Aid: A Factor of Evolution*, Black Rose Books, Toronto, Canada. (Originally published 1902.)

5 Gregor Johann Mendel (1822–84), Austrian biologist whose work became the basis for modern genetics.
6 See Richard Dawkins, 1976, *The Selfish Gene*, Oxford University Press, Oxford, England.
7 See Gordon Rattray Taylor, 1983, *The Great Evolutionary Mystery*, Secker & Warburg, London.
8 Attributed to American novelist William Burroughs.
9 See Richard Leakey and Roger Lewin, 1978, *People of the Lake, Man: His Origins, Nature and Future*, Penguin Books, New York. See also Richard Leakey, 1981, *The Making of Mankind*, Michael Joseph, London.
10 From Bill Devall and George Sessions, 1985, *Deep Ecology: Living as if Nature Mattered*, Peregrine Smith Books, Salt Lake City, Utah, USA, quoting Henry David Thoreau (1817–62), American essayist and poet, the 'hermit of Walden'.

EXCHANGE   Giving one thing for another.

In many parts of the world people are meeting in ad hoc groups for a variety of exchange purposes – to exchange visions of the *future*, to exchange goods and services on a mutual basis outside the flow *economy*.

EXCLUDE, EXCLUSION, EXCLUSIVE   Shut out person, thing, from place, society, privilege; make impossible.

A key *value* of *grey culture*.

Greens reject exclusion in favour of *inclusion*. If exclusion becomes necessary, there is something wrong with the *structure* which causes the situation.

<u>Relationships</u>   **terminal culture, compression, Impossible Party.**
<u>See also</u>   **inclusive, values.**

EXIST   To have a place in reality.

EXISTENCE   Being, existing. A random proposition: a short interval in eternity. State in which a thing takes form (see **morphology, evolution**).

EXISTENTIALISM   Philosophical theory with emphasis on the individual as a sovereign, *free* and *responsible* agent; belief in individual existence as the basis of meaning. ('I am, therefore I exist'? – see **Cartesianism**.)

The emphasis that existentialism puts upon individual responsibility and experience fits well with green thinking, but the idea that only human intervention can give true meaning to nature is anathema to green thinkers, especially deep ecologists.[1]

CONCEPTUAL EXISTENCE   If something exists only in our *minds*, does it have a place in *reality*?

Things which we create first exist in our *minds* (see **meme**). Many people – the deeply religious, or those whose lives are dominated by fantasy – live their lives in a reality which consists, in the main, of things which exist only as concepts. In science and *philosophy* we speculate about ultimate realities such as the size and *nature* of the *universe* beyond the observable horizon, or about the *nature* of existence itself.

The *problem* of human existence is the perpetual *problem* of distinguishing between *vital reality,* optional *choices* and *terminal* fantasies. Our difficulty is that it seems to be easier to realise *terminal* fantasies than to accommodate ourselves within the vital *reality* of our circumstances.

Relationships   **being, life, universe**.

See also   great **cycle** of **life, reality, creation, evolution**.

References

1 John Button, 1988, *A Dictionary of Green Ideas*, Routledge & Kegan Paul, London.

EXPECT   Look forward to *event*; regard as likely to happen.

EXPECTATION   Anticipate as likely to happen; the belief in fulfilment; favourable judgment of probability.

Our expectations of *life,* particularly its material parameters, and of the *values* and *assumptions* of others, as reflected in their behaviour, are fixed by *nurture* within our particular *culture*. Expectations form part of that largely unquestioned basis of *life* that serves to fulfil individuals on the one hand and maintain the direction of *culture* on the other.

To *change culture* we need, among other things, to *change* our expectations, to question much of what we presently take for granted. What do/can we legitimately expect of ourselves and *life* in a *sustainable future* (see **needs, wants**)?

Relationships   **mindset, assumption, culture**.

See also   **anticipation, event, morphology**.

EXPLOIT   Utilise for one's own ends, work, use.

EXPLOITATION   The process of exploiting something.

Exploitation is only reasonable if it is mutual, i.e. *symbiotic,* and part of a *cyclic* process which enhances life, i.e. is synergistic. Otherwise it is always unreasonable; it lacks *mutuality* and consent, and denies equity.

The *economic system* of *grey culture* is based upon the exploitation of *finite* resources (see **energy**). A significant part of the *terminal* problem is that exploitation is seen as a *natural* legitimate *process*, underwritten by a monotheistic belief that the world is at man's disposal. Thus we *consume* the *environment* and take the *web of life* apart around us.

Greens seek *way of living* which avoid exploitation. Eventually this will require an entirely new *economic system* as well as a realignment of individual *consciousness*. *Sustainability* requires that we live within the possibilities of *life*; that we enhance our lives in concert with all *life*; that *finite resources* are used as if they had to last for ever. And that our fellows have equality within *sustainable* parameters, and all *life* has defined mutual *rights*.

Relationships   **symbiosis, resources, rights, limits**.
See also   **economy, creativity, sustainability**.

EXPONENTIAL   Mathematical: of exponent, a symbol indicating to what power a factor is to be taken, e.g. $E=mc^2$ where c, the speed of light, is to be squared, that is multiplied by its self, $c \times c$. Astronomical figures are generally given factorially to make the numbers manageable.

EXPONENTIAL GROWTH   An ever increasing rate of *growth*, the rate of increase depending on the factor. Also expressed as a compound rate of *growth*, or the doubling time of a process.

> Suppose you own a pond on which a water lily is growing. The lily plant doubles in size each day. If the lily were allowed to grow unchecked, it would completely cover the pond in 30 days, choking off the other forms of life in the water. For a long time the lily plant seems small, and so you decide not to worry about cutting it back until it covers half the pond. On what day will that be? On the twenty-ninth day, of course. You have one day to save your pond.[1]

The concept is relevant because most *life processes*, if given the chance, express themselves exponentially. Thus the time the human population takes to double gets shorter and shorter. If a population increases at 10 per cent per year, as some do, it will take seven years for the total to double. (To get the doubling time divide 70 by the percentage increase. Thus a 1 per cent increase would double the population in 70 years, the average lifetime).

The frightening *nature* of exponential growth applies to every *process* involving continual *growth* – of *population, economics*, rates of *consumption*, and so on. The arithmetic is clearly unsustainable, and when the *natural* factors which maintain the numerical *balance* between species are removed it becomes disastrous. Most human endeavour since settling to agriculture has been directed at removing the constraints on the growth of human numbers (see **numbers**).

> People at present think that five sons are not too many and each son has five sons also, and before the death of the grandfather there are already 25 descendants. Therefore people are more and wealth is less; they work hard and receive little.[2]

The terrifying *nature* of exponential *growth* is that, in the time before the last *catastrophic* doubling, people are looking back to a previous time (see **past**). There is no indication from their experience of the nature of the *process* of which they are part. If you wait for evidence, it is too late.

<u>Relationships</u>   **numbers, environment, limits, growth**.

<u>See also</u>   **environment, assumptions, evolution**.

<u>References</u>

1 Donella H. Meadows, Dennis L. Meadows, Jorgen Randers, William W. Behrens, 1972, *The Limits to Growth: A Report for the Club of Rome's Project on the Predicament of Mankind*, Pan Books, London.

2 Han Fei-Tzu, *circa* 500 BC, quoted in 1.

EXTENSION   From the time when the first claw, hand or beak used something as a *tool*, various *forms* of *life* have extended their control over their *environment*.

The use of *tools*, of *technology*, extends our influence into the *environment*; in a very real sense we extend ourselves into and beyond our *environment*. Television radiates out into space, carrying *cultural* gems into the *future* to far galaxies, where other *life forms* may appreciate the Muppets or 'I Love Lucy'. The phenomenon has been described by Herbert Giradet:

> We have become both man and machine. Late 20th century 'amplified man' is not the fusion of man and horse immortalised by Greek sculpture and mythology in the image of the 'centaur'. Horse power drove our forefather on through two millennia and one could say we remained 'centaurs' until the emergence of the internal combustion engine. This opened a whole new Pandora's box. Since then, our dependence on and association with machines has become so complex that it is hard to think of one image to portray what we have become, though the 'robot' of science fiction fame probably comes closest.
>
> Our metabolism today is no longer characterised primarily by

the throughput of biological matter harvested from the surface of the Earth. Our sustenance are ores and fossil fuels from deep within the crust. Each year each of us swallows many tons of coal and oil. Our breath is no longer just what we exhale from our mouths but also the exhaust fumes from our cars, factories and power stations. We excrete the wastes of our own bodies as well as the poisonous discharges of the machines with which we have fused.[1]

The *process* of extension is apparent in most areas of human *life*. We are all, at least in the industrial world, *amplified* by its effects; it is a *cultural* phenomenon that affects us all, regardless of ability or *choice*. Marshall McLuhan[2] noted many dimensions of human extension: *clothes* as extensions of the skin; the wheel of the foot; the book of the eye; electric circuitry of the central nervous system. It even has a sexual dimension; the gun as an omnipotent penis – 'happiness is a warm gun' – and the enticing swaying skirt as a visible extension of the hidden labia.

The characteristic of the *process* is that it involves *institutional forms* that extend our endeavours from the *past*, into the total *environment*, and far into the *future*. The implications of these *forms* and *processes* are profound. *Institutions* may be regarded as the extensions of people (see **institutions**).

<u>Relationships</u> **meme, institutions, evolution, economy.**

<u>See also</u> **extra-genetic, potential, morphology.**

<u>References</u>

1 Herbert Giradet, 1990, *Being Fair to Posterity*, paper given to The Council for Posterity, 24 Abercorn Place, London NW8 9XP.
2 Marshall McLuhan and Quentin Fiore, 1967, *The Medium is the Massage*, Penguin, London.

EXTINCTION The end, termination, of a form of activity or life.

In *life* forms extinction is an irreversible process. We do not know how many different forms of *life* there are on earth, but it has been estimated that, If the present trends continue through the 1990s, 20 per cent will become extinct by the end of the decade.[1]

Extinction has been outrun by speciation in the past. The resulting incredible *diversity* has produced a *dynamic*, yet *stable*, *environment* modified by the *processes* of *life* itself. Humanity is now reducing this *diversity* at a literally disastrous rate, reducing the capacity of all *life* to maintain the *environment*, possibly to the point of total extinction.

The picture of *life* in the last decade of the 20th century is like a jelly on the edge of a table; some is inevitably slipping over the edge, but the amount used to remain roughly constant. We have tipped the table, and more is slipping off all the time. The question is, has so much already gone that nothing can prevent the rest following?[2]

See also   **terminal**.

References

1 Lee Durrell, 1986, *The State of the Ark*, The Bodley Head, London.
2 Colin Johnson, 1991, *The Green Bible: Creating Sustainable Life on Earth*, Thorsons, London.

FAMINE   see **casualty problem**.

FARMING   see **food, chemiculture**.

FEDERAL   A system of government wherein a *unity* is created by separate parts which each retain a degree of independence in internal affairs; a means of association for independent bodies.
FEDERATE   To join together for a common purpose; means of political, economic, etc., organisation.
FEDERATION (also **confederation** – con=with – a looser form of federation, sometimes used to imply dubious motives)   A body, political, economic, social, of separate parts, joined for a common purpose.

Greens see federations as *natural organic means* of organising society for the expression of *potential* and the fulfilment of *need*. Such arrangements need not be based on geographical location, and would tend to be based on *communities* federating for particular purposes in transient arrangements. Thus the society of the *future* would consist of shifting *networks* of federations of interest which would form and dissolve as *needs* or desires arose and were fulfilled.

Relationships   **matrix, ad hoc, community, politics**.
See also   **anarchy, co-operation, hierarchy, institution**.

FEEDBACK   *Information* which modifies (controls) a process or *system* by the results or effects of that process or *system*; return of part of output to an earlier stage of the output process; response, as of audience to performer. Modern origin in cybernetics (science of systems of control and communications, as in computers and robotics). The means is generally described as a feedback loop.

Feedback is an essential feature of *stable dynamics*. Positive feedback is taken as inhibiting output, negative feedback as increasing it. Thus, as an engine slows down, negative feedback is given to the governor, which acts to increase its speed. It should be

101

noted that in *social dynamics* and behaviour situations the reverse is true; positive feedback (reward) increases the behaviour which provokes it.

The textbook example of feedback is of the lavatory cistern, where the level of water controls the level of water. Flush, and the lowered level opens the valve, allowing water in. The increasing water level progressively closes the valve, until the cistern is full and the water level causes the valve to shut. A full cistern is its normal *stable*, self-maintained, state.

Feedback is an essential part of all *cyclic processes*; it either serves to maintain their *inherent stability*, or informs them of *growth or reduction circumstances*. Thus the capacity for feedback is a measure of the *potential* for *anticipation* within a *system*. Feedback is absent from *linear processes*. In such a *system* the lavatory cistern would either flood or cease to work when the water supply was exhausted.

Grey culture is characterised by *linear processes* and minimal feedback. Where feedback is present, it tends to be negative, as in population *growth* leading to further population *growth*; *economic growth* demanding further *growth*; and so on. This is in contrast to every biological *system*; biology achieves coherent *change* and maintains *homoeostasis* through the constant activity of feedback loops (see **exponential, numbers**).

Feedback is a *vital* concept. A *green culture* would be characterised by a *matrix* of feedback loop with every part of the *biosphere* and physical *environment*. Without these connections, *balance* and *sustainability* would not be possible. The *Gaian whole* (excluding humanity) is characterised by such interactive *matrices*; this is how relative *stability* is maintained over long periods of time. We do not have to create the feedback loops; they are a part of *nature*. We have to appreciate, understand, and get back into the *natural systems* of the earth.

Connecting with the existing *networks*, with feedback systems which are intelligible and obvious, would both predict and monitor the effects of human activity in the *biosphere*, enabling *choices* to be made for the benefit of the *whole*. Without comprehensive feedback, *progress* will remain blind, its *linear* direction *terminal*.

Relationships   **cycle**, **Gaia**, **morphology**.

See also   **sustainability, limits**.

FEMININE   Of women.

FEMININE VALUES   Generally accepted as predominantly those of caring, sharing, co-operating; of intuitive knowledge, wisdom; life-centred.

The proposition that future *communities* should be based on feminine rather than masculine values has much currency in *green* thinking.[1] It is essentially a reflection of earlier human tribal structures, where the core group of gatherers (females) would contain the young, the old (and wise) and the sick or injured, while the males would hunt or scavenge on the perimeter, acting as a protective screen. The cellular analogy is obvious; the vital knowledge and reproductive material at the centre, with the expendable/replaceable membrane enclosing the whole.

FEMINISM   Advocacy of women's rights; belief in equality of sexes.

The belief that discrimination on the basis of sex (sexism) is unacceptable, and that the social roles of women should not be based upon sexist presumptions.

There is an instinctive suspicion of all -isms. While they may summarise a body of belief and its practical expressions, too often the reaction is as extreme and unreasonable (unreasoned) as the provocation (as in capitalism and communism). An -ism is frequently an invitation to dogma, and the belief that an opposite discrimination will counter the one to which there is objection (see **thematic compatibility**).

Relationships   **community, evolution, matrix, rights, sexual dimorphism values.**

See also   **intuition, structure, synergy.**

References

1 James Robertson, 1978, *The Sane Alternative: A Choice of Futures*, James Robertson, The Old Bakehouse, Cholsey, Wallingford, Oxon OX10 9NU, England.

FIELD   A defined area or three-dimensional space; a region of influence, within which the effects of a *process* or force may occur.

FIELD POTENTIAL   The capacity for a *process* or force to include a space, region or *time* within its influence. Every form of *existence* has a field; its potential may be its degree of influence under various circumstances, or its capacity to *change* under varying circumstances (see **formative causation**).

The combined expressions of the field potential of the *processes* of Western industrial *culture*, particularly in its *institutional economic forms*, generates the present *global predicament*.

For the *future* we need to understand the capacity for influence of the *processes* we initiate. In an interconnected world everything has the *potential* for effects beyond those intended or immediately predictable.

Field theories[1] will become increasingly important as we seek to create a *sustainable future* which includes the field potential of all *life* and its *potential* for interactions and *future* expression (see **holism**).

<u>Relationships</u> **formative causation, morphology, extension, potential, change.**

<u>See also</u> **evolution, anticipation, synergy, symbiosis.**

<u>References</u>

1 Rupert Sheldrake, 1983, *A New Science of Life: The Hypothesis of Formative Causation*, Granada, London; David Bohm, 1980, *Wholeness and the Implicate Order*, Routledge & Kegan Paul, London; G. Spencer Brown, 1969, *Laws of Form*, Allen & Unwin, London.

FINITE   Limited, bounded, of fixed quantity.

FINITE RESOURCE   Much of the material stock of the planet, the inanimate *resources* of the *Gaian whole*. A large range of such materials, in the form of essential minerals, are necessary to *life* cycles.

Ultimately all planetary resources are finite. Those which are of principal concern to *grey culture* are *fossil fuels* and metallic ores. The latter are refined, many joining oil products in being oxidised in a one-shot use. We can see the end (in between ten and 100 years' time) of the known reserves of silver (Ag), gold (Au), copper (Cu), mercury (Hg), manganese (Mn), molybdenum (Mo), lead (Pb), platinum (Pt), tin (Sn), tungsten (W) and zinc (Zn).

Industrial *processes* and the material Western *way of life* depend upon these resources. *Grey culture* is in the position of the classic cartoon character – sitting out on a branch while cheerfully sawing it off the tree. Nor is it a simple matter of resource exhaustion; industrial *processes* using metals often involve their being refined and released into the *biosphere*, which can result in highly *toxic* and persistent residues accumulating in the *food chains*, as with mercury. Additionally, the processes can remove from *life cycles* substances such as molybdenum that are absolutely essential to the *growth* of every living cell. When combined with *flow economics* the whole industrial *process* is an un-*balancing* and exhausting recipe for disaster; further combine this with the indiscriminate production of *artificial* substances, and the *terminal* finishing touch is almost guaranteed.

As scarcities become apparent, the technical warfare *power* of the *First World* will be increasingly applied to other areas of the planet in ever more desperate attempts to command *resources*, to maintain the *unsustainable* to the end (see **institutions**).

We have to treat all finite resources as if they had to last for ever, and use them in the fullest possible knowledge of the effects and implications for the *future* (see **utility**).

Relationships   **entropy**, **mindset**, **economy**, **Impossible Party**, **sustainability**, **rights**.

See also   **numbers**, **expectations**, total **toxic** overload.

References

See The Ecologist, 1972, *A Blueprint for Survival*, Penguin, London; Barbara Ward and René Dubos, 1972, *Only One Earth: The Care and Maintenance of a Small Planet*, Penguin, London; Paul R. Ehlich and Richard L. Harriman, 1971, *How To Be a Survivor: A Plan to Save Spaceship Earth*, Pan/Ballantyne, London.

FIRST WORLD   The industrialised Western world, where relative political *freedom* is combined with disproportionate consumption of *resources*; for example, the USA, where 2 per cent of the global population consumes 25 per cent of *resources*.

From the idea that the world is divided into three definable sectors, with a *Fourth World* as an emerging desirable future option.

The First World, with its *terminal assumptions* and *expectations*, as maintained by refined *institutional socio-cultural* mechanisms. Home of the *Impossible Party* of ever increasing *consumption*. The First World dominates the Second and *Third*, and paradoxically contains the seeds of the *Fourth* (see **Third**, **Fourth Worlds**).

Relationships   **economy**, **exponential growth**, **terminal**.

See also   **institutions**, **expectations**, **mindset**.

FLOW (also **flux**, see **economy**)   Directed or contained movement; change of shape or *nature*. Generally a one-way *linear process*.

Expression in matter or *energy* of the basic forces of *existence* (see **chi**).

Matter seeks *stability* as a reaction to the universal flow;[1] *energy* flows as an expression of *entropy*; *life* seeks to overcome *entropy* through *synergy* and *growth* (see **entropy**).

As part of human *extension* into the *environment*, to express

105

further our *potential* for *growth*, we have *created* a global *economic system* dependent on *energy* and based on flow (see **economy**). In so doing we have failed to appreciate the implications; the flow of *finite resources*, from *environment* to *waste*, is *unsustainable*. *Life processes* are *cyclic* and the *processes* upon which they depend must also be *cyclic*, compatible with the basic motivation of *life*.

For the *future* we need to distinguish between *processes* which unavoidably involve flow and must be as efficient as possible, such as the use of *energy*; those essential *life processes* which must be *cyclic*; and those which must be based upon *stock*, such as those involving *finite resources* or high initial *energy* inputs.

(*Time* is also a flow phenomenon, deriving from the *energy* of motion.)

Relationships   **energy, life cycles, utility**.

See also   **economy, finite resources, turning point**.

References

1 David Bohm, 1980, *Wholeness and the Implicate Order*, Routledge & Kegan Paul, London.

> Flow is, in some sense, prior to that of the 'things' that can be seen to form and dissolve in this flow ... There is a universal flux that cannot be defined explicitly but which can be known only implicitly, as indicated by the explicitly definable forms and shapes, some stable and some unstable, that can be extracted from the universal flux.

FOOD   Substances ingested that are fundamental to maintain *life* and *growth*. All animals and some plants eat other living things; something dies so that another may live. The basis for the concept of original sin may be the realisation that we have to kill to live – 'all our food is souls'.[1]

Grey culture seeks to reject such propositions by regarding food as a product. Thus the *reality* of the lamb becomes a film-wrapped, portion-packaged, attractively coloured, cooled and presented life-source-denied chop.

Greens believe food must be regarded as a sacrament.

> Human responsibility is to ensure the best for all life in the knowledge that it is all one, that life supports life. The health of people and planet is intimately linked with the way we feed ourselves; neither can be achieved by poisoning food chains and polluting the environment, or denying the reality of other species.[2]

The current order makes the fate of food animals hell on earth; it distorts the genetics of all food so that it becomes dependent on that order, and thus locks us into dependency in the most *vital* area of *life* (see **chemiculture**).

If there is to be a schism in the *green movement* it will be over food: between those who eat animals and those who do not; between those who believe it is right and those who believe it is wrong. If we accept that all *life* has *rights* there can be little moral distinction between the *form* of *life* one chooses to kill. Until our *philosophy* and *morality* are further developed, the only sound *moral* presumption is that each should be prepared to kill that which they wish to eat – 'No death that is not somebody's food, no life that is not somebody's death.'[3]

Those who seek to avoid consuming any animal products are denying *reality* as much as those who demand food as a sterile product. The whole *cycle* of *life* and *death* within the *Gaian whole* forms one network where distinctions in diet are a matter of *nature* and *choice*; *choices* have effects, and to choose against your *nature* is to distort that *nature*. *Vegans* step outside the *natural cycles of life* and so distort them, although the *nature* of the distortion is open to debate, and the integrity of their position beyond doubt.

Those who cannot kill yet demand meat make a fundamental contribution to the divorce between humanity and *nature*. In the gap between desire and ability humans have *extended structures* which fulfil the desire at the price of dependency and global distortion.

FOOD CHAIN   Series of organisms dependent one on the other for food.

A concept which reflects the *linear* thinking of *grey culture*. Food web, a current *ecological* improvement, acknowledges the multiple inputs and outputs of a variety of organisms, but is still incomplete.

More *green* and *holistic* is the concept of a food network, where the diet of a particular species is selected from the total food *matrix*.

FOOD CYCLES   Recognises the reality of food, that all the materials and molecules of *life* are in a constant *cycle* in the *Gaian whole*.

Under the influence of *life, energy* and matter constantly interchange levels and forms in the interactions of food cycles within the *web of life*. At the interface between animate and inanimate, bacteria and plants convert basic substances into *living* parts of the *web*, and in so doing make them available to other *life forms* (*life anticipates life*). Food cycles are dependent on the basic physical *cycles* of the planet; of air and water, the climate, and their inter-action with the land. *Pollution,* whether intentional or otherwise, disrupts the *function* of these *cycles* and introduces *toxins* to the food network.

The equation is simple: the *health* of planetary *life* equals the *health* of the food cycles. Humans take food from many of the most concentrated parts of the cycle, so poisons in the cycle become concentrated in us. To simplify further, the *health* of the person is the *health* of the planet, and vice versa.[4]

In the *natural* food cycle nothing is *wasted,* nothing lost; *forms* and *energy* levels *change,* and *life evolves.* At least, all this was so until recently. Human activity is disrupting the food cycles and taking the *web of life* apart.

It takes some profound and very basic errors to cripple such bounteous and global *nature.*

FOOD/ENERGY   We derive *energy* from the food we *consume.* Modern industrialised food production is part of a larger *energy* equation (see **energy**).

It has been estimated that to produce and deliver one unit of food energy uses between three and seven units of *fossil fuel energy.* This is obviously a recipe for disaster. However, since it is assumed that *fossil energy* will last at least for the lifetime of present policy makers, the problem is ignored.

The food/energy equation is part of the dependency equation we have created. Modern food production is characterised by *insti-tutional provision;* that is, the means of providing food primarily satisfies *institutional needs.* Nutrition, the *health* of the *biosphere,* the maintenance of *food cycles,* quality in provision, are discounted by a *system* which generates surpluses and malnourishment, *waste* and unfulfilled *need.*

FOOD/POPULATION   There is much debate on the question of how many people the world can feed. The answers generally owe more to prejudice and emotion than reason or knowledge of farming. The broad parameters are that while species are being driven to extinction by human activity, we are taking too much, our *numbers* are too high, our demands excessive. If we accept *rights* for all *life,* then we have to allow space and *resources* for the exercise of those *rights.*

FOOD SOURCES   Modern industrialised food is a minefield. It is polluted, adulterated, denatured, processed, preserved and pack-aged. Every part of the chain detracts from the objective – to provide nutrition for *consumers.* In many ways such food is a *health* hazard, for the planet, for the food sources involved, as well as for *consumers*.[5]

Food should be *organically*[6] produced for local *consumption*. (I must declare my position; when not writing I am an organic farmer producing mutton, wool and beef, and planting as many trees as I can.)

Given that farming is an unnatural act, organic *farming* is the only *morally* and *environmentally* acceptable means of producing food. It works by selectively enhancing beneficial *natural cycles* rather than by disrupting or destroying harmful ones. By avoiding the *need* for and use of drugs and refined *chemical* inputs (or contaminated feed – *organic* animals are fed *organic* food), the *organic* farmer retains the integrity of the food cycles, and thus the *health* of those who eat *organic* produce (see **organic**).

The tragedy of the *need* to fight to establish *organic* farming and get *organic* food to *consumers* is that the *organic* farming cycle was only recently broken. The demand for *more* and cheaper food led to reliance on refined *chemical* fertilisers (NPK) and drugs as substitutes for good husbandry and basic animal welfare. The result is plenty of food of poor or dangerous *quality*; adding basic *chemical* fertilisers disrupts the *natural* fertility *cycles* which generate all the other nutrients derived from the soil. And in their absence we have malnourishment amid plenty. The widespread use of drugs means, not *healthier* animals, but animals kept in conditions in which they could not otherwise survive, while humans get the drug residues (and the drug-resistant bugs). Not that modern *chemiculture* is totally to blame for breaking the *organic cycle*; humanity has a long history of doing it by over-*exploitation*.

Fortunately the food message is increasingly accepted, and safe, nutritious, *organic* food is now more widely available.[7] But the majority of the farming *community* still h∩s to make the *choice* and return to *sustainable* ways.[8]

EXTEMPORARY FOOD   Food without preparation, gathered from *natural sources*.[9]

In the long term the majority of food will have to be from extemporary sources, as part of humanity's return within the *cycle of life*. The current trend towards genetically tailoring food (and the *biosphere*) to humanity's *needs* is *philosophically* unacceptable; arrogant in the extreme, in that it *assumes* limited *relationships* and effects of the *life* forms it *creates*; presumptuous in that it denies the reality of *biosphere*. *Sustainable* food sources, compatible with the *rights* of other *life* forms, will be from *natural* sources.

EXTENSIVE FOOD   Comprehensive, in the sense of multi-crop symbiotic farming. The opposite of intensive.

A step back from *grey culture* tendency for mono-crop *chemiculture* and intensive drug-dependent animal production.

Extensive farming combines animals and plant production in the traditional manner, and is acceptable as a means of returning to complete *organic methods*.

Relationships   **life, rights, organic, cycle of life**.

See also   **numbers, chemiculture, consumers**.

References

1 Inuit saying.

2 Colin Johnson, 1991, *The Green Bible: Creating Sustainable Life on Earth*, Thorsons, London.

3 Gary Snyder, 1983, quoted in Bill Devall and George Sessions, *Deep Ecology: Living as if Nature Mattered*, Peregrine Smith Books, Salt Lake City, Utah, USA.

4 Theodore Roszak, 1981, *Person/Planet, The Creative Disintegration of Industrial Society*, Paladin, London.

5 See Eric Millstone, 1986, *Food Additives: Taking the Lid Off What We Really Eat*, Penguin, London.

6 For standards of organic produce and other information contact The Soil Association, 89 Colston Street, Bristol, England. They produce a journal, *The Living Earth* of general interest and have published, 1991, *The Soil Association Handbook* (Macdonald Optima, London).

7 For British sources of organic food see David Mabey and Alan and Jackie Gear (eds), 1990, *Thorsons Organic Consumer Guide*, Thorsons, London.

8 See Richard Body, 1987, *Red or Green for Farmers (And the Rest of Us)*, Broad Leys Publishing, Saffron Walden, Essex, England.

9 Richard Mabey, 1986, *Food for Free*, Peerage, London.

FOREST   Tract of land covered with *trees* and associated *life* forms; unenclosed woodlands.

Forests are *biological* powerhouses, forming active reservoirs of *life*, expressing the *potential* of *photosynthesis*, *biological growth* and *creation*. They play major roles in *cycling* planetary carbon, nitrogen and oxygen, in addition to the interacting water and mineral *cycles*, thus modifying and stabilising climate.[1] Forests are the hearts, lungs and souls of the planet. Many *natural peoples* have names for *trees* which translate as 'tall people'.

Forests are essential for planetary well-being. We are realising this now that the most magnificent and *diverse* reservoir, the tropical rainforests, are threatened by human activity. European forests were felled to clear land for farming long ago, consigning many species to local and total *extinction*. Sherwood, home to legendary Robin Hood, once covered the spine of England, but where is it now? The highlands of Scotland can either be seen as gaunt grandeur or rock exposed by soil eroded into boggy valleys after the trees were stripped to create sheep ranches. While we pressurise the Brazilians to save the Amazon, what are we doing at home?

Forests have come to be seen as either plantations (coniferous blight) or *tree* reserves (museums). Forests for the *future* need to be places where the *natural cycles* of the forest itself may be expressed, from scrub and pioneer species, through several centuries of development through the climactic change and the decline of dominant species, to the recolonisation by scrub. For this forests need space for the reserves of scrub and colonisers, as well as the 'waste' of the climactic change. They need to be left alone.

<u>Relationships</u>   **acid rain, greenhouse effect, numbers, economy, restoration.**

<u>References</u>

1 Norman Myers (ed.), 1985, *The Gaia Atlas of Planet Management*, Pan Books, London.

FORM see **function, structure, morphology**.

FORMATIVE CAUSATION   Theory of the interaction of form and cause in existence.

In *A New Science of Life*,[1] Rupert Sheldrake develops a theory of formative causation which has profound implications for the *future*. Based on the proposition that we are part of an *evolving universe* in which everything is *evolving*, including what are presently regarded as 'immutable' laws of *nature*,[2] the theory holds that once circumstances have produced an *event*, similar circumstances will tend to produce the same *event*.

Thus once something has *evolved* it will tend to reproduce; further, after the initial *emergence*, reproduction will become easier as the *process* of generation itself *evolves*. The example Sheldrake gives is of newly created *artificial* substances which are difficult to crystallise; once they have been crystallised, that is a regular molecular structure has emerged, subsequent attempts to crystallise the same substance becomes easier, until eventually it becomes commonplace. (Questions of communication, or learning capacity, raised are dealt with under **morphology**.)

Formative causation describes a mechanism for *stability* in *existence*, amounting to a habitual response to circumstances. Yet things do *evolve*; *stability* is not constant. The mechanism of *change* proposed is that of optional pathways (*potential*) within the habitually expressed form. Thus *evolution* is an expression of inherent *potential* (once things start to *evolve*, their *potential evolves*, hence greater complexity in *life*); in response to changing circumstances a new form will emerge. The *process* is essentially one of expression of *field potential*; every form of *existence* has a field. Sheldrake proposes *morphogenetic fields* to describe the inherent fields of *existence* and of their *potential(s)* which may be expressed under *changing* circumstances (see **field**).

Those concerned with the *future* have greeted the implications of formative causation with both despair and hope; despair because it seems to mean that things will simply maintain their present course to *terminality*, and hope because awareness of our situation seems to mean the capacity for *change*, for the *emergence* of other forms of *sustainable* living. In the present period of *change*, circumstances favour the emergence of new forms.

Relationships   **evolution, morphology, potential, model.**
See also   **life, anticipation, expectation.**
References
1 Rupert Sheldrake, 1983, *A New Science of Life: The Hypothesis of Formative Causation*, Granada, London.
2 Thus the laws of physics, which describe the way things interact, depending upon a range of variables such as mass, velocity, position, etc. rather than being descriptions of the way things always have and always will happen, are summary descriptions of the way things happen now, within circumstances at their present state of evolution. This is true even of assumed 'universal constants', such as the speed of light, which may be seen not as a constant but as a summary effect of all the influences upon light at this stage of the universe (see **universe**).

FOSSIL FUELS (see **energy**)   Non-living, ancient carbon or hydro-carbon-based source of energy via combustion – oil, coal, gas, peat, shales. Formed by the decomposition of previous *life* forms which have locked up *life* and solar *energy*. Non-renewable sources of *energy* whose use creates the *greenhouse effect* when there carbon content is oxidised to produce carbon dioxide, CO_2 as a by-product.

FOURTH WORLD   An emerging world based on small nations, *communities* of self-reliance, and *life* on a human scale.

The concept draws on many strands of *green* thought and desire, including the self-sufficiency of John Seymour,[1] the human scale of Kirkpatrick Sale[2] and social ecology of Murray Bookchin.[3] The concept is focused on in the *Fourth World Review*,[4] 'For Small Nations, Small Communities and the Human Spirit', wherein the debate about emerging decentralised self-governing *alternative*,

native and natural *communities* continues. Contributors are as diverse as HRH Prince Charles and myself.

There are also assemblies. The eighth was held at the University of Toronto in 1989, with forums on *bioregionalism, community economics*, personal and *community power* and community strategies. See announcements and reports in the *Fourth World Review*.

Relationships   **community, human scale, self-reliance, spirituality**.

See also   **anarchy, bioregion, numbers**.

References

1 John Seymour, 1976, *The Complete Book of Self-Sufficiency*, Faber & Faber, London.

2 Kirkpatrick Sale, 1980, *Human Scale*, Secker & Warburg, London.

3 Murray Bookchin, 1980, *Towards an Ecological Society*, Black Rose Books, Toronto, Canada.

4 *Fourth World Review*, 24 Abercorn Place, London NW8 9XP.

FREE STANDING   In economics, an *entity* which is self-sufficient or self-reliant.

'*Economic* alternatives need to become free standing; self-sufficiency is a *Green* economic virtue.'[1]

Relationships   **co-operative, community**.

See also   **briarpatch, economy**.

References

1 Derek Wall, 1990, *Getting There; Steps Towards a Green Society*, Green Print, London.

FREEDOM   Personal, civil liberty; independence; power of self-determination; to act, possess, of right.

A slippery concept; freedom from is clearly different from freedom to, yet each is essential to the integrity of the other. Definitions also stress acting of one's own volition, on the basis of independent will.

Since no one exists in isolation, freedom is always a relative property, yet paradoxically it only makes sense if expressed in absolute terms.

Freedom from the various webs of *exploitation* and machination that humanity weaves for its fellows is obviously a desirable prerequisite for a *sustainable future*. Freedom to *create* such a *future*, unencumbered by the trammels of the past is essential. And the two *ideas* merge in the reality that, before denying the propositions of *terminal culture*, it is essential that *sustainable alternatives* are freely available to take their place. Otherwise our attempted *shift* will simply add to the *sink* (see **creation**).

Freedom must be *balanced* by *responsibility*; the classic proposition is that 'My freedom ends where another's begins'. This may be interpreted as the need for a defensive perimeter, of freedom determined by deterrence. Blended with *responsibility*, the need for defence can be removed; my freedom can only exist when there is no conflict with another's (see **rights**).

Access to *information, knowledge* and *opinion* in the debate concerning a subject is essential for freedom and the exercise of *responsibility* in any society. In this respect freedom is a *function* of *social structure*; the *structure* either facilitates freedom or restricts it, and ultimately freedom can only be conditional in the *responsibility* of its use, and that in turn is a *social (philosophical)* question (see **philosophy**).

Greens believe that *life* in *autonomous communities* will provide the most suitable *structure*, with an accessible *community* constitution and open administration. In essence this is a modern form of Rousseau's *social contract*, an answer to his original and still relevant observation, 'Man is born free; and everywhere he is in chains'.[1]

As well as freedom to *consume information*, we also need freedom of expression (see **censorship**).

Greens are also concerned with the freedom of other species. The question of *human relationships* with the rest of the *biosphere* has *philosophical* relevance to the *structures* we *create* for *life* as a *whole* (see **culture**).

Relationships   **anarchy, rights, responsibility, community**.

See also   **culture, institutions**.

References

1 Jean Jacques Rousseau (1712–78), Genevan political philosopher, educationist and essayist. Author of, 1762, *Contrat Social*, which attempted to solve the problem posed by its opening sentence 'Man is born free ...' by postulating a social contract by which citizens' rights and possessions are part of 'general will' which, undivided by private or sectarian interests, would necessarily aim at the general good. With its slogan 'Liberty, Equality, Fraternity', the *Contrat Social* became the bible of the French Revolution.

FULFILMENT   see **potential**.

FUNCTION (see **structure, system, morphology**)   Proper activity; mode of action or activity by which a thing or person fulfils a purpose.

The function of things – other *life* forms – within the *natural* order tends to be respected by *greens*, and seen as something to be over-ridden, dominated, conquered, destroyed, by the *grey.*

In *social dynamics* it is important to distinguish between function and *position.* Current social arrangements, dominated by *hierarchical forms* of *organisation*, place emphasis on *position* rather than function. The more traditional a society, the more important *position* becomes, as in those societies based on genetic *elitism*, where being born into a particular family confers a *position* and rewards regardless of function.

Green community-based society will emphasise the function(s), talents, of individuals as a measure of their contribution to the *community*, rather than accidents of birth, dispositions of *power* or opportunism.

FUNCTIONALISM   The emphasis on function rather than aesthetics in design.

Functionalism is relevant for the *future* because it encourages the *maximum utility* of materials and *finite resources.*

Relationships   **mindset, matrix, ad hoc, relationship**.
See also   **hierarchy, morphology**.

FUNDAMENTAL   Essential, primary, original; source from which others are derived; principle, *value*, rule from which a *system* is derived.

FUNDAMENTALISM   Strict adherence to, maintenance of, traditional orthodox religious or other beliefs, such as the unquestionable infallibility of scripture, the literal adherence to texts.

A search for the *future* in the *past.*

Green fundamentalism is a belief *system* in which *green* concerns are paramount and *ecological* issues influence all decisions (see **questions**).

Fundamentalism may be acceptable if based upon *philosophy*; that is, as an active, developing view of *existence*. It becomes coercive when based upon dogma.

Relationships   **philosophy, mindset**.

FUTURE   Of time to come; everything beyond now; that which may be expected to happen.

The results of what we have done in the *past* influence what will happen in the future; human activity has reached such a pitch that the *process* can become overwhelming.[1] Despite our current *predicament*, there is an *inherent* continuity in things which confers *stability*. Normally this is a desirable feature of *existence*; it brings a measure of security in *anticipating* the future. If the future we *anticipate* is undesirable, *terminal, unsustainable,* or a combination of these, then *stability* and continuity become disadvantageous.

Grey culture consumes the future; our *extensions* into the *environment* also colonise the future (see **economy**). We are disposing of options, species, materials, the very fabric of the planet, with no consideration for tomorrow. Living within the *limits* of the *biosphere* will require developing the capacity for now-centred living, that is accepting that the span of our influence should be restricted by the *rights* and options of those sharing now and what may be required by those who will follow.

Creating a desirable future requires a break with the *past,* or, more properly, many breaks in many *fields* at different times. The future *evolves,* it is not an instant proposition. The future requires that we understand what of our *past* may be retained and what should be abandoned; this requires a *philosophy* that guides such judgments and gives a framework for *sustainable extension* into the future.[2] In addition to breaking with the *past,* greens have to have ideas, *models,* of what is required for the future. By *creating* suitable *models* of future *existence* now, and propagating them in the *minds* of our species, we both *change minds* and *create* a different future. Engineering a *shift* from *terminality* to *sustainability* requires visualising and focusing on what we desire, spreading the *anticipation* of a different future so that it becomes reality (see **choice**).

<u>Relationships</u>   meme, **formative causation, human evolution, anticipation, potential**.

<u>See also</u>   **dreamtime, compression, morphology**.

<u>References</u>

1 Alvin Toffler, 1970, *Future Shock*, Pan Books, London.
2 Colin Johnson, 1991, *The Green Bible: Creating Sustainable Life on Earth*, Thorsons, London.

GAIA, GAIAN The concept of the planet as a whole living *entity*; of that concept.

> In the beginning, as the Greeks saw it, when chaos settled into form there was a mighty sphere, floating free within the moist gleaming embrace of the sky and its great swirling drifts of white cloud, a vibrant globe of green and blue and grey, binding together in a holy, deep-breasted synchrony the temperatures of the sun, the gases of the air, the chemicals of the sea, the minerals of the soil, a breathing, pulsing body that was, in the words of Plato, 'a living creature, one and visible, containing within itself all living creatures.'
>
> To this the Greeks gave a name: Gaea the earth mother.[1]

The modern development of Greek insight offers a total, *holistic*, view of the planet, inspired by the view of *earth* from space. It postulates that the physical and chemical conditions of the planet, under the influence of *energy* from sun and moon, have been actively modified by *life* to suit its needs in a continual process of *global symbiosis*.

The Gaia hypothesis[2] offers the insights that the planet is alive and that all earthly life *functions* as a single organism, much as if it were a single super cell.[3] The *biosphere* defines and maintains conditions necessary for its survival by influencing the major *cycles* of the planet, from rocks and weather to molecular *cycles*, via a myriad of interacting *feedback* loops which literally girdle the globe in series of interacting *matrices* – the *dynamics* of the *web of life*. *Life* on this planet is one super organism, and humans together with the millions of other species are as cells in its tissues.

Gaia is a scientifically based exposition of the old notion of Mother Earth as the nurturing and *sustaining* source of *life*. In coming of age the idea has grown to describe the *inherent awareness* of the *biosphere*. The implications are far-reaching. The Gaia hypothesis provokes a view of the earth where:

1 Life is a planetary phenomenon. On this scale it is immortal and has no need to reproduce.

2 There can be no partial occupation of a planet by living organisms. It would be as impermanent as half an animal. The presence of sufficient living organisms on a planet is needed for the regulation of the environment. Where there is incomplete occupation, the ineluctable forces of physical and chemical evolution would soon render it uninhabitable.

3 Our interpretation of Darwin's great vision is altered. Gaia draws attention to the fallibility of the concept of adaptation. It is no longer sufficient to say that 'organisms better adapted than others are more likely to leave offspring'. It is necessary to add that the growth of an organism affects its physical and chemical environment; the evolution of the species and the evolution of the rocks, therefore, are tightly coupled as a single indivisible process.

4 Theoretical ecology is enlarged. By taking the species and their physical environment together as a single system, we can, for the first time, build ecological models that are mathematically stable and yet include large numbers of competing species. In these models increased diversity among the species leads to better regulation.[4]

Seeing the planet as an *aware* organism with the capacity for maintaining *stasis* over long periods of *time*, raises the question of its reaction to the disruptive activities of humanity. Could, or is, Gaia, with human help, making the planet unfit for human (or all mammalian) survival? Those the gods wish to destroy ...

Greens accept the Gaian hypothesis as the best available description of the *dynamics* of earth *life*. To *create sustainable ways of living* for the *future*, humanity has to accept the *limits* of those *dynamics* (as well as those imposed by *finite resources*) and devise *ways of living* and *means* of fulfilment within the Gaian *whole*, accepting our *rights* and *responsibilities* as part of a coherent *web of life*.

We share one *earth*, one destiny.

GAIAN CONTRACT (see **life contract**)   A concept which derives from Rousseau's social contract and the idea of a *life contract*; in essence, that we have to understand the terms on which we have to live within the Gaian *whole* (see **limits, morphology**).

<u>Relationships</u> **life, holism, philosophy, formative causation, evolution, limits.**

<u>See also</u>   **feedback, cycle of life, perception, sustainability**.

<u>References</u>

1 Kirkpatrick Sale, 1985, *Dwellers in the Land: The Bioregional Vision*, Sierra Club Books, San Francisco, USA.

2 J.E. Lovelock, 1979, *Gaia: A New Look at Life on Earth*, Oxford University Press, Oxford, England.

3 Lewis Thomas, 1980, *The Lives of a Cell*, Allen Lane, London.

4 J.E Lovelock, 1989, *The Ages of Gaia: A Biology of Our Living Earth*, Oxford University Press, Oxford, England.

   See also Michael Allaby, 1989, *Guide to Gaia*, Macdonald Optima, London.

GAME (see **model**)   Contest according to rules to test skill, strength, or the outcome of chance.

Means of analysing the dynamics of a series of propositions, usually by changing variables (rules), as in computerised war games.

Games are important means of testing the outcome of propositions, or the *dynamics* of *models*, before they are unleashed into the real world. Children do this all the time as 'play', an essential part of the *growth process* which will fit them to their *life* circumstances.

The *future* requires that we invest more in developing complex games to represent things which are proposed. *Grey culture*, with its ethos of blind *progress*, simply allows things which are conceived to be *created* with minimal regard for effects on *life* and the *environment*. *Green culture* will require more careful exploration of proposals, by means of *models* and games, before they are accepted and *created*. If we had played 'nuclear electricity' instead of going straight to 'nuclear power' we would not have had either, or the terms and implications would have been clear at the outset. Games are good for exposing strengths and weaknesses and illuminating the true *agenda* of *processes*.

<u>Relationships</u>   **creativity, paradigm, feedback**.
<u>See also</u>   **change, growth, perspective**.

GENE   Unit of heredity in chromosome, controlling a particular characteristic, or the operation or timing of the *function* of other genes. Each cell of a gene-based entity contains a complete set of genes for the total entity – its genetic complement. Because of its structure the gene is also known as the immortal double helix.

The double helix molecular structure of the chromosome is composed of DNA (deoxyribonucleic acid). This directs protein synthesis, and a wide range of *life* processes, through the action of RNA (ribonucleic acid).[1]

GENE POOL   The total genetic complement of species, *environment*, or planet. Some human activities disrupt the gene pool, such as the release of radioactive material or other *pollution* into the *environment*. Others simply reduce it by driving species to *extinction* (see **diversity**).

Humans have irrational attitudes to gene pools; whereas much is invested in altering that of, say, horses or pet goldfish, that of humanity itself is left to chance or random modification. Our *philosophy* of *life* is inconsistent in this area.

GENETIC   Of, or to do with, genes.

GENETIC ENGINEERING (aka **biotechnology**, **'biotech'**, **reproductive technology**)   Process whereby the genetic code of a *life* form is physically altered to give subsequent forms specific characteristics. For example, bacteria may be altered so that they can ingest particular substances. By similar techniques the sex, etc., of offspring can be predetermined.

The *process* of genetic engineering is *philosophically* rejected by *greens* because it amounts to a further and *potentially* disastrous distortion of *nature* in its most fundamental form to suit man. Together with *nuclear energy* and *artificial* chemistry, genetic engineering is a hazardous gamble with the *future* in the casino of blind *progress*.

> (Biotechnology) represents the ultimate negation of nature, ... a final testimonial that ... all of the physical and biological world has been put there for our exclusive use ... The problem is that biotechnology has a beginning but no end ... (it) legitimises the idea of crossing all species' barriers and undermines the inviolability of discrete, recognisable species in nature.[2]

Genetic engineering has the *potential* to become the most highly refined but grossest form of bestiality yet discovered.

GENETIC POTENTIAL   All genetic processes represent a *potential* before the *anticipated function* is fulfilled. Fulfilment requires conditions within the organism and in the external *environment* to be compatible with the inherent expectations of the gene or genetic system. If these expectations are not met, the organism will suffer illness or congenital disability, or fail (die) (see **health**).

The *future* requires a directed *process* of human *evolution*. Whether this may be achieved within our current genetic repertoire is a matter of debate which will be resolved by the *future*. However it is fact that within the human genetic array, those who have been decoding the *functions* of groups of genes, or even of individual genes, have found what amounts to incoherent or scrambled genes. These either fulfil *functions* of which we are presently unaware or they may represent blank capacity for the *future*.

EXTRA-GENETIC Extra-genetic inheritance refers to those features which are transmitted by cellular material rather than genes. It is one reason for the mother having greater influence than the father; the offspring receive, for example, extra-genetic input from the ovum.

The term is also relevant to forms of *existence* which rely upon gene-based *life* forms, which *exist* as an *extension* of the *life* form, usually (although not essentially) with a degree of *utility*. Thus nests are extra-genetic *extensions* of birds.

The concept is particularly relevant to humans, as we *extend* extra-genetic *structures* which have de facto lives of their own, *existence* beyond their creators, in the form of the *institutions* which dominate modern *cultures* (see **institutions**).

Relationships   **life, biosphere, existence, meme.**
See also   **extension, potential, evolution.**
References

1 See J.A.V. Butler, 1959, *Inside the Living Cell,* Allen & Unwin, London, for a good basic description of genetic and cellular components and processes.
2 Jeremy Rufkin, 1985, *Declarations of a Heretic,* Routledge & Kegan Paul, New York, USA.
    See also Richard Dawkins, 1976, *The Selfish Gene,* Oxford University Press, Oxford, England.

GENERAL SYSTEMS THEORY   see **system.**

GEOTHERMAL ENERGY   see **energy.**

GIFT ECONOMY   see **economy.**

GLOBAL   worldwide, affecting the whole planet.

GLOBAL CULTURE   *Created* by things which are repeated on a worldwide basis, as pop (music) *culture,* Coca-Cola *culture, pollution, consumption.* The present global *culture* is the sum of those aspects of Western industrial *culture* which lead to uniformity and *create* the *global predicament.*

Greens believe that a global *culture* based on *sustainable, life-enhancing philosophy* and *practice* is essential for the *future.* Under its thin umbrella many *diverse* local and *bioregional sub-*

cultures may co-exist (see **community, culture**).

'Acting locally, thinking globally'.[1]

GLOBAL PREDICAMENT   Condition of impending *terminality,* generated by the *philosophy* of *reductionism* combined with prevailing religious views of Western industrial *culture* (see **Cartesianism, economy**), and perpetrated by the *institutional forms* and mechanisms which that *culture* has *extended* into the world (see **institutions**).

GLOBAL SYMBIOSIS (see **Gaian contract**)   *Symbiosis,* association of two different organisms, living attached or one within the other for mutual benefit.

The *co-operative* implications of living together for mutual benefit have *extended* the meaning of symbiosis beyond its original narrow meaning. It is now taken as a *co-operative* and mutually beneficial association.

Global symbiosis, the mutually beneficial association of all the elements (with the exception of modern industrial man) of the *biosphere* (see **Gaia**).

GLOBAL WARMING   see **greenhouse effect**.

Relationships   **Gaia, culture, economy, institutions**.

See also   **extension, morphology**.

References

1 Hazel Henderson, 1978, *Creating Alternative Futures: The End of Economics,* Berkeley Windover, New York, USA.

GNOSIS   Knowledge of spiritual mysteries.

GNOSTIC(S)   *Spiritual anarchists,* the arch rebels of Christian society from the 2nd to the 4th centuries. For Gnostics forming a church (*institutionalisation*) is/was as contradictory as *anarchists* forming a *political party.* The Pauline Christians of Rome crushed the Gnostics and handed over an obedient and conformist church to the Roman emperor. The Inquisition was invented to ensure the dispatch of later manifestations; rejection and persecution by the established church continues today.

Knowledge is seen as a dangerous thing.

The Gnostics were part of a vast European underground, the faith of the underdog, the saint and the revolutionary. It broke out again in the sixteenth and seventeenth centuries through the Anabaptists, the Hutterites, the Mennonites, the Family of Love, Jacob Boehme and finally the Quakers. We think of Gerrard Winstanley in connection with the Diggers, his role as a Gnostic prophet has yet to be properly recognised.[1]

GNOSTICISM   The thread of gnostic *spiritualism* passed on via, among others, Blake ('To see a World in a grain of sand ...'[2]) and Jung.[3] It is relevant to *spirituality* for the *future* in its concentration on *knowledge* rather than dogma or subjective experience. Also in its perception of the *needs* of the *future*:

> If you bring forth what is within you, what you bring forth will save you. If you do not bring forth what is within you, what you do not bring forth will destroy you.[4]

<u>Relationships</u>   **anarchy, spirituality, intuition.**
<u>See also</u>   **philosophy.**
<u>References</u>

1 Peter Cadogan, in 'Gnostics as Anarchists of Old', published in *Freedom*, Volume 51, Number 14, 14 July 1990, Freedom Press, Angel Alley, 84b Whitechapel High Street, London E1 7QX. *Note*: I would like to acknowledge that this entry is based upon knowledge kindly passed on by Peter Cadogan. Any errors, of abridgement or otherwise, are mine.
2 William Blake (1757–1827), *Auguries of Innocence:*
   'To see a World in a Grain of Sand,
   And a Heaven in a Wild Flower,
   Hold Infinity in the palm of your hand,
   And Eternity in an hour.
3 Carl Gustav Jung (1875–1961), 'Religion, it might be said, is the term that designates the attitude peculiar to a consciousness which has been altered by the experience of the numinosium.' (of a numen – a local or presiding deity – indication of the presence of a divinity) *Psychology and Religion* from 1990 *The Basic Writings of C.G. Jung*, Princeton University Press, Princeton, New Jersey, USA.
4 Jesus Christ, *Gospel according to Thomas*, 45: 29–33.
   See also Elaine Page, *The Gnostic Gospels*, Pelican, London.

GNP   see **gross national product.**

GRASSROOTS   From the bottom of society, the basic level.
   A concept which, while apparently implying egalitarian social *processes*, actually reveals the privileged *position* of those who see the grassroots as something separate, to be conditionally included, rather than as distinct equals who should have the *choice* ('have', differentiated from 'be given'). A *symptom* of the *terminal mindset* (see **mindset**).

> Grassroots democratic politics means an increased realisation of decentralised, direct democracy. We start from the belief that the decisions at the grassroots level must ... be given priority.

> We grant far-reaching powers of autonomy and self-administration to decentralised, management grassroots units.[1]

The words may sound fine, but the underlying attitudes must be rejected. That there exists a superior group who will 'give priority', who will be in a position to be able to give, even, is a negation of equality. Similarly the arrogance of 'we grant' (and decide how far 'far-reaching' is); those who have the *power* to grant also have the *power* to withdraw.

The concept of grassroots is a part of thought which sees society as a *hierarchy*, of *power* and powerlessness, of superiors and inferiors, of the *included* and the *excluded*, of 'them' and 'us'. A means of seeing people in terms of clichés: 'rank and file', the 'working class' etc. ('classify me to deny me' – Bob Dylan). Such terminology should be rejected by *greens* in favour of dealing with people as individuals, on the basis of equality, of *function* within *community*, of *freedom* and *responsibility* within the wider *matrix* of *being* (see **community**).

Relationships   **hierarchy, power, terminal culture**.
See also   **thematic compatibility**.
References
1 *Die Grünen*, quoted in Fritjof Capra and Charlene Spretnak, 1986, *Green Politics*, Grafton, London.

GREAT CYCLE OF LIFE   see **cycles, life**.

GREEN   The colour of plant life, of chlorophyll; one of the primary colours of light, between blue and yellow in the spectrum.

In the human context green is anything which is life-enhancing in the widest sense; respect for the *earth*, all its *life* and physical make-up, and the *cycles* which maintain it; the desire for *knowledge* of *ways of life* compatible with the *life* of the *Gaian whole*, (going green); a person who exhibits such *values* and desires; also of processes acceptable to such a *way of life* (see **green philosophy**).

Relationships   **life**, the **universe** and everything.
See also   **philosophy, Gaia, limits**.
References
See Jonathon Porritt, 1984, *Seeing Green: The Politics of Ecology Explained*, Blackwell, Oxford, England.
    Also John Button, 1989, *How to Be Green*, Century Hutchinson, London.

GREEN COMMITTEES OF CORRESPONDENCE (GCoCs)
American groups circulating ideas and proposals on green issues. Centred on 10 key values: *ecological wisdom*; *community-based economics*; personal and *social responsibility*; respect for *diversity*; *grassroots democracy*; *decentralisation*; *post-patriarchal values*; *non-violence*; *future focus/sustainability*; *global responsibility*. GCoCs started in 1984, although the Corresponding Society in Britain of the 1970s is an earlier precedent (see **GreenNet**).

GREEN DILEMMA   see **institutions, casualty problem**.

GREEN ISLANDS   Any part of a new *sustainable future* emerging from within *grey terminal culture*. *Changes* in individual *consciousness*; activities arising from such *changes*.

GREEN MOVEMENT   The *shift* towards *green* thoughts, ideas, *consciousness, philosophy*, etc.; people who subscribe to such.
    The growth of the green movement is reflected in the increasing numbers of people joining green organisations. *Greenpeace* has seen its membership grow from a handful of founders in 1970 to 327,000 two decades later, while in Britain alone, Friends of the Earth grew from 39,000 in 1988 to 190,000 in 1989. Beyond such specific organisations many include older established conservation groups, such as the World Wide Fund for Nature, National Trust, etc., in the green movement. However such organisations pre-date *green* concern, and this is reflected in many anomalies, such as the support for the hunting rights of privileged classes.
    Also the *political shift* towards green parties and policies. After the 1989 European Community elections, greens held 39 out of 518 seats. As Die Grünen in Germany have found, the *nature* of the established *political process* makes it difficult to remain *green* as you sink in the *grey* swamp.[1]
References
1 See Saral Sarkar, 'A Third World View of the German Green Movement', in *The Ecologist*, Volume 20, Number 4, July/August 1990.

GREEN PHILOSOPHY   Philosophy: seeking wisdom or knowledge, especially that which deals with ultimate reality.

Philosophy consists of speculation on matters as to which definite knowledge has, so far, been unascertainable; but like science, it appeals to human reason rather than authority.[1]

Philosophy exists in no-man's land, between the definite *knowledge* of science and the dogma of theology. In this dangerous and disputed territory philosophy may be led, attacked, adopted or rejected by either or both.

In essence philosophy is that which is believed to be correct. Philosophy has also come to mean the expression of *values*, attitudes, belief (dogma), and a way of living.

Green philosophy cannot be presented as a finished body of belief, indeed it is unlikely ever to be so, since it will *evolve* with changing circumstances and increasing *wisdom*. Fundamental precepts can be stated upon which green philosophy is based: that all *life*, and all *existence*, has fundamental *inherent value*; that all *life* has *rights*; that humanity must live within the *limits of nature* (the *great cycle of life*) and *finite resources*, or fail without. That humanity has the *responsibility* of *stewardship* (as opposed to management) of the planet; that to *fulfil* our *potential* as *stewards* we need to undertake an act of *conscious evolution*; that the objectives of *sustainability* and the enhancement of all *life* should be our primary concerns.[2]

Philosophy is important because it is the intellectual engine room of *culture*. Most people inherit the philosophy of their *culture* in the form of shorthand *assumptions* and *expectations*, beliefs about the way things are and how *life* should be lived, without ever questioning the source. To *create* a *green culture* we need to establish a *viable* green philosophy which will guide the *principles* and *practice* of our lives. Attempting to '*green*' grey *culture* with its underlying incorrect, *exploitive*, and *terminal philosophy* simply will not work. The controls in the *cultural* engine room will allow for, counteract or absorb such superficial actions. '*Greening*' may *change* the appearance, but the content will remain the same. Actions compatible with green philosophy are essential for the *creation* of a *green culture*; there can be little compromise, *means* and *ends* must become one in a *sustainable future*.

Many strands from the *past* contribute to the *green* vision of the *future*, as the (far from comprehensive) references to entries in this book indicate. An essential task for the *future* is to gather these threads and ensure their revival and survival in the new context. The *green movement* needs its testament of the *past*, the ideas, the *intuitive* ahead-of-time insights, the wisdom and beauty that is undeniable, the flowers of our *creativity*.

Relationships   **evolution, culture, intuition, principles, practice.**
See also   **mindset, assumptions, expectations.**

References
1 Bertrand Russell (1872–1970), 1946, *History of Western Philosophy*, Allen & Unwin, London.
2 See Colin Johnson, 1991, *The Green Bible: Creating Sustainable LIfe on Earth*, Thorsons, London.

GREENHOUSE EFFECT (aka **global warming**)   The increase in the earth's temperature due to the emissions of 'greenhouse gases', particularly carbon dioxide (CO_2), methane (CH_4), oxides of nitrogen (NO_2, NO_3), CFCs (chlorofluorocarbons), and low altitude *ozone* (O_3) formed by reactions between hydrocarbons, oxides of nitrogen, and sunlight.

'In the next forty or fifty years, the greenhouse gases in the atmosphere will double and the world will get warmer by between 1 and 4.5°C.'[1]

These gases, emitted by the vast number of combustion *processes* using *fossil fuels*, and from biological processes such as farming and breathing, disrupt the planet's climate regulatory *systems*. In the simplest case CO_2 traps incoming infra-red radiation from the sun, thus leading to a temperature increase – as in a greenhouse.[2]

In 1970, in the first issues of *The Ecologist*, Jean Liedloff noted that atmospheric CO_2 had been increasing by 0.2 per cent since the beginning of the *Industrial Revolution* and, if allowed to continue unabated, would cause polar ice meltdown and coastal area flooding and erosion.

It should be noted that the warmth induced by the greenhouse effect is not a new thesis; it was first proposed by Swedish chemist Svente Arrhenius (1859–1927) in 1896. In 1957 the Scripps Institute of Oceanography in California showed that around 50 per cent of CO_2 was being trapped by the atmosphere. 'Humanity was engaged in a great geophysical experiment.'[3]

Unthinking people have welcomed the warmth induced by the greenhouse effect as a benefit. Climatic disruption will, however, be disastrous. Our present means of *food* production leans heavily on present climatic patterns; disrupting these will cause shortages and famine to become far more widespread. Disruption is already evident in many parts of the world. It is typified by short periods, 'spikes', of unseasonably high or low temperatures within patterns of seasonal shift; mild winters, hotter summers. The spikes disrupt plant *life* and thus *food* production. Also global warming is causing sea levels to rise, through melting glacial and polar ice and expansion of the oceanic water mass. Most of the world's major cities and a large proportion of the present population live at or near the present nominal sea level.

The temperature increases involved may seem small (between 1.5 and 5.5°C) however, 125,000 years ago, when the temperature was just 2°C warmer, hippopotami lived in the Thames valley. Similarly a drop in temperature of 3°C would be enough to initiate another ice age.[4] Climatic *stability* depends on very small changes in temperature.

Every combustion *process* – burning petrol in cars, gas, oil or coal in central heating, indirect combustion via the use of electricity, whatever – burning anything containing carbon produces carbon dioxide (CO_2), which accounts for 50 per cent of the problem. The only answer is to burn less, to use less *fossil fuel energy*. There is no other way around this basic problem. Human activity has hit a fundamental *limit* of the *nature* of the planet[5] (see **energy**).

Deforestation also contributes to the greenhouse effect as *trees* remove carbon dioxide from the atmosphere and lock it up in their *structure* (see **forests**).

Global warming is a classic *cul-de-sac problem*; the longer corrective action is avoided, [6] the more serious (i.e. irreversible) the *problem* becomes. Just to stabilise atmospheric concentrations of greenhouse gases at present levels requires a 60 per cent cut in emissions NOW. Yet while the *First World* is becoming *aware* of the *nature* of the *catastrophe*, the *Third World* is demanding more: more *energy*, more *consumption*, more goods, more greenhouse gases. Resolution demands different solutions to human *need fulfilment* (see **economy**).

Relationships   **limits, economy, energy, Gaia, growth.**

See also   **numbers, acid rain, terminal culture.**

References

1 From the *Guardian*, quoted in P.H. Collin, 1988, *Dictionary of Ecology and the Environment*, Peter Collin Publishing, Teddington, Middlesex, England.

2 John Gribben, 1989, *Hothouse Earth: The Greenhouse Effect and Gaia*, Bantam Press, London.

3 See *The Ecologist*, Volume 20, Number 4, July/August 1990. *The Ecologist*, Worthyvale Manor Farm, Camelford, Cornwall PL32 9TT, England.

4 Jonathon Porritt (ed.), 1987, *Friends of the Earth Handbook*, Macdonald Optima, London.

5 Bill McKibben, 1990, *The End of Nature*, Viking, London.

6 'The Changing Atmosphere' international conference held in Toronto, 1988, issued this statement:

An initial global goal should be to reduce carbon dioxide emissions by approximately 20 per cent of 1988 levels by the year 2005. Clearly, the industrialised nations have a responsibility to lead the way, both through their national energy policies and their bilateral and multilateral assistance arrangements.

Despite this, the British government announced that it was not prepared to act until after yet another report, from the UN-backed Intergovernmental Panel for Climate Change in 1990 (quoted in 4, above). The content of the latter, with its warning that a 60 per cent cut in emissions was necessary immediately, caused then Prime Minister Margaret Thatcher to contort ineffectually, claiming that Britain would reduce CO_2 emissions by 20 per cent by maintaining the level that they would reach in 1992, thus achieving a reduction in relation to what the level would have been in 2005 if the government had not acted so courageously. It should be noted that the USA refused to accept even this pathetic target. (See George Orwell [Eric Arthur Blair, 1905–1950], 1959, *Nineteen Eighty Four*, particularly 'doublespeak' and 'doublethink'.)

GREENING   Originally of specific environmental projects, e.g. planting trees and conservation. Now of the *process* of *creating sustainable ways of living* or contributions to that objective.[1]

Greening can too easily become superficial activity to make the *unsustainable* seem not only acceptable, but desirable, such as solving the *environmental problem* by driving a Volvo estate on unleaded petrol (see **consumerism**). Thus is appeals to those who wish to have their *ecological* cake and eat it. Also as a cypher in the commercial PR repertoire of *grey economics*; 'our product is greener', 'we are seeking sustainable development', etc.[2] Also the attempt to convert the *grey* to the *green*, by PR, camouflage, assertion, advertising, confusion, and so on. Criteria for judging the reality of greening are the basic *future* questions (see **questions**). With the activities of corporate entities, ask to see their plan for *devolution* to *human/community scale* enterprise, (see **institutions**), and their propositions for converting their activities from *flow* to *stock* (see **economics**).

Most current *green* greening activity is directed towards *changing* policy and *politics* within the framework of existing *systems*.[3] *Greens* are said to have forced conventional political parties to become 'green'. Greening is said to be characterised by woolly thinking, the exploration of irrelevancy, and seeking shelter in *cul-de-sacs*; such criticism is best ignored. Times and *processes* of *change* are characterised by minor *shifts* and *disruptions* before new patterns, new *forms*, emerge (see **morphology**).

Relationships   philosophy, principles.

See also   creativity, culture.

References

1 See Charles Reich, 1970, *The Greening of America*.
2 John Elkington and Tom Burke, 1987, *The Green Capitalists: How to Make*

Money – and Protect the Environment, Gollancz, London.
3 David Icke, 1990, *It Doesn't Have to be Like This: Green Politics Explained*, Green Print, London.
4 See also G. Tyler Miller, 1983, *Living in the Environment*, Wadsworth, Belmont, California, USA.

GREENNET   A commuter-based *information* and communications *network*. Part of a *federation* of seven *green networks* covering Australia, Brazil, Britain, Canada, Nicaragua, Sweden, USA; more are planned. Open to individuals at reasonable fees; all you need is a computer, a modem and a telephone line. Further details: GreenNet, 25 Downham Road, London N1 5AA (071-249-2948).

GREENPEACE   Founded from the Don't Make a Wave Committee (1970) arising from *peace* (anti-nuclear) and emerging *environmental* concerns.

The US government's testing ground on Amchitka in the Aleutian Islands, on the Pacific volcanic ring, led to the idea of sailing a boat into the test zone, to bear witness against this unacceptable activity. This set the pattern for action in the Pacific, during which Greenpeace became such an embarrassment that the French government sank the *Rainbow Warrior* in an act of *war* (or international terrorism) in Auckland harbour, New Zealand, with the loss of one life, photographer Fernando Pereira.

Greenpeace came to wider public attention in the mid-seventies with its campaign to Save the Whale. This brought the organisation into direct conflict with the governments of whaling nations on the world media stage, and at the same time exposed activists to danger in some of the most perilous parts of the oceans. The courage of such activities captured the hearts, minds and pockets of many. Campaigns have been progressively extended to cover many *environmental* and animal issues, sometimes in highly controversial ways, such as: 'It takes up to forty dumb animals to make a fur coat. But only one to wear it.'

Greenpeace has become known around the world for its courageous, positive confrontation over *environmental* issues. Their many imaginative actions have captured massive media audiences around the world, making many aware of issues which would normally not surface through the 'business as usual' *processes* of *terminal culture*.

Now using the slogan 'thank God someone's making waves', 'Greenpeace is a force for good and also a force for hope, the hope that we can find a solution to the environmental problems that beset us. By taking action it reminds us that change is possible. It is also essential.'[1]

If you have some *time* or resources to spare, or want to do something positive with your *life* contact: Greenpeace, 30-31 Islington Green, London N1 8XE (071 354 5100). Or start a Greenpeace group where you are.

> When the earth has been ravaged and the animals are
> dying a tribe of people from all races, creeds
> and colours will put their faith in deeds not words
> to make the land green again; They shall be known as
> the Warriors of the Rainbow.
> Protectors of the Environment.
>
> *Hopi Indian Prophecy*

References
1 Michael Brown and John May, 1989, *The Greenpeace Story*, Dorling Kindersley, London.

GREENS   People subscribing to green *values*, ethos, *philosophy*, etc. In *politics*, supporters of 'green' parties or policies.

There are growing numbers of sub-divisions (see **eco-**) – visionary, *holistic*, *peace*, left-wing, Christian, etc. – greens. Jonathon Porritt has also defined the difference between light and dark *greens*;[1] light are reformers, political realists, whereas dark are fundamentalists, radicals.

References
1 Jonathon Porritt (ed.), 1987, *Friends of the Earth Handbook*, Macdonald Optima, London.

GREY, GRAY   Intermediate shade between black and white, coloured like ashes or lead; depressing, dismal; anonymous, unidentifiable.

Grey is used as a generic description for anything associated with the current *unsustainable terminal culture.*

GREY CULTURE (see **terminal**)   *Culture* based upon the present ethos of *growth, environmental* destruction, increasing *consumption.* Derived from the *reductionist philosophical* tradition and the *homocentric* view of the planet as being at man's disposal.

Relationships   **global predicament, economy, numbers.**
See also   **growth, consumption.**

GROSS NATIONAL PRODUCT (GNP)   The measure, in monetary terms, of *flow* through a nation's *economy*. The chalice on the altar of *growth economics*. *Symptomatic* of the emphasis on *quantity* rather than *quality*.

A *linear* concept, GNP measures everything that increases *consumption* as 'good', thus a disaster which destroys houses is a good, because it will stimulate *flow*, of building materials and construction work. *Polluting* and then cleaning up (if possible) is a good. However, inventing a *means* of *energy* or *resource* reduction is a bad, since it will reduce GNP. Economists and politicians are happy when GNP goes up, and miserable when it does down. Part of the underlying insanity of *terminal culture* (see **economics**).

GROWTH   Increase in size or complexity; also (economics) in value.

Growth is typical of *life processes*. *Problems* arise because we have failed to differentiate between *processes* which may be *extended* indefinitely and those which are subject to *natural limits*. We have projected simple *assumptions* (more = better) into every area of *life*, especially *economics*, with little regard for the consequences (see **exponential growth**).

There are *limits to growth* in every form of *existence*. *Limits* are a natural part of *interdependent systems* which ensure the survival/ *stability* of the *structure* against the excesses of its parts; they are an aspect of *synergy* which receives little attention in a *culture* dedicated to 'more' (see **balance**).

ECONOMIC GROWTH   The belief that we can each go on *consuming* more, of more things and more *energy* indefinitely; the illusion of a world without *limits*. A *linear* concept which will carry us outside *life* (see **finite resources**). Every industrial *economy* is based upon the presumption of continual growth, or 'more'. This is the built-in route to *terminality*; in a *finite* world continual growth is *unsustainable*[1] (see **Impossible Party**).

NEGATIVE GROWTH   The proposition that more can be had from *less*, of refinement of *material* and *energy* use. Negative growth would be a feature of conversion from the *flow economy* to one based on *stock* (see **economics**). Although reducing *consumption*, it need not mean a decline in facilities, and is likely to increase fulfilment as human activity becomes once more integrated with *life processes*.

PERSONAL GROWTH   Personal growth is continual *change*. Few of us live in *natural communities* where we grow into means of *ful-*

filling our *needs* from our immediate *environment*; modern people have lost the innocence of *natural peoples*. As yet, the majority fail to find themselves.

We grow up in a *culture* which *nurtures* us for its *needs*, which fits us for *institutional forms* of *existence*. Part of the trouble is our highly adaptable *nature*: the accident of our place and circumstances of birth are irrelevant; we fit into what we find. We are as adaptable as Lorenz's ducklings[2] to the patterns placed in front of us; we fit obligingly into the little boxes of our *culture* (see **education**).

But no matter how well culturally adapted, the nagging question of individual identity can remain: 'What am I?'

Questions of human nature become more relevant as we seek to fulfil our *needs* and *potential* while *creating sustainable ways of life.* The exploration of self, *needs* and *nature* is part of the ground demanding more attention.

Current personal growth centres on *therapy* intended to adjust people to the *reality* of *self* in *terminal culture*. This *model* should be rejected: 'Do not adjust yourself, reality is at fault.' Rather we should be exploring, preparing to go on into directed *evolution* which will enable us to live in the *future*. Standing on the brink of space, the greatest adventure lies within us (see **change, potential**).

POPULATION GROWTH   see **numbers**.

Relationships   **carrying capacity, feedback, life, limits**.

See also   **consciousness, community, culture**.

References

1 See Donella H. Meadows, Dennis L. Meadows, Jorgen Randers, William W. Behrens, 1972, *The Limits to Growth: A Report for the Club of Rome's Project on the Predicament of Mankind*, Pan Books, London.

And Stuart McBurney, 1990, *Ecology into Economics Won't Go: or Life is Not a Concept*, Green Books, Hartland, Bideford, Devon, England.

2 Konrad Lorenz, Austrian zoologist, acknowledged as the founder of ethology, the study of animal behaviour in natural environments. Primarily concerned with instinctive behaviour. Lorenz described the process of 'imprinting', by which a variety of stimuli determined behaviour patterns in newly hatched birds. The classic example was of ducklings following the first thing(s) they saw upon hatching, in this case various coloured wellington boots, in the apparent belief that they were mother. His later work dealt with the evolution of behavioural patterns for survival.

GUARANTEED BASIC INCOME (GBI) (aka **social wage, social income,** also **basic income, citizens' wage**)   The idea that everyone should have an automatic income, or access to a means of living. A derivative of Marx's: 'From each according to his abilities, to each according to his needs.'[1]

Seen in the primary context of *Gaian needs*, with human *needs* secondary, the idea may be reworked in the form of a *universal credit economy*, where each person is given credit, not to *consume*, although that may be the case, but in accordance with the degree of *sustainability* of their *way of life*. Thus the meek may inherit the earth (see **universal credit economy**).

<u>Relationships</u>   **economics, ways of living, sustainability.**

<u>References</u>

1 Karl Marx (1818–1883), 1977, *Critica del Programa de Gotha*, Progress Press, USSR.

HARMONY   Agreeable effect of apt arrangement of parts.

The result of positive *synergy* in a *system*; one of *life's objectives* within the *environment.*

Relationships   **sustainability, creativity, potential, limits**.

See also   **agenda, synergy, symbiosis**.

HAZARDOUS WASTE   see **pollution**.

HEALTH   Soundness of body and/or mind.

A more positive definition of health has proved an elusive quarry. Over the past two decades the search has been *extended* to include the ability to *function,* to fulfil *needs,* and finally to fulfil *potential.*

A *holistic* definition has to encompass all levels of *being,* and the effects of their interaction. Thus it starts with the notion of health as the fulfilment of *anticipation,* in a *being* or *system.* This *extends* from the molecular, in terms of the *need* for (*anticipation* of) *nutrition,* breathing and drinking, and the ability to expel *waste*: all the interactions we must have with our *environment.* But whereas such a definition may be adequate for, say, a plant, it falls short for more complex, more highly *motivated life* forms. These require additions. First, of the fulfilment of *anticipation* (expectations) within *socio-cultural structures,* especially in a *way of life* based upon *assumptions* about those *structures.* Second, of conditions which allow the fulfilment of *potential*; to be able to become all they are capable of becoming.

Yet these additions over-shoot. Presently, our *socio-cultural dynamic* actively works against health and, while in *evolutionary* terms fulfilment of *potential* is acceptable, humans can become so many things which are injurious to their own health and that of others that 'fulfilment' has to be qualified. Health then becomes a conditional in expression, dependent upon *morality,* in the *choice* of *potentials* expressed in *relation* to the possible inhibition of the *potential* of others, and also dependent upon *philosophy,* simply because that which we wish to express must be acceptable in the widest context of *life*.

Health, then, is the ability to meet *anticipated needs* and to fulfil those *potentials* which are not injurious to the health of others.

The classic statement of the requirements of health was made by Thomas KcKeown:

> The requirements of health can be stated simply. Those who are fortunate enough to be born free of significant congenital disease and disability will remain well if three basic needs are met. They must be adequately fed; they must be protected from a wide range of hazards in the environment; and they must not depart radically from the pattern of personal behaviour under which man evolved – for example by smoking, over-eating, or sedentary living.[1]

The Greek injunctions from the temple wall at Delphi, 'know thyself' and 'nothing to excess', can provide the starting points for practical behaviour in a *culture* devoted to patterns of behaviour which both deny our basic *nature* and discount the requirements of our *evolution*.

Terminal culture actively denies the proposition of health. Whenever we think 'health', *illness* appears in our *minds*. Any discussion of health almost invariably centres on disease, on cures, on preventatives, on *symptomatic* relief, etc., rarely on health as a positive attainable state. Even the most *green policy* manuals talk, under the heading health, about how they will deal with sickness.[2]

The *problem* is that sickness and health are not part of the same continuum; health can co-exist, and dominate, in bodies which have serious flaws or disability. There is an indirect connection between the two, but the absence of one does not automatically equate with the presence of the other. In *social* terms if we wish for health, then we have to create consciously the conditions necessary for it; treating *illness*, while necessary, is not the same thing at all (see **illness**).

Health (and *illness*), is the result of identifiable factors in *life*. It is not a matter of luck, except *genetically*, or a mother's bad health or nutritional state influencing her baby, or of fate beyond influence. If we want to be healthy, we need to *create* conditions for healthy *living*. We understand that this is true for pot plants or domestic animals, but fail to connect the same logic to the human condition. In *socio-cultural* terms, health is a *structural problem*: get the *socio-cultural* (*life*) *structure* right and health will result.

In the most general sense we cannot expect to be healthy as individuals of a species standing minutes from the brink of nuclear extinction, while the *natural* ground which supports us is being dissolved by our various excesses and swept away by our presumptive ignorance. The health of the person is the health of the planet;[3] the two are inseparable and will succeed or fail together. There will always be individuals whose health is failing; this is part of the *natural cycle* of things. Similarly, we will never be entirely free of a vast number of conditions which are provoked by other *life* forms or the conditions under which we live, combined with our susceptibility to their effects. However, we cannot hope to *create* the maximum of individual health while we maintain conditions of *life* which deny it to others of our species, or to *life* in general. If our well-being is bought at the cost of degeneration or demise for others, it is *unsustainable*, and we will fail when they can no longer support us. Health is a concept which must be universally applied; we share one *earth*, one destiny, in one *life*, whatever we choose to make of it.

HEALTH CARE   A general description of the care of illness; usually little to do with health per se (see **illness**).

> Nothing has changed so much in the past twenty-five years as the public's perception of its own health. The change amounts to a loss of confidence in the human form. The general belief these days seems to be that the human body is fundamentally flawed, subject to disintegration at any moment, always on the verge of mortal disease, always in need of continual monitoring and support by health-care professionals.[4]

Part of a negative *process* described as the medicalisation of society.[5]

HEALTH FOOD (see **food**)   A non-concept *symptomatic* of *terminal culture*. All *food* should be 'health' food.

Relationships   **food, environment, needs, rights**.

See also   **culture, mindset**.

References

1 Thomas McKeown, 1976, *The Role of Medicine: Dream, Mirage or Nemesis?*, Oxford University Press, Oxford, England.

2 See David Icke, 1990, *It Doesn't Have to Be Like This: Green Politics Explained*, Green Print, London. 'A green health policy would obviously need more resources spent on the NHS in the early years', page 181.

3 Theodore Roszak, 1981, *Person/Planet: The Creative Disintegration of Industrial Society*, Paladin, London.

4 Lewis Thomas, 1977, 'On the Science and Technology of Medicine', in John H.

Knowles (ed.), *Doing Better and Feeling Worse*, W.W. Norton, New York.
5 Ivan Illich, 1976, *Limits to Medicine: Medical Nemesis, The Expropriation of Health*, Marion Boyars, London; Arabella Melville and Colin Johnson, 1982, *Cured to Death: The Effects of Prescription Drugs*, Secker & Warburg, London.

HEAVY METALS   see **pollution**.

HIERARCHY   Organisation with grades or classes ranked one above another.

Hierarchies are projections of primate socio-cultural *dynamics*, via the patriarchal family organisation, into the world at large. They are not the common form of organisation that *grey culture* would have us believe: 'The seemingly hierarchical traits of many animals are more like variations in the links of a chain than organised stratifications of the kind we find in human societies and institutions.'[1]

The hierarchy is the characteristic *structure* of *institutional* forms of organisation, indeed hierarchical formation leads almost inevitably to the *institutionalisation* of *function* (see **structure**). Once formed, *function* becomes secondary; for those in the hierarchical *structure*, *position*, conformity to rank, *agenda*, and the ethos of the *institution* take priority. Hierarchies have the apparent benefit of focusing *power*; individuals surrender *freedom* for the protection of the *structure*. Much of the *power* generated by the *synergy* of the *whole* is directed to its own survival and the survival of its constituents. The price is conformity and dependence upon the *structure* and active interest in its perpetuation, the denial of individual *needs*, including *morality* and *ethics*, in favour of servicing the *needs* of the organisation (see **institution**).

Hierarchies *create* dependence, they suffer the *inherent waste* of internal *competition*. They also deny individuality, reject talent, *function*, and abilities – except those which may serve the *structure*.

Hierarchies do not create *sustainable life structures*. Rather they are a distortion of a minor primitive mechanism which projects dangerous forms and forces into the *biosphere*.

The only valid application of hierarchy (apart from the breeding decisions of more basic *life* forms) is in logic, where sequential *choices* may create successive *choices*, which if pursued indefinitely produce the familiar pyramid *structure* – the logic hierarchy we all carry in our minds.

Greens believe that the hierarchy should be rejected in favour of the *matrix* (see **matrix**). Also, that the substitution of many *matrices* offering a wide variety of *networks* to fulfil many *func-*

tions is part of the *conscious evolutionary process* we have to achieve for the *future* (see **evolution**).

It may be argued that, within *matrical structures*, hierarchies will arise to focus *power*, to fulfil specific purposes. This may be unavoidable, but acceptable providing it is transient, based upon a clear *function* or *need*, and any *institutionalisation* of the *structure* and the *power* it generates are rejected (see **ad hoc**).

Relationships   **structure, position, competition, institution.**
See also   **holon, matrix, function.**
References

1 Murray Bookchin, 1982, *The Ecology of Freedom: The Emergence and Dissolution of Hierarchy*, Cheshire Books, Pal Alto, California, USA.

HOLISM, HOLISTIC, WHOLE, WHOLENESS, WHOLES   Tendency in nature to form wholes that are more than the sum of the parts, by process of ordered grouping (see **synergy**).

In *Holism and Evolution*,[1] Jan Christian Smuts formulated the insight of an invisible but powerful organising force *inherent* in *nature*, that of holism. He observed that if we did not look at wholes we would fail to take account of *nature*'s drive towards ever more complex forms and organisation (see **morphology**).

Despite the fact that holism is a description of phenomena which we observe all around us, its implications are rejected by *grey culture*. The *reductionist ethic*, with its reliance on analysis of simple cause and effect, its view of *relationships* as isolated and *linear*, is a denial of such observation. Paradoxically, the rejection owes much to the fact that, while such *relationships* may be observed, they cannot be subjected to the experimental methods of 'objective' *reductionist* science. *Life* and *existence* are not as *grey culture's philosophy* holds them to be; hence the *terminal nature* of the *culture* it *projects* and the numerous disasters caused by the 'unexpected' effects of things, ranging from *artificial* chemicals to large dams.

Holism is a primary component of *green philosophy*. The *green* understanding of holism is as a universally *inclusive* concept; everything is *related* to everything else, nothing *exists* in isolation. Essentially holism is about *relationships*, about the ways things interact, and about the motivation in *nature* to form wholes (see **anticipation**).

Holism offers a totally *inclusive* way of thinking about *existence*; everything we perceive *exists*, if only in that perception, and holism allows the possibility of understanding the *dynamics* of the interactions between our inner perceptions and outer *existence*, of the effects we have upon *creation* and *reality*. In its understanding of *relationships* and motivation, holism also holds the key to the *dynamics* of *life* and *existence*.[2]

As with many powerful yet simple ideas, holism has been appropriated. Initially, and logically, it was applied to *health*. Holism was used to refute the *Cartesian mechanistic* view of humans as divisible entities, with separate bodies, *minds* and *spirits*. Instead it proposed that we *function* as integrated wholes, each part affecting and affected by the rest. It was held to be important to treat the whole person; then later to look at their *life* situation, *environment*, etc., until eventually the concept was resolved into 'the health of the person is the health of the planet.'[3] However, along the way many 'holistic' side shoots were produced; holistic herbals, cookbooks, hairdressers, gardeners, etc., most of which, by linking the most *inclusive* general concept with an *exclusive* particular, seemed, *philosophically* at least, to cancel themselves out.

Despite these excursions, holism is an essential part of the *future mindset*. Smuts was right. We have to look at wholes to appreciate the *dynamics* of *nature* and of ourselves. And we require sufficient detachment to understand the *interactions*, both within humanity and between humanity and the rest of the *biosphere*. Without both we cannot *create* a *sustainable future* for all.

The *potential power* of holism was expressed by Kenneth Pelletier:

> Perhaps it is just as well that humans have yet to comprehend fully the wonder of their own beings, otherwise they would probably spent all their time in the celebration of life and have no time for anything else.[4]

Relationships   **philosophy, anticipation, morphology, synergy, structure.**

See also   **Gaia, field potential, holon.**

References

1 Jan Christian Smuts (1870–1950), 1920, *Holism and Evolution*. Twice prime minister of South Africa, Smuts participated in the founding of the United Nations, but the preamble he wrote proclaimed rights which were denied to the majority of his fellow South Africans.

2 See David Bohm, 1980, *Wholeness and the Implicate Order*, Routledge & Kegan Paul, London.

3 Theodore Roszak, 1981, *Person/Planet: The Creative Disintegration of Industrial Society*, Paladin, London.

4 Kenneth Pelletier, 1979, *Holistic Medicine: From Stress to Optimum Health*, Dell Publishing Company, New York.

See also Colin Johnson, 1991, *The Green Bible: Creating Sustainable Life on Earth*, Thorsons, London.

HOLON 'A sub-whole; a stable, integrated structure, equipped with self-regulatory devices and enjoying a considerable degree of *autonomy* or self-government.'[1]

Holons are thus identified parts of *systems*, of *wholes*, which in turn form parts of further *wholes*.

While primarily used by Arthur Koestler to describe biological entities which contributed to the form of particular *beings*, it has wider *potential* applications. The social *communities* envisaged in *future green culture* would *exist* as holons of the total social *structure*.

The holon concept is most useful as a bridge between the rigid concept of *hierarchy* and the totally open one of *holism*. By allowing discrete entities to be described, the *nature* of their *relationships* with the immediate *whole* may be determined. Whereas *hierarchy* assumes the independence of its own *structure*, *holism* understands the illusion of this proposition, while at the same time allowing for the *existence* of *hierarchies* within a wider *whole*.

Relationships   **hierarchy, holism, matrix**.
See also   **existence, synergy**.
References

1 Arthur Koestler (1905–1983), 1978, *Janus: A Summing Up*, Hutchinson, London.

HOMOCENTRISM (see **anthropocentric**)   Human-centred; the belief, and resulting behaviour, that the world and all its contents (and by implication all of *existence*) are placed at, or were created for, humans' disposal. Part of the *terminal mindset*.

Relationships   **grey/terminal culture, unsustainability**.
See also   **consumerism, Impossible Party**.

HOMOEOSTATIS   Tendency towards relatively stable state of *balance* or equilibrium between interdependent elements in a *system*.

Most living *systems*, whether cells, single *beings*, or the *whole* planet, have complex *feedback loops* built into their *structure*. These enable them to maintain the *relationships* between the parts and exert control over their internal conditions and external environments, with the object of achieving/maintaining *optimum life* conditions.

Homoeostasis is a *dynamic* state of *balance*, of constant monitoring of many interdependent variables; of flexibility which may differentiate *live* from non-live *existence* (see **life**).

Human activity has disrupted planetary homoeostasis. In *creating sustainable life* our activities will be limited by the constraints of *finite resources*, *ambient energy* use and the maintenance of *Gaian* homoeostasis. When our disruption of planetary *systems* ceases we will have moved back inside the *great cycle of life*.

Relationships   **balance, dynamic, sustainability**.
See also   **holism, Gaia**.

HONEST, HONESTY   Fair and righteous in speech and act; open; dealing with people or things with integrity. Being true to yourself in relating to others.

A necessary quality for the *future*. Without honesty humanity will revert to its old *terminal agenda*, to the protection of privilege and *position*, to *exlusivity* and secrecy, to *exploitation*, and the demands of *ego*. With honesty we may understand ourselves, our actions and their effects upon the *future*.

Relationships   **community, politics, agenda**.
See also   **nature (human), evolution**.

HOUSING   Buildings for human habitation or shelter. One of the five basic needs (see **needs**).

In *grey culture* housing is frequently *extended* into property, a means of *creating*, investing or displaying *wealth*, and of indicating social *position*, as 'having an OK address'.

Greens believe that housing should be a *function* of *community*, that provision should be made within the overall *life structure* for the *function* of housing the members of the *community*.

The design of housing, in terms of *structure* and *function*, is important. It can facilitate a socially cohesive and enjoyable *way of life*, or lead to social and individual disruption. As Alice Coleman put it, 'social breakdown, like charity, begins at home.'[1] Housing for a *community* should be designed by that *community* to fulfil its *needs* and desires. The *structure* reflects the *functional* intentions: pro-people, pro-life, socially *inclusive* rather than *exclusive*, and the *whole* integrated within the *dynamics* and *resources* of the immediate *environment* or *bioregion*.

Housing should either be built to last indefinitely, be capable of efficient repair etc., or designed as a modular, Lego-type system of components capable of many arrangements and re-arrangements within *changing needs*. Otherwise it should have zero *environmental* impact, like the totally *green* igloo, or be made from fast growing, readily replaceable, *natural* materials.

Present housing is a reflection of the *economic* system which produces it; it is designed to exist on a *flow* of purchased inputs and outputs. *Energy, food,* water, etc. are bought in, and *waste* and *pollution* expelled into the *environment*. *Future* housing *needs* to be designed to plug into *natural cycles* of provision and re-circulation; using *ambient energy,* producing *food* and water on a *community* basis and eliminating *waste* and *pollution* safely.

Relationships **community, self-sufficiency, cities**.

See also **food, clothing, care, transport**.

References

1 Alice Coleman, 1985, *Utopia on Trial,* H. Shipman. In this collection of studies, the factors in housing design which positively or negatively influenced social behaviour were identified. Its findings were of little interest of British authorities concerned with providing public housing.

HOUSING CO-OPERATIVE see **co-operative**.

HUMAN ECOLOGY see **ecology**.

HUMAN NATURE see **nature**.

HUMAN RIGHTS see **rights**.

HUMAN SCALE Life and provision within the scale of people as individuals.[1]

Human scale living requires both getting back into ourselves, to rediscover the reality of *human nature* and design *life* within manageable proportions for participation in the light of whatever we discover, and structuring our lives in the *environment* in *relation* to our *needs*. It also requires containing human affairs with human scale in *relation* to the *needs* of the local *bioregion* and the *Gaian whole*. Responding to local circumstances while acknowledging the *whole*: 'acting locally, thinking globally.'[2]

Human scale living implies rejection of *institutional* scale and its *needs* in favour of those of people. The focus should be on *purpose* rather than *power*, on *responsibility* and direct accountability.

Relationships **ego, community, culture**.

See also **institution**.

References

1 Kirkpatrick Sale, 1980, *Human Scale,* Secker & Warburg, London.

2 Hazel Henderson, 1978, *Creating Alternative Futures: The End of Economics*, Berkeley Windover, New York, USA.

HUNDREDTH MONKEY   A parable of change.

Observing the learning habits of monkeys on a remote Japanese island, anthropologists scattered sweet potatoes for them to eat. One day a monkey dropped a sweet potato in the water and, retrieving it, found it tasted better when washed free of dirt and sand. She proceeded henceforth to wash her sweet potatoes and taught her sisters to do the same. The practice spread throughout the colony. When the hundredth monkey began to wash his sweet potato in the sea, the practice appeared simultaneously on another island colony.[1]

The monkey phenomenon was first reported by Lyall Watson in *Supernature*,[2] and put as a parable by Ken Keyes in *The Hundredth Monkey*.[3]

Similar phenomena have been observed, notably in rats (described by Rupert Sheldrake in *A New Science of Life*)[4], but also in trees. Where trees under attack by caterpillars produce a substance toxic to caterpillars, it was observed that nearby trees not under attack also produced the toxin. This occurred even when unattacked trees were totally physically isolated from those under attack. The phenomena raises the question of the effects of the observer; are the observed subjects responding to the behaviour of the other subjects, or to the *expectation* (*anticipation*) of the observer? (See **morphic resonance**.)

The *process* described as a behavioural *shift*. Once initiated, behaviour patterns build up in a *system*, as with *genes*, or in a species as in the examples above, until a change occurs through the population. The means of communication is a matter of hypothesis (see **morphology**).

Relationships   **shift, morphology**.

See also   **formative causation**.

References

1 Joanna Rogers Macy, 1983, *Despair and Personal Power in the Nuclear Age*, New Society Publishers, USA.
2 Lyall Watson, 1973, *Supernature*, Sceptre, Sevenoaks, England.
3 Ken Keyes, 1981, *The Hundredth Monkey*, Living Love Publications, USA.
4 Rupert Sheldrake, 1981, *A New Science of Life*, Blond & Briggs, London.
    See also M.B. Hesse, 1961, *Forces and Fields*, Nelson, London.

HYDRO-ENERGY   see **energy**.

IDEA (see **meme**) Many strands of the *green movement* are impatient with ideas[1] in the sense of theories, hypotheses, conceptualisation, of intellectualism.

Yet the *creation* of a *sustainable future* requires new ideas, new understanding, a new *philosophy* which encompasses the *needs* of all *life* and *existence*. We have to go head first into the *future*; we are the problem, we have to *change*. And while we have to *change* much around us, the essential *change* is within.

Relationships   **perspective, creation**.

References

1 The demand is for action. Although this may have immediate appeal when confronted by realisation of the full horrors of *terminal culture*, or even particular aspects of its death-centred ethos, one moment of thought reveals that such action is in fact reaction. It has its historical parallels in the peasants' revolt in England in 1381 and aspects of Pol Pot's regime in Laos/Kampuchea, where intellectuals or even the minimally educated were killed, probably as an expression of rejection of the culture they represented. However, in rejecting *terminal culture* we should not throw out the baby with the bath water, a lesson people had to learn during earlier social change. 'The front is long'; action against excesses and the unacceptable behaviour by our fellows is essential at times, but it is no substitute for the *creation* of a *sustainable future*, and such a *future* requires new ideas.

ILLNESS, SICKNESS Unhealthy condition of body or mind, state of being. The disruption of *anticipation*, the failure to fulfil *potential* (see **health**).

The concept of illness can be applied to any part of a *being*, from the chemical/molecular and cellular/organic, and *extended* to the socio-cultural milieu and the *environment* in which *beings exist*. It can also apply to *extended cultural structures*. A sick society or *terminal culture* is as ill in reality as a sick person or other life form. In the sick planet, humans are the disease agents (see **global predicament**).

Grey culture treats all illness *symptomatically*. That is, causes of conditions are ignored and the results produced addressed. Medicine waits for avoidable disease to occur before treatment and politicians perpetuate the errors of the *past*. Thus the *progress* of illness, either personal or *cultural*, always outruns the application of *symptomatic* relief:

> In tackling the problem of illness in man or beast a common approach is to seek specific remedies for specific disease, through drugs, injections, antibiotics and so forth, to protect crops by using specific pesticides to kill specific pests and by engineering works to save the soil from being blown or washed away. This failure to recognise fundamental relationships, coupled with the piecemeal treatment of symptoms, is likely to result in a race between the emergence of new forms of sickness and the discovery of new materials to combat them. If so, man will be fighting a losing battle.[1]

This prediction has proved correct. Far from *creating health*, or even a lack of illness, *symptomatic* relief has had the opposite effect. Each year more people are dependent upon drugs to fulfil their everyday *functions*,[2] more are chronically sick and, while it is true that crude mortality[3] has declined, chronic disease has advanced spectacularly. Under the aegis of modern medical care, people are not so much living longer as taking longer to die.

What have been erroneously called 'the diseases of civilisation' (as if people fortunate enough not to suffer were somehow uncivilised) are now intractable parts of the illness profile of all developed societies. These diseases[4] should be called exactly what they are: diseases of *culture*. These conditions, manifesting themselves in significant proportions of the population, are, in turn, *symptoms* of the malaise of the *culture* of those populations.

Relationships   **culture, terminality**.

See also   **synergy**.

References

1 Professor Lindsay Robb, in *The Ecologist*, Volume 1, Number 1, July 1970.

2 Arabella Melville and Colin Johnson, 1982, *Cured to Death: The Effects of Prescription Drugs*, Secker & Warburg, London. Quotation based on the government's *General Household Survey, 1977*. (In the intervening years the proportion of the British population suffering from chronic and short-term illness has increased.)

> Fifty-six per cent of all men and 70 per cent of women reported that they suffered from chronic health (illness) problems. Of these, moreover, 67 per cent of the men and 71 per cent of the women reported that they had to take some form of special care *all the time* because of their chronic ill health. In rough round figures (for Britain), this means that of a population of 56 millions, 35 million people now consider themselves chronically ill. And 24 millions of the population of Britain are constantly preoccupied with the special care they need because of their poor health.
> Within this special care category of weakened and enfeebled individuals are the

33 per cent of men and 40 per cent of women (excluding contraceptive pill use) who constantly have to use some form of medication for their chronic health problems.

3 While it is true that of those who are born more now survive to maturity, an increase in life expectancy for mature people over the course of this century has been of a few years only. If illness and disability statistics are studied in detail the picture which emerges is a recent decrease in active life; people are spending more time as invalids before they die. See [2] above.

4 The 'diseases of civilisation' are: heart disease, including hypertensive and circulatory conditions; cancers of all types; diabetes; allergic reactions; mental disorders; auto-immune disease; and iatrogenic disease, literally 'doctor caused disease', usually induced by drug treatment. See [2] above.

See Brian Inglis, 1981, *The Diseases of Civilisation*, Hodder & Stoughton, London.

ILLUSION Deception, delusion, a false belief or perception of nature or reality of thing, circumstances, outcome; misapprehension of the true state of affairs.

The belief in *grey culture* that things, or most things, can stay the same, while a *green, environmental*, gloss is applied to business and life as usual.

Relationships   **culture, mindset**.

See also   **change, unsustainability**.

IMBALANCE (see **balance**)   The loss, or change in state, of *integrity* in a form, *system*, or *relationship*.

IMPLICATE ORDER (see **holism**)   A *model* of *existence* in which every part of what *exists* is enfolded within every other part – the *existence* of previous and subsequent forms are inherent properties of *existence* (see **anticipation**).

As David Bohm, Professor of Theoretical Physics, has put it: The order is not to be understood solely in terms of a regular arrangement of objects ... or as a regular arrangement of events. Rather, a total order is contained, in some implicit sense, in each region of space and time.[1]

The proposition of implicate order, as with that of *formative causation*, offers a view of *existence* which appears to be pre-ordained. In both we confront the difference in the *nature* of *life existence* and non-life *existence*. To an unknown degree *life* can regard the proposition of implicate order as a *potential* rather than a fixed property (see **evolution**).

Relationships   **holism, evolution, existence**.

See also   **universe, synergy**.

References

1 David Bohm, 1980, *Wholeness and the Implicate Order*, Routledge & Kegan Paul, London.

IMPOSSIBLE PARTY   The privileged *way of life* in the north,[1] the excessive *consumption* of the *First World*, the *unsustainable way of life* of ever more of everything, *way of life* based on increasing *consumption* of *finite resources* and of converting the *environment* to *waste*.

Life style based upon *institutionally* supported superficial *values*; greed, selfishness, *ego*, and their demand for expression in *consumption* and display. Those unfortunate things about *terminal* culture which draw others to copy despite the lack of *sustainability*.
Relationships   **terminal culture, mindset, economy, exponential growth**.
See also   **being, consumption**.

References

1 The Brandt Commission, 1983, *Common Crisis North-South: Co-operation for World Recovery*, MIT Press, Cambridge, Massachusetts, USA.

See J.K. Galbraith, 1958, *The Affluent Society*, Hamish Hamilton, London.

Also Vance Packard, 1960, *The Waste Makers*, Penguin, London. Also see *The Status Seekers*.

INCLUDE,   INCLUSIVE,   INCLUSIVITY Comprising   or embracing, thing or person, as part of whole; open, accepting.

Inclusivity is a key *green value*. In human affairs every aspect of *social, economic* and *political* life should be open to those who wish to be included. If this is 'impossible' there is something fundamentally wrong with the *structure, scale* or form of the organisation involved.
Relationships   **community, ad hoc, freedom**.
See also   **structure, system**.

INDUSTRIAL DEMOCRACY   see **co-operative**.

INDUSTRIAL REVOLUTION   Period from late 18th century to present when the combination of *fossil energy*, materials technology and innovative design produced the *mass society*. Increasing productive capacity led to increasing *consumption* and the initiation of the present phase of the population explosion. The unseen cost was the *creation* of *terminal culture*, a *way of life* based upon assumptions of unlimited *resources* and *infinite away* to absorb its waste.

While not rejecting industrial *processes* or *technology* out of hand, *greens* respond ambiguously to industry. Industrial activity, along with most human activity, needs to be directed by a *philosophy* of *sustainability* and the *economics* of *stock* rather than *flow.*

INDUSTRIAL SOCIETY (aka **consumer society**)   *Mass society* wherein the population is dependent upon *institutionalised* industrial *processes* for its sustenance (see **consumer**).
Relationships   **economy, consumer, mass.**
See also   **techology.**
References

See L.T.C. Rolt, 1947, *High Horse Riderless,* 1988 edition by Green Books, Ford House, Hartland, Bideford, Devon, England.
Also Edward Goldsmith, 1988, *The Great U-Turn: De-industrialising Society,* Green Books, Bideford, Devon, England.
And Murray Bookchin, 1974, 'Towards a Liberatory Technology', in *Post-Scarcity Anarchism,* 1974, Wildwood House, London.

INEVITABLE, INEVITABILITY   Unavoidable, sure to happen, bound to occur or appear.
'There is absolutely no inevitability as long as there is a willingness to contemplate what is happening.'[1]
See also   **choice, formative causation.**
References

1 Marshall McLuhan and Quentin Fiore, 1967, *The Medium is the Massage,* Penguin, London.

INFINITE   Boundless, endless, without limit. Mathematical: greater than any assignable number, the ultimate more.
Grey culture depends on the assumption of infinite *energy, materials, natural* capacities and *growth.* It is this *unsustainable assumption* which makes the present *culture* a *terminal* proposition.
INFINITE AWAY (see **away**)   The *assumption* of *grey economics* and much personal behaviour that anything unwanted, used, surplus, etc., may be thrown 'away'. There is no such place, everything goes somewhere, and something lives, or used to live, everywhere (see **pollution**).
Relationships   **economy, culture, mindset.**
See also   **cyclic, environment.**

INFORMAL ECONOMY   see **economy.**

INFORMATION (aka **data**)   Informing, telling, thing told, news about something.

Today information is increasingly data, the *reduction* of facts or *quantities* to electronic streams. Such data streams are the life-blood of the *institutions* of *grey culture*. Part of the protective mechanism of *institutions* is to translate information beyond the reach of those outside the *structure* (as with professions and jargon). Alternatively it is produced as an unmanageable swamp (Alvin Toffler's 'information overload'[1]); critics of *institutional* behaviour, such as the objectors to a proposed nuclear reactor, are buried in information in support of the proposal.

It is important to differentiate clearly between information and *knowledge*. Information can be any sensory input, the scent of a flower or an electronic data stream. Before it can mean anything information must be converted in our minds, or via an *extension* like a computer. Within that *process*, *knowledge* may be produced (see **knowledge**).

In the age of the computer and information overkill, with the phenomenon of the unending data stream, it is crucial to retain faith in *human values* and increase our familiarity with the *philosophy* which drives human affairs. Our *intuition*, experience and relevant accumulated *knowledge*, to which selected *information* may be added, allow us to be *wise*. The *linear focus* on information destroys this *quality*; information *technology* is producing a generation who know how to push buttons but little else, even the meaning of the data they so assemble. *Balance* within a broad *philosophical* understanding is essential if the accumulation of information is to serve rather than continually demand service.

Information is *institutional* lifeblood (see **institutions**).

The fact that General Motors may have a larger intelligence organisation than Australia will yield it no power when most of us cycle or walk to work and choose to stay at home on our holidays.[2] (see **consumer**).

Relationships   **technology, institutions, philosophy**.
See also   **networks, knowledge, (money) economy**.
References
1 Alvin Toffler, 1970, *Future Shock*, Bantham Books, New York, USA.
2 R.E.F. Trainer, 1985, *Abandon Affluence*, Zed, London.

INHERENT   Existing in, capacity or characteristic which may emerge under certain circumstances.

Properties of the *nature* of *existence*, of things, including of *nature* itself (see **holism, implicate order, evolution**).

INSTITUTION   Originally establishment (of person) in cure of souls; established law, custom, or practice; body exercising established law custom, etc., for charitable or public purpose.

In his essay 'Discourse on Inequality',[1] Rousseau 'held that "man is naturally good, and only by institutions is he made bad" – the antithesis of the doctrine of original sin and salvation through the church.'[2]

The meaning has become colloquialised to include all bodies corporate, such as joint stock companies, the organs of the nation *state*, and other corporate ventures. The primary characteristic of an institution is that it outlives its founders, it has a de facto life of its own. Other characteristics include *hierarchical* organisation and *bureaucratic* rigidity.

We live in a *culture* populated by institutional *forms*. They developed in parallel with human civilisation, indeed some believe institutions are the essential mark of civilisation. The earliest formed around tribal heads and ritual functionaries, amplified into monarchs and priests by the new *social dynamic* which emerged after settlement to agriculture. In this more intense *social* climate, heads of *hierarchies* constructed protective institutional shells around their *positions*. Over the past 20,000 years modern humanity has grown in increasingly close *symbiosis* with the institutional forms it has *created*. So much so that they are literally taken for granted.

Murray Bookchin has warned that the *green movement* could 'become institutionalised as an appendage of the very system whose structure and methods it professes to oppose.'[3]

It is time to re-assess this *relationship*, for it is at the core of the *global predicament*. Most people in industrial or *First World* countries rely upon institutions for their means of livelihood. For the majority, *symbiosis* has changed to dependence. *First World* countries retain their relative *position* in the world order because of the strength of their institutions. Multinational corporate institutions, acting in concert with those of the nation *state*, *function* as global conveyors, bringing the natural *resources* of poor (institutionally weak) nations to the rich. In return the weak nations are given the means to develop strong central institutions. Such trade/aid is compatible, not with the *needs* of the populations of such nations, but with the *needs* of the global institutional *hierarchy*.

Contained within the institutionalised nation *state*, individuals are dependent for all their *vital needs* upon institutional provision. At every important point in *life* individuals confront institutions; it may be in appearance a face-to-face confrontation, but the reality is of an isolated person on one side and the corporate representative on the other. The *structured* inequality of such encounters refute *political/economic* claims (made by institutional representatives) of a free world, of societies based upon notions of equality, individual '*freedom*' and opportunity.

Most of us have dual roles. Outside institutions, our lives and *relationships* are as dependent *consumers* of institutional provisions, while inside, as secure employees, we have *position* and *status*. Outside we are *potential* victims, while inside we mimic the institutional *agenda* of *competition*, struggling for relative *position* and command of *resources*, and/or *power*, the addictive drug of the *hierarchical structure*. As institutional forms increase their dominance of *life*, we even become dependent upon them for social *relationships* (the reason many give for wanting a job). Those outside institutional *structures* (chiefly discarded members of society) are left isolated and *powerless*, living in social gaps not worth institutional attention.

The reality of *grey culture* is that institutional *values* always take precedence over human/*life values*. In the *terminal grey economic system* it is institutions which are converting the *environment* to *waste* in their demand for continual *growth* and *exponential exploitation*. It is the institutions of *grey culture* that are its *means* of *progress* to *terminality*.

While we can describe the effects, what can we say of cause; what is the nature of the *catastrophe*?

Hypothesis: *life* is a particular form of *energy* which seeks to overcome *entropy* by its *synergistic* expression (see **life**). Within the general objective of all *life*, that of immortality, institutions have *evolved* as a peculiarly human *means* towards this objective. Institutions are vehicles for immortality.

But because the form has the *potential* to take on a de facto *life* of its own, develop its own *synergy* and *agenda*, institutions amount to *evolutionary successive* forms, much as we are the *successive* forms of the cells which, at some point in *evolution*, aggregated to form complex bodies. Because they are *successive* forms, they exercise increasing dominance over human *life* and affairs.

In analogous *evolutionary* terms, humans are parallel to the *genetic* material inside cells and institutions are similar to complex cellular *structures*; at some point in *evolution* replicating molecules *extended* a cellular membrane to enclose and protect them from the *environment*. Institutions perform a similar *function* for those inside in the more complex human *socio-cultural* and *natural environments*. Seeing institutions in this way illuminates much of the conflict of the *global predicament* and human attempts to mitigate its causes.

The *motivation* for institutionalisation is very deep. So much so that it may be a primal *inherent* characteristic of the human form. The earliest, most *dynamic* and enduring institutions have been those concerned with saving souls for *eternity* – the pursuit of immortality beyond the *limits* of earthly *existence*. But institutions are the *means* of pursuit of the *hidden agenda* of our particular form of *life*.

Institutional *growth* has been promoted by the rejection of half of human *nature*. The battle for souls centres on concepts of good and evil, of the continual battle within us between gods and devils. Logic, and reality, tell us that our extremes of good and evil, rather than opposing *entities*, are simply different ends of the same spectrum of *potential*, of *inherent* properties of human nature. The original institutional *assumption*, that the conceptualisation of evil leads automatically to its expression, may have been valid in earlier times. Paradoxically, today it is institutional *power* which facilitates the expression of the most extreme evil which humans can conceive. However, thinking and believing are not the same as expression, and full exploration of our inner *potential*, whatever *value* may be placed upon it, is essential for humanity's understanding of its own *nature*.

By denying 'bad' and concentrating on 'good' we are misled about our true *nature* and *potential*. By concentrating on good (with the carrot of the promise of heaven and life everlasting, or the stick of hell and something very nasty), we are pushed off *balance*. The impossible attempt to reject half our *nature* (and with it the rest of the *biosphere*) allows the supporting branches of institutionalisation, hypocrisy, duplicity, dishonesty, and secrecy, to *grow* and flourish. Such recurring features of institutional *life* are not unfortunate aberrations, rather they are revelations of the essential *structure*. It is the *imbalance* within the human state, and the constant conflict with self, which allows institutions to flourish.

Human concern with the institutional form is not new. It is to be found in every expression of rebellion against the established order. *Intuitive*, unclear of purpose, such rebellion is characteristic of human *creation*; the art of the artist rejected at the time[4] becomes institutionally respectable when its message is no longer a threat. The *bureaucratic* rejection of new *ideas* and forms continues, until and unless they can be moulded to compatibility with institutional purpose[5]. (Herein lies the *green* rejection of *revolution*, of the ultimately pointless *competition* between different institutional forms which wish to cast the *future* in their particular mould.)

The first clear statement of adverse institutional effects was made by Rousseau.[6] In an essay (not that quoted above) on whether the arts and sciences had a purifying effect upon morals he maintained that they did not, because they seduced man from his *natural* and noble estate (an equally unbalanced reaction). In later work he re-emphasised the *natural* goodness of man and the corrupting influence of institutionalised *life*. In this context, his *Contrat Social* may be seen as an attempt to devise a *structured* way out of the mesh of institutional *culture*, with *life* in *community* based upon 'liberty, equality and fraternity'. Later still, his views on monarchy and government institutions, emphasising the primacy of people over *state*, outraged the establishment. His writings on *natural* religion forced him to flee to relative obscurity.

In recent times, concern over the institutional giantism of modern society, with multinational corporations dominating the globe, has been expressed, although it has not been precisely focused. Expressions have been in terms of the need for human scale[7] in human affairs and for the creation of a *Fourth World*.[8,9]

However, the emergence of institutional forms has continued on the *autopilot* of blind *progress*. The most reactive and volatile form is the modern business corporation, with its many layers of protection for shareholders and successive denial of *responsibility* at every level of its activity. Institutional forms offer advantages; the obvious, *power, position* and *wealth* from the *flow economy*; and the covert, the implication that those within will survive while those without will perish. Increasingly refined institutions, and their integrated *relationships*, particularly between those of *religion, economics* and *politics* are fundamental to *terminal culture*.

Creating a *sustainable future* requires that we shed the institutional form. It is an *evolutionary cul-de-sac*, a form which demands the destruction of the *environment, life* and humanity. Human *evolution* into *sustainability* thus demands a most unnatural act to counter that part of our *nature* which seeks immortality through the institutional form; we must step back in *evolution* before we can go forward. Back from the edge of *terminality*, back from the mechanisms of the *terminal culture* which blindly carry us over that edge. Back to the point where we can once more live on human terms.

The heart of the *green dilemma* is, how do we de-*structure* institutional forms without destroying ourselves? The obvious answer is in the acts of *creation* required for a *sustainable future*; by returning human affairs to human scale, to self-reliant, *community*-based *life*, integrated into *bioregion* and *biosphere*, and by accepting *natural limits* without denying *human nature*.

Institutions of course fight back, making life for individuals on the outside increasingly difficult. Rural depopulation can be seen as the result of the institutional *economic structure*, the pressure on the young to pass exams, get qualifications, compete for *position*, conform or become destitute. Small, human scale entities, whether farms or stores, *communities* or associations, are rooted out by the *power* of the larger, more powerful institutional forms.

Greens can claim to have been first to realise and describe the *symptoms* of the *global catastrophe*, and to act to avert it. The *future* requires faith in the human *qualities* which inspired that vision and action; faith in human ability to *create* a non-institutional *future*, where human and *life values* may predominate, so that the *future* may regard our institutional excursion as the last phase of our primitive *evolution*, when, although we knew not what we were doing, we realised that it was pointless to save our souls if the price was to lose the *earth*.

INSTITUTIONAL PROCESS   The essence of the institutional process is that the opposite of what is generally desirable results.

This perverse effect is the product of the *synergy* within the *structure* of the institutional whole. It is an *inherent* property, part of the expression of the nature of the institutional form. Forestry authorities talk of broadleaved natural *forests* while spreading coniferous blight; business people talk of *freedom* of *choice* while *creating* monopolies; politicians preach public accountability while strengthening institutional *powers*. The net effect is the betrayal of human causes, human *values*, in favour of institutional necessity. All are *symptoms* of the institutional *process* at work.

The process involved achieves institutional objectives. While so doing the body will claim neutrality, *balance*, impartiality, debate, reason, inevitability, etc. – or even to be *green*. Resource economist John Boden cites the Audubon Society (a US environmentalist group) which owns lands in several areas of the United States as 'wildlife sanctuaries', but allows oil and gas extraction and cattle grazing on some of its land in order to generate income for the organisation.

Things are loaded in favour of the institutional process. *Resources* are available to exhaust those who oppose it; opponents are going against the dominant flow in *terminal culture*. Opposition usually has a predictable outcome. Public planning inquiries are notorious examples. Others are: the process of appearing in court to prove innocence which has the same effect upon the accused whatever the verdict (unless subjected to judicial murder. Note that institutions have this ultimate sanction – and there is no redress against errors – 'They never make mistakes'[10]). Similarly, the refutation of personal attacks, say in the media, for non-conformist behaviour, may achieve a retraction, 'there is no truth in the allegation that ...' which has the effect of reinforcing the attack.

Emerson may have been right, that 'an institution is the lengthened shadow of one man'.[11] We have been captured by our shadows, they move and we follow, their motivation is no longer ours.

Relationships   **evolution, culture, field potential, mindset, terminal**.

See also   **hierarchy, power, formative causation**.

References

1 Jean Jacques Rousseau (1712–1778), 1754, see 6 below.

2 Bertrand Russell (1872–1970), 1946, *History of Western Philosophy*, George Allen & Unwin, London.

3 Murray Bookchin, 1980, 'An Open Letter to the Ecology Movement', quoted in Bill Devall and George Sessions, 1985, *Deep Ecology: Living as if Nature Mattered*, Peregrine Smith Books, Salt Lake City, Utah, USA.

4 For example, the work of Vincent van Gogh, (1853–1890), whose Sunflowers, 1888, anticipated the contortions seen in plants sprayed with herbicides, while the message implied by 'Skull with Cigarette' was resisted until very recently, and is still hidden from the Third World.

5 See the excellent intuitive expression of the institutional process by Mick Farren and Edward Barker, 1972, *Watch Out Kids*, Open Gate Books, London:

The system, it cannot even be tied down to individuals, that rules our planet is corrupting and polluting the land, sea, and air. Animal life is being destroyed. Humanity is being misused and *distorted* until it is almost impossible for it to live with anything but a pretence of dignity. In the West a generation is being turned into criminals, in Asia, Africa and South America the same generation is having its land, its home, its standard of living, in some cases its very life destroyed by the global chess game that is an apparently essential part of the system. (My emphasis.)

And:

We will all compromise in order to survive and the system will still continue.

The feeling of community* that was about to emerge three years ago has shattered and split. If that singleness of purpose can be recaptured and developed it might enable us to survive and hold tiny pieces of territory in which we could live according to our own ideals, and by living in this way we may remind the population that an alternative to the system actually exists.

(Pages not numbered, appears opposite Massacre at Attica illustration.)

*See Theodore Roszak, *The Making of a Counter Culture*, Faber & Faber, London.

6 Jean Jacques Rousseau (1712–1778), 1750 essay competition set by the Academy of Dijon, which Rousseau won, 1754–5, 'Discours sur l'origine de l'inégalité parmi les hommes', 1762, *Contrat Social* Prometheus Books, Buffalo, New York, USA (1988), and *Émile* Basic Books, New York, USA (1979).

Favourably interpreted, Rousseau's views greatly influenced Kant, but were subsequently perverted (re-institutionalised) by Hegel into his Philosophy of Right, which gave birth to modern totalitarian theories of the state.

7 Kirkpatrick Sale, 1980, *Human Scale*, Secker & Warburg, London.

8 See *Resurgence*, Ford House, Hartland, Bideford, Devon, England,and *Fourth World Review*, 24 Abercorn Place, London NW9 9XP.

9 See Leopold Kohr, 1957, *The Breakdown of Nations*, 1978 edition, E.P. Dutton, New York. Leopold Kohr is originator of many human scale, small is beautiful, concepts.

See also Colin Johnson, 1991, *The Green Bible: Creating Sustainable LIfe on Earth*, Thorsons, London. Chapter 13, 'The Final Model', is an expanded discussion of the original and biological parallels of the evolution of institutions and their implications.

10 Aleksandr Isayevich Solzhenitsyn, 1973, *The Gulag Archipelago*, English edition, Harper Collins, New York, USA. Solzhenitsyn's life in Russia was one long battle against the institutional processes of that state.

11 Ralph Waldo Emerson (1803–1882), 1983, *Essays and Lectures*, Press Syndicate of the University of Cambridge, Massachusetts, USA.

INTEGRITY   Wholeness, soundness, uprightness, honesty.

A desirable property of *existence*, essential moral for a *green* future (see **politics**).

INTERCONNECTEDNESS   Property of connection, nature of *relationship*.

Ultimately everything is connected with everything else; nothing exists in isolation. Consequently whenever one thing changes, all about it must also change.

By understanding *relationships*, the *nature* of the interconnectedness of things, we understand the *nature* of *life* and *existence*.

Relationships   **holism**.

See also   **interdependent**, **synergy**.

INTERDEPENDENT, INTERDEPENDENCE Things which depend upon other things; form of existence which is reliant upon its source.

Property of *system, life*, etc., from same source, wherein similar *entities* are dependent on each other and/or the same factors or circumstances. Hence, the interdependence of planetary *life*.

Independence can never be total; it is an illusion to believe that a person, group or species can live in isolation. As John Donne (1571–1631) put it in *Devotions*, 'No man is an Island, entire of itself; every man is a piece of the Continent, a part of the main.'
<u>Relationships</u> **symbiosis, community**.
<u>See also</u> **self-reliance, self-sufficiency**.

INTERMEDIATE TECHNOLOGY see **technology**.

INTUITION Immediate apprehension by the mind without reasoning; immediate apprehension by a sense; immediate insight.
'What is now proved was once only imagined.'[1]

The phenomenon of intuition is frequently dismissed in *grey culture* in favour of analysis, reason, logic: *values* dominant in male-orientated *philosophy* and science. Intuition, again as part of its derogation, is held to be a predominantly female attribute.

The *philosophical* rejection of intuition can be traced to Hegel,[2] who rejected the insights of the post-Renaissance romantics in favour of reason. It is regrettable that the insights of his colleagues and contemporaries, particularly those of Schelling,[3] were rejected by the mainstream of thought in *grey culture*.

Intuition may be seen as the product of mental *processes* to which we have no *conscious* access; a complex of cognition which occasionally surfaces. The mystic tradition of deprivation, meditation, the use of drugs, etc., may be seen as seeking ways to release such expressions. Those who experience intuitive insights may have the ability to 'see' ahead, within or across the boundaries of the *morphogenic* boundaries of *life*, to *anticipate* the unfolding of our collective unconscious, our shared *morphology*, or to view the *reality* of other *existence*. Intuition also produces views of the *past*; the property amounts to a detachment of *perception* from *time* to form.

Intuition is dismissed because it appears to be beyond logic, yet that is precisely why it is important. Most intuitive insight is recorded in products of the *spirit*, in *creativity* on and beyond the front edge, expressed in forms which are rarely appreciated at the time of their *creation*. Wherever humans explore, despite the claims of logic and contemporary science, intuition leads; logic and reason follow.

It is also an everyday thing for many people; making the right choice a significant number of times in various circumstances, simply because of some prompt below the level of *conscious* recognition.

For the *future* we need to give more attention to the human intuitive ability, ideally to learn to understand intuitive 'language', to select from the revealed *potential* that which is relevant, desirable, essential for our chosen *future* direction. Many people intuitively understand that this is why *freedom* of expression is vitally important. When *creativity* is *institutionalised* it is rendered sterile, insight into *future* or other perspectives is switched off in favour of consolidation of *past* or conforming continuity of present. This may be understood by those who favour *censorship*. The price of *freedom* of expression may be horrors of bad taste and much offence, but the benefits are a greater understanding of our *nature*, of other *existence*, and priceless insights into the *future*.

Intuition is a route beyond now, to *future*, to *past*, to other spheres, and to the *infinity* of our inner selves. It is the path to transcendence of the *limits* of *existence*; the means by which we can touch the universe beyond our reach, and by touching expand both it and ourselves. By allowing ourselves to reach out, we also reach in, to that *centre* where all we are and all we may become is fixed. In the experience of transcendence all becomes one; intuition reveals each as part of the *whole*. There is in each of us the possibility to see each step of the path of *existence*, to choose our path, to extend the journey of the *future* as long as we may.

<u>Relationships</u>   **creation, morphology, potential.**

<u>See also</u>   **future, anticipation, knowledge.**

<u>References</u>

1 William Blake (1757–1827), 1966, *The Marriage of Heaven and Hell*, in *The Complete Writings of William Blake*, Oxford University Press, Oxford, England.
2 Georg Wilhelm Frederick Hegel (1770–1831), 1802, *Kritishe Journal der Philosophie* (see **rational holism**).
3 Friedrich Wilhelm Joseph von Schelling (1775–1854). Schelling began his philosophical career as an adherent of Fichte's principle of the ego as the supreme principle of philosophy (the root of existentialism which was to grow through Heidegger and Sartre, but also to be subverted into the Nazi national egoism of the *Herrenvolk*), but in the *Philosophy of Nature* and *The World Soul*, 1797–1799, he supplements the concept of 'absolute ego' by showing that the whole of nature may be regarded as an embodiment of a process by which spirit tends to rise to a consciousness of itself (see **Gaia**).

INVESTMENT   Investing of money, in property, etc., provision for future.

Part of the mechanics of *flow economics*, whereby money is used to increase the *flow*, usually by *consuming* the *future*. The old meaning of invest, to lay siege to, gives a better idea of the *process*.

ETHICAL INVESTMENT

Ethical investment can be seen as a way of window dressing the whole consumer-capitalist destruction in a typically reformist way; combining ethics and the market rather than challenging the system fundamentally.[1]

Conservationists and environmentalists seem to approve of ethical investment (see **slice**). David Bellamy is a chairperson of a committee of the Trustee Savings Bank's environmental trust. And in the City of London:

Green issues sprout from every window ... The TSB's recently pulled in £12 million with its new environmental trust... The insurance company, Laurentian Life, yesterday announced that its Rainforest Fund will donate £2 towards the preservation of the forests of south-west Cameroon for every new policy written.

However, the businessmen have a more realistic view of their motives: 'Greenness is a useful marketing tool, to say otherwise would be stupid,' confirms Alan Gadd at Hendersons. The Henderson Green PEP has pulled in more than £1 million in three months.[2]

In *ecological* terms ethical investment is as much a contradiction as *green consumerism*. Money invested still has to generate income. It does this by increasing the *flow* through the *economic system*. True it might generate less *flow*, or *flow* of a less damaging sort, but it is still contributing to a *system* which *consumes* the *environment* and generates *waste*. The only really ethical investment would be in *stock economies* centred on the *needs* of local *communities* and fulfilled *co-operatively*, but fund managers, sales reps and the vast army of non-productive beneficiaries could not make much of a living from that.

Relationships   **economics, flow**.

See also   **change, alternative**.

References

1 Derek Wall, 1990, *Getting There: Steps Towards a Green Society*, Green Print, London.

2 Martin Baker in *The Independent*, Saturday 2 September 1989.

-ISMS Means of summarising, encapsulating body of belief, attitudes, etc. As in communism, feminism, capitalism. Often an indicator that dogma has set in and *institutionalisation* is on the horizon.

JOY Vivid emotion of pleasure, gladness.
An essential component of *life*, discounted by *institutions*.
<u>Relationships</u> **values, spirituality, ecology.**
<u>See also</u> **life, living (art of).**

KNOW, KNOWN   Have in mind, to be able to recall, to be aware of, something learned.

KNOWING   Awareness of what is known.

As our *potential* unfolds we become aware of more; that which was novel becomes commonplace, the revelation of one age becomes the normality of another. What is known is *anticipated* in the knowing of others as part of our *symbiosis* with *culture*. The *anticipation* of knowing, where an *intuitive* statement precedes reasoned exposition, reveals knowing as the *synergy* of the unfolding *morphology* of our species.

But there is much we do without knowing, without realisation of the *nature* and effects of our actions; the problem of the *hidden agenda* of *processes* within the *synergy* of our species. 'O! what men dare do! what men may do! what men daily do, not knowing what they do!'[1]

KNOWLEDGE   Knowing, familiarity gained by experience; a person's range of *information*; theoretical or practical under-standing of something, as opposed to opinion of same.

Kant's claim that 'though our knowledge begins with experi-ence, it does not follow that it arises out of experience'[1] initiated the *philosophical* inquiry into how we know what we know (or what we think we know). His proposition of 'the thing in itself', of *existence* independent of our knowledge of it, seems obvious in the light of subsequent scientific discovery, but the nagging doubt about the *nature* of knowledge (see **objective**), the inner sensory *process* and interpretation, remains.

As *terminal* society becomes more *compressed*, knowledge is replaced by *information*, and the ability to exercise *wisdom* in judgment lost in favour of data manipulation.

For the *future*, knowledge of *process* is of paramount import-ance. Without such understanding we can only experience the *events* produced by *processes*, and be victims of their unpredicted effects such as the destruction of the *ozone* layer by *CFCs* in hairsprays. If we know what is being done, and how, its effects and desirability may be judged.

The problem with all knowledge, all knowing, is that we don't know what we don't know. Hence the *green* attitudes of caution, of respect, for other *existence*. We do not wish to get into the *terminal* proposition of having to be forgiven because we know not what we do; better not to do until we have some idea, and then to proceed with more caution and respect, until we think we are sure we know what we are doing.

The *ethic* of knowledge in *grey culture* is that what is known is all there is to be known. History shows this to be bunk, nevertheless *grey culture* acts as if selected (convenient) parts of current knowledge were all, refusing to speculate where this may lead (see **culture**).

Relationships   **mind, mindset, intuition, morphology**.

See also   **education, information**.

References

1 William Shakespeare (1564–1616), 1598, *Much Ado About Nothing*

2 Immanual Kant (1724–1804). Kant reacted against Hume's reduction of knowledge to things and causation to habitual associations of sense impressions (knowing what we expect to know, seeing what we expect to see). This was clearly in conflict with the knowledge of logical deduction. In his *Kritik der reinen Vernunft* ('Critique of Pure Reason'), 1786, he shows that the immediate objects of perception are due not only to the evidence provided by our senses but also to our own perceptual apparatus which orders our sense impressions. Kant held that knowledge of 'things in themselves', that is of that which would exist without our knowledge of it, is impossible since we can only know our ordered sensory impressions. The point revolves around the propositions of knowledge opposed to knowing, of conscious reason and irrational intuition. Much philosophical effort in reductionist culture has been devoted to defining the fine line between the reality of that which may be reasoned (known) and that which may not.

LABOUR CREDITS (see **universal credit economy**)   A system of ascribing relative value to various sorts of work; generally higher value for necessary jobs which no one wants to do and lower for the popular things. Used in *communes* and other *co-operative* groups as a practical, if inequitable, means of getting things done. Concept described and refined in Skinner's *Walden Two*.[1]

<u>References</u>

1 Burrhus Frederick Skinner, 1948, *Walden Two*, Macmillan, New York, USA. US psychologist, foremost contemporary exponent of behaviourism, ibid, 1976, *About Behaviourism*, Random House, New York, USA.

LAND   Solid part of *earth*'s surface; ground, soil. The most basic *resource*, foundation of the real *economy* of *life*. Land is both a *finite* resource, in that there is only so much of it, and one capable of indefinite use in the right circumstances. Modern humanity has yet to *create*, or more correctly to restore, a *sustainable relationship* with land (see **retrospective innovation**). *Terminal culture* has produced the opposite; *flow economics consumes* land, *chemiculture* sterilises it, *climate change* washes it away.

LAND ETHIC   *Moral relationship* with land and its use in relation to the *needs* of all *life*.

The human obligation of *stewardship* centres on *symbiosis* with the land. It is our *right* to live on the land; it is our duty to restore/ enhance its bearing capacity, its *diversity*, its *balance*, while conserving the *resources* of its *structure*. I am as equally appalled by '*greens*' wearing gold or rare minerals for which the *earth* has been torn apart as I am by the genocidal practices of *chemiculture*.

LAND REFORM   Humanity has developed the concept that it may possess the land, that individual people and *institutions* may own and have dominion over it, that the interests of all other terrestially dependent *life* may be ignored. At the heart of a *sustainable human culture* is the question of land reform. *Green* land reform recognises that land cannot be owned as an *exclusive* commodity. This means a complete re-stucturing of our *relationship* with land,

165

and also with our interrelationships with other *life* forms. Land use must be *inclusive*; based upon *bioregional* and *community values*; *greens* believe this offers the best hope for *sustainable* land use.

Relationships   **Gaia, culture, sustainability**.
See also   **restoration, community**.

LANGUAGE   A vocabulary and way of using it prevalent in one or more countries; method of expression or communication; words and their use. Languages are a *extension* of vocal communication.

The meaning of language has *extended* beyond that centred on words. The focus is increasingly on communication. We now understand that we communicate in many more ways than verbally. Body language, make-up, behaviour, non-verbal sound, scent and so on, all form part of our repertoire of communication.

Beyond ourselves every medium develops a language ('I exist, therefore I communicate'). Humans have *cultural* languages, which may be seen as the language of artefacts, of architecture, of art and music; the languages of *technology*, from road signs to electronic data streams. Communication by the many languages we use simultaneously is a complex, multi-faceted phenomenon, and our languages have *potential* and *dynamics* of their own. Problems arise because things have to be simplified in translation from one form to another; frequently meaning is lost or changed, or reduced to lowest common multiple symbols or ciphers.

Languages are our means of classifying and ordering the world; if our linguistic range is restricted, so is the sense we are able to make of things. They are also our means of manipulating *reality*, or being manipulated by it. In a fast communicating *culture*, the slow tend just to get carried along. The *structure* of languages and their uses influence that which we realise; if those languages are *inherently* inaccurate (i.e. founded on erroneous *assumptions*) then they mislead. 'If the rules which underlie our language system, our symbolic order, are invalid, then we are daily deceived.'[1] When our many languages are those of a *terminal culture* then the deception threatens to become complete.

The dominance of inherent *cultural values* in language is illustrated by the number of *de* and *non-* words *opposition* has to use. This reinforces the implied positive *value* of the *status quo*. In many desirable areas we simply have no language to express the order desired. We have no language for *health*, but encyclopaedias of disease; we have little language for *peace*, but volumes on *war*.

Language reflects *institutional* priorities, and has itself become *institutionalised*; its form (*position*) is more important than communication (*function*), and words are used to contain rather than communicate. Linguistic *institutionalisation* is a means of sterilisation; new ideas and new expressions are rejected, ideas and their descriptive language inhibited. Teaching in formal *education* becomes a means of fixing, of *stability*, rather than *growth* or exploration. In this the British excel; the *education* system either produces semi-literates or conformist elites. The mass media, in relying on the lowest common denominator in language, become their own message,[2] propagating the closed circuit communication of cliché and *assumption* – you know what I mean?

The *motivation* for this and other similar books is to break out of the *institutional* trap of language sterilisation, to promote the new, the desirable, in *ideas* and words which communicate them so that they may become *options* for the *future*.

The language of the *future*, with positive terminology of what is desired rather than negative reference to that which is *opposed*, may be difficult to *create* and spread. It is important that we persevere; new language spreads new *ideas* and new *ideas* create a different *culture*. Despite the complexity of new *ideas* and the cacophony of multi-medium communication, *green culture* needs to strive for the most simple, direct and unambiguous forms of communication. We have to understand exactly what we wish to communicate, and also what else we may be communicating (see **agenda**). The achievement of clear understanding may mark the separation of the *sustainable* from the *terminal*.

Relationships   **information, education, meme, morphic resonance**.

See also   **honesty, function, institution**.

References

1 Dale Spender, 1985, *Man Made Language*, Routledge & Kegan Paul, London.
2 Marshall McLuhan and Quentin Fiore, 1967, *The Medium is the Massage*, Penguin, London.

LAW   Body of enacted or customary rules recognised by the *community* as binding.

Although laws are the basis for the exercise of authority, society, in the form of a body of diverse individuals, cannot avoid law. We make agreements which we must honour if association and society are to have *coherence* and meaning.

The problem with law in *institutionalised* society is that it becomes part of the *institutional structure*, removed from individuals and *community.* It fails to meet the real *needs of the community* when people cannot understand the rules by which they are expected to live; the law becomes not only an ass, but a meaningless ass.[1]

Under the *institutional process* the law becomes, not a means of protection and facilitation, but a means of oppression, of safeguarding privilege and *position.* Thus multinational *environmental* crime is rewarded and victimless artistic expression is punished. The amount of law a society or *culture* needs can be seen as a measure of the failure of that society or *culture.*

Greens believe the law should mean 'customary rules recognised by the community'. In *future community* the law should be accessible to every member, both for application where necessary and modification where agreed.

The wider *green culture* requires the retraction of law from its *homocentric* concerns of property and *institutionalised* justice, and its *extension* into *ecological* law (see **principles, rights**). Basically, *ecological* law requires the acknowledgement of the *rights* of *life* and the properties of *existence.* The application of law in this context would be as a means of ensuring the *potential* of the *future.*

<u>Relationships</u>   **community, rights, anarchy, democracy.**

<u>See also</u>   **structure.**

<u>References</u>

1 Charles Dickens, (1812–1870), 1837–39, *Oliver Twist,* ' "If the law supposes that," said Mr Bumble, ... "the law is a ass – a idiot." '

LEAD-TIME   The time between the initiation of a *process* and the completion of the event it generates. Usually seen as a nuisance because of the delay involved in completing projects, acquiring goods, etc.

In many *processes* the lead-time is characterised by an apparent lack of *change,* until at some point unmistakable signs emerge. The *global predicament* is the sum of such *changes,* usually from unpredictable causes. Unfortunately, in an unknown number of cases, by the time the *symptoms* emerge it is too late to arrest the cause. What is also unknown is how many *processes* are running through their lead-times to present further problems in the *future.*

<u>Relationships</u>   **global predicament, change, process.**

<u>See also</u>   **anticipation, feedback.**

LEARNING CURVE   A time-based illustration of the period required to assimilate new ideas, skills, techniques, etc. The general shape is of an 'S'; the *process* starts slowly, accelerates and then reaches a plateau where no further improvement can be made.

Learning a new skill often requires learning a sequence of things, and 'curve' actually applies only to the simplest task. The actual process is characteristically stepwise; periods of stability, lack of progress, punctuated by rapid progress.

The solution to *dynamic problems*, typically those based on *exponential growth*, requires a learning curve which outruns the *growth* curve of the *problem*. Those concerned with the *future*, or with *problems* which are annihilating it, see humanity on a learning curve. *Greens* want to get up the curve as quickly as possible; *greys* want things to stay as they are.

The first part of the curve of the self-directed act of human *evolution* for the *future* is to achieve recognition of the *need* for such an act.

'Chance favours the prepared mind.'[1]

Relationships   **adaptation, anticipation, change, creativity**.

See also   **lead-time, evolution, institutions**.

References

1 Attributed to Louis Pasteur (1822–95), the French chemist who discovered the microsphere of life and developed means, such as heat treatment ('Pasteurisation'), and innocuation, of modifying its effects.

LESS   Of smaller quantity, not so much or so many.

The *First World* has a responsibility to *consume* less, to be more *efficient*, particularly with *energy*, as a preliminary to *changing* from a *flow (grey) economy* to one of *stock (green)*.

We have to shed the primitive desire for the new and shiny, and cherish with pride the old and venerable. In going for *quality* rather than *quantity*, things can be made to last longer (see **finite resources**).

Questions of how much each is entitled to inevitably lead into our ideas of the very *structure* of human society and its *relationship* with the *natural world*. It is obvious that so many of us cannot continue *consuming* our *environment* at the present rate; that if we wish everyone to have the best possible life in a *sustainable future*, indeed if we are to have a *future* at all, the *question* of population must be consciously and comprehensively addressed. Fewer people is the primary planetary need (see **numbers**).

'Less is better – think more, use less' – *green* graffiti.

Relationships   **consumer, quality, efficiency, economics**.

See also   **balance, critical mass**.

LETS (local exchange trading system) Means whereby *communities* can organise and achieve necessary work, desirable objectives, skills exchange, outside the cash *economy*. The idea can also be *extended* to the exchange of produce and materials. Problems arise within *grey culture* where LETS try to issue their own currency or *create* currency units.

Relationships **community, exchange**.
See also **economy**.
References
See Derek Wall, 1990. *Getting There: Steps Towards a Green Society*, Green Print, London.

LEVELLER (see **Digger**) Person who would abolish social distinction, advocate of equality, one who rejects genetic *elitism* and privilege. Proto-democrats in England 1647–48.

LIFE State of functional activity and continual *change* peculiar to organised matter; manner of existence. In *grey* Christian *culture*, 'life (may be seen) as a pilgrimage towards death, as the end of the beginning.'[1]

Life may be defined as any *process* which increases the complexity of *structures*, providing these *structures* have the ability to convert *energy* or matter.

The molecules upon which life is based are built from atoms which are the product of a failed star; we are star-stuff,[2] the *processes* of life the result of *chemical evolution* in a complex but delicate *environmental balance*.

Life can be seen as a bridge between matter seeking *stability* and *energy* seeking *entropy*. Life seeks immortality, the biological variant of *stability*. Its vehicles are endlessly *evolving* species which constitute the *Gaian whole*. Individuals, indeed entire species, are transient phases in the continuity of the *whole*; each experience a point in *eternity* when they are the particular focus of *synergy* within a form of *energy* and matter.

The unique *quality* of life is that it actively opposes *entropy*.

Humans must become sensible to all other forms of *life*. What we have in common is far greater than the differences which distinguish us.

LIFE-CENTRED Beliefs, attitudes, *philosophy*, etc., which are focused upon the experience, *needs*, of life; behaviour which reflects such an *ethic*.

Green philosophy seeks to describe the beliefs etc., upon which a life-centred *culture* may be created.[3]

In *terminal culture* the current order is under-pinned by an orientation on *death*. People are encouraged to suffer and accept, eventually to receive their reward after life in one of a number of versions of heaven (valhalla, happy hunting ground, etc.) (see **institution**).

LIFE CONSPIRACY Every form of life is selfish, each tries to convert as much of its *environment* as possible into replicas of itself.

The short-lived success of one form at the *terminal* expense of others is prevented by the *balance* within the *whole*. In stepping outside the constraints of *nature* humanity threatens destruction of the *whole*, and ultimately of itself. The human life conspiracy has carried us into the *cul-de-sac* of our specific *hidden agenda* (see **institutions**). We either learn to live within the *balance* of the *whole* or we fail without (see **holism**).

LIFE CONTRACT Every form of life has an *inherent* contract with the *Gaian whole*. None can *exist* in isolation; all require the *global environment created* by the others; each is dependent on others for *food*.

In fulfilling our duties within the life contract we contribute to the *stability* of the *global environment* (or more correctly the consensual direction of its *evolution*). The *web of life* can be seen as the expression of the implied contractual *relationships* of all of the parts. Some elements of the contactual *network* can be spelt out in basic terms, the atmospheric interaction between animals and plants for instance:

Respiration (plants and animals)
$$(CH_2O)_n + {}_nO_2 > {}_nCO_2 + {}_nH_2O + \text{heat}$$
carbohydrate plus oxygen produces heat (energy) plus carbon dioxide plus water

Photosynthesis (plants)
$${}_nCO_2 + {}_nH_2O + \text{light} > (CH_2O)_n + {}_nO_2$$
carbon dioxide plus water plus sunlight (energy) produces carbohydrates plus oxygen

This not only illustrates the *sustaining* trade-off of oxygen and carbon dioxide between plants and animals, but also the essentially *cyclic nature* of all life contracts.

The most important element of the life contract is *food*.

Humans, through farming, have *extended* and formalised this contract (we are not the only species to do so; for instance, ants farm greenfly). One of the main roots of the *global predicament* can be traced to our broken contract with our *food* sources; we no longer nurture them in *symbiosis*, we pervert and abuse the species upon which we are dependent (almost as if punishing them for our dependence), *polluting* their *environment*, and so poisoning the entire *food* chain (see total **toxic** overload). While one can appreciate that flock animals, such as sheep, would associate with a shepherd to gain care, despite the depredation they would suffer anyway, this is not the same as the crescendo of genetic and intensive abuse such animals suffer today in *terminal culture's chemiculture* production units (see **food**).

Our broken contract with the *food network* is part of our undeclared *war* with *nature* as a *whole*. In pursuing its separate, isolated route to immortality humanity has divorced itself from *nature* and broken the life contract with the *Gaian whole* (see **institution**).

LIFE CYCLE   Each individual life has a cycle; arising from the cumulative *potential* of the *past*, each individual life will fulfil its own *potential*, to a greater or lesser degree, from conception/inception, through a *growth*/increasing complexity *process*, to *death* and the return of its components to the greater planetary *cycle* of life. This *cycle* is typical of most forms of *existence*: life is a *cyclic* phenomenon in a *cyclic universe*, the stages of each life cycle are *extended* as far as possible by the material propensity for *stability* and the biological quest for immortality (see **cycle**).

Each life is dependent upon, influenced by and contributes to, the many *cycles* within the *biosphere*. These *cycles* in turn are generated by the motion of the *earth* around the sun and the moon around the *earth*; the constant *cycles* of heaven on *earth* (see **universe**).

LIFE DYNAMIC   The forces generated by the life cycle of an individual, by the interactions of members of a species, and of life with the *environment*.

The most basic dynamic is that of *evolution*; each form of life seeks to *extend* its command of the *environment*, eventually to *shift* to a successive *form*. Humans' life dynamic includes the forces generated by their *extended social*, *cultural*, and *institutional environments*.

As with every expression of force, there is a reaction. With life dynamics this is not the classical Newtonian 'equal and opposite' reaction, but the reaction to life will result in one of three outcomes. It may be the maintenance of a *stable dynamic balance.* Or it may be an either/or *change* in the *balance. Change* will either result in increasing dominance of one species at the expense of others, or to a new state of *balance.* The former, if continued, will eventually result in the degeneration of one or more species, and/or the *environment* in general. The situation we currently confront is one of the human life dynamic overrunning that of the planet as a *whole* (see **balance**).

It is possible to illustrate various expressions of life dynamics as *function* diagrams (usually called a dynamic curve, from its original typical shape illustrating the graph of power outputs against revolutions of engines). That of a typical male individual in *terminal culture* is given below.[4] It shows a typical pattern of *energy* output and the mode of failure common with cardio-vascular problems. For *healthy function* the individual should *cycle* up and down the front face of the curve, producing more performance against increased arousal – but resting when the point of fatigue is reached. The *dynamics* of *grey culture* lead people both to believe the intended arousal/performance line is achievable, and, since it is not, to point 'P' where *catastrophic* breakdown is unavoidable. Hence the epidemic of culturally generated heart disease; it is an inherent *function* of the culturally induced life dynamic.

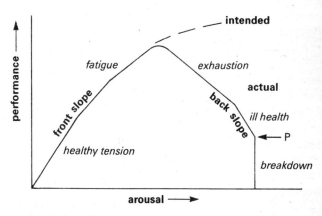

Male function curve

The dynamic of an individual *life cycle* may be similarly illustrated. From the point of conception *growth* occurs up to a climactic point when the *potential* of the form is fulfilled, and the individual declines, dies and is re-absorbed into other *life cycles* of the *environment*.

Human life is more complex. It is characterised by stages of *growth* (steps) and *stability* (plateaux). These occur and overlap in the many dimensions of the specifically human life dynamic. Steps are superimposed on the basic life curve, as *growth* and the decline we experience prior to *death*.

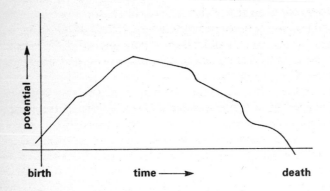

Simplified human life dynamic

Our species dynamic is a familiar picture.

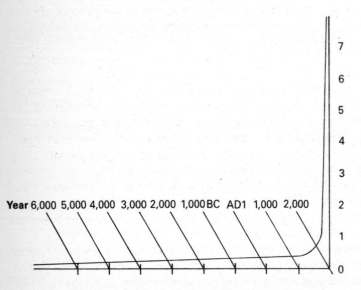

Human species dynamic (population) curve

It is the human population graph, which shows our departure from a *balanced* dynamic to a destination which is unknown but clearly and predictably disastrous (see **numbers**).

The *future* requires adjusting our internal dynamic (*conscious evolution*), modifying our behavioural dynamic so that it does not induce disease, and drastically altering our species dynamic so that it does not destroy the planet. Beyond a reduction of human *numbers*, our dynamic needs to incorporate the *restoration* of the dynamic of our species with the dynamics of the *whole* (see **morph mapping**). We have to break out of the terminal *cul-de-sac* represented by diagram 3, and *create* a dynamic which is compatible with the totality of the *great cycle* of planetary life. This is the very essence of *green* purpose.

LIFE ENHANCING   Anything which increases the capacity or potential of all life; increases the size or duration of the *cycle* (see **balance**).

The *grey cultural* view is that anything may be regarded as life enhancing which appears to make human life easier or more superficially rewarding.

Life enhancing in the *green* sense is anything which adds to the capacity of life to fulfil its *potential* while maintaining the overall *balance* of the *biosphere.*

Life can only be enhanced as a *whole*; the enhancement of the lot of one individual, species or *bioregion* at the expense of other elements of the *whole* is not enhancement, only a *shift* away from balance (see **restoration**).

LIFE FORCE   The *flow* of *energy* through matter in its living state. The motivation resulting from such *energy.*

The *dynamics* generated by the life force are *inherent* properties of certain arrangements of matter, which may be expressed in certain circumstances, e.g. *genes,* matter in stages fusion reactions. The biological life force expresses itself in the *extension* of forms, as in *evolution* and the extra-*genetic extension* of *interdependent* forms, as in human *institutions* (see **chi**).

LIFE-POSITIVE   Attitudes, *values* and behaviour which favour other life; rejection of current *terminal, death*-oriented, *cultural values,* in favour of *restoration, balance* and *sustained ways of living.*

Such attitudes and behaviour are related to *principles* which form the basis of *ecological law.* Barry Commoner[5] has defined four *principles* of *ecology* which underwrite life-positive beliefs (see **principles**).

LIFE POTENTIAL   Expression in *evolution* which is compatible with the *Gaian whole.*

The unfolding *morphology* of each stage of a *cycle* of *existence,* of each part of each *being,* of each species, each *symbiotic relationship,* and the *synergy* of the *whole.*

Within *terminal culture,* much of human *potential* is negatively directed; it assists the *terminal process. Grey* human *culture* is incompatible with the *synergy,* the direction of the life force, of the *Gaian whole* (see **global predicament**).

LIFE STRUCTURE   All those permanent factors of a *way of life* produced by a species in response to its *environment.*

Every life structure is contained within, and contributes to, the *environment.* Humans have *extended* their life structure by means of social, *cultural* and *institutional forms,* into the *environment.* This both increases the scope of the human *environment* and transfers more of the external *environmental resources* into the human sphere (see **institutions**).

A *green sustainable culture* will rely upon a diversity of structures, consciously constructed to be compatible with the *environment* upon which they depend (see **community, matrix**).

For individuals to accept *responsibility* for life structure they need to examine *assumptions* and habits in every area of life, discover the underlying *processes,* and *change* them where necessary. The broad objectives are to move away from a life structure based on *institutional* dependence, towards *ways of life* based on personal and *community self-reliance.*

LIFE STYLE   The myriad of everyday choices we all make contribute to our general life style, although the parameters may be set by circumstances which we cannot control, e.g. prison life style.

Popularly used to differentiate between choices and actions said to be 'healthy' or 'unhealthy,' thus 'a healthy life style'.

Grey culture nurtures the belief that we each make free *choices,* but this is only correct within the range of options provided by that *culture.* Our life styles are contained within the *limits* of *culture* and the resources available to individuals within the *culture* (see **consumer**). While the *culture* is *unsustainable* our *choices* will unavoidably contribute to that *unsustainability.* It is practically impossible to live a *green sustainable* life style in a *terminal culture* (see **green islands**).

Nevertheless, every *choice* we make is relevant. Like raindrops in the storm, running to the stream, flowing to swell the tide that washes ever higher, every *choice* we make either contributes to the disaster or helps lessen it.[6] But making such *choices* is not the same as positive counter-action; the life style remains contained within the disaster *culture*. Minimising the disaster requires fundamental *change*; the *creation* of a different *culture* which gives real *choice* in life styles.

Our aim should be to live lightly on the *land*, taking only necessities, leaving only footprints.

CARBON-BASED LIFE (Carbon: non-metallic chemical element occurring as diamond, graphite and charcoal, in carbon oxides and carbonates and in all organic compounds.)

All life on *earth* is based on the agreeably cohesive *nature* of the carbon atom. The successively larger and more complex molecular arrangements of living matter are held together by the carbon atom; it acts as the permanent scaffolding for all forms and stages of life.

Fossil fuels – coal, oil and natural gas – are based on the carbon remains of previous life. Lost by chance beneath tectonic tides, the weight of the overburden squeezed out most of the other elements, leaving carbon and closely associated *chemicals*.

Carbon has no liquid state, it exists as a solid or is oxidised, giving off heat and forming carbon monoxide and dioxide (the primary *greenhouse* gas). Compounding carbon with other substances influences the temperature at which it will oxidise. Burning carbon-based fuels (coal, oil, methane, wood and other biomass products) on the present global scale is completely distorting (overwhelming) the *Gaian natural* carbon *cycle*; humans are taking massive amounts of carbon life stock atoms out of store and causing climatic and wider *environmental imbalance*. The *unsustainable way of life* of the *First World* is based on *finite resources* of *fossil fuels*; that is a significant part of its *unsustainability*. One hiccup at the oil wells and millions are in trouble.

Carbon-based *fossil fuels* also produce the feedstock for the modern *chemical* industry (see **artificial**). The polymer *chemical* industry uses carbon atoms in compounds to assemble further molecular *structures*. By using carbon in this way it is locked outside the life cycle, perhaps for ever. Burning *artificial* molecules causes *problems* because the carbon which holds them together oxidises at relatively low temperatures, either releasing the molecular side-chains or leaving them to form into other arrangements. Some are highly *toxic*, all are *pollutants*. Some such substances, having been deprived of their carbon atoms, have a high affinity for the carbon in living tissues, or for molecules that will end up in

177

the *food* network. This is why each of us is contaminated by an unknown, but increasing number and quantities, of such substances. We are playing molecular Russian roulette with life on a massive scale.

GREEN LIFE   The basis of reverence for green life, as a *symbolic value* for all life, is because green plants re-convert carbon dioxide (CO_2), by combination with water in the presence of sunlight, into carbohydrates, thus bringing carbon out of the atmosphere and back into *food* networks (see **food, life contract**).

$$_nCO_2 + {_n}H_2O + light > (CH_2O)_n + {_n}O_2$$

carbon dioxide plus water plus light (energy) produces
carbohydrates plus oxygen

While *terminal grey culture* worships carbon in its eternal crystalline form, destroying reaches of the planet in the search for diamonds, *greens* see the real *wealth* of life in the vast diversity of *green* life forms and their miraculous interaction with animal life. They could survive without us, but we could not live without them.

'If the doors of perception were cleansed, everything would appear as it is, infinite.'[7]

QUALITY OF LIFE see LIFE ENHANCING

WAY OF LIFE   The means by which life is maintained; principle features of such means. The way of life which identifies various groups of people.

The way of life characteristic of the *First World* is that of *institutional* employment, provision and dependence.

Whatever ways of life we choose in the *future*, two questions govern the overall validity of our *means* of *existence*: Is it *sustainable*, and does it *enhance* life? Anything which does not fill these requirements is part of the *terminal problem* and should be seen as such.

To *create sustainable* ways of living we need to map the *morphology* of *Gaian existence*, so that the parameters of human *morphology*, from individual to *community*, *culture* and species, may be integrated into the *dynamics* of the *whole* (see **morphology**).

WEB OF LIFE see **Gaia**.

Relationships   cycles, death, evolution, Gaia, potential.

See also   cultural, morphology, terminal, sustainable.

References

1 The Right Reverend Jim Thompson, Bishop of Stepney, speaking on BBC Radio 2 Jimmy Young Programme, 4 October 1990.
2 Carl Sagan, 1983, *Cosmos*, Random House, New York, USA.

3 Colin Johnson, 1991, *The Green Bible: Creating Sustainable Life on Earth*, Thorsons, London.

4 Arabella Melville and Colin Johnson, 1985, *The Long-life Heart: How to Avoid Heart Disease and Live a Longer Life*, Century Hutchinson, London.

5 Barry Commoner, 1971, *The Closing Circle*, Knopf, New York, USA.

6 See Bernadette Valleley, 1989, *1001 Ways to Save the Planet*, Penguin, London.

7 William Blake (1757–1827), 1966, *The Marriage of Heaven and Hell* in *The Complete Writings of William Blake*, Oxford University Press, Oxford, England.

LIMIT   Bounding line, terminal point; point beyond which *function* or form loses continuity; factor(s) which serves to define possibilities.

Everything has *inherent* limits, of size, duration, complexity, etc. *Existence* occurs within the *inherent* limits of the *form* involved, or those of its *vital processes*. As part of the *evolutionary dynamics* of *life*, each form seeks to expand the limits into which it has emerged, in preparation for the next *evolutionary* step. This is why humans find it difficult to come to terms with the concept of limits, with the idea that all things may not be possible, that the prospect of the 'more' *consumer life ethic* is *unsustainable* and may be genocidally flawed.

Various limits are of particular relevance to *green* thought and the *future*.

LIMITING FACTOR   The thing which limits the range size, scope etc., of a system, process or form of existence.

The current *culture* is ambivalent in its regard to limiting factors. The mechanistic tradition accepts that they exist; in structural design the weakest component, the limiting factor on the performance of the *structure*, is determined by analysis and beefed up or fined down. The *process* is repeated so that there is no single limiting factor and under predicted extreme circumstances the *structure* acts *synergistically*. However in *natural processes*, with limiting factors of which we are largely ignorant, no such procedure is even attempted. *Nature*, and its *processes*, are assumed to be *infinite*, without limit (see **away**).

Even if we could determine *natural* limiting factors, it is unlikely (even if it were desirable) that they could be increased in the way structural strength can be increased. The *dynamics* of *natural processes* are not simple, or mechanical. Altering one factor will affect all the others. *Natural* limiting factors may be seen as the point of *balance* of a *system*; the *whole system* must be enlarged, to increase its total capacity, rather than attempting to increase capacity by altering its limiting factor. Thus, although the limiting factor remains the same, increasing the total capacity of the *system* retains its *balance*, its *coherence* and its *integrity* – provided the increased capacity of one *system* does not distort or overrun the limits of others.

LIMITS OF CYCLIC PROCESSES   Human activity has already taken the *biosphere* beyond the limits of many of the *cyclic processes* which maintain *biospheric stability*. The *natural cycles* of the physical *environment*, of sunlight, rainfall, gases, all the substances required by *life* to construct the *food network*, all the factors upon which *life* depends, have limits. While it may be possible to push one, or more, to its upper limit or even beyond, for a time, *life* cannot continue indefinitely even if only one factor is running in the red. *Sustainable life* requires that we determine which of the many factors is closest to its limit, and either increase its capacity, in *balance*, or reduce the demand upon that factor. *Grey culture*, in denying limits, is pushing everything far beyond into the red, shutting off its senses and flying blind. The end results are predictable.

The *greenhouse effect*, climatic disruption, species *extinction*, resource depletion, *pollution*, over-population, etc. are all *symptoms* of the disruption of *balance* by human activity among the *cycles* upon which planetary *life* depends. Whether the integrity of these *cycles* may be restored is the *question* of the *future*.

For a *sustainable future*, all factors of human *life*, all our *needs*, *wants*, the demands we make in fulfilling our *future potential*, have to be confined within the flexible but limited parameters of global possibility. The truth of our *existence* is that we either learn, *evolve* to live within the limits of *nature*, or we fail without.

LIMITS OF FINITE RESOURCES see **finite resources**.

LIMITS OF GAIA   The *natural* world has a *network* of interacting and *interdependent cycles* which describe its limits and maintain its *stability* (see **feedback loops**). The *Gaian whole* is limited (excluding an unpredictable astronomical event) by the *life cycle* of its sustaining star, or the degradation of *life* caused by human activity.

The *life* of *Gaia*, and its *diversity* of biological *functions*, is limited by the rate at which physical and biological *processes* can *cycle* critical nutrients through the planetary system while retaining overall *balance*. Imbalanced human intervention, as in agriculture, with the application of massive amounts of *chemical* nutrients (nitrogen, potassium and phosphate) to plant crops, short circuits many *natural cycles*. The '*food*' produced may have greater mass, but it lacks nutrients, causes malnourishment, and reduces the soil to sterility, eventually to be blown or washed away. Overrunning the *natural* limits produces deserts.

LIMITS TO GROWTH   The acknowledgement of limits to human activity, specifically in *economic* and *numerical* expansion (see **exponential growth**).

In money *economics* the reality of *growth*, particularly in *future investments* such as pension funds etc., was put succinctly by Herman Daly:

> Contrary to the implications of some economic growth models, the best evidence from geographers is that the diameter of the earth in fact does *not* grow at a rate equal to the rate of interest![1]

The classic study which set out the proposition of limits to human activity was initiated by the *Club of Rome*, which produced *The Limits to Growth*.[2] The present human *culture* demands continual growth in *food* production, human *numbers* and their *expectations, consumption* of non-renewable resources and the capacity of the *biosphere* to absorb *pollution*. The conclusion of a detailed computer model study of each of these parameters, and their interaction, was that the short doubling times of many of humanity's activities, combined with the immense *quantities* being doubled, will bring us close to the limits of growth of those activities surprisingly soon. The *Club of Rome* study was initiated in 1968, and its results published in 1972. Almost two decades have passed, and *grey culture* still insists upon displaying its *terminal nature* by ignoring the fundamental truth: THERE ARE LIMITS TO GROWTH.

All politicians, economists, religious leaders, all those at the head of the *institutional structures* of the present world order, depend upon unlimited growth, upon the *ethic* of ever more of ever more.

It is the demand for *economic growth*, for more *flow* from *environment* to *waste*, for uncontrolled population *growth*, for greater individual *expectations*, that produces the *terminal global predicament*. We have to accept limits; there is no *alternative*. As the authors of *The Limits to Growth* stated:

> We are convinced that realisation of the qualitative constraints of the world environment and of the tragic consequences of an overshoot *is essential* to the initiation of new forms of thinking that will lead to a fundamental revision of human behaviour

and, by implication, of the entire fabric of present-day society.'
(My emphasis)

HUMAN LIMITS (see **numbers**)   As was noted above, within the
evolutionary dynamics of *life*, each form seeks to expand the limits
into which it has emerged, in preparation for the next *evolutionary*
step. This is why humans find it difficult to come to terms with the
concept of limits, with the idea that all things may not be possible,
and that even if they were, many of them would be both pointless
and undesirable.

Humanity finds itself in a peculiar position. Whereas our physical
evolution seems to have slowed or stopped (it is a relative
process), that of our *minds* and their *socio-culture extensions* has not.
Over our recent *evolutionary past*, while our bodies have not
changed, the size of our brains has continually increased. This has
contributed to the imbalance we project into the *natural world*. We
have an *inherent* internal conflict; limits imposed by our physiology are not accepted by our *minds* (see **life structure**).

While *grey culture* has concentrated on limiting the expressions
of humanity's animal *nature*, it has tended to ignore the *question* of
limits on the *processes* or products of our *minds* (except where
these involve more basic animal *functions* – see **censorship**). The
future requires that our limiting parameters be redefined.

Limits to expression of our animal *nature* need to be liberated
within a different understanding of *rights*, while the products of
our *minds* require expression in isolated surroundings which will
control their projection into the *environment* at large. This would
have the effect of removing inner limits from human discovery,
while maintaining protection for the *biosphere* from the effects of
those discoveries. A new *philosophy* is required to guide the *process* of the expressions of human development into the world at
large, combined with a greater understanding of ourselves.

The present *imbalance* of limits produces a negative and distorted effect; most people in the *First World* live significant parts of
their lives in the inner world created by mass media fantasy and
endless distracting trivia which blind them to the reality of outer
processes.

Our species has to accept limits to its *numbers*. The traditional
liberal concept of the objective of human endeavour as the greatest
good for the greatest number needs rethinking. If humanity insists
on *life styles* based upon high material *consumption*, we will have
to rationalise what happens now by default – the greatest good for

the smallest number – and limit *numbers* which restrict the *consumption* of the few (by making it *environmentally* or morally unacceptable). If we choose *sustainability,* with rational population levels, then the limits to *numbers* become set by different criteria (see **critical mass**).

NATURAL LIMITS see LIMITS OF GAIA, **cycles.**

PERSONAL LIMITS (see **freedom**)   The classical statement of the limits to personal behaviour, that 'my *freedom* ends where yours begins', needs restating. Limits, between people, species and bioregions which do not have space between them, require control and defence. Such limits inhibit *growth* and the expression of further *potential. Terminal culture* has removed the space between inherent limits; rather than the possibility of *peace* it produces mutually assured destruction, instead of *growth* it has generated *compression.* In place of the expression of *potential* we are buried under *problems* of our own *creation.*

At the root of the *problems* we *create* are the inner *processes* of our *minds.* It is conventionally believed that our *minds,* our imagination, the inner *universe* we all possess, need accept no limits; that the possibilities of our inner space are *infinite.* Experience of the last 200 years (if not the period of recorded history) indicates that we need to understand the precise difference between inner acts of *creation* and the outward expression of what is conceived. As a matter of urgency we need to understand the *dynamics* of the psychological processes existing within our species (see **morphic resonance**), so that what is conceived within may not be *projected* into the world unless it is acceptable within a new *sustainable philosophy.* We may be capable of anything, but the ability will continue the destruction of blind *progress* unless it is combined with *wisdom* which allows us to select consciously from the possibilities open to us.

The conceptions of *infinite* human imagination cannot be endlessly converted into reality from a planet of *finite resources.* We have to describe limits and simultaneously to choose directions. Humans have to make conscious decisions in the *knowledge* of limits, to *evolve consciously* towards *sustainability* within the limits of the *nature* of which we are a part. If the *future* produces a *green* religion it will probably *centre* upon a doctrine of limits:

the word 'limit' has a negative connotation, but the virtue of limits is they are part of the self-regulating process that leads to community homoeostasis.[3]

<u>Relationships</u>   **cycles, finite resources, sutainability, rights**.
<u>See also</u>   **numbers, growth, potential**.
<u>References</u>

1 Herman Daly, in Michael Tobias (ed), 1985, *Deep Ecology*, Slawson Communications, San Marco, California, USA.
2 Donella H. Meadows, Dennis L. Meadows, Jorgen Randers, William W. Behrens,
1972, *The Limits to Growth: A Report for the Club of Rome's Project on the Predicament of Mankind*, Pan Books, London.
3 William Ophuls, 1977, *Ecology and the Politics of Scarcity.*

LINEAR   Of or in line; involving one dimension only. A defining
characteristic of *processes* in *terminal culture.*

   Green philosophy requires acknowledgement of the *cyclic nature*
of *existence*, and the incorporation of human activities into *cyclic
processes.*

LINEAR ACCOUNTING   Profit is determined by accounting for a
small linear part of the actual *process* involved. By ignoring the
irreplaceability of *finite resources* – the *environmental* destruction,
including species extinction, *inherent* in their extraction; the *pollution* involved in extraction, conversion, use and ultimate disposal;
substitution and *restoration* costs (if this is possible) – industrial
societies can claim to be profitable – even 'soundly based'.

LINEAR ECONOMICS   see **economics, flow.**

LINEAR MODEL/PARADIGM   The idea that for every effect (singular *event*) there is a cause. Although the linear model accepts the
notion of multiple causes and even multiple and unpredictable
effects, they are still held to operate with sequential tidiness, rather
than *synergistic* randomness. The lineal model is a way of trying to
rationalise *nature* and its *processes* by fitting them into a model
with which our *minds* can cope.

   Part of our required act of *conscious evolution* involves
changing our linear model of the *dynamics* of *existence* to one
based on the *synergy* of *networks* and *matrices* (see **mind**).

LINEAR PERSPECTIVE   *Life values* and *assumptions* based on the
linear model and linear thought.

   Terminal culture is based upon a linear view of *existence*, of
simple isolated causes and effects. All its *processes* reflect this view,
especially *flow economics.*

LINEAR THOUGHT   The thought process encourage by the
analytical tradition of mechanistic reductionism (see **Cartesianism**).

   Linear thought is sequential, one thing at a time, in what is
assumed to be a logical order, rather than a parallel or *matricial* (see
mind).

Linear thought is dominated by its one-dimensional character-istic; thus the search for a single cause to *problems*, for the single simple answer. Such searches fail because things just are not as linear thought assumes they are. Linear thought denies the *inherent connectedness* of things and ignores the propositions of *holism*.
Relationships   **mindset, terminal, culture**.
See also   **cycle, sustainability**.

LIVING, ART OF   Creative self-fulfilment; understanding all that we are capable of becoming; choosing to express those capabilities which add to the joy of others, experiencing the *ecstasy* of *ecology*, using abilities to add to the capacity of all *life.*

Within the deadening *cul-de-sac* of *terminal culture* we each have to cultivate the art of living, of maximising our once-in-eternity experience in concert with all others sharing the same time-slot. Building *green islands* for the *future*, starting from where we are and *extending* outwards until we join together into a *sustainable global green culture*.

'We are always getting ready to live, but never living.'[1]
Relationships   **life, being, potential**.
See also   **limits, cycles**.
References
1 Ralph Waldo Emerson (1803–1882), *Journals*, 13 April 1834.

LOCAL CURRENCY (see **LETS**)   A *community*-based means of *exchange* of goods, skills, etc. Local currencies presently operate on the basis of the nation state. *Greens* believe that, in parallel with *political devolution, economic devolution* will require a local currency within a global currency. This reflects the belief in the necessity for a *global culture* within which local *diversity* may thrive (see **universal credit economy**).

LOVE   None of the references I have used for conventional defini-tions and meanings were much help with love. It seems to be one of those words which we all use very widely, to describe reactions from mild inclination to consuming irrational passion, or feelings from habitual preference to the most devastating emotional experi-ence. It is one of those words which we all understand when we use it.

In an attempt both to summarise and to extend the concept of love I conclude that it is best expressed as the feeling of being one with; with your desires, feelings, with their possible reciprocation by another being or thing.

Thus the experience of being one with another describes the feelings of being in love most of us hope to experience. It also allows for the extremes of a preference for habitual behaviour – loving tea, etc. – and for the ultimately fatal becoming one at the extremes of passion – as the moth with a flame, the disciple with deity, the one for others. 'Greater love hath no man than this, that a man lay down his life for his friends.'[1]

The rational ancient Greeks regarded love as an *illness* that could approach madness. *Terminal culture* has *extended* this view; love, and particularly its expression in sexual activity, has provoked contrary reactions. It is necessary for the continuation of the species, but oh so dangerous to the *institutions* of the *culture* because it offers a universal unclosable route to transcendendance of self, of being one with others, of realisation of uncontrolled *potential*. In face of such possibilities, *institutions* opt for control by every means, from primal guilt to issuing licences for those parts of the inevitable *process* they could not stop. The result is perversion, of love turned back upon self and frequently expressed as hate for that which is desired, of degradation of feelings, of a cash *economy* in what should be free, of guilt constraining joy, of false *limits* which ultimately insulate the feelings of humanity from those of other *life* and *existence*. The whole prospect has been turned, with much else of human *nature*, on its head. As Oscar Wilde observed:

> Yet each man kills the thing he loves,
> By each let this be heard,
> Some do it with a bitter look.
> Some with a flattering word.
> The coward does it with a kiss,
> The brave man with a sword![2]

Intuitively we feel that love should not be destructive and, while its expression in *creativity* inevitably involves some measure of destruction, yet we know things in general should not be as they are. As Petra Kelly of *Die Grünen* in Germany put it, 'love must become an integral part of all areas of society so that it can halt the forward march of isolation, separation and a hostile social order.'

Love is one of the basic human *needs*; we all *need* to love and be loved, to experience the feeling of being one with others. The feeling must begin with the self; if we cannot love ourselves, in the fullest understanding of what we are, we are unlikely to be able to *extend* the experience beyond ourselves. Being one with the self is contrary to the separation of being *inherent* in the *reductionist* tradition which generates *terminal culture*; this is why the perceptions of *holism* are important. We must become one with ourselves and develop a full appreciation of our *relationships* with the rest of *life* and *existence*. As Iris Murdoch put it, 'We need a moral philosophy in which the concept of love, so rarely mentioned now by philosophers, can once again be made central.'[3]

Love of self, once established and turned outwards, can become an all embracing experience, of others, of all *life* and *existence*, of the *ecstasy* of *ecology* and of simply *being*. The experience becomes transcendental; we experience *being* one to the maximum *extent* of our *potential*.

Finally, we need to encourage all expressions of love; it is an attempt to be human, to be what we are, to stand against the tide in a non-human, anti-life milieu.

Relationships   **being, life**.

References

1 The Christian *Holy Bible*, St John, 15:13.
2 Oscar Fingal O'Flahertie Wills Wilde (1854–1900), 1898, *The Ballad of Reading Gaol*.
3 Iris Murdoch, 1970, *The Sovereignty of Good*, Ark Publications, London.

MALTHUSIANISM From British clergyman/economist Thomas Robert Malthus (1766–1834), who propagated the view that a population always tended to increase faster than its means of subsistence, published anonymously in 1798 in *Essay on the Principle of Population*. Although not the originator of the idea,[1] Malthus presented it in a coherent and logical way. Darwin is said to have remarked, 'on reading Malthus' *On Population*, natural selection was the inevitable result of the rapid increase of all organic beings', presumably believing that such rapid increase necessarily led to a struggle for existence which would result in the survival of the fittest (see **compression**).

Malthus advocated sexual restraint as a means of birth control.

References

1 See Bertrand Russell (1872–1970), 1945, *History of Western Philosophy*, George Allen & Unwin, London, pages 694/5, where the original idea is attributed to French philosopher Condorcet (1743–94); 'Malthus's father was a disciple of Condorcet, and it was in this way that Malthus came to know of the theory' (see **myth appropriation**).

MARKET Gathering of people for the purchase and sale of provisions, livestock, etc.; the demand for particular goods or services; means of giving value to things.

May also been seen as the means of underwriting the *structural* conformity of the *economy* and society. Place where money speaks, and *life* is silenced.

MARKET ECONOMY The heart of the *economic* religion of the western industrialised nations. Assumed to be a 'free market economy', but in fact a mass of habits, rules, exclusions, prohibitions, cartels, monopolies, etc., which have the effect of consolidating *institutional wealth* and *power*, against the interests of *life*, *community*, people and the *environment* (see **economy, flow**).

The theory behind market economies is that man's *wants* are infinite, and can only with difficulty (continual struggle) be fulfilled. Since this proposition involves continual *growth* in the rate of *consumption* of the *environment* it must be rejected. Yet production must also be controlled, since, if the market were satiated, demand would fall and profits could not be maximised. Controls in the 'free' market are: starvation; bribery, either direct or in the form of subsidies, favourable contracts, make-work schemes, etc., which all off-set the *political* inconvenience generated by the real operation of the market; and monopolies or cartels, which ensure that the market operates favourably for those selling rather than those who may be in the position of having to buy.

Currently *grey economists* are trying to add '*green*' bolt-ons to the market heart of *flow economics*, for instance by adding an *environmental* cost, or by taxing *pollution*. This nonsense is naturally welcomed by governments and their supporting *institutions*, but no one has yet explained how you cost the priceless or tax for the irreplaceable. It is *symptomatic* of the arrogance of those whose present *philosophy* is destroying the *earth* that they believe that they understand all the effects of their *economic processes*, that all factors can be reduced to monetary terms, that money can restore the *environment*, replace lost and damaged lives, buy back lost species.

Some *greens* are led on to this slippery and irrational slope; it is assumed that the 'peace dividend' of reduced arms-spending following the rapprochement between the Superpowers can be spent on *environmental restoration*; that is, that the damage caused by *flow economics* can be healed by maintaining the *flow*, but redirecting it.

The market is a means of avoiding *responsibility*, of suffering and encouraging the exercise of irrational *power*. If it is true that you can't buck the market, the market must be replaced by a *system* that responds to *need* rather than money, to *sustainable values* rather than destructive *power*. The market, to paraphrase Oscar Wilde, is the place that knows the price of everything and the value of nothing.

Relationships   **economy, terminal culture**.
See also   **needs, wants**.

MASCULINE   see **sexual dimorphism**.

MASS   Coherent body of similar constituents, of matter, people, etc., of indefinite shape; dense aggregation of objects, colour, relating to large *numbers* of persons of things; action by large *numbers*; gathering into or of large *numbers*.

Mass is most frequently used as prefix for things which are intended to be applied to large *numbers*, or to the result of use by large *numbers*.

MASS DESTRUCTION   The crowning achievement of *terminal culture*. *Life* on *earth*, or an unknown but significant part of it, lives minutes from the prospect of mass destruction via the application of science, *technology* and enormous amounts of *finite resources* to weapons. The logical outcome of a *death*-orientated *culture*.

Mass destruction is also the result of the application of various *processes* on a mass scale for ends which, of themselves, may not be bad.

MASS MEDIA   The provision of *cultural values, information*, etc., to mass audiences.

According to Marshall McLuhan,

Societies have always been shaped more by the nature of the media by which men communicate than by the content of the communication. The alphabet, for instance, is a technology that is absorbed by the very young child in a completely unconscious manner, by osmosis so to speak. Words and the meaning of words predispose the child to think and act automatically in certain ways. The alphabet and print technology fostered and encouraged a fragmenting process, a process of specialism and of detachment. Electric technology fosters and encourages unification and involvement. It is impossible to understand social and cultural changes without a knowledge of the workings of the media.[1]

McLuhan went on to describe *life* in a media-modified 'electronic global village'. The problem with the unification encouraged by mass media is that it inevitably works on lowest common multiples. *Culture* is based on the slight ebbs and flows of identical media trivia. Mass media are *inherently exclusive*, the self-perpetuating *institutional* minority speaking to and on behalf of the unrepresented majority, the *cultural consumers*.

Mass media produces the paradox of individual isolation in the mass. Fired by the perpetual quest for involvement, mass *societies* become addicted to the trivia provided by mass media. There is a further dimension to the paradox; it is that of fragmentation within the mass, of incoherent boundaries within coherent *wholes*. The *nature* of the control exercised by mass media may be the use of personal emotional involvement as a means if disrupting or directing the *potential synergy* of the mass.

Yet the vision of an individual or *community*-based *network* of open access electronic media does create the possibility of unification and involvement. It would benefit the *future* if it were based on the idea of a globe of villages, rather than a global village. (The *institutional* electronic global village already exists; money is an electronic global data stream, resource manipulation, inter-state communication, and commerce is on these *networks.* What is excluded are people, society, *needs*, etc.)

MASS PRODUCTION (see **economy**) Rationalised production of identical goods to exploit mass markets. The means of removing *creativity* from *work* in the provision of goods. Invention attributed to Henry Ford with his 'one man, one task' rationalisation of car manufacture on the assembly line ('man and machine in perfect harmony'), but the idea actually owes more to armament manufacturers, such as Samuel Colt, who made gun components within standard tolerances so that any part would fit any gun.

MASS PROVISION The *grey* institutional answer to basic human *needs*. The soul-destroying uniformity of mass housing is typical of the lack of individual human *values* in mass provision. A logical outcome of mass societies.

MASS SOCIETY (see **numbers**) The reactions of society in the mass inevitably tend towards the primitive, the instinctive, the unthought emotional reaction. People in this state are more susceptible to manipulation, to division, to irrationality.

CRITICAL MASS From nuclear physics; the amount of fissile material necessary to initiate a nuclear chain reaction.

Also used in theories of population *dynamics.* There is an upper critical *limit* which, if passed, will cause a population either to *sink* to a degraded remnant or to *shift* to a new *evolutionary* form. If a population falls below its lower critical *limit* the species will fail because of lack of *numbers* (see **morphology**). The populations of most species *cycle* between the upper and lower *limits,* held in *balance* by the *dynamics* of other *life* within the *environment.*

For humans the relevance of critical mass population is to discover the minimum *numbers* of each of the diverse races, with their various *ways of life,* necessary for each race to continue. The true application of *knowledge* should not be to enable us to overwhelm the *earth* by continually *shifting* our upper critical *limit* at the cost of everything else, but rather that we continually decrease the lower *limit,* to the benefit of all *life,* especially the *biosphere* upon which we depend (see **numbers**).

Relationships   **human scale, community, culture**.
See also   **shift, formative causation, mindset**.
References

1 Marshall McLuhan and Quentin Fiore, 1967, *The Medium is the Massage*, Penguin, London.

MATRIX, MATRICES   Womb, place in which thing is developed; formative part of animal organ; mass of rock; mathematical, rectangular array of *quantities* in lines and columns which may be treated as a single *quantity*.

The idea of the matrix has yet to settle in *green* consciousness. While it is often used, sometimes instead of *network*, it is frequently avoided, possibly because of its *inherent* female connotation, of the womb, equally perhaps because of its implicit denial of *hierarchy* and ejection of the irrevocable focus of *power*.

> Matrix is a conspicuous warning signal ... It has a number of precise specialised meanings,[and] a conveniently hazy general meaning ... as something within which something else originates, or takes form, or develops ... But when somebody uses the word outside its jargons in general speech, it is a strident warning to listen suspiciously because somebody may be showing off.[1]

Oh dear, does the *green movement* really need such pompous petty strictures, such patronage of inhibition, against showing off, or is it really aimed at the protection of other *values*?

The convenient general meaning best focused on is that of a support lattice work of *interconnected* things, options or *values*. Everything originates in something else and many things, particularly living things, require nurture. The *extension* of the concept of womb to greater organs of nurture appears both logical and reasonable. Thus one can talk of the *Gaian* matrix of *life*, and mean the complex of *sustaining* and nurturing (lattice or web of) interactions of the *whole* planet within its solar *environment*.

For *greens* there are two important applications of the matrix. One is as a *model* for human *social structures* and the *dynamics of relationships* within those *structures*, and the second is as a *model* for *future* ways of thought.

The *structure* of *future* human society revolves around the concept of *life* in *community*, of *communities* in *federation*, of *community relationships* in *confederation*, of a matrix of *communities*. Within a *green global culture*, *communities* with *diverse cultures* will form *networks* of interest and *need*; such *networks* will arise from selection from the available matrix. Similarly individuals within *communities* will select their *networks* of options from the available *socio-cultural networks.*

Such a *structure* is a rejection of that of *terminal culture,* of monolithic *institutional* nation states, with *inherent hierarchical power structures* and *privilege* based on *position.* Matrical *structures* should be *inherently green, inclusive* rather than *exclusive,* the *way of life* based upon *function* and the maintainence of human *values,* individual *freedom* and *responsibility,* and the proposition of *life* within *human scale* and within the *limits* of the *biosphere* (see **structure**).

The second area of relevance for the concept of matrix is that of *conscious human evolution.* This requires addressing not only what we think, but the way we think. Current patterns of thought are *linear* and/or *hierarchical.* In this they reflect primitive *dynamics* of primate *life.* For the *future,* patterns of thought need to reflect the actual patterns produced within the organ of thought, the brain.

Within the brain a matrix of interconnected neurones produces many concurrent *networks* of consensual activity (see **mind**). These produce or monitor a variety of perceptions and activities. The inner matrical *processes* may ultimately be the source of the pattern of human *life* which it would be both desirable and logical to project into the world at large. 'If you bring forth what is within you, what you bring forth will save you. If you do not bring forth what is within you, what you do not bring forth will destroy you.'[2]

The concept of the matrix, as a description of the supportive *nature* of *existence* both without and within, should be wholeheartedly embraced. It is interesting to observe that in *terminal culture,* the heads of *institutional hierarchies* form a de facto matrix of mutual support. *Power* elites, the establishment, [3] the *status quo* of every society, while forcing competition at the base of their *structures,* generally settle for their *slice* of the cake at the top via a *co-operative network* arising from the matrix of interests in the *culture* they form.[4]

<u>Relationships</u>   **network, community, function, evolution.**
<u>See also</u>   **ad hoc, hierarchy, limits.**
<u>References</u>

1 Phillip Howard, 1978, *Weasel Words,* quoted in, John Button, 1988, *A Dictionary of Green Ideas: Vocabulary for a Sane and Sustainable Future,* Routledge, London. 'Showing off' is a crime peculiar to the British way of life. It is behaviour which

indicates you either do not 'know your place' (your pre-ordained station in life) or, worse still, do not accept it. Showing off is the sort of behaviour which other societies use to judge aspiration, inclination, ability and talent. The British prefer pretension and position based on genetic elitism – a culture of nurtured (good) losers.

2 Jesus Christ, *Gospel According to Thomas*, 45: 29–33.

3 Term applied by historian A.J.P. Taylor (1906–90) in the 1950s to describe the matrix of historical and conformist elites which controlled Britain.

4 See Anthony Howard, 1962, *The Anatomy of Britain*, Hodder & Stoughton, London; also Jeremy Paxman, 1990, *Friends in High Places*, Michael Joseph, London.

MEANS The way by which something is achieved; process employed.

In *terminal culture* the continual question is: 'Do the ends justify the means?', usually by way of justifying immoral, unacceptable, behaviour. The doctrine of expediency – a little evil for a greater good.

For *greens, sustainable life* requires that the means becomes the end. Our means of fulfilment must in themselves be fulfilling. We achieve *sustainable ways of life* by *living* in *sustainable* ways.

Relationships   **process, sustainability, philosophy**.

See also   **efficiency, economy**.

MEAT   see **food**.

MEME   Having an *idea* is frequently illustrated as a light coming on. A meme is *process* and product, the switch, the cable and the bulb shedding light, which comes from within our *mind* in connection with our *culture*. Memes emerge in our consciousness when we see the light. The meme of the meme was originated by Richard Dawkins:

> I think that a new kind of replicator has recently emerged on this very planet. It is staring us in the face. It is still in its infancy, still drifting clumsily about in its primeval soup, but already it is achieving evolutionary change at a rate which leaves the old gene panting far behind.
>
> The new soup is the soup of human culture. We need a name for the replicator, a noun which conveys the idea of a unit of cultural transmission, or a unit of *imitation*. 'Mimeme' comes from a suitable Greek root, but I want a monosyllable that sounds a bit like 'gene'. I hope my classical friends will forgive me if I abbreviate mimeme to *meme*. If it is any consolation, it

could alternatively be thought of as being related to 'memory', or to the French word *même*. It should be pronounced to rhyme with 'cream'.

Examples of memes are tunes, ideas, catch-phrases, clothes fashions, ways of making pots or building arches. Just as genes propagate themselves in the gene pool by leaping from body to body via sperm or eggs, so memes propagate themselves in the gene pool by leaping from brain to brain via a process which, in the broad sense, can be called imitation. If a scientist hears, or reads about, a good idea, he passes it on to his colleagues and students. He mentions it in his articles and his lectures. If the idea catches on, it can be said to propagate itself, spreading from brain to brain. As my colleague N.K. Humphrey neatly summed up an earlier draft of this chapter: '... memes should be regarded as living structures, not just metaphorically but technically. When you plant a fertile meme in my mind you literally parasitize my brain, turning it into a vehicle for the meme's propagation in just the way that a virus may parasitize the genetic mechanism of a host cell. And this isn't just a way of talking – the meme for, say, 'belief in life after death' is actually realized physically, millions of times over, as a structure in the nervous systems of individual men the world over.[1]

Memes arise in the *matrix* of our individual *minds*. We have ideas which spread through the greater *matrix* of the common *consciousness/subconsciousness* of our species. Those memes which survive, which are repeated, if only in our *minds*, make up our *culture*. Because of the differential in human *evolution* between our physiology and our brains, we live in a world populated by the products of our *minds*. These are *extended* into the *global environment*, either as artefacts, the products of art or industry, or as conceptual forms, in *values* such as honour, integrity, justice, possession, or as *extended structures* in the many *institutional* forms we project into the *environment* (see **institutions**).

Once more we confront the importance of *philosophy*. It is the prime motive force which drives the *culture* it projects. In the *dynamic symbiosis* between *philosophy* and *culture* and that between *culture* and individual, the foundation memes of the *culture* are propagated, usually without us being aware of their transmission or activity, much as we are unaware of the activity of our *genes*. Yet, as well as projecting our *culture* and *way of life*, *philosophy* also gives us the *tools* with which we may judge and *choose* those memes which arise. It should guide our *choice* of those things which we *extend* into the *global environment.* Our ways of *life* are projected by a *philosophy* which generates a *terminal culture.*

> I conjecture that co-adapted meme-complexes evolve in the same kind of way as co-adapted gene-complexes. Selection favours memes which exploit their cultural environment to their own advantage. This cultural environment consists of other memes which are also being selected. The meme pool therefore comes to have the attributes of an evolutionarily stable set, which new memes find it hard to invade.[2]

Hence the resistance of *terminal culture* to *change*, the resistance of *grey* society to alter its *unsustainable ways of life*, to end the *Impossible Party.* The *terminal* memes of *grey culture* may be the result of the over-specialised and erroneous *evolution* of the human brain. We confront the *compatibility* of the *terminal whole*, with its own disastrous logic and *inherent synergy*. Human *progress* to date confronts us with *life's* search for immortality in the *extended agenda* of *genes* and memes. This is why we cannot *change* one thing and leave others alone; the *future* requires humans to adopt a new meme *mindset.*

A *green* and *sustainable culture* requires the spread of *green* memes, such as those of *sustainability*, of *life* enhancement, of living within the *sphere of life*, of the necessity of establishing *life* based on *green philosophy* and its derived *principles* and *practices.* The task may seem impossible, but there may yet be time: 'in general memes resemble the early replicating molecules, floating chaotically free in the primeval soup, rather than modern genes in their neatly paired, chromosomal regiments.'[3]

Our required act of *conscious evolution* amounts to a *conscious* degree of alignment of memes for the *future.* The broad *choice* is simple; we either choose to align our species with the *nature* of the *biosphere* upon which we depend, *consciously* aiming for eternity, or we allow the *processes* of blind *progress* to carry us over the edge into *terminality.*

The *problems* of the world are human *creations*, they are our products, our *problems.* We can equally well choose answers and then *create ways of life* which do not repeat *terminal problems.* The *problem* is within; so is the answer. For the *future* we need to develop and spread *green* memes, to ensure their survival as the means to our survival, to *create* a *sustainable global culture* based on *green philosophy*.

Hopeful meme: there is absolutely no inevitability as long as there is a willingness to contemplate what is happening. 'We, alone on earth, can rebel against the tyranny of the selfish replicators.'[4]

Relationships   **change, anticipation, potential, morphic resonance, evolution**.

See also   **culture, mindset, formative causation**.

References

1 Richard Dawkins, 1976, *The Selfish Gene*, Oxford University Press, Oxford, England, page 206/7 of the 1978 Paladin edition, Granada, London.
2 Page 213/14 of 1 above.
3 Page 211 of 1 above.
4 Page 215 of 1 above.

METAMORPHOSIS   *Change* of form, *nature*, or character; *change* into new form.

The most common, although far from completely understood, *process* of metamorphosis is that of insects. Eggs are laid by adults, these hatch, producing a larval form (as grubs, maggots, etc.) and these subsequently metamorphose into the adult form.

Just as the *morphology* of the insect *changes* at distinct stages of its *life cycle*, so the *morphology* of other *life* forms *changes* over time. For most it is a relatively straightforward *process* of *growth* and *decay*. For humans metamorphosis is centred on our *socio-cultural extensions*. The *changes* we are projecting concern the shape and *structure* of our *cultures* and their *institutional* forms.

The metamorphosis *greens* seek is in the *nature* of human *culture*. The need is to *de-institutionalise*, to return to *human scale* and *values*, and to *emerge* in a *sustainable form*.

Relationships   **change, evolution, morphology**.

See also   **structure, culture, philosophy**.

MIND   Source of *consciousness*, thought, feelings, motivation. What we experience, as well as the many functions of which we are unaware, of the living activity of the brain. The focus and expression of that activity.

Grey culture, with its *reductionist philosophy*, believes in the separation of mind, body and *spirit*; that is, they may be treated as unrelated entities. This nonsense is slowly fading from the surface of the *culture*, but it remains embedded in its founding *philosophy* and *institutional* behaviour (see **Cartesianism**).

Green holistic beliefs accept that the mind, body and *spirit* are interactive parts of the *whole* person, that there are *limits* to the degree to which they may be regarded as separate entities. Similarly there are *limits* to the extent to which members of species may be regarded as separate entities; there is a continual *feedback loop* between individual mind and the shared species consciousness (and probably between species and *Gaian whole* – the concept of life as a singular phenomenon dependent on diverse expressions), which means that individual will has *limits* in the will of others, as part of the *collective subconscious* of our species.[1]

The *dynamics* of mind within species raises the question of the degree to which our mental *functions* are predetermined. Some *holists* believe that the mind is best seen as a *systematic symptom* of our form of *existence*, an inevitable result rather than an optional initiator. If the classic *Cartesian* statement 'I think, therefore I am' is turned around – 'I am (*exist*) therefore I think' (express logic) – the property of mind as a logical expression of a particular form of *existence* can be *extended* almost infinitely. But the *inherent* logic of *existence*, of one form *anticipating* the *existence* of others, is not the same as the ability to manipulate sense *perceptions* (indeed to *create* sense *perceptions*), to take *decisions*, make *conscious* *choices* and have the ability for *creative* acts. Of course if it is believed that *creation* is itself a matter of realisation of that which is within, then the degree of activity of the mind becomes a matter of the degree of *potential* between various forms of *existence*; there is a continuum between the regular (logical) arrangement of molecules into compounds, crystalline forms and amino acids, and Beethoven's Fifth Symphony, the wheel, *institutional structures* and concepts of *existence* beyond experience or observation. Subjective and objective alternate in a flickering *perception* show.

Despite the *reductionist analytical tradition* of *grey culture*, very little exploration of the mind has been undertaken. Indeed it appears as if each age and *culture* of humanity sees its inner *processes* as reflections of its *cultural morphology*. Inquiry into the nature of *mind* produces, not the mind, but a reflection; the mind presents itself in terms of its collective products – thus the medieval mind populated by demons and angels, the Victorian by the mechanical dominance of the human will over *nature*. Today it is seen as a holographic computer analogue, tomorrow as a reflection of the external *Gaian matrix* of consensual planetary *existence*. We seem unable to penetrate our own mental processes beyond the reflective coating produced by *cultural symbiosis*.

Current *culture* shares with present *green thinking* the inability to resolve questions of differences between the male and female mind. Are they equal and *potentially* the same, only differentiated by *nurture,* or are there *inherent,* and presumably complementary, differences? Dangerous ground for speculation (see **sexual dimorphism**).

Such propositions as 'I have a mind, but I am not my mind',[2] in seeing the essence of *existence* in the expression of will, itself the *function* of the mind, raises the question of the *nature* of the *existence* of the human mind. It may best be seen as a reflection of the conic *model* of *evolution* (see **evolution**). Our mental *morphology extends* backwards to an unknown component of *past evolutionary* phases, and forwards to the front edge of our collective unfolding *morphology,* where the will may be occupied with what we believe to be desirable. The front edge is wide and amorphous; some people are ahead of their time, others *exist* in the *past,* most live in the recent *past* from where continuity may be *rejected* with minimal effort.

Once again the question of determinism; do people choose to live in the recent *past,* or is it simply *inherent* acceptance of the *hidden agenda?* How far are we *free* to make up our minds, or do they come ready made? The *future* requires that we believe that our mind(s) is an indeterminate '*free*' agent, capable of *creating* its own parameters of *future* possibility, which may be *infinite,* but also capable of rationalising its own capacities of achieving *harmony* in its *choice* of reality and *projections* of *existence.*

Green faith lies in both determinism and the indeterminate, faith in the determinism of the wider *life-logic* of which we are a part and acceptance that we can select from the indeterminate *potential* open to us; and in belief that the present shall, in *future,* be seen as an abhorrent excess, similar to many other excesses in our *past* from which we have withdrawn.

In such beliefs we find expression of the *spiritual* capacity of the mind, a property with which the current *culture* is uncomfortable. Scientists of the *grey culture* pray on Sunday that they may find incontrovertible, objective, logical proof of things on Monday. *Greens* need suffer no such destructive contradictions; *existence* has an *inherent spiritual* dimension as part of the property of *being.* 'For everything that lives is holy, life delights in life.'[3]

Standing on the brink of space, the greatest journey remains within. Our act of *conscious evolution* amounts to persuading our minds to reveal what is within.

MINDSET   That raft of assumptions, beliefs, expectations, prejudices, unthought-out reactions, upon which we float our lives.

Series of internal *models* of reality, *existence*, etc., which has become dogmatic, fixed, so that modification may be a traumatic *process*.

When confronted with information which does not fit the mindset, the subject will modify the data or the *perception* of the data, so that it becomes consistent with the prevailing mindset (see **model**). Data modification can range from that of a total world view, our *perception* of reality, to minor details, seeing () as 0 where we expect to see 0 and () does not match our mindset.

Relationships   creativity, **being, formative, causation.**

See also   **evolution.**

References

1 Carl Gustav Jung (1875–1961) developed the concept of an impersonal, or extrapersonal, collective subsconsious, where the inherited archetypes of our species were stored. There is no reason to suppose that this collective capacity is a passive property; indeed, observation of collective reactions indicates that it can have highly co-ordinated active expression under suitable circumstances.

2 Roberto Assagioli, 1974, *Act of Will*, Penguin, London.

3 William Blake (1757–1827), 1966, *America: A Prophecy*, in *The Complete Writings of William Blake*, Oxford University Press, Oxford, England.

MODEL (also **paradigm**, see **meme**)   Representation in three dimensions of existing or proposed *structure* built to a smaller scale; simplified description of a *system* to assist calculation and prediction, usually as mathematical models; conceptual description of *relationships* or interactions, as social or behavioural model.

A *paradigm* is an example or pattern (originally of sound), now used to describe internal pictures of the *mind*, mental models, of reality, *processes*, beliefs etc.

We each have an immense library of common *cultural* models which enable us to share beliefs, thoughts and behaviour without the continual need to restate everything from the beginning. They enable us to communicate internalised experience of common *perceptions* from the external world, so that words before you, e.g. Eiffel Tower, Charge of the Light Brigade, ice-cream, mountain, and so on, instantly produce internal images coloured by individual experience of the things associated with the words. The *process* also works for products of the *mind* itself; concepts formed and modelled in the *mind* are subsequently projected into the world. Concepts such as possession, ownership, inheritence, *law, value,* duty, nation, regarded as the immutable reality in which our *lives* are set, are in reality only the external fulfilment of shared internal models – represented by language and graphic symbols, themselves highly sophisticated shared models.

We construct models in our *minds* to enable us to make sense of experience, *anticipate events*, manipulate *processes*, predict the outcome of actions and for the pure fun of intellectual exploration. *Culture* is projected from many interacting models, so the *creation* of new or modified models is an essential part of the means of achieving *future culture*. However, it is important to remember that models are simplifications of the reality they represent; they have the *inherent* drawback of *excluding* much which may prove relevant. Becuase of this, models are best seen and used as successive approximations, or approaches, to reality (see **mindset**).

It is always desirable, particularly with models of *social dynamics* or behaviour, that there be more than one model of things. Nothing should be accepted without question.

The *paradigms* given by *education*, being both singular and historical, help perpetuate *culture*. The more difficult we find the construction of a suitable internal model of external experience, the more inflexible the achieved model tends to be. For most situations we prefer to accept the dominant models and *paradigms* of our *culture* rather than construct our own.

Models are derived from a variety of internal sources. Some derive from our collective unconscious, the shared archetypes noted by Jung as common to much of our species, the ancient source of our interpretation of reality. From this base models are modified by experience and intellect. The *creation* of new models may be the result of intellectual/spiritual exploration, or the natural unfolding of the *morphology* of our species, or an interaction of all of these.

Models are the means by which we create our *future*. Every *system* of belief generates conceptual models of the way the *system* interprets the experience of *existence* for believers, and of the way *existence* would be conducted to comply with the requirements of belief. Dogma freezes models and *creates* the danger of a closed unadaptable *system* (see **mindset**).

An ideal *philosophy* would allow a *dynamic synergy* between the elements of *existence*, experience, belief and the internal models generated, such that the models and *paradigms* which affect our belief *structures* and behaviour would be continually modified as the *philosophy evolved*. The failure of the present is rooted in the *institutionalisation* of beliefs and models which fixes them irrespective of effect or circumstances. The effect of *institutionalisation* is to divorce *cultural paradigms* from *philosophy*, so that, right or wrong, they become effectively beyond *change* (see **philosophy**).

The predictive use of models enables propositions (other people's models) to be tested for *philosophical* compatibility, e.g. a proposal for a *process* which may have effects which are not immediately apparent, or may *consume* excessive resources in relation to assumed benefits, and so on. *Knowledge* of *process* is essential for understanding and criticising propositions; the ability to construct parallel models is essential for the criticism of *grey* and propagation of *green*.

Every *philosophy* develops descriptive models of its extremes of understanding, of cosmology and *consciousness*, the understanding of the *universe* without and self within. While seeking these extremes, the *green* focus tends to be on *life*, the phenomenon which unites the *diversity* of both. As a *life-centred* reflection they will encompass areas of 'not known' which may persist indefinitely, since it is unlikely that we will ever know everything.

The *process* of modelling, then, is essential for the *future*. It falls into three parts: a critical examination of those models we have absorbed from *grey culture*, generally under the headings of 'the way things are' and 'what is/is not possible'. Then for a *sustainable future* we *need* models of what is there in the *biosphere*, and how it works, understanding of its *processes*, and beyond *life*, in the *universe* and everything, to the totality of our *existence*. We may then go on to build on to our models of *sustainable cycles* and *life processes*, human *extensions*, things and ways of *life* which are compatible with *whole* (see **morph mapping**).

Relationships   **perception, philosophy, culture**.

See also   **mindset, meme**.

References

See Colin Johnson, 1991, *The Green Bible: Creating Sustainable Ways of Life of Birth*, Thorsons, London.

MONKEYWRENCHING   Of monkeywrench, a large wrench with adjustable jaws, usually known as Stillsons in Britain. A (mainly USA) successor to sabotage, the dropping of a wooden shoe (French 'sabot'), into the machinery, and the traditional British 'spanner in the works'.

The concept was inflated in this generation's green *consciousness* by Edward Abbey in *The Monkey Wrench Gang*[1], which described the property destruction rampage of ecoguerrillas through the American west. The present movement for such tactics is centred around the American journal *Earth First!*[2] 'No compromise in the defense of Mother Earth!'.

The concept of violent destruction is of dubious validity, even against inanimate property. Faith in the *future* may indicate that much of it should be *recycled* for better use. If something is actively harmful, such as a radioactive *waste* outlet, the question becomes more complex; once *created* such *waste* will *exist* somewhere; plugging the pipe will not *change* that.

Relationships   **means.**

See also   **philosophy.**

References

1 Edward Abbey, 1975, *The Monkey Wrench Gang*.
2 *Earth First!*, PO Box 5871, Tuscon, Arizona 85703, USA.

MORAL   Value concerned with goodness or badness of character, behaviour, *choice*, or with the distinction between right and wrong in *choices* or behaviour.

MORALITY   Particular *system* of morals; degree of conformity to moral *values*; assumed *system* of normal *values*.

In *grey culture* morality, driven by religious dogma, has become focused obsessively upon sexual behaviour. In this area norms are generally related to *limited* sexual expression within a heterosexual licensed context. The fact that this does not match the reality of people's behaviour is a perpetual source of conflict, guilt, hypocrisy and frustration (see **institution**).

Beyond sexuality, morality is expressed in *exclusive* terms – things are either good or bad. Reality, however, is rarely so obliging; few things are either wholly good or totally bad, most things have a variable mix of both depending upon context, use and our *perception* of them. Moralists are frequently on a reality avoidance course; the option of purity or perfection may simply be a way of avoiding difficult *choices*, or compromise, or of upping the stakes. Similarly, regarding something as evil or unacceptable may simply be a means of dismissing it and avoiding the painful mental *processes* necessary to come to terms with things.

For *greens* morality is a matter of total *life ethics*. It involves honouring the *life contract*, being consistent and *honest*, and requires expressing *values* and *choices* which enhance *life* rather than degrade it.

Being moral in this sense is not a matter of dismissing 'bad' things, nor does it allow a refuge from reality in perfection; rather it involves *positive confrontation* with all the factors of *life*, and resolving the pain of the necessary compromises. That is not to say that anything is acceptable, but that the *limits* of the compromise must be clearly defined in terms of *values* which rely on sound *principles*, which in their turn are derived from a *consciously* considered *philosophy*.

To come to terms with a personal morality we must be prepared to think the unthinkable. Personal *freedom exists* between the *limits* set by our concepts of good and bad, of the acceptable and the unacceptable. Our *relationships* with others and our social behaviour will reflect the compatibility of our views with those of others, the agreement on the *choices* we make from the options available to us. Since these views are important, and differences inevitable, the *social structure* of *life* in a *diversity* of *communities*, each with their own different emphasis of *values*, would provide a variety of *ways of life* from which individuals could select.

Thus *greens* seek a morality based upon a common *philosophy*, but expressed in terms of *free choice*. An imposed morality requires arbitrary enforcement by *authority* and is *unsustainable*; a morality of *free choice* is *self-sustaining*.

<u>Relationships</u>   **freedom, choice, human nature, community, philosophy**.

<u>See also</u>   **institutions, mindset**.

MORPH MAPPING (see **morphology**)   A comprehensive descriptive model of the interactions of all forms of life, their *cycles* and *processes*, within the context of those of the *Gaian whole*.

A means of understanding the totality of *life*.

MORPHOLOGY   Study of the form of things; in biology, study of the form of animals and plants; in philology the study of the form of words and the system of form in a language.

The definition given in *The Encyclopaedia Britannica* includes the following elements: of the relationships within the structure of forms; to describe the function related to form. Morphology encompasses the study of biological structures over a tremendous scale, from the molecular to the macroscopic.

The key to the *evolving* use of the concept is in its basic meaning, that of shape or form.

In this sense morphology can mean the shape or form of anything. But when used to describe living things, with the idea of *function* linked to form, then morphology becomes a descriptive tool of the *dynamics* of the *whole*, whether of a cell, *being* or species, and their respective *life processes*. Since all *life* is connected, the morphologies of all forms of *life* may be linked until eventually the *whole* morphology of *life*, with its *matrix* of interactions, may be described (see **morph mapping**).

We presently have no adequate means of describing the morphology of various forms of *existence*, although we may be aware of particular expressions, e.g. when the morphology of mice is expressed in our house, or that of moles in the lawn. The science urgently needs development to fulfil the *potential* of the concept for the *future*. Morphology describes the results of *ecological processes*; when its *potential* is fulfilled it will become the descriptive science of *existence*.

Like many concepts vital for our understanding in the *future*, morphology has impeccable credentials from the past. As Charles Darwin put it:

> We have seen that members of the same class, independently of their habits of life, resemble each other in the general plan of their organisation ... The whole subject is included under the general terms of Morphology. This is one of the most interesting departments of natural history, and may almost be said to be its very soul.[1]

It was perhaps predictable that under the aegis of *reductionist philosophy*, natural history, along with much else *projected* by that *philosophy*, would lose its soul.

Greens intuitively know that when *knowledge* loses its *spiritual* content it is reduced to *information*, and loses any chance of becoming *wisdom*. It is crucial that the soul be restored to *life* sciences, that they be redirected away from *exploitation*, and directed towards understanding of the total *life* context. The *tools* are available; they are based on *green values* – of *synthesis* rather than analysis, of *dynamics* rather than statics, in general of the *principles* of *holism* rather than *reductionism*.

The concept of morphology offers a total *change* in the way we understand and relate to other *living* things. It also gives a different dimension of our understanding of our own species, the *dynamics* of our *lives* and the interaction of our species with others, and ultimately a different *perception* of our place in the *Gaian whole*.

With detailed interactive *models* of the morphology of all *life*, we will have access to *dynamic* predictions of the effects of human actions upon the *biosphere*, in detail and on the *whole*. With such *models* we will be able to fulfil our role in the *restoration* of what remains of the *biosphere*, now and, as *stewards* of its *dynamic balance*, into the *future*.

Thus morphology is a concept which embraces all expressions of *life*. Again, Darwin outlined its earliest concerns:

> What can be more curious than that the hand of a man, formed for grasping, that of a mole for digging, the leg of the horse, the paddle of the porpoise, and the wing of the bat, should all be constructed on the same pattern, and should include similar bones, in the same relative positions?[1]

Many of these questions have been partially answered by the science of *genetics*, but *genes* of themselves do not provide the whole answer. However, inquiry into the arrays of proteins ordered by the *genes* takes us further; protein molecules are characterised by their *inherent* property of bundling themselves up into complex shapes (see MORPHOGENESIS). At the other extreme, *environmental* influence, with its *dynamic matrix* of interacting factors, provides the final morphology of all planetary *existence*.

Thus as a *life* science morphology has the *potential* to describe the *dynamics* of *existence* at all levels from the molecular to that of the *Gaian whole*. For example, the shape of the *green* vision of human *life* in *communities*, each a part of a *global matrix* from which *networks* of interest may be selected and *federations* formed, is clearly a different morphology for that of the present *chaos* of *institutional* nation states competing for *resources*, permanently on the brink of *war* and heading nowhere, either through *inherent unsustainability* or genocide.

The scope of morphology means it may clarify things such as the mechanisms of *creation* and *evolution*, both descriptively and predictively. Beyond *life* it may be used in the same way for physical phenomena, and within *life* to describe the shape and *relationships* of concepts. In a development from its base in philology, morphology may be moved from the *structure* of words to the *structure* of their meanings. This presents us with the possibility of mapping the *structure* of thoughts, and possibly of thought, and thus assisting our *evolution*.

Morphology has recently been given a modern context by the work of Rupert Sheldrake and his hypothesis of *formative causation*.[2] In this it has been both *extended* and resolved under various sub-headings, as follows.

MORPHIC FIELD   The concept of morphic fields derives from the proposition of formative causation (see **formative causation**).

Formative causation holds that once something has happened in a certain way it will tend to happen that way again. An *event* tends to result from and reinforce a *process*; the more any *process* is repeated the more habitual it becomes, whether it involves *events* in human society, the formation of stars, or the behaviour of sub-atomic particles. *Process* and *event* project the morphology of the form of *existence* they *created.* *Energy* will transform into matter and vice versa in the same ways, crystals adopt the same form, and the cosmos probably *cycles* through time and dimensions in a habitual sequence. *Life* habitually reproduces in the same way. Yet we know *changes* occur; *processes* are not infallible, habit is not immutable, everything is subject to *evolution,* to changes in its morphology.

Formative causation holds that, in an *evolving universe,* every-thing *evolves.* As Sheldrake[2] points out, even what we popularly regard as the immutable laws of physics with their '*universal*' constants are subject to *evolution.* Yet if *creation* is not governed by absolute laws, we must hypothesise a guiding force which both maintains continuity, containing habit, yet allows *change.*

In *formative causation* it is proposed that the *nature* of things depends upon morphic fields. Like the known fields of physics (e.g. electro-magnetic, gravitational), morphic fields are non-material fields of influence *extending* in space and time. Every *system of existence* has a morphic field describing the shape and *nature* of its *existence.* When a state of *existence changes* in response to an alteration of *energy* pattern within its *system,* the organising field *changes.* It may become another field, be incorporated in a larger field, or form a composite of many interacting fields. Compositing fields, that is producing increased complexity, is typical of all *life forms* and their *extensions.*

Morphic fields guide the *processes* of *systems,* and describe the *limits* of the *potential* of form. Yet within many forms *exists* the *potential* for further forms to emerge as part of the *evolutionary process.* Morphic fields express the *dynamic* properties of memory, *relationship* and communication of the *systems* they describe. Memory within a morphic field is cumulative, which is why all things tend to become increasingly habitual through repetition. This phenomenon implies the property of *anticipation* in *systems.* All *existence anticipates,* that is to say expects, other similar forms of *existence,* that is, of things with similar morphic fields. The greater the similarity, the greater the *anticipation*; nothing *exists* in isolation. It is within this capacity that the paradox of *change* within *stability* arises. When the degree of *anticipation* includes the unusual and then, in the random probability of things, this arises, then *change* in the form of the unusual may occur. The property of *anticipation* is particulary relevant to the possibility of human *evolution* and the *creation* of a *sustainable future*. Is our morphic field, or its *potential*, up to the task?

MORPHIC POTENTIAL   The capacity between morphic fields for combination with other fields, and/or for extending further fields.

Relationships between morphic fields are a matter of *universal* experience. They produce the form/*function relationship* observed in *nature*; the more closely the morphology of an organism matches its *vital functions* within the *environment*, the more successful the organism will be. Field compatibility may be expressed as the morphic potential of any *system*. Carbon atoms have a high potential to form *relationships* by merging their fields with many others to form, among other things, the molecules upon which *life* is based.

Morphic potential may be expressed in the *creation* of entirely new fields, allowing for the emergence of new forms of *existence* outside the habitual. The precursor of an *evolutionary* step may be seen as the circumstances which stimulate the emergence of new morphic fields. For example *green philosophy*, stimulated by the predicament of the planet, emerges as a new field of thought (see **spontaneity**).

In Taoism it is held that there is a 'way of unfolding' which is *inherent* in all things.

MORPHIC RESONANCE   Morphic fields and their *potential* are both expressions of *existence* and the means whereby *existence* facilitates its expressions. They *extend* the *anticipation* of *existence*, that there will be other, similar, *existence*, as well as having the potential to *extend existence* into new *forms* and new arrangements. These properties imply some means of communication.

The proposition within the theory of *formative causation* is that there is communication between morphic fields by morphic resonance. Thus involves the transmission of *formative causal* influences, of morphic fields and *potential*, through *time* and space. It allows the cumulative memory of *past* habits, interfield *information* exchange and *anticipatory* sensing of *future* options, to be spread among like and compatible fields. Experimental observations which confirm these properties include the long-term study of learning rates in different rat colonies around the world, and the propagation of fashion ideas in human society (see **memes**).

The finding of the rat experiments is that the more rats learn a particular task, the quicker other rats learn the same task, even when thousands of miles apart and separated by several generations. The rat morphology had been modified by the learning *process*; its field had *changed*, and the modified field had emerged as part of *future* rat *nature*. The phenomenon of fashion, where the same new style appears in different parts of the world simultaneously,[3] has also been observed in other fields of invention and investigated inconclusively for industrial espionage because of the large amounts of money involved.

MORPHIC SHIFT (see **shift**)   A *change* in form and related *function* of a *system* or organism. Emergence of new way of living, shape of *existence*.

The human species is undergoing morphic shifts at decreasing *time* intervals. For the first two million or so years since the emergence of the *homo* form, human morphology was expressed in the gatherer/hunter *way of life*. Around 20,000 years ago a morphic shift occurred as humanity settled to agriculture. Roughly 2,000 years ago the urban *way of life* was established, with a further shift. Two hundred years ago the *fossil energy*-based *Industrial Revolution* transformed the world, and in the 1960s computers and cybernetics began to *change* society. The morphology of each form of *social organisation* has developed from the previous form, producing a complex unfolding morphology which, while *extending* a new dimension, may include many previous elements in a variety of mixes and influences in the everyday lives of individuals.

MORPHO-DYNAMICS (see **morphic shift**)   A description of the *process* of *change* from one form to another.

MORPHOGENESIS   During recent *socio-cultural evolution* human *genes* have remained the same. Yet the most profound *changes* have occurred against this static *genetic* background. The dominant *changes* in our *way of life*, and the forms we have *projected* into the world, are attributed to morphogenesis. This is the *potential inherent* in a form to *extend* itself or to be *extended*. It is the most novel of the various areas of morphology and requires more consideration (see **extension**).

RELEVANCE OF MORPHOLOGY   Morphology enables us to describe the shape and *dynamics* of *existence* in all of its manifestations.

This is particularly important for complex *living systems* which, if they are to *sustain* themselves, must achieve or be maintained in a *dynamic state* of *balance*.

There are embryos of the techniques envisaged in the diagrammatic representation of *human life dynamics*. These should be developed, with computer and artificial intelligence *models*, with the objective of achieving an *anticipatory model* of the *Gaian whole*. Again there is an embryo of the *process* in the *models* used to predict weather and seismological *events*.

With such *tools*, humans would be in a position to judge the effects of proposals for *processes* or *resource use*, in the fullest possible understanding of every factor involved. Morphology, and its various related areas of descriptive *dynamic* science, is not only essential for global *stewardship* in the long term, but also for *restoration* of the remaining *biosphere*.

At present it is possible to use the terminology of morphology to understand the *global predicament*, especially the human role as both generator and victim of the *problem*. The morphology of *terminal culture* is characterised by *compression* caused by excessive human *numbers*; the *natural balanced* state of humanity within the *biosphere* has been distorted, the *disruption* so caused resulting in chronic ill-*health* among populations of developed nations. The successive morphic shifts we have experienced have brought us to the point where we confront ultimate *limits*: those of the very *nature* of the *biosphere* of which we are still an integral dependent part. In further *extending* ourselves, via *institutional* forms and *structures*, we project the *dynamics* of *terminality*. The *choice* we confront on the edge of *terminality* is either to *extend* ourselves beyond the capacity of *life* as a *whole* into a *catastrophic sink* which may amount to *extinction*, or to re-design our morphology so that it has a *sustainable* form which is compatible with that of the *Gaian whole*.

The morphology of concepts is important for the *future* because the development of a *green philosophy* and *culture* is a matter of what happens in our heads. *Changing* the way enough of our species thinks may spread *sustainable memes* through morphic resonance, *creating* an inner *matrix* of thought which will project *sustainable ways of living* throughout our species. *Culture* is that which is repeated; it is also that which is believed.

One implication of *formative causation* is that the possibility for *change* is severely restricted. However in an *evolutionary* and unfolding *universe* it may be proposed, since our *socio-cultural evolution* provides examples, that there is a morphological script of *existence* similar to the *genetic* script in biological *life*. The irresistible force of an idea whose time has come is derived from its compatibility with the morphic script; it appears at the right time and place. The unfolding morphology of the human species within that of its planetary context may be bringing us to an age of *balance*, of *sustainability*. Our *anticipation* of such an age may help *create* it; our *conscious choices* will consolidate that *anticipation*. If human *life* is significantly different from any other it is because it can appreciate its situation and act to *change* it.

As Darwin put it, and it is worth repeating although the context was different, 'The whole subject is included under the general term of Morphology. This is one of the most interesting departments of natural history, and may almost be said to be its very soul.'[1] It may be that the possibilities of morphology have been ignored by *grey culture* because it seeks to deny the proposition of soul to everything except man. The exploration of a science of *life* which itself has the property is likely to reveal what *greens* know *intuitively*, that among all *life* what there is in common is immeasurably greater than any differences which may divide it.

<u>Relationships</u>   **life, dynamics, ecology, existence, balance, Gaia.**
<u>See also</u>   **extension, institution, limits.**
<u>References</u>

1 Charles Robert Darwin (1809–1892), 1859, *The Origin of Species By Means of Natural Selection*, Penguin, London.
2 Rupert Sheldrake, 1983, *A New Science of Life: The Hypothesis of Formative Causation*, Granada, London.
3 Fashion designer Katherine Hamnett gave me the example of a design of 'a ridiculous pair of trousers'. She was absent-mindedly sketching one day and produced a design for a totally unmarketable pair of trousers. She forgot about it until some months later she was looking at the design sketches of an Italian designer, when she was amazed to find a sketch identical to hers. On checking she was even more surprised to find that the identical ridiculous designs had been produced at around the same time, several thousand miles apart.

See David Bohm, 1980, *Wholeness and the Implicate Order*, Routledge & Kegan Paul, London; and George Spencer Brown, 1969, *Laws of Form*, George Allen & Unwin, London.

MOTHER EARTH (see **Gaia**)   A concept that recognises the fact that we derive from the *earth*. Perhaps in view of the essential *nature* of water to *life* we should think of Mother Sea.

Some *greens* tend to emphasise the mother aspect and discount the essential *earth*-ness. The concept of Mother Earth is embraced as if the planet were an ever-open welcoming refuge with a particularly warmhearted response for humans: 'You can throw yourself flat on the ground, stretched out upon Mother Earth, with certain conviction that you are one with her and she with you.'[1] The rosy glow could be dispelled if you try it on ground occupied by ants or wasps. Alternatively, the re-integration could be complete if you were moved to express the urge in the fast lane.

References

1 Erwin Schrödinger, 1964, in Alan Watts, 1973, quoted in John Button, 1988, *A Dictionary of Great Ideas: Vocabulary for a Sane and Sustainable Future*, Routledge & Kegan Paul, London.

MOTIVE Tending to initiate movement, concerned with movement; that which induces a person to act, such as fear, desire, circumstances, etc.

MOTIVATION The need to express a motive. Force resulting in emergence of *inherent potential* under particular circumstances; as in the *evolution* of *life*, form of *existence*.

The basic motivation in *existence* is for matter to seek *stability*, and for *energy* to diffuse through *entropy*. *Life*, through *synergy* between *energy* and matter, is motivated to *survive* and, beyond that, to seek immortality.

Greens believe that *life* must be seen as a *whole* and its motivation resides in a shared purpose within a shared *environment*. The implication is that expressions of *potentials* are governed by the likely effects of one expression upon others, particularly of those of one species on others. Humans therefore need to understand their motivations, to explore the logic of *existence*, and accept the problems of *choices* which will be revealed. We cannot proceed blindly; that is the route to *terminality*. Being human involves making *conscious choices*.

Relationships **rights, morality, sustainability**.

See also **agenda, institutions**.

MULTINATIONAL (see **institution**) Large business corporation whose activities extend across national boundaries; aka international corporation, multinational company or corporation, transnational company or corporation.

Multinationals tend to use the differences between national *laws* and circumstances to enhance their profitability, for example by setting up *polluting-process* subsidiaries where controls are lax, buying where commodities or labour are cheap, and selling products where incomes are high. It is because they wish to manipulate these factors to their advantage that such businesses, and the *political systems* they support, favour 'free' trade and the GATT (General Agreement on Trade and Tariffs) *process.*

MURPHY'S LAW   'If anything can go wrong, it will.' Regrettable omission from technical *education*, particularly in the *nuclear* industry.

MUTUALITY   The expression of compatibility of purpose, form, feeling, desire, etc.

Green belief in *co-operation* rather than *competition* is founded on the mutuality of human *needs* and purpose; *greens* see mutual aid as the best *means* of their fulfilment.

The classic statement, produced in opposition to the popularisation of Darwin's theory of *evolution* as 'the survival of the fittest', is Kropotkin's *mutual aid*,[1] which holds that in human affairs, and those of *life* generally if not the *whole* of *existence, co-operation*, mutuality and altruism are far more important and effective factors in *survival.*

Relationships   **co-operation, dynamics.**

See also   **limits, finite resources.**

References

1 Prince Petr (Peter) Kropotkin (1842–1912), 1902, *Mutual Aid: A Factor in Evolution*, undated edition by Extending Horizons Books, Boston, USA.

MYTH   Traditional account of events, usually involving supernatural factors and characters; embodiment of popular ideas, wisdom, etc., of natural or social phenomena.

The repeated myths of a society form their earliest *culture.* In modern *culture*, institutions actively seek control by myth appropriation. In totalitarian states history, *cultural mythology*, is rewritten to suit the *cultural* form the heads of the *institutions* wish to project. In more open societies the behaviour is less blatant; for example, in the case of the night people from east and west Berlin danced around the Brandenberg Gate, and the 'official' opening *event* some weeks later, which will history record?

In myth appropriation the actions of people are discounted in favour of those of the *institutions*, unless an individual can be *institutionalised* by the myth. Take for example the inventor of the compression ignition engine. Everyone who plays Trivial Pursuit knows it was invented by Herr Dr Diesel. Wrong. The diesel engine is a prime example of myth appropriation. Dr Diesel was actually trying to make an engine that would run on coal dust (fine carbon suspended in compressed air). The compression ignition engine was invented by a chap called Herbert Ackroyd Stuart, who produced 'diesel' engines in 1892. This predated Dr Diesel's work by some five years. Although Vickers in Barrow-in-Furness used a troublesome (it tended to explode) oil engine developed by Dr Diesel in submarines during the 1914–18 war, the essential features which we associate with the modern high-speed diesel engine were all Ackroyd's. Unfortunately, although the world might have lived with 'The Ackroyd Engine' (even buying gallons of Ackroyd), because he called his engine the Cold Start Solid Injection Compression-Ignition Engine (CSSIC-IE) he didn't stand a chance. Diesel's engine was cleaned up, lightened, and given to the world as 'the diesel'.[1]

Herbert Ackroyd Stuart's request to the Institute of Mechanical Engineers in 1923 that the word 'diesel' be dropped from the description of such engines was rejected – the myth was already established. He retired to Australia where he died a disappointed man. In his will, he directed that all his papers be burned.

Institutional myth appropriation is important because it *changes culture* and denies human reality.

<u>Relationships</u>   **culture, institutions**.

<u>See also</u>   **information, education**.

<u>References</u>

1 I am indebted to William Melville, F.I.Mech.E., for the Ackroyd Stuart story, based upon a paper by Rex Wailes, The Newcomen Society, May 1977. Any errors in abbreviation or detail are mine.

NATIVE PEOPLE   Native: local inhabitant; derogatory as: member of non-European or less civilised indigenous people.

Greens have to some degree used the term 'native people' to describe long-term inhabitants of particular *bioregions*. However, because the word 'native' has been given inferior or derogatory connotations, the term should be dropped in favour of the more positive 'natural people', as in the *natural people* of Australia, or the *natural people* of the Sioux nation (see **natural people**).

NATURAL (see **nature, human nature**)   Existing in or by *nature*, not *artificial*; innate, inherent; uncultivated.

Humans and their acts have become so divorced from the natural world that the only safe definition of what is natural may be that which occurs without human influence. If this is rigorously applied very little *exists* in its virgin natural state. Human activity has reduced 'natural' to a relative proposition.

The term has been perverted in many ways by *grey culture*; by use as a description of something *inherently* good, or better, as in 'natural *health care*', 'natural skin cream'. Not everything that is natural is good, either of itself or in the *quantities* encountered; ask any rattlesnake or remember the last time you had flu. Natural is also a matter of context. 'Natural' has become used to give almost anything a *market* edge, so much so that we have to define separately those things with which we have interfered least, e.g. '*organically* grown': no added yuk, etc. Natural is also used as a cop-out, a means of avoiding *responsibility* and/or *choice*, as 'It's only natural' (like stupid or destructive behaviour or *nuclear fission*), or *myths* of *culture*, like 'natural population *growth*', or 'natural rates of unemployment'.

Natural is a concept which requires recapturing. For *greens* the concept of natural is most important in consideration of the *processes* by which we live. The most fundamental natural characteristic is that it is a *process inherent* in the *environment* or a part of it. As such it is part of a *self-sustaining cycle*. *Living* within natural *limits* then requires adjusting human *ways of life* to fit within the capacities of such *sustainable cycles* (see **cycles, rights**).

Where humans modify natural *cycles*, as in agriculture, mining and refining, *creating artificial* substances, etc., this should be in the full *knowledge* of the effects of the *processes* involved, and their long-term effects. Such un-natural acts should also be subject to a discipline which is compatible with the overall objective of *sustainability* (see **restoration, numbers**).

The most important *function* of *green philosophy* is to provide both a guide to our intervention in natural *processes*, and a way out of our dependence on the un-natural and *unsustainable*.

NATURAL CHILDBIRTH   see **parenting**.

NATURAL PEOPLES   Preferable term to 'native' peoples.

A term used to describe long-term inhabitants of particular *bioregions*, as the natural people of Australia, or the natural people of the Sioux Nation, unless such groups make it known that they wish otherwise.

Natural people is preferred to the term '*native people*' because it does not carry derogatory connotations.

NATURAL SELECTION   see **evolution**.

Relationships   **Gaia, existence, sustainability, inherent**.

See also   **finite resources, feedback loops**.

NATURE (see **life**)   Innate quality of things, *existence*; the expression of such qualities.

Commonly thought of as the rest of *life*, the *environment*, wildlife, the physical *dynamics* of the *environment*, as weather, the oceans, etc.

A more *inclusive* definition of nature is the expression of the *infinite potential* of *existence*. 'Perhaps we have to spend more time listening to the music of nature.'[1]

Life and nature are sometimes seen as the same thing, yet nature, as the *inherent* properties of *existence*, obviously has many sub-divisions, of which *life* is one. Within the cosmic – the nature of all *existence* – local nature can be divided into two spheres of particular interest: that of the *global* natural; and the superimposed nature of humans.

Human nature has, literally, become dominant. From our position as part of the natural scheme of things our influence has become universal, our destructive ways a threat to the rest of nature.

Taken in its entirety, the increase in mankind's strength has bought about a decisive, many-sided shift in the balance of strength between man and the earth. Nature, once a harsh and feared master, now lies in subjection, and needs protection against man's powers. Yet because man, no matter what intellectual heights he may scale, remains embedded in nature, the balance has shifted against him, too, and the threat that he poses to the earth is a threat to him as well.[2]

Our view of the natural world and its importance is undergoing a *shift*. We are moving from the view of nature as something repugnant, perpetually red in tooth and claw, to be avoided by acts of civilisation, towards the realisation of dependence, of recognition of the need for *integrity* within the *Gaian whole*.

Greens seek to accelerate this conceptual *shift* as part of the reintegration of our species with nature.

HUMAN NATURE   When proto-humans left the shrinking forests and stood up in the emerging savannah (substituting terrestial bipedialism for arborial brachiation – walking rather than swinging in the trees – as the specialists put it), the human course for divorce from nature was set. Becoming upright produced a less efficient way of moving which generated more heat; we lost our fur (and probably initiated the exaggerated sexual *dynamics* of our species). In resorting to *clothing* we assisted the *process* of *extending* ourselves. Our expansion from sub-tropical to temperate climatic zones depended upon further *extension* of our abilities; when humans began to use fire, and eventually developed agriculture, our domination of nature was well under way (see **extension**).

What can we say of our nature? As a crude indicator of the influences which have shaped our nature, the numerical picture is clear:

of the estimated 80 billion people who have ever lived out a life span on earth, over 90 per cent have lived as hunter gatherers; about 6 per cent have lived by agriculture and the remaining few per cent (and that in spite of the current population explosion) have lived in industrial societies.[3]

The numerical picture has to be viewed against the *compression* of time; the 90 per cent were spread over 2 to 3 million years; 6 per cent as agriculturists over 20,000; while the industrial age has occupied the last 200 years of the human story.

The *changes* in our *ways of life* have been accompanied by *changes* in *life structure.* From our biological foundation, *social, cultural* and *institutional structures* have successively emerged. The complex *whole* has a *synergy* which leaves individuals feeling isolated, powerless, bereft of confidence, lacking understanding of human nature in relation to the *existence* they experience.

The conventional discussion of the nature of humans divides into two broad streams: those who believe it is deterministic,[4] that is whatever we are and do is derived from influences largely outside our control, such as *genes* or deities (we are what we are); and those who see humans as creatures determined by will, *creating* human *morphology* by *choice* and *conscious* influence (we are what we think).

As is frequently the case with the analyses produced by *grey culture,* both positions bear some truth, yet miss much. Human nature is a compound of all the influences of our *evolution.* It arises from the instinctive, ranging from those influences deeply embedded in our *genetic* core to the *nurturing dynamics* of the *culture* in which we in our turn find ourselves embedded. Much may be predetermined – all those processes which our nature *anticipates,* from the *relationships* of *form* and *function,* from the molecular to the interaction with others of our species. But much more is not, and remains in the realm of our will.

Whatever else we may be, we are highly adaptive. Like many other aspects of our nature, this has both good and bad sides. The good is obvious; we have learned to survive in all *environments* of the planet, and can tolerate a wide range of conditions. The bad is that we too easily accept the conditions in which we find ourselves. A generation born in squalor or poverty, or under other unsatisfactory conditions, accepts those conditions as the norm; our *morphology shifts* readily so that we change to accommodate the unacceptable. We have yet to define conditions for human *life* in relation to the planetary whole; the *green* debate is about creating such conditions.[5]

The contradictions *inherent* in the human condition lie in the perpetual battle with ourselves. Because there is no clear definition between determined and wilful behaviour, and the mixture is volatile, we experience the extreme expression of our nature, of that of which we are capable. Hence the *need* for taboos, morals and *ethics.* These may be seen as attempts to hold the line between the resurgence of the worst aspects of deterministic behaviour and the expression of our higher (human) *values.*

Our nature presents us with a *potential problem* in seeking conscious *evolution* into the *future*. It is not a new *problem*, predictably perhaps it is the oldest *problem* – coming to terms with the extremes of good and bad in our nature. If the conic *model* of *evolution* is accepted, then the *creation* or emergence of a successive larger area of *consciousness* in the *future* will have the effect of amplifying those past layers of our *evolutionary* make-up. How far the *future* is coupled to our *past* is *unknown*, but expanding *consciousness* will inevitably increase our capacity for good and bad. Unless we *anticipate* and allow for this, we will simply amplify our expression of *problems* as well as answers, achieving the same *imbalance* but at a more intense level of expression.

Our *future* lies in coming to terms with the primitive residues of our nature, for they will never leave us, and our acts may serve to *extend* their *potential*. At the same time we must understand the nature of our present *terminal dynamics* and seek to reverse them.

We must go head first into the *future*, accepting the challenges and hazards of *conscious evolution*, rather than attempt to modify aspects of the *past*. We can choose what we emphasise; we can provide for animal expressions while increasing our focus on *nurture*, but for this to be successful we must construct appropriate *cultural structures* which meet all the *needs* of our nature without the expression of those *needs* harming the nature of other *life* or its *environment* (see **needs**). To paraphrase Martin Luther King,[6] our objective must be 'a species at peace with itself, a species that can take its natural place in a world at peace with its own destiny'.

To summarise: human nature and nature per se demand a mechanism of *interrelationship* which allows for the complexity and *needs* of both. We are different, and we must contain that which is specifically human so that it may fit within the greater sphere of *nature*, whose wider yet less flexible *limits* we must observe. Understanding the *structure* of nature as a *whole* is fundamental to the *future*, for it is this *structure* which will carry us to eternity, not that of human *extended institutions*. We have to break out of the double-bind we have initiated, break out of the human/*institutional cul-de-sac*, and break back into *sustainable* nature.

The successive *shifts* involved in our changing nature, from gatherer/hunters to cybernetic technologists, have progressively *extended* our species beyond the natural world. Our *extension* of *institutional forms* means in effect that we have become involved in a sort of double double-cross takeover bid in our *relationship* with the rest of nature (see **morphology, institution**).

Nature has naturally reacted to the *processes* we have initiated. The *changing* climate, resurgence of infectious disease, and other *symptoms* of *terminality*, may be seen as nature giving humanity, if not all mammalian *forms* of *life*, the yellow card, preparatory to sending them off as a mistake in the overall *evolutionary* scheme of things.

(In discussing human nature I have generalised, rather than distinguished between male and female. The differences between the sexes of our species are discussed under **sexual dimorphism**.)

Relationships   life, **culture, evolution**.

See also   **consciousness, inherent, potential**.

References

1 An anonymous US tax attorney, remarking on the case of American recluse Elmer Clegg, 'discovered' living in his woods with animals and no 'essential' modern services 30 miles from Dallas, Texas.

2 Jonathan Schell, 1982, *The Fate of the Earth*, Picador, London.

3 Robert Prescott-Allen, quoted by Edward Goldsmith in *The Ecologist*, Volume 20, Number 4, July/August 1990. *The Ecologist*, Worthyvale Manor, Camelford, Cornwall PL32 9TT, England.

4 See Edward O. Wilson, 1975, *Sociobiology: The New Synthesis*, for a recent expression of the ideas of biological determinism; also 1978, *On Human Nature*, Harvard University Press, Cambridge, Massachusetts, USA, and 1981, *Genes, Mind and Culture*; Charles J. Lumsden, 1983, *Promethean Fire*, Harvard University Press, Cambridge, Massachusetts, USA.

5 See Colin Johnson, 1991, *The Green Bible: Creating Sustainable Life on Earth*, Thorsons, London.

6 Martin Luther King (1929–68), speech after the successful black civil rights march from Selma to Montgomery, Alabama, in the south of the USA, in the early 1960s. King said 'people'; I have substituted 'species'.

NEED (also **necessity**, see **vital need**)   Circumstance requiring action for fulfilment.

Human needs are a complex reflection of *human nature*. Basic physical needs are straightforward; humans need *food*, clean water, unpolluted air, shelter and *love* (which may be equated with care) (see **health**).

All of these are necessary if we are to survive and fulfil our *potential. Terminal culture* is progressively *disrupting* each of these basic necessities: the *food networks* are being taken apart and poisoned; water is increasingly *polluted*; air is contaminated (this is particularly important because, whereas we have defences against some *polluted* food and water, no *life* form has *evolved* to cope with *polluted* air); the homeless are increasing; and isolation is a universal fact of modern *life*.[1] We have created an *institutional social milieu* which is not good for people or other parts of the *biosphere*.

Human needs extend beyond the basics. We also need social *structures* which facilitate human *social* interactions and express our common *values*, while at the same time allowing space for solitude and differentiation of expression.

Creativity is also essential to humanity; it is part of our *spiritual* dimension and necessary to the fulfilment of our *potential.* Within *terminal culture* many people have their *creative* ability reduced to the production of order, to meaningless repetition; many more are inhibited by lack of fulfilment of their basic needs. Under these circumstances the common thread of *creativity* through *reproduction* survives. Indeed, the more *compressed* and desperate the situation, the more it seems to be expressed, as in population explosions in refugee camps. *Compression* and deprivation seem to *create* conditions which generate further *compression* and deprivation (see **compression**).

Greens seek to *create social structures* which both fulfil human needs and maintain *balance* within the *biosphere.* The focus on *life* in *community*, on *economics* which do not *consume* the *earth*, on human rather than *institutional relationships*, and on *values* and *ways of life* which are *inherently sustainable* rather than *catastrophically terminal* are, in themselves, the deepest expression of human needs combined with appreciation of the needs of all *life.*

Humanity needs to question the way all of our needs are fulfilled to ask, 'Is it *sustainable?*' and, 'Does it enhance all *life*?' The focus changes from human needs per se to the needs of humanity in *relation* to the *biosphere* and the *resources* of the planet. In this respect the basics are simple: we need to reduce human *numbers* drastically; to focus on *being* rather than having[2]; to reduce our *consumption* of *finite resources*; to stop *pollution* and eliminate *waste*; to maintain (restore) the integrity of the *food networks*; consciously to design human *communities* to meet human needs. It is no surprise that human needs and the needs of humanity in *relation* to the planet are more or less the same. In fulfilling both areas, only 'Yes' is the acceptable answer to both the above questions.

Beyond needs, our wants must be fulfilled within a *philosophical* framework which divides clearly the acceptable from the unacceptable.

<u>Relationships</u>   **rights, limits, potential**.
<u>See also</u>   **assumption, expectation**.

References

1 'Although more common and intense among teenagers, nevertheless one in four adults confessed to feeling very lonely or remote from other people', David Weeks, principal psychologist at the Royal Edinburgh Hospital, Scotland, reported in *Freedom*, Volume 51, Number 19, 6 October 1990, Freedom Press, Angel Alley, 84b Whitechapel High Street, London E1 7QX.
2 Eric Fromm (1900–80), 1976, *To Have Or To Be?* Harper & Row, New York.

NEGATIVE FEEDBACK (see **feedback loop**)   In cybernetics and *systems* theory negative feedback encourages *processes*. In *social/* group *dynamics* it is sometimes used the other way round.

NEO   see **new**.

NET ENERGY PRINCIPLE (aka **NEP**) Means of *energy* accounting in *system* or *process*. The amount of *energy* used or lost in making something or achieving a *purpose* is measured or calculated as a means of determining the most effective – that is, *energy efficient* – option. *Green* accounting will involve assessment of *energy* efficiency, *resource* depletion, *bio-assimilability* of by-products and end results, and possibly some *relationship* to a means of *exchange*, such as money, credit, etc. (see **energy**, **economy**).

NETWORK   Arrangement with intersecting lines and interstices similar to those of a net; complex interconnecting *system*, as of paths, roads, railways, or communications, etc., also of people or organisations with particular interests.

In the *green* sense networks are seen as a means of organising without *creating* permanent *power centres* or *instititutional hierarchies*. In fragmented *terminal culture*, networks of diffuse association have replaced active *social* life in *communities*; many people have a network of friends around the world while knowing little of their immediate neighbours.

Some *greens* place great faith in the network *principle*:

Networks are co-operative, not competitive. They are true grass roots: self-generating, self-organising, sometimes even self-destructing. They represent a process, a journey, not a frozen structure ... a network is both intimate and expansive ... Networks are the strategy by which small groups can transform an entire society.[1]

While networks may have those *potentials*, they can also be *exclusive*, self-perpetuating, a means of maintaining an inward-looking dogma. Networks are *tools* for *social* organisation; what those *tools* may be used for is not an *inherent* property of the *tool*. At best it may be more suitable for some things than others. A network is essentially a selection from the available *matrix* of options.

Relationships   **ad hoc, matrix, structure**.
See also   **federation, community, information**.
References
1 Marilyn Ferguson, 1982, *The Aquarian Conspiracy*, Granada, London.

NEW (also **neo-**)   Not existing before, the first, created, brought into *existence*, etc.; previously unknown. Also (*neo*) new, modern, later, revived.

The wider *green movement* is peppered with 'new' things, such as: new *economics*, new *games*, new international this and that, new left (a more traditional 'new'), new local *economic* order, new physics, new right (a new left), new settlers, etc. These are sometimes grouped under the generic nouveau heading of New Age.

'New' has inherent appeal, as washing powder manufacturers know; it is always more powerful, always more valued. The new appeal is a deeply embedded part of our psychology; from the birth of successors to our pursuit of immorality.

The problem with calling anything 'new' as part of its title, rather than merely as a current description of its status, is that it lacks perspective; everything ages and is superceded by another 'new'. The folly of the practice is very near to me. When the foliage dies down in winter the signs that a house once stood at the corner of one of our fields emerge; the gap in the hedge where the gate was set, the lines marking old stone walls and the eroded terraces of the small garden. This plot is fixed with the name 'Ty Newydd', Welsh for 'New House', because once it was. It was demolished nearly a century ago, yet it is fixed in perpetuity on maps and minds as 'new'.

Defining anything as new also means that it is inevitably compromised to some degree by comparison with the old, with that of the *past*. Few things are genuinely new in the sense of being original *creations*; if they are, they are usually marked by a description which in itself is new, as 'jet' rather than 'new aero engine'. Beware anything 'new' which cannot stand on its own.

NEW AGE   While describing the *future* as a new age may be valid, to call it the New Age is an error flavoured with a mixture of arrogance and smart marketing. Thus while Kirkpatrick Sale may reasonably speculate, 'It seems clear that future historians will mark a new age beginning somewhere within our lifetimes. The question is: what sort of new age will it be?'[1], to set out rules (and claim guardianship if not property in the *future*) is not. David Spangler seems to do both:

> Anyone who moves into such a consciousness [of planetary awareness] is stepping into a New Age. It doesn't matter whether they are living at Findhorn or whether they be anarchist, Baptist or Buddhist. If they seek to serve humanity in a way that we know inwardly will help the potential of humankind emerge, then essentially they have a grasp of what the New Age is.[2]

I am afraid on that basis I have no grasp of what a New Age may be. Unfortunately, such loose assertion of assumptive *values*, whether they be 'new' or otherwise, lay the *green movement* open to the justified charges from its opponents of woolly thinking, arrogance and *philosophical* incompetence. At best, expressions of 'New Age' manifestations seem to be necessary as an emotional cocoon from the realities of the passing age.

NEW AGE CONSPIRACY (aka AQUARIAN CONSPIRACY) The proposition that *environmental/ecological* concerns may be co-opted into a conspiracy of *grey culture* management *ethics* which see the *earth*, as in the *past*, as a resource for human exploitation. Followers of Teilhard de Chardin[3] and Buckminster Fuller[4] are held by some *deep ecologists* to uphold the appeal of *anthropo-centrism* (human-centredness) and the direction of a god in human affairs.

> Many New Age thinkers conclude that humans' role as partner with Earth's natural processes 'need not be vile' but co-equal.[5] The ultimate New Age fantasy is the metaphor of the spaceship Earth. Humans from spaceship Earth will move to totally man-made and manipulated spaceships carrying colonies of humans to Mars, and the expert – the technologist – will be the hero.[6]

Relationships   **past, future, hidden agenda**.
See also   **creation, change, formative causation**.
References

1 Kirkpatrick Sale, 1980, *Human Scale*, Secker & Warburg, London.
2 David Spangler, 1973, *The Laws of Manifestation*.

3 Teilhard de Chardin (1881–1955), see 1965, *The Phenomenon of Man*; and 1971, *Man's Place in Nature*, Fontana, London.
4 Buckminster Richard Fuller, aka Bucky Fuller (1895–1983), described himself as an 'explorer in comprehensive anticipation design', Works included *Ideas and Integrities: A Spontaneous Autobiographical Disclosure*, 1963 (see **synergy**).
5 James Lovelock, 1979, *Gaia: A New Look at Life on Earth*, Oxford University Press, Oxford, England, quoted in 6 below.
6 Bill Devall and George Sessions, 1985, *Deep Ecology: Living as if Nature Mattered*, Peregrine Smith Books, Salt Lake City, Utah, USA.

NON-   Prefix used to give negative sense.

The use of non-, in the sense of not doing something, has the regrettable effect of focusing attention on the thing which is not to be done. For example, 'non-violence' serves at best to convey an inhibition rather than to give a positive picture of other possibilities.

Examples of non-s used in the *green movement*, such as non-*competitive*, non-directive, non-intrusive, non-nuclear club, non-renewable, non-sexist, and non-violence (with its trail of sub-derivatives, -direct action, -intervention, -revolution), all serve inevitably to emphasise that which they oppose (see **thematic compatibility**).

NON-VIOLENCE (also NON-VIOLENT DIRECT ACTION, NVDA)   The rejection of the imposition of will by violence. A means of maintaining the moral imperative in conflict. (Can become morally dubious when used with the intention of provoking violence.) 'The ideally nonviolent state will be an ordered anarchy.'[1]

The essence for non-violent activists is that they are prepared to suffer, even be killed, rather than use violence in conflict. Seen as using good to overcome evil and as the expression of *moral* courage rather than force.

Non-violence as a *conscious choice* has been used most effectively in modern times by Mahatama Gandhi in ending the British rule of India (now Pakistan, India and Bangladesh), and by Martin Luther King and others in rejecting the *institutionalised* racism of the southern states of the USA.

The essence of NVDA is that it presents the opponent with a *choice*. The classic example comes from the anti-*nuclear* movement of the 1960s. The *nuclear* bomber is about to take off, the non-violent activist wishes to stop it. The options are to disable the plane, say by throwing yourself into an engine, or to sit in front of the wheels. Sitting in front is the correct (although possibly less immediately effective) means because it forces the pilot to make a *choice*; it places *moral responsibility* upon him. Disabling the plane imposes your will by denying his *choice*; nothing has *changed*, he will go and get another plane.

Forcing opponents to confront the reality of their *choice* is essential, whether it be of the judge to jail you, or the pollutor to poison you, or the executor to kill you. NVDA does have practical weaknesses in that it relies on the possibility of face-to-face confrontation, assumes minimal *institutional* contexts, and requires faith in the non-genocidal tendencies of fellow humans.

'Non-violence' suffers from negative emphasis. In my opinion it would serve better if it were described as '*positive confrontation*'.

For the future it is essential that positive, self-contained, descriptive terminology be used. Defining things in terms of that which is opposed prolongs the life of that which should be rejected: *co-operation* instead of non-competitive, *free* instead of non-directive and so on.

<u>Relationships</u>   **culture**, **mindset**, **affinity group**.
<u>See also</u>   **meme**, **new**.
<u>References</u>
1 Attributed to Mahatma Gandhi.

NUCLEAR   Of, relating to, a nucleus, the central part of a thing around which others form. Usually used in terms of atomic *energy*, the *energy* derived by changes in the nature of the atomic nucleus (see **energy**).

Greens reject the present use of nuclear *energy*, since it is based on the *hidden agenda* of the production of materials for use in nuclear weapons, while the problems of the production of long-term high-toxicity radioactive wastes have not been resolved. Whether these objections may be overcome in the *future* is an open *question* (see **pollution**).

NUCLEAR DETERRENCE   The theory that if everyone has nuclear weapons this will stop anyone using them; best described by its acronym MAD (mutually assured destruction). Critics point out that the nuclear deterrent has not upheld the *peace* since the end of the Second World War.

Proponents would no doubt say that if all these states had nuclear weapons the wars would not have happened.

NUCLEAR FASCINATION   All governments are attracted to nuclear weapons. Each desires its own thermo-nuclear virility symbol. The problem is that while the '*responsible*' states maintain that they have a perfect *right* to nuclear weapons, that *right* cannot be

Cartoon by Donald Rooum, Freedom Press, Angel Alley, 84b Whitechapel High Street, London E1 7QX.

denied to others. They are candles to *institutional* power-addicted moths.

There seems to be a universal fascination with nuclear *energy*. The number of times the totally familiar mushroom cloud appears on TV, in everything from documentaries to pop videos, indicates its primal attraction. It is as if we see in the release of fundamental *energy* our own genesis; we are star-stuff; the complex molecules of *life* were formed in the nuclear *processes* of failed stars. It is also as if we seek to *anticipate* our end, a nuclear nemesis, *created* by man under the hand of his gods; here beginning and end become one, and *life* is reduced once more to nuclear debris awaiting a new beginning.The logical outcome of *death-centred culture*.

Relationships   **energy, terminal culture**.

See also   **institutions, hierarchy**.

References

See Rosalie Bertell, 1985, *No Immediate Danger: Prognosis for a Radioactive Earth*, The Women's Press, London.

NUMBERS   Plural of number; symbol representing quantity in cumulative order, series, count, sum, aggregate, etc.

HUMAN NUMBERS   *Green* concern is with human numbers, the sum of the world population of our species.

Human numbers generate the *problems* which threaten all *life* on *earth*. However we try to wriggle around the equation, there are simply too many people. Even if we all demanded much less, it would still be too much for the *biosphere* to bear. The debate of the *problem* is significant for its almost universal absence on the current *grey agenda* and its muffled and confused appearance on the *green*.

At a celebration of the bi-centenary of the invasion of Australia (1789), the descendants of one convict couple came together. After seven generations there were 24,000 of them. Half the population of Australia is under 30; in many *Third World* countries the average age is under 20. When this stage of the population bomb detonates ...

In Washington, DC, at the corner of Connecticut Avenue and 18th Street, there was (may still be) a world population indicator. On the 21 April 1980, at 10.25 am, it read 4,509,075,595. Each minute another 114 was added to the total, representing the net increase when deaths were subtracted from births. Ten years earlier the net rate of increase shown on a similar machine in Philips Electrical's Euvalon[1] in Eindhoven, Netherlands, had been 60 per minute. So not only are human numbers rising rapidly, but the rate at which they are increasing is itself increasing (see **exponential growth**).

Now (October 1990) world population is estimated to be increasing at a net rate of 177 per minute (274 births minus 97 deaths). This means there are one million more humans every four days.[2]

These examples and numbers produce the most frightening and disastrous illustration of the human and *global* condition – the human population graph.

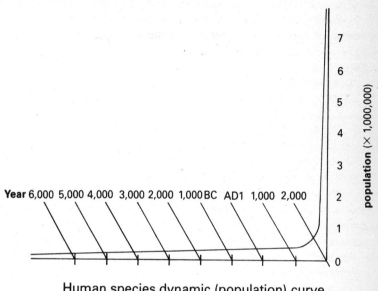

Human species dynamic (population) curve

The rate of increase of human numbers is so rapid that in many parts of the world it quickly destroys the local *environment*, initiating a total disruption of the supporting *ecosystem*. People caught up in these population brush fires either flee or die where they are. In the *Third World* over the course of the past century the demographic trap has been sprung on most traditional stable societies; while death rates have fallen dramatically, birth rates have not. It is totally erroneous to believe that falling child mortality can be equated with falling fertility or birth rates – there is a delay until other factors impose fresh *limits*; that is the nature of the trap.

The numbers trap is one that now embraces us all. Over-population affects every region of the *earth*; the west may not feel the trap while *institutional* conveyors import *food* and oil and export poverty and famine, but one hiccup at the oil wells or a bad harvest has noticeable effects everywhere.

All populations increase their numbers to some maximum; numbers constantly push the *limits*, while ingenuity seeks to expand those *limits*. This is the nature of our *progress*. Presently we seek to remove the *limits* imposed by *knowledge* of the *problem*; to seek any rational means which allows the 'humans good, there-fore more humans, better' equation to survive in our *mindset*. In *nature* numbers are security against the unforeseen hazards of the *future*; but humanity has removed many hazards from the *natural* world (or rather indulged in hazard substitution), and the need for meaningless numbers no longer exists. They are best seen as the pursuit of the *hidden agenda* of our species.

When populations reach *limits*, there are three possible courses. First, at a low limit, of *stability* within the *biosphere*. Second, a *sink*, where a population reaches a climactic maximum and crashes, suffering disrupted behavioural patterns as part of its *com-pression* within the *limiting* factors. After the crash a remnant may remain to repeat the *cycle* once more. Third, *compression* within the population may initiate a *shift*, to a further successive *evolu-tionary* form. In its pursuit of the *life agenda* of immortality humanity seems to be gambling that numbers will produce a *shift* before we *sink*. The *problem* is that our embryonic successive form, and our action in promoting it, is destroying much of the *biosphere* (see **institutions**).

Rationality demands that we reduce our numbers; *survival* with human *values* intact dictates it. Global population is currently around 5,500 millions and is expected to reach 6,300 millions by the year 2000, and 8,500 millions by 2020.[2] Thereafter guesswork becomes dominant; some believe human numbers are likely to reach 10,000–15,000 millions in the absence of extreme action to control numbers. Whatever future predictions, the simple fact is that numbers are beyond *sustainable limits* now. In allowing them to rise higher we may (if we have not already) consume our *environment* beyond *restoration*, commit to *extinction* so much of the *web of life* that the whole may no longer be viable.

In these circumstances any agency which *limits* or reduces human numbers should be accepted as part of a *natural process* of redress. As it is unlikely that we can avoid a disastrous population crash, the logical thing to do is to devote energy to preparations to minimise its severity by reducing the numbers involved, and for post crash *sustainability* (see **casualty problem**).

At what population level could humans achieve *balance* with the *biosphere*? Nobody knows; we can only speculate. Whatever theoretical number is chosen, if our desires continue to expand, our numbers must continually decrease. Consider the question another way. How much of the available biomass is ours by *right*? Clearly, with an unknown number (estimated at between three and 24) of species becoming *extinct* every day, our demands are suicidal. We cannot *consume* the *web of life* and *survive*.

The most constructive and *sustainable* approach would be to reverse the question. Instead of asking how many people the *biosphere* can bear, we should ask what is the minimum number each segment of our variegated species needs to survive in its *bioregional* context? What are the smallest numbers of people which can *sustain* ethnic variation and *cultural diversity* compatible with *sustainable ways of life*? These are the numbers we should discover and aim for as quickly as possible (see **parenting**).

How do we decrease numbers? Starvation, disease, *war, choice* and disaster are the current means. By *choosing* to reduce numbers, fewer will be lost by other means. *Sustainability* requires the universal acceptance of one woman one child, but the world will be saved by those women and men who, for the next two or three generations, choose to have no children. Is the paradox acceptable? Is it in the best interests of our species that those who respond to *need* give way to those less able to do so?

Human close-*affinity groups* have devolved as our *socio-cultural structures* have *evolved*. We have moved from tribe to *extended* and then nuclear families; today single parent families and individuals living as singles are on the increase. Families express the *instinctive need* for isolated couples to attempt to rebuild their tribe. Whatever the *motivation, consciousness* must be focused on its denial; we must understand the *need* and seek other means of fulfilling it. If our excursions into *technology* have one value, it should be that we no longer *need* crude numbers as our means of hazard manipulation, nor do we *need* ever more young hands to provide for the aged. If we were totally rational the resources devoted to arms would be redirected to *global* birth control, for the truth is that, if we do not control our species, *nature* will.

Living once more in *self-sustaining socio-economic communities* would help *limit* human numbers. People would be more directly connected with the reality which *sustained* them. In *terminal culture, flow economics* and its *institutional* conveyors hide the fact that a child born in a rich country sucks nourishment from poorer regions. Excessive numbers are a *global* problem; none of us can afford them and the *biosphere* cannot *sustain* them.

All *life* is selfish, all *life* seeks to convert its *environment* into replicas of itself. Humanity has no *choice* other than to come to terms with itself and temper primitive *instinct* with *global consciousness.*

<u>Relationships</u>   **genetics, human nature, evolution**.

<u>See also</u>   **stability, sink, shift**.

<u>References</u>

1 The Euvalon was a futuristic 'flying saucer' building housing a technology and science exhibition. It was, I believe, one of the first places to have exhibits aimed at the pollution problem caused by waste and dumping. Unfortunately now closed, as Philips, under the pressure of international competition, needed to redevelop the site.

2 Figures kindly supplied by Population Concern, 231 Tottenham Court Road, London W1P 9AE, 071–631 1546.

NURTURE   To bring up, train, care, nourish.

The meaning has been *extended* in the debate concerning the influences on *human nature* and behaviour. 'Is man nature or nurture?'; that is, are we the products of predetermined influences or of the nurture of our *culture*, in the summary effects of family influence, socialisation, *education* and so on? While the most realistic answer is that we are a blend of both, in modern society the nurturing influence of our *culture* has become dominant. It is no accident that there are few muslims in Ireland or catholics in Israel; it is a *function* of *culture* imposed upon the geographical accident of birth. Most people accept the nurture of the *culture* in which they find themselves, and try to live minimal lives in the recent *past.*

A *green culture* will generate *green* nurture for those within, but they should be encouraged to rebel, to *question*, to develop their own answers. If the *culture* and its underlying *philosophy* are correct, the answers will be compatible with an *evolving green way of life* (see **balance**).

<u>Relationships</u>   **community, culture, philosophy**.

<u>See also</u>   **education, mindset**.

NVDA   see **non-violence**.

OBJECTIVE   Belonging not to the *conscious* or the perceiving or experiencing subject, but *inherent* in the subject of *perception* or experience of itself.

Also of a person or writing, description, picture, report, discussion; dealing with the facts or appearance uncoloured by feelings or belief.

And thing to be achieved; object of exercise.

Objectivity, in the sense of detached or unemotional, is practically impossible. Everything is modified by *perception* and/or the means by which it is perceived.

SCIENTIFIC OBJECTIVITY   Is founded in the measurement of an effect that can be repeated by any challenger by replicating precisely the conditions which produced the measurement.

The doctrine of reproducibility, of the 'facts' of a particular experiment, are the basis of the scientific proof of any proposition. Many of the policy decisions relating to science and *technology*, or to their effects, are based on the presumed infallibility of scientific objectivity.

The ideas behind such reliance in *terminal culture* are based on the *mechanistic assumptions* of that *culture*. The reproducibility of experimental data implies a deterministic state of *existence*, with immutable scientific laws which are awaiting discovery by man. Unfortunately, things are not quite like that (see **formative causation, nature**).

The scientific tradition, with its illusion of objectivity, reached its deterministic conclusion when the French scientist the Marquis de Laplace,[1] following the success of Newton's *mechanistic model* of gravity, proposed that the *universe* was completely deterministic. He believed that there were a set of scientific laws which would allow the prediction of everything; we only had to discover the laws. This notion was initially resisted because it was felt to infringe upon God's *freedom* to ordain things. Nevertheless, Laplace's proposition remained a standard *assumption* of science until the early part of this century.

Quantum theory was to be its downfall. In order to make sense of rates of radiation *energy* emitted by hot bodies, Max Planck[2] proposed that such radiation was emitted in coherent packets which he called quanta. In developing quantum theory to predict the position and velocity of particles, Werner Heisenberg[3] found it necessary to formulate his famous uncertainty principle. The nub of this means that the more accurately you try to measure the position of a particle, the less accurately you can measure its velocity, and vice versa. Heisenberg's uncertainty principle is a fundamental inescapable property of *existence.*

> The uncertainty principle had profound implications for the way in which we viewed the world. Even after more than fifty years they have not been appreciated by many philosophers, and are still the subject of much controversy. The uncertainty principle signalled the end to Laplace's dream of a theory of science that would be completely deterministic: one certainly cannot predict future events exactly if one cannot even measure the present state of the universe precisely![4]

Uncertainty lead to the development in the 1920s of quantum mechanics, which instead of a single 'objective' outcome, predicts a number of different possible outcomes and *limits* prediction to the likelihood attributable to each. The result is stated in terms of probabilities, and a large number of such predictions produces a probability curve.

What relevance do the outer reaches of particle physics have to everyday life? Simply that no matter how objectively we think we are looking at something, both it and we are subject to *inherent* variations which remove the final basis for an objective truth. The subject produces the object of the exercise; in reality, where everything is interconnected, nothing can *exist* in isolation, unaffected by other *existence.*

Mechanistic objectivity may be seen as a current town street map. For many purposes, and for some time, you can get around with it, particularly if repeatability is the objective rather than that which is repeated. But things *change,* and the map of objectivity is only a representation, not reality itself. Scientific objectivity overlooks its own *limits* in pursuit of its *agenda*; of 'safe' *nuclear* power, safe *biocides,* etc., of seeing only the benefits of its *processes* while discounting any other possibilities. It sees things from one point only on the probability curve. Drug disasters and techno-failures, *toxic* hazards and insoluble *environmental problems* testify to the short-sighted illusion of such objectivity (see **Murphy's law**).

Scientific objectivity is also used as a screen for the disposal and destruction of *nature* and other *life forms*. The objectivity of animal experiments is dubious, the morality unacceptable. There is no absolute truth to be gained from such practices, except perhaps that *terminal culture* man is unacceptable to the *community* he abuses.

<u>Relationships</u>   **terminal culture, mindset.**

<u>See also</u>   **Cartesianism, exploitation.**

<u>References</u>

1 Pierre Simon, Marquis de Laplace (1749–1827), French mathematician and astronomer.

2 Max Karl Ernst Planck (1858–1947), German theoretical physicist, formulator of the quantum theory.

3 Werner Karl Heisenberg (1901–76), German theoretical physicist, developed quantum mechanics and formulated the revolutionary principle of indeterminacy in nuclear physics, 1925. Heisenberg showed that the uncertainty in the position of the particle times the uncertainty in its velocity times the mass of the particle can never be smaller than a certain quantity, which is known as Planck's constant.

4 Stephen W. Hawking, 1988, *A Brief History of Time: From the Big Bang to Black Holes*, Bantam Press, London.

ONE   Single quantity expressing a whole unity. Also the detached self – 'One may become interested in the environment.'

ONENESS   Experiencing unity with something – self, other thing or *life* form. Experiencing the connectedness between things; the hunter at one with the prey, feeling part of the *web of life*, the *whole* of *existence*.

OPEN   Initiate process; give or have access to; unfold, develop, expand, extended.

OPEN MINDED   A liberal quality of *grey culture*.

Being open minded has a double meaning. Open mindedness, in the sense of giving access, can too easily result in, or be a refuge for, indecision, being an uncritical sponge that soaks up anything. Attempting to be reasonable in all circumstances produces a woolly response, usually based on *assumptions* rather than assessment.

The more positive sense is that anything will be considered, nothing is unthinkable. This ability is essential for the *future* (see **censorship**).

OPENNESS   Being open (or being open to being open).

Openness implies the value of *inclusivity*, rather than *exclusivity*. Openness is essential in all public/ *social functions*. A lack of openness is usually a mark of hypocrisy, of protection of *position*, of *exclusivity*; the closed group and closed mentality are hallmarks of *grey culture*. People do have a right to a private life, which should be absolute within the *law* (and could be in a society based on public *function* rather than public *position*). Whatever an individual does within the *community*, a non-public *life*, a right to privacy and isolation, is essential.

Relationships   **inclusivity, culture, evolution, mindset**.

See also   **rights, honesty**.

References

For examples of the lack of openness in British society and institutions see Peter Laurie, 1970, *Beneath the City Streets*, Allen Lane, London (sub-titled *A Private Enquiry into Government Preparations for National Emergency*); Nicholas Hilyard, 1981, *Cover Up: The Facts They Don't Want You to Know*, New English Library, London; Tony Bunyan, 1976, *The History and Practice of The Political Police in Britain*, Julian Friedmann, London.

OPPOSITION   To set against person, thing, force, proposal, etc., a contrary proposition, opposite thing, etc.

Part of the dynamics of *grey culture*; an established thing and opposition to it, especially in conventional *political systems*. There is a government and an opposition; they are essential parts of the same *system*; both form a de facto alliance; that is the *system*. Anything which falls outside the *system* is rejected by both. Thus *political* opposition is conditioned by having first to gain access to the *system*; in so doing, opposition inevitably becomes part of the *system*. Working within the *system extends* the *system*; opposition refines proposition, it does not replace it.

The *green* objective is not to oppose, although at times that may be necessary, rather the emphasis is on *creating* different *ways of living*, other means of fulfilment.

Beware the opposition of *thematic compatibility* – a plague on both their houses.[1]

Relationships   **thematic compatibility, anticipation, structure**.

See also   **potential, stability**.

References

1 William Shakespeare (1564–1616), *Romeo and Juliet*
  A plague o' both your houses!
  They have made worms' meat of me.

ORGANIC   In chemistry: of compounds and polymers formed around the carbon atom (see **carbon-based life**).

In medicine: physiology, of organs of a body.

In farming, gardening: using natural, biological, methods (see **food**).

In organisation: a structure which is held to be inherently natural.

The senses most commonly used in the *green movement* are those of farming and *food*, and of organisation (see **structure**).

ORGANIC FOOD (see **food**)   Food which is produced by methods generally compatible with *nature*. The objective is to produce nourishing complete foods, free from contamination by drug, *chemical* and *biocide* residues (see **chemiculture**).

The motivation for the organic movement was the understanding that the *health* of people was intimately linked with the *health* of the soil and the plants and animals grown for *food*. It has *extended* into general concern for animal welfare, the preservation of *natural genetic* varieties, and concern for the *environment* in the widest sense.

Given that humanity will have to continue farming *food* for the foreseeable *future*, there is only one sustainable answer to the world *food* problem – sound husbandry, based on small extensive mixed farms and organic practices. Small farms support more *life*, in every sense (see **life contract**).

ORGANIC FOOD PRODUCTION   All systems of organic farming aim to enhance the *life cycles* of the *food* animals and plants involved; in so doing they enhance other *life cycles* in the *environment*.

There are various definitions of organic food and parameters for its production. For example the International Federation of Organic Agricultural Movements (IFOAM)[1] defines organic agriculture with a set of aims:

1 To work as much as possible within a closed system and draw upon local resources.

2 To maintain the long-term fertility of soils.

3 To avoid all forms of pollution that may result from agricultural techniques.

4 To produce foodstuffs of high nutritional quality in sufficient quantity.

5 To reduce the use of fossil energy in agricultural practice to the minimum.

6 To give all livestock the conditions of life that conform to their physiological needs and human/ethological principles.

7 To make it possible for agricultural producers and their families to earn a living from/through their work and develop their potentialities as human beings.

8 To maintain the rural environment and also preserve non-agricultural ecological habitats.

The IFOAM aims for organic agriculture are derived from a *philosophy* of the *relationship* between humans and the *environment* they use to produce *food*. As such they describe a *way of life* rather than *rules* for farming, although the rules are implicit. Point 3 is particularly significant, since presumably it *extends* to all *artificial* chemical products, such as *plastics* and paints. Point 6 however is disappointing, since it reflects the *reductionist assumption* that animals may be regarded as 'physiology', that they have no *needs* of *mind* or *spirit* in their *existence*. (My experience as an organic sheep farmer leads me to believe that these *needs exist* for all sentient beings. Young lambs get tremendous pleasure from the endless games to be invented around a tree bole in their pasture; mothers become frantic at their limitless energy; family groups have long-term *relationships* which should be preserved – for instance daughters seek mothers at times of stress such as lambing, and so on.)

The United States Department of Agriculture defines organic agriculture thus:

> Organic farming is a production system which avoids or largely excludes the use of synthetically compounded fertilisers, pesticides, growth regulators and livestock feed additives. To the maximum extent feasible, organic farming systems rely on crop rotations, crop residues, animal manures, legumes, green manures, off-farm organic wastes, mechanical cultivation, mineral bearing rocks, and aspects of biological pest control to maintain soil productivity and tilth, to supply plant nutrients and to control insects, weeds and other pests.
>
> The concept of the soil as a living system that develops the activities of beneficial organisms is central to this definition.

Not so much a definition, more an outsider's description of organics, in terms of the prevailing *ideas* of *chemiculture*, of the things involved, with no indication of an understanding of the reasoning behind or *dynamics* of the practice. It is a start that the concept is recognised, although this carries with it the danger of its *institutionalisaton* and perversion (see **institutional process**).

The British Organic Standards Committee in their Standards document published by the Soil Association (details below) define organic agriculture as follows:

The enhancement of biological cycles, involving micro-organisms, soil fauna, plants and animals is the basis of organic agriculture. Sound rotations, the extensive and rational use of manure and vegetable wastes, the use of appropriate cultivation techniques, the avoidance of fertilisers in the form of soluble mineral salts and the prohibition of agro-chemical pesticides form the basic characteristics of organic agriculture.

Although the Standards published by the Soil Association are rigorous, and become more so each year, they appear to contain contradictions in detail, and signs of improvisation. The organisation is characterised by the ethos of British amateurism and woolly *philosophy*. It is as though it is sure of its ground, but not sure where that ground is in *relation* to its wider *philosophical* (or *socio-cultural*) context.

The common complaint about organic food is that it is expensive. But it is bound to be in comparison to *chemicultural* produce. Organic food requires *time* and care, especially for animals, and farmers both highly skilled and attuned to the *processes* they are encouraging. The result is *food* which is pure and contains more of the essential micronutrients than *chemiculture* produces, animals who live '*natural*' lives, and a *life enhanced environment*. That is what you pay for. (Except at present much of the retail premium is absorbed by monopolies and entrepreneurs, and little of it gets to the farmer. A 15 per cent premium to the farmer is typical.)

Although price comparisons may be important to *consumers*, they are not on a like-with-like basis. Ordinary food is effectively half price through subsidies at many points of the *chemiculture process*. *Consumers* pay both overt subsidies and for the other effects of chemical farming, for example in cleaning up the nitrate-*polluted* water supply, as well as for the effects on the wider *polluted environment*.

The following is an indication of the depth of the peculiar *institutional* insanity which runs through farmer/animal *relationships* in conventional *chemiculture* farming:

> Improving the welfare of the pregnant sow is one of the next research projects at Terrington [a British government Ministry of Agriculture, Fisheries and Food experimental husbandry farm]. A three-year project will investigate how her welfare is affected by feeding regimes and offering straw for foraging behaviour.
>
> The work, which is being carried out in conjunction with the

Scottish Agricultural Colleges, will also investigate whether farrowing sows can be given more freedom.[2]

Those the gods wish to destroy ...

Organic food is becoming increasingly available as *consciousness changes*. For sources in Britain see *Thorsons Organic Consumer Guide*.[3] To grow your own, or convert your flower garden, see Lawrence Hill's classic *Organic Gardening*.[4]

Because of increasing demand (and higher prices), not all *food* sold as 'organic' is organic. The best guide to authenticity is the Soil Association symbol and the producer's certificate number.

The UK government and EC (European Community) are becoming involved through UKROFS (United Kingdom Register of Organic Food Standards), a body representative of many interests including some opposed to the organic *philosophy* who wish to dilute the standards (see **institutional process**).

The Soil Association is the principal focus for organic interests in Britain. It was founded as a charity in 1946 by Lady Eve Balfour,[5] in the belief that human *health* depends upon the *quality* of *food*, and that this in turn depends upon the *health* of the soil. It encourages an ecological approach to agriculture and promotes organic husbandry as the real long-term option for *food* production. The Soil Association has local groups, produces a quarterly journal, *The Living Earth*, for members, and is a source of information and advice. It is at 86–88 Colston Street, Bristol BS1 5BB, England. There will be equivalents in most countries[1].

ORGANIC SELF   Taoist concept; the self in balance with others. In the unfolding of self-awareness, it is essential to maintain *harmony* and *balance* within the *whole*. This is not the same as the expectation or imposition of order; rather it *anticipates* the *chaos* of *creativity*, of individuality, and trusts to the greater order beyond the immediate vision (see **morphology**).

Relationships   **permaculture, food, health, rights, environment**.

See also   **life contract, chemiculture, pollution**.

References

1 IFOAM (International Federation of Organic Agricultual Movements), Kozentrum Imsbach, D-6695 Tholey-Theley, Germany.

2 Feature, 'Pigs in Perspective', in *Farmers' Guardian*, Friday 28 September 1990, published by Lancashire Evening Post Ltd, 127 Fishergate, Preston, Lancs, England. I am indebted to fellow organic farmer Ann MacKenzie (who could save Terrington three years work by a simple introduction to her free ranging and happily foraging sows), for drawing this item to my attention, amid gales of laughter provoked by despair and incredulity.

3 David Mabey and Alan and Jackie Gear, 1990, *Thorsons Organic Consumer Guide*, Thorsons, London.

4 Lawrence D. Hills (1911–90), 1977, *Organic Gardening*, Penguin Books, London; also, 1983, *Month-by-Month Organic Gardening: The Green Gardener's Calendar* (actually a book), Thorsons, London. (I learned while writing this entry that Lawrence Hills had died. His work has been an inspiration to many, providing a practical and rewarding, literally down-to-earth, entry into green concerns; fortunately his inspiration will live on.)

5 Lady Eve Balfour, 1975, *The Living Soil and the Haughley Experiment*, Universe Books, New York; see also Nicolas Lampkin, 1990, *Organic Farming*, Farming Press Books, Ipswich, England; Richard Body, 1987, *Red or Green for Farmers (And the Rest Of Us)*, Broad Leys Publishing, Widdington, Saffron Walden, Essex, England; Sedley Sweeney, 1985, *The Challenge of Smallholding*, Oxford University Press, Oxford, England; John Elkington and Julia Hailes, 1988, *The Green Consumer Guide: From Shampoo to Champagne, High Street Shopping for a Better Environment*, Gollancz, London.

For details of the problems of conventional chemiculture farming, see the titles referenced under **chemiculture**.

OVER   Direction, usually other than intended, as fall over; over and above.

Over is another of those words (see **new, neo**) used, usually as a prefix, with another word to *change* its meaning, generally to imply too much, as in over-explain.

Overs of concern to *greens* are numerous – over-capacity, overdeveloped, overfishing, overpopulation, etc.

Overs in the sense of *more* are generally to be avoided (see **balance**).

OVERPOPULATION   see **numbers**.

OZONE O_3, poisonous form of oxygen.

Ozone in the upper atmosphere acts to screen out ultraviolet radiation. Holes have been discovered in this screen, first in Antarctica, recently over the Mediterranean and Arctic, caused by the catalytic action of *artificial* gases, particularly CFCs.

At ground level ozone is formed when hydrocarbons and nitrogen oxides emitted by car exhausts, factories, power plants, or other combustion sources, react with sunlight. Ozone is *toxic* to humans at concentrations above 0.1 parts per million; the maximum WHO 'safe' limit is 75 parts per billion. Ozone is harmful to green plants and can kill *trees*.

Ozone is created in the stratosphere by the effect of ultraviolet radiation from the sun on oxygen. Ozone also splits and becomes oxygen (O_2) again as part of a continuous cycle of chemical change. It is destroyed by reaction with nitric oxide (created by burning fossil fuel) or water or chlorine compounds (from chlorofluorocarbons used in aerosols and packaging). The reduction of ozone in the stratosphere by any of these reactions creates a thin area or 'hole' in the ozone layer. The ozone layer in the stratosphere acts as a protection against the harmful effects of the sun's radiation, and the destruction or reduction of the layer has the effect of allowing more radiation to pass through the atmosphere with harmful effects (such as skin cancer) on humans.[1]

Britain's hot summer [1990] has seen ozone *pollution* peak in rural areas. Ozone at low altitudes, a pollutant which contributes to photochemical smog, rose above World Health Authority 'trigger' levels during July.

Worst affected regions included East Sussex, Devon, Derbyshire and Hertfordshire. At Lullingworth Heath, in East Sussex, the government's Warren Springs Laboratory recorded a maximum hourly average of 115 particles per billion molecules on one day in mid-July. A site in Derbyshire, at Ladybower, and another at Yarner Wood, near Exeter, each registered 100 particles.[2]

Relationships   **cycles, health, pollution.**
See also   **limits, balance.**

References
1 *Dictionary of Ecology and the Environment*, 1988, Peter Collins Publishing, Teddington, Middlesex, England.
2 *The Independent*, 24 July 1990.

PARADIGM (see also **model**)   Example or pattern, especially of sound; inflexion.

The pattern meaning has been extending, particularly in the sense of pattern of thought.

Kuhn[1] gives the example of the pre- and post-Newtonian patterns of thought. The post-Newtonian paradigm was an innovation; its terms of reference and conclusions would have made no sense to those familiar with the earlier, scholastic 'paradigm', whose world view was dominated by the dogma of ecclesiastic law.

A paradigm is a pattern of thought which makes sense of our *perception* of *existence*. The post-Newtonian paradigm, the beginning of our current mechanistic *reductionist* view of *existence*, represented a *shift* from the previous paradigm to something entirely *new*.

Greens seek to initiate a similar *shift* in patterns of thought. Believing that the current paradigm has self-evidently reached its *limits*, a *shift* to a *sustainable* world-view is the only option open to us.

<u>Relationships</u>   **perception, mindset.**
<u>See also</u>   **reality, existence.**
<u>References</u>

1 Thomas S. Kuhn, 1962, 1970, *The Structure of Scientific Revolutions*, University of Chicago Press, Chicago, USA.

PARENT   One who has begotten or borne offspring, father or mother; foremothers or fathers; one who has adopted a child; animal, plant or cell from which others are derived; *institution* which has produced subsiduaries.

For *greens* the *function* of *being* a parent is more important than the *genetic relationship* of child to mother/father. Ideally parent(s) and child are *related*, but this is not essential, nor are the sex, race, age or *relationships* of the parent(s) seen as important.

PARENTING   The function of having, supporting, children.

In an *overpopulated* world it is important that women are not made to feel guilty or negative about not giving birth.

It is equally important that each child born has, can *anticipate*, a satisfactory *life-context*, of *relationships* and fulfilment of *potential* within the wider control of *sustainable life* in *balance* with planetary *needs* as a *whole* (thinking globally and acting locally).

Ideally the *future* demands that each woman has no more than one child. With shared *nurture*, as well as the experience of pregnancy and birth, within *community*, the more pleasurable aspects of birth and *nurture* may be repeated without the traps of drudgery and *overpopulation*. The mother in *grey culture*, locked away in her breeding box with no escape from the demands of children, literally sacrifices her life, her *potential*, for her children. The *dynamics* of *life* in *community* should be able to offer the best of many worlds, rather than the continual demand of many sacrifices for singular achievements. Such a *way of life* would reflect our ancestral tribal habits, which gave the best of both worlds, of parenting and *nurture*, without isolation and despair. It would also remove the need for each woman to seek to rebuild a tribal *morphology* from her individual womb.

Perhaps, in view of the large excess of people, adoption should be a primary *green* objective. As far as repeat breeding is concerned, to paraphrase Henry Thoreau,[1] 'those parents are best which parent least, – that parent is best which parents not at all'.

GREEN PARENTING

> As parents, whatever the odds against us we have to try to bring up children who are competent and internally happy, free from the treadmill of a compulsive drive for acquisition, over-excitement and selfness. Instead they will have energy, zest for life and the confidence (self esteem) which will help them to restore the planet and at least some of its occupants to a state of wellbeing. Sometimes it may seem like an uphill struggle. It would be easy to give in to the temptation to buy another toy to keep Johnny amused, or to stick him in front of the video with a polystyrene carton of junk food. Sometimes we're bound to find ourselves doing this. But it is in order to be better able to resist making this way of life a habit that we require more confidence in our own ideas than we have ever had.[2]

Although well-intentioned, such expressions ring alarm bells. It is always hazardous to predict, to expect, what 'they will' do or have. Despite the best or worst intentions, some children have a way of deciding for themselves and escaping the parental straitjacket, no matter how worthy it is, and they are all very worthy according to parents.

The only *green* attitude to parenting and *nurture* is to encourage *green* attitudes and behaviour, to explain why you believe what you believe, but encourage *freedom* and exploration. Ultimately you will only keep your children if you are prepared to let them go, and return if they wish of their own free will. You cannot expect your children to live your life for you, or to save the world for you.

Relationships   **numbers, potential**.

References

1 Henry David Thoreau (1817–62), *On Civil Disobedience*: 'I heartily accept the motto – "That government is best which governs least", and I should like to see it acted up to more rapidly and systematically. Carried out, it finally amounts to this, which also I believe – That government is best which governs not at all.'

2 Juliet Solomon, 1990, *Green Parenting*, Macdonald Optima, London.

PARTICIPATE   Have a share in, take part in, thing or process or event.

PARTICIPATION   In vogue in the 1960s and 1970s; used mainly by the establishment as a means of heading off calls for the *devolution* of *power* and decision making. Participation was offered, but *power* withheld. At a meeting sponsored by various bodies interested in *industrial democracy*, held at Essex University in the wake of the student/worker 'disturbances' in France in 1968, French students listened with increasing disbelief as British trades union speakers made impassioned pleas to be allowed to participate in the *processes* to which their members devoted their lives. After tea, the French students had cheered up; across the back of the room they had hung a banner. It said:

je participe	nous participons
tu participes	vous participez
il/elle participe	ils/elles PROFITENT

Participation is valid if it is an option among equals, and encompasses all aspects of the *process* to which it is addressed.

Relationships   **co-operative, democracy, community**.

See also   **process**.

PAST   Gone by in time.

Most people prefer to live in the safety of the recent past, where things are predictable and the *future* too far away to provoke anxiety.

The past went that-a-way. When faced with a totally new situation, we tend always to attach ourselves to the objects, to the flavour of the most recent past. We look at the present through a rear-view mirror. We march backwards into the future. Suburbia lives imaginatively in Bonanza-land.[1]

<u>Relationships</u>   **time, present, future**.
<u>See also</u>   **anticipation**.
<u>References</u>
1 Marshall McLuhan and Quentin Fiore, 1967, *The Medium is the Massage*, Penguin, London.

PEACE   Freedom from or cessation of *war*. Another desirable concept defined in terms of its opposite. But

peace is not simply the cessation of hostilities, [it is] a state of being in harmony with all of life. The peace we seek in the world and our own lives goes deeper than agreeing not to shoot at each other. Silencing the guns is a necessary first step.[1]

Grey culture performs a similar mental reflective trick in the way it perceives peace as it does *health*. Whenever *greys* discuss peace they think and speak defence and armaments (see **nuclear, health**).

Greens believe that peace, or the conditions in which it may be given a chance, are a *function* of the *structure* of human society. The belief in *communities* of *human scale*, in *federations* and *networks* selected from the available *matrices*, of population levels which are *sustainable* at minimal levels, where *life* is not *compressed*, are essential prerequistes. Hence also the *green* belief in the *need* for a *global philosophy* sheltering a *diversity* wherein no unit is large enough other than to self-destruct. But of themselves they will not produce peace; as Gandhi said, 'There is no way to peace; peace is the way.'[2] It may be that we have to build a *life structure* for our species that allows for some expression of a need *war* (see **war**).

The present *terminal culture*, of *hierarchical institutions* focused on *competitive* nation *states*, has *war* as an *inherent* part of its *structure*. *War* is the *health* of the *state*.[3]

<u>Relationships</u>   **philosophy, culture, structure**.
<u>See also</u>   **community, diversity**.
<u>References</u>
1 Michael Lindfield, 1986, *The Dance of Change: An Eco-Spiritual Approach to Transformation*.
2 Mahatma Gandhi (1869–1948), quoted in Fritjof Capra and Charlene Spretnak,

1984, *Green Politics*, Grafton, London.

3 Attributed to Heinrich von Treitschke (1834–1896).

> Without war no state could be. All those we know of arose through war, and the protection of their members by armed force remains their primary and essential task. War, therefore, will endure to the end of history, as long as there is a multiplicity of states.

PERCEPTION   Inner facility of awareness, *intuitive* recognition of truth, quality or nature of thing or self. Action by which *mind* registers its interpretation of sensory experience. 'Man's desires are limited by his Perceptions; none can desire what he has not perceived.'[1]

Perception is the result of the inner *processes* by which we interpret and order *existence.* 'If the doors of perception were cleansed, everything would appear to man as it is, infinite.'[2] We seem to have essential screens to our perception; being confronted by *infinity* is likely to blow mental fuses, to dissolve our present perceptions of reality and replace them with something we are not yet ready to comprehend.

The brain's perceptual shut-down *systems* operate in the mid- and hind-brain, and appear to have *evolved* to protect the higher parts of the *mind* from confusing *information* overload. These mechanisms may be needed less with the *growth* of the *processing* capacity of the neo-cortex through *human evolution.*

There are *inherent systems* in the brain which prevent the full range of *information* that impinges on our sensory organs from entering *conscious* levels of the *mind.* LSD (lysergic acid diethylamide) interferes with the action of these blocks, allowing more *information* into *consciousness* than normal. LSD clobbers habituation, removes *assumptions,* so that everything appears new, significant, exciting or terrifying (the bad trip). The effect is both to allow perception of things that would normally go unnoticed, and to produce remarkable *changes* in learning and beliefs which can endure long after the drug effect has worn off.[3]

The effect of *cultural nurture* is to shape further the parameters of perception, to create additional filters and blocks. The trick of a 'good' *culture,* its means to *survival,* is to induce the perception that there are no such filters, that the doors are clear. Yet we know, by comparison with others and by the historical continuum of which we are a part, that *cultures* act *symbiotically* with the *mindset* of their participants. Different *cultures* perceive the same *events* in different ways; hence misunderstanding.

The *relationship* between individual and *culture* is complex. At times when *culture* is dominant, people are quiescent, things are *stable*. At times of *change* people become dominant, there is upheaval, and *culture changes*. It is *changing* perceptions of reality or possibility which cause people to ascend above and dominate their *culture* (see **paradigm**).

Changing perception, *personal growth* and species *evolution* are part of the same *dynamic*. The *natural* view of the *evolutionary process* involved is that as we are able to cope with larger slices of *infinity* – they are discovered or revealed. (Evolutionary chicken-and-egg conundrum: Which came first, ability or capacity?) In this sense our *evolution* may be seen as the continual *process* of removing or changing the internal screens and filters between us and reality.

Conscious evolution equates with increasing our perceptive capacity. This may not amount to a blanket increase in total perception so much as increasing the depth of perceptive pathways, of increasing their capacity in specific areas. *Greens* feel that 'seeing green' is a necessary precursor to the next stage of *human evolution*.

Relationships   **mind, culture, evolution**.
See also   **stability, change**.
References

1 William Blake (1757–1827), *There is no Natural Religion*.
2 as 1, *The Marriage of Heaven and Hell*, in *The Complete Writings of William Blake*, Oxford University Press, Oxford, England.
3 Arabella Melville, PhD thesis, University of Birmingham, 1974.

PERMACULTURE   An integrated system of perennial agriculture, designed to enrich rather than destroy local *ecosystems*, which is as far as possible *self-sufficient* in *energy* needs. Many of the techniques of permaculture were developed by the Tagari Community in Tasmania, where the term was first used; there are now associations promoting permaculture ideas in several countries.[1] In spreading, the *idea* has extended from integrated gardening to vernacular semi-temporary dwellings.

The *green perspective* is that the planet was/is a permaculture. We have to rejoin, to become part of the permaculture of the planet, that is the essence of *sustainability*, of living within the capacity of the *biosphere*, of increasing human capacity by increasing that of all *life*.

Relationships   **sustainability**.
See also   **restoration**.

References

1 John Button, 1988, *A Dictionary of Green Ideas: Vocabulary for a Sane and Sustainable Future*, Routledge, London; see Bill Mullison, 1990, *Permaculture One* and *Permaculture Two*, Island Press, Washington, USA; also 1988, *Permaculture – A Designers Manual*, A.G. Access, Davis, California, USA.

PERSONAL GROWTH (see **growth**, **personal**)   Usually associated with various therapies concerned with self-awareness.

In *grey culture* personal growth amounts to getting into fast-forward as quickly as you can, leaving *away* behind, being seen to be a successful sensation seeker as we all shoot over the edge.

If the term has any general relevance it is in the importance of defining areas in which human *growth* may be unlimited, and conversely those where *limits* must be accepted.

The difference between growth in *grey culture* and that within a *green perspective* is that, as far as possible, the latter is a *consciously* directed process. It is a process which involves both *past* and *future* as parts of our continuous whole. We need to become aware of our *past*, its conditioning and connection with our *culture* and *relationships*. We also need *perception* of our *potential*, of desirable possibilities. Between the two may be found pathways, maps, of the *process* of growth. The *potential* is glimpsed through contact and opening to 'known' unknown within us to reveal the vision of who and what we are – our *potential* selves.

Growth then is a *dynamic* interplay (*process*) between the two poles. But instead of it being a deadening conflict, growth is *co-operating* with the *dynamic process* that these poles create.

Relationships   **psychosynthesis**, **growth**, **evolution**.

See also   **perception**.

References

I am grateful to Charleen Agostini for assistance with this entry; any errors or faults are mine.

PERSPECTIVE   Aspect of a subject and its parts as viewed by the *mind*; hence of limited perspective, a single perspective.

The *reductionist philosophy* of *terminal culture* seeks the single perspective, as part of absolute truth, of a thing or subject. A single perspective generates a dogmatic view of *existence*.

Greens believe there are many possible aspects, and seek *means* and *structures* which allow these to *co-exist*. It is undesirable that perspective becomes fixed; things need to be seen in different ways under a variety of circumstances – at times with narrow, concentrated focus, at others with a broader perspective. Only in this way can *relationships*, and their *changes*, be appreciated.

This is not the same as the *shifting* perspective of the opportunist; the connection with a *philosophy* which enables judgments to be made of what is perceived is crucial.

BIOCENTRIC PERSPECTIVE   Personal *ecological consciousness* that recognises intellectually and feels emotionally the *inherent* worth of other species, of all other *forms* of *existence*. Necessary as a preliminary to becoming *one* with the *biosphere*. A view of *existence* which rejects the *homocentric values* of *grey culture*.

Relationships   **culture, mindset, perception.**

See also   **change, consciousness.**

PESTICIDE   see **biocide, chemiculture.**

PHILOSOPHY   Seeking after *wisdom* or *knowledge*, especially that which deals with ultimate reality, or with the most general causes and principles of things and *ideas* and human *perception* and *knowledge* of them.

Philosophy is of supreme relevance to the *global predicament* because philosophy is the foundation upon which *culture* is built, and it is *culture*, with its principal components of *economics, politics* and religion, which produces the *way of life* which typifies a particular *culture*.

Trying to *change politics, economics,* or religions will be impossible unless the foundation upon which they stand is *changed* first. Without a different philosophy, the *agendas* of the old foundation will re-assert themselves in those elements of *culture* which it *projects*.

> The world view and value system that lie at the basis of our culture and that have to be carefully re-examined were formulated in their essential outlines in the sixteenth and seventeenth centuries. Between 1500 and 1700 there was a dramatic shift in the way people pictured the world and their whole way of thinking.[1]

Western industrial *culture* is a product of philosophical influences which have been grouped under the general terms of mechanistic and *reductionist*, and summarised as *Cartesian dualism*, after French philosopher Réné Déscartes (1596–1650). Other main contributors to the mechanistic tradition of *Cartesian dualism* were Isaac Newton (1642–1747)[2] and Francis Bacon (1561–1626).[3]

The essence of this tradition is analysis; every problem or proposition is broken down (reduced) to successively smaller parts, and *linear* (mechanistic) *relationships*, of cause and effect, are sought. The belief is that at some point the ultimate truth of the *nature* of things will be revealed. Unfortunately, while the analytical tradition has much to offer, things, particularly living things, do not reveal their ultimate truth by these means. The dissected animal tells you little of the *dynamics* of its species; understanding of its biochemical *processes* reveals nothing of the part played in the *cycles* of the *biosphere*. The mechanistic analogy used to refute mechanism is that of the watch: take the pieces apart and the essential *function* is lost; it can only be understood by considering the *whole* in its intended *dynamic* state.

Philosophy has also been defined as 'that which is correct'.[4] It is now widely recognised that the philosophical engine which drives our *culture* is not correct; the world view it induces and the resulting *way of life* is unsustainable. With the *synergy* of the major elements of Western culture – *death*-oriented religion, *flow*-based *consumption economics*, *politics* reliant on *institutional* forms – and the *whole* being blended into the *compressed mass* we presently experience, *unsustainability* becomes active *progress* towards *terminality*.

An ideal philosophy would allow a *dynamic synergy* between the elements of *existence*, experience, belief and the internal *models* generated, such that the *models* are being continually modified as the philosophy *evolves*. The failure of the present is rooted in the *institutionalisation* of beliefs and *models*, which fixes them irrespective of effects or circumstances. The effect of *institutionalisation* is to divorce *cultural paradigms* from philosophy so that, right or wrong, they become effectively beyond *change*.

Despite this, *green* philosophy does not reject the analytical tradition. Rather it seeks a different *perspective*, a further *shift* in the way we view the world, which will give predominance to *synthesis*. The essence of *synthesis* is that it seeks to understand the *relationships* of things, of *holons* and *wholes*. Whereas analysis is *linear* and *static*, *synthesis* inevitably involves *matrices* and *networks* and the *dynamics* of the *vital* interactions within them. *Synthesis* is the route to understanding *life processes*.

Green philosophy is not yet a coherent *whole*; indeed, in the *nature* of things, it is never likely to be complete; it will *evolve* with our changing understanding of things. However there are major components which form a framework which may be *extended* and modified in the *future*. These are *holism*, the *gaia* hypothesis, the understanding of *formative causation*, the embryonic science of *morphology*, with its twin roots in biology and *structuralism*, and *deep ecology*.

From these components, *principles* may be derived which act as guides for practice. For consistency in the *future* it is essential that we do not lose sight of our philosophical base. It should be used to ensure that propositions contribute to *sustainability*, and that compatibility is maintained between philosophy, *principles* and practice.

Green philosophy will *change* the way we think. In accomplishing this *change* we will *project* a different human *culture* into the world. I believe that the most urgent task confronting humanity is to establish a *global green culture* from a philosophical base which will supercede all present belief and dogma without destroying that which is valuable from the *past*. The philosophy must be capable of including and containing the *past* while actively projecting the *future*. We have to create a *green global cultural* umbrella which will shelter the *diversity* of human expressions while at the same time directing humanity to *sustainable ways of living* within the *natural limits* of the *Gaian whole*.

The objective of *green* philosophy must be to guide our journey from here to eternity, and in so doing *create* the possibility of heaven on earth for every expression of *life* which shares the journey with us. Moving ever closer to some unseen edge, over which much has already gone for ever, there is little point in aiming for anything else.

Green philosophy will grow from unexpected sources:

> Academic philosophy has often before been out of touch with the most vigorous thought of the age, for instance, in the sixteenth and seventeenth centuries, when it was still mainly scholastic. Whenever this happens, the historian of philosophy is less concerned with the professors than with the unprofessional heretics.[4,5]

Relationships   **culture, mindset, perception, assumptions**.
See also   **question, stability, shift, model**.
References
1 Fritjof Capra, 1982, *The Turning Point: Science, Society and the Rising Culture*, Simon & Schuster, New York.
2 Brewster's *Memoirs of Newton*.
  'I do not know what I may appear to the world, but to myself I seem to have

been only like a boy playing on the sea-shore, and diverting myself in now and then finding a smoother pebble or a prettier shell than ordinary, whilst the great ocean of truth lay all undiscovered before me.'

3 Francis Bacon (1561–1626), *The Advancement of Learning*
'If a man will begin with certainties, he shall end in doubts; but if he will be content to begin with doubts, he shall end in certainties'.
4 Bertrand Russell (1872–1970), 1945, *History of Western Philosophy*, George Allen & Unwin, London.
5 For an example of the philosophy of an unprofessional heretic, see Colin Johnson, 1991, *The Green Bible: Creating Sustainable Life on Earth*, Thorsons, London.

PLASTIC   Amorphous property of substance; capable of assuming any shape.

PLASTICS   Substances made predominantly from polymers of artifical molecules, mainly derived from coal and oil by-products. Polymers – repeating patterns of molecules – are formed around the agreeably cohesive nature of the carbon atom.

The concept of plastics is problematic for *greens*; the reality of them is problematic for the *environment*. (In a local shop, when I refused a plastic bag, the assistant retorted, 'Better than cutting down trees'. Later I recalled that neither was necessary.) The attractions of plastics as materials is that they can produce apparently desirable results for low costs; however, they do this in ways which are completely incompatible with *green philosophy*.

It is nothing more than a convenient illusion that plastics are *stable* long-life materials. Flexible plastics actually have a very short useful life; they become brittle and tear and/or become opaque and no longer transmit light. Their short useful *life* may be followed by an eternity as useless *waste*.

This is because of the very *nature* of the materials involved. Plastics are made by 'organic' chemists from life-based materials. In the process of manufacture these life-molecules are locked away from *life cycles* for ever; the materials become permanent *pollutants*, even if they are inactive in the *environment*. Secondly, they contain many unstable components which actively *pollute* the *environment* as they leach out of the plastic. There is also the incidental but serious *pollution* problem generated when people burn plastics, producing dioxins which are *toxic* even in minute quantities.

These problems arise because of the way plastics are *formed*. They are *artificial* substances produced by polymerising, that is *creating* long-chain molecules (polymers) with endlessly repeated *structures.* This *process* is supplemented by adding other molecules (co-polymers) to vary the structural properties of the plastic.

To get a picture of a plastic *structure* it may help to envisage them as molecular fences – lots of long poles cross-linked by many short connectors. However, as early polymer chemists discovered, a tangled fence does not make very good flexible membrane or solid product. So other substances are added to *create* desired *qualities.* These range from dyes and ultraviolet stabilisers to substances intended to modify the finished product. Plastics are made more flexible by adding monomers, substances which are only partially involved in the polymerisation process.

Modern flexible plastics are very sophisticated things. Perhaps rather than a fence they should be seen as a wet sponge; the body formed by the polymer *structure* is *stable* and long lasting, the liquid is the sponge making it transparent (or coloured) and maintaining the resilience and flexibility of the whole. But the sponge dries out; all those chemicals filling the voids in the *structure* are released into the *environment,* soon to be followed by the partially degraded *structural* remains (see **pollution**).

There is no evidence that all the millions of tonnes of *artificial* molecular debris released enter the *food network,* or indeed that they are directly harmful to any organism – they may be, they may not. As with so many *artificial* things, we simply do not know. What can be said is that they have the *potential* for harm; for instance by overloading immune *systems,* or by forming unpredicted combinations with other substances.

Plastics pose particular difficulties for *organic farmers* (see **food**). Plastics can in no way be described as a means of *life/environment* enhancement. They are based upon concepts which are derived from opposing and probably irreconcilable *life philosophies.*

That is not to say that plastics as such need be unacceptable to *green philosophy.* To be acceptable they must fulfil two criteria: they must either have an indefinite useful *life*; or they must be totally *biodegradable.* Imperial Chemical Industries (ICI) recently announced the first genuine *biodegradable plastic.* It has limited uses, naturally, and best serves to illuminate the false claims of all the others. The best others have done is to cause the 'sponge' to break down into particle *pollution.*

Recycling plastics is possible, but it generates *pollution* in *re-processing* the remains. I have been told that *re-processing* causes more *pollution* than new manufacture. There is also the loss of the replaced monomers. In practical terms we live in a country which cannot organise the *recycling* of a range of high-value materials, so what hope for 'cheap' plastics?

Cost is the primary attraction of plastics, particularly in agriculture. Many *organic* growers say plastics are cheap, save labour, and are convenient. But here their *philosophy* breaks down, for this is what ordinary *chemiculture* farmers say about chemical fertilisers, drugs and *biocides*.

Perhaps the lesson of plastics is one that has widespread relevance to the *global predicament*; we should not try to do things on the cheap, because if we do the *environment* pays the price in the end.

Relationships   **pollution, economics**.
See also   **artificial**.

POLITICS (also **political**)   Science and art of government; means of expression of will of people, community, etc.; theory, of *social* management, of *means* of conducting affairs within and between states.

Politics is the *means* by which groups of people focus *power* for specific ends. In those societies generally termed '*democratic*', this usually means contributing to centralised *institutional structures* by forming *institutions* intended to give a degree of public *participation* in affairs.[1]

Modern political parties are *mass participation institutions* which act to deny individuals and *communities* control over their lives and affairs. A political party becomes progressively more *exclusive* as a *hierarchy* rises from the support of those the party represents. In conventional politics there is a government party or coalition, and an opposition. Together they *form* a *whole* which acts to *exclude* other influences; political matters must be channelled through 'the *democratic process*', which of its *nature* ensures that *ideas* which would *change* the *structure* of that *process* are *excluded* (see **thematic compatibility**).

POLITICIAN   'Someone who only acts rationally when all other possibilities are exhausted.'

GREEN POLITICS   The means of expression and administration of the will of people in *community* and in concert with *life* as a *whole*.

Greens are confused over politics. Some see entering the *grey* political arena, gaining *power*, exercising benevolent *green* influence (or dictat) from the *institutional* heights as the only way to *change* society. They may be right; this could be the way to *change* society, but it is doubtful if it would *change* the *culture* of that society (see **philosophy**). This view overlooks the price in conformity of entering the present arena, the effect on individuals of meshing with established *structures*, and the perverting resilience of the *institutions* they wish to conquer.

To believe that placing *green* politicians at the head of *grey institutions*, while leaving the *institutional structures*/logic intact, will bring *fundamental change* is just old-fashioned naiveté. It is *symptomatic* of old ways of thought, of the *autopilot* re-exerting the old course. Similarly, to believe that achieving the commanding heights of *institutional* monoliths will enable them to be remade misunderstands the *nature* of the path to the top, that of the *structure* which it climbs, and the effect of ascending upon those who climb. The politics of *green culture* must reject the *institutional exclusive* impersonal forms which serve to disenfranchise all but a minority; they must be based on universal personal and *inclusive forms*.

Other *greens* believe that the way to achieve the political (and *social, economic, cultural*, etc.) ends desired is to *create* them now. Instead of seeking central *power*, they seek to redraw the political map on *community* and *bio-regional* bases, and seek political control within these *structures*. The next step is to *create* a *federal structure* to link them. *Changing* policies within even small areas would then lead by example rather than centrally imposed *green* dictat (see **anarchy**).

History has shown that to regionalise or empower *communities* (decentralise) by reinforcing or refining the mechanisms of centralised *power* is an unlikely outcome (see **power**).

<u>Relationships</u>   **power, structure, community, anarchy**.
<u>See also</u>   **institution, hierarchy**.
<u>References</u>

1 See Anthony Sampson, 1962, *Anatomy of Britain*, and, 1965, *Anatomy of Britain Today*, Hodder & Stoughton, London; also Sandy Irvine and Alec Ponton, 1988, *A Green Manifesto: Policies for a Green Future*, Macdonald Optima, London; and David Icke, 1990, *It Doesn't Have to be Like This: Green Politics Explained*, Green Print, London.

POLLUTE   Destroy the *purity* or *integrity* of *environment*.
POLLUTION   That which pollutes; matter in a polluted state.

Pollution may be given four classifications: *natural* substances occurring in unnatural *quantities*, e.g. silt deposits or volcanic ash; refined *natural* substances whose *bio-assimilation* is impaired by their refined state; *artificial* substances which are not *bio-assimilable*; substances which are *inherently toxic*, which may be purpose made, such as *biocides*, or the result of unpredictable actions, such as combination with other substances.

Pollution used to be seen as a regrettable and largely local effect, as the result of accident or obvious excess. Today it is recognised that it is an *inherent future* of the way *terminal* society uses *technology* to fulfil its *agenda* of *growth*. Pollution is a *global* phenomenon whose effects will continue unpredictably for decades or (in the case of *nuclear waste*) millenia.

Industrial *consumer* society is rapidly running out of capacity for its pollution. According to the studies by the *Club of Rome*,[1] humanity is likely to fulfil its *terminal progress* by fatal overload of the *life* support *systems* of the planet.

> Over the last two centuries – a mere instant of geological time – industrial societies have altered the earth's chemistry in ways that may have staggering ecological and economic consequences within our lifetimes or those of our children. Three stand out as particularly threatening and costly to society: diminished food security from a changing climate, the demise of forests from air pollution and acid rain, and risks to human health from exposure to chemical pollutants in the environment. These consequences arise from everyday activities that collectively have reached a scale and pace sufficient to disrupt natural systems that evolved over millions of years.[2]

There is no answer to the pollution problem. We have to stop producing it and, as far as possible, clean up that which we have already scattered.

<u>Relationships</u>   **economy, energy, waste, acid rain**, total **toxic** overload.

<u>See also</u>   **artificial, chemiculture, numbers**.

<u>References</u>

1 Donella H. Meadows, Dennis L. Meadows, Jorgen Randers, William W. Behrens, 1972, *The Limits to Growth: A Report for The Club of Rome's Project on the Predicament of Mankind*, Pan Books, London.
2 Sandra Postel, 1987, *Worldwatch*.

For regular updates on pollution and other environmental matters, see *The Environmental Digest*, Environmental Publications Ltd., Panther House, London WC1X 0AP.

POPULATION   see **numbers**.

POSITION   Place occupied by person or thing; point occupied for strategic purposes.

In *grey culture social* position is important. Many people occupy positions in *social hierarchies* as their means of livelihood. The most extreme examples are in *genetically elite* societies, where being born in the right position is enough to ensure wealth or *social* support. In many professions the *social* position conferred is at least as important as the *function* the professional is supposed to fulfil (see hidden **agenda**).

Position becomes more important the higher up the *social hierarchy* it occurs. (During the French Revolution some servants tried to persuade aristocratic masters and mistresses to dress in ordinary clothes and learn a few simple household tasks, as a means of avoiding arrest and the guillotine; most said they would rather die, and had their wish granted.) At the bottom of the scale, people who perform the essential *functions* for the *life* of society, of the *community*, have little *social* position.

Greens believe *social function* is more valuable than *social* position. What people do is of more importance than their accident of parentage, or the position they manage to acquire (see **universal credit economy**).

<u>Relationships</u>   **values, hierarchy, institution**.
<u>See also</u>   **function, potential**.

POSITIVE CONFRONTATION   Alternative term for non-violence, which avoids negative connotations of non-violent civil disobedience (NVCD), non-violent direct action (NVDA), non-violent revolution (NVR), etc (see **non-violence**).

POSITIVE FEEDBACK   see **feedback loops**.

POST-INDUSTRIAL FUTURE   The concept of an emerging society which is not dominated by dependence upon, and the *needs* of, manufacturing industry.

Some advanced societies are shedding heavy basic industries at present; jobs in services are replacing those in manufacture. This should not be seen as the same thing as the *creation* of post-industrial society. Industry has moved elsewhere for cheaper materials and labour. The *system* still depends upon *flow*; it has become *global* rather than local (see **institution**).

The *creation* of a post-industrial future requires *change* in almost every area of human activity. In *economics change* from *flow* to *stock*, the acknowledgment of *limits*, particularly to human expansion and *numbers*; the *creation* of *ways of life* within *human scale* which have other means of fulfilment than material *consumption*.

The *future* focus will be on *being*, on the *arts of living*; of fulfilment of the biological, *social*, *spiritual*, aesthetic, emotional and intellectual *needs* which are peculiar to our species, while doing nothing to hinder the fulfilment of others.

<u>Relationships</u>   **future provision, economics, human scale.**
<u>See also</u>   **change, creativity, potential.**
<u>References</u>

See Edward Goldsmith, 1988, *The Great U-Turn: De-industrialising Society*, Green Books, Hartland, Bideford, Devon, England; also Murray Bookchin, 1974, *Post-Scarcity Anarchism*, Wildwood House, London; and Leopold Kohr, 1957, 1978, *The Breakdown of Nations*, E.P. Dutton, New York, USA.

POTENTIAL   Capable of coming into being, of form, *energy* or action; latent property; something which is possible but which has not (yet) happened.

The potential of any thing is part of its *inherent* properties. These properties emerge under favourable (which may mean extreme) circumstances. Within the hypothesis of *formative causation*, this is expressed as the emergence of a new field of possibility (see **field potential**). In *evolution* it is expressed as the emergence, via a *shift*, of a new form (see **morphology, evolution**).

In *grey culture* the emergence of potential is ascribed to a mixture of *natural* and divine forces, generally expressed as: 'That's progress', implying that what is coming into being is beyond human control, not a matter of *choice*. *Greens* reject this view of human potential, primarily because it is *inherently terminal*; its potential is for a variety of means of *extinction*.

Greens have implicit faith in human potential. The *problems* of the world are of our *creation*; the ability to solve them lies within human potential. The belief in the need for an act of *conscious evolution* is reinforced by the knowledge of blank *genetic* capacity in our make-up (see **genetic**). The fact that we can appreciate our predicament is in itself an indication of the ability to *anticipate* the need for solutions. The emergence of the *green movement* can be seen as an expression of potential solutions.

Humans are creatures of extremes. The expression of all that is within our potential is recognised as unacceptable; hence the emergence of *morals* and *ethics*, of *rules* of behaviour with *limits* and proscription. We understand that we may not become all that we have the potential to become. This is why the *philosophy* which *projects* human *culture* is of *vital* importance. *Philosophy* guides our choice of *limits* and acceptability, of that which should be encouraged and that which must be rejected (see **philosophy**).

The potential humans must explore as a matter of *vital* urgency is that of our capacity for *sustainability*; for *creating sustainable means* of fulfilment, and *sustainable life dynamics* for our species in *balance* with the *dynamics* of the *Gaian whole*.

Relationships   **inherent, morphology, evolution**.
See also   **extension, change, creativity, conscious**.

POWER (see also **politics**)   Ability to do or act; particular faculty of body or *mind*.

Power is central to *grey culture*; propositions which do not offer power, or magnify it, are usually rejected, whatever their intrinsic worth.

The *principle* which illuminates such choices is, 'Power tends to corrupt, and absolute power corrupts absolutely. Great men are almost always bad men.'[1] Power is addictive; it is desired for its own sake. The effects can be seen in the madness expressed in the horrific behaviour of absolute rulers.The same *process* continues in more subtle ways in current society; power is the drug which drives the institutional *social* engine.

'We must guard against the acquisiton of unwarranted influence ... by the military industrial complex. The potential for the disastrous rise of misplaced power exists and will persist' (General, later 34th US President, Dwight D. Eisenhower [1890–1989], in his farewell address). It is regrettable that men seem able to warn of the danger of power only when they are no longer in a position to influence events.

Powerful people do not readily, and of their own volition, release their grip on power. Heads of *hierarchies* have an *inherent* advantage; their *position* enables them to maintain their *position*. Power is only relinquished to superior power; thus power propagates itself, maintaining its destructive distortion of human affairs. Any *system* of *social* or *economic* organisation which requires the relinquishment of power by one individual to another will involve the possibility of corruption, if only through apathy.

In *terminal culture* power has become *institutionalised.* Power, in the *social* sense of being able to focus *energy* to achieve particular ends, has been replaced by the ability to maintain *position* in *hierarchy*, and of the expression of the will of various *institutions*. People as individuals have effectively been disenfranchised and rendered powerless. The areas of important *choice* in *life* have been given/taken by another authority (see **institution**).

The perversion of power is a result of both scale and form in *terminal culture*; it is also a *function* of the *nature* of power. Because power is recognised as an ultimately non-fulfilling addictive perversion, with 'more' as its only rationale, *greens* believe that human society must be *structured* in such a way that *limits* the accumulation of power and prevents its *institutional* consolidation; thus a *culture* of *bio-regional diversity* with *self-reliant communities* on a *human scale*, combined in *federations* of *need* or interest. The *future* requires *networks* selected from the available *matrix*, rather than arbitrary nation states and transnational corporations.

For individuals it is important to distinguish between power (that which may be exercised or imposed, external to *self*) which is necessary to maintain *life* and potency (the power within of understanding, expression, *creativity*, of fulfilment of acceptable *potential*). Power is something which must be kept very close and used with utmost discretion; potency should be developed to enhance the *life* of all. Power must be carefully (and openly) focused among *communities* for transient purposes, and the focusing *structure* dissolved once the object is achieved; potency should be maximised during an individual's lifetime for the benefit of one or all.

Will *greens* be able to avoid the trap of power, and its inherent addiction and perversion? (See **politics**.)

Relationships   **hierarchy, politics, economics, competition**.
See also   **matrix, community, morphology**.
References

1 Lord Acton (John Emrich Edward Dalberg, 1st Baron Acton of Aldenham, 1834–1902), *Historical Essays and Studies*, *Appendix* Gordon Press, New York, USA; see also Leopold Kohr, 1957, 1978, *The Breakdown of Nations*, E.P. Dutton, New York.

PRESENT (see **past**)   Now; the result of the *past*.

The only point from which we can influence the *future*. Many people may find it necessary to adjust their perceptual focus; *living* in the present to seek *sustainable* routes into the *future* is becoming more urgent.

Relationships   **future**.
See also   **evolution**.

PRINCIPLE   Fundamental source, primary element; fundamental truth as basis for reasoning. General guide to action.

The accepted understanding of a principle is inadequate. Because the fundamental source from which principles themselves are derived is *philosophy*, the belief that derived principles are themselves fundamental allows them to be plucked from the air as required and disposed of when they become inconvenient. Thus when a principle, as a guide for action, is incompatible with or unconnected to *philosophy*, duplicity and/or hypocrisy may arise. Similar problems, such as inconsistency, may arise because the *philosophical*base has become over-*extended*and is no longer appropriate. That these *problems* are common features of 'principled' behaviour in public life indicates how far society has become divorced from a suitable *philosophical* base.

Consistency with respect to principles depends upon two factors – *integrity* and the acceptance of a *coherent system* of *philosophy*.

Green principles fall into four broad categories: those which are specific and directly compatible with *green philosophy*; reversed principles, that is those which produce *terminality* and would produce *sustainability* if reversed; adopted principles, those which should be taken from the *past* and continued in the *future*; and embryonic principles, those which if further developed could become compatible with *green philosophy*.

ADOPTED PRINCIPLES   Adopted principles are those which derive from those elements that are generally regarded as the source of our humanity. Generic headings for these principles are *altruism*, *love*, *freedom* and *responsibility*. The first filter for application is that principles under these headings should be *life-positive*.

While the essence of our humanity may be described in terms of such shared noble principles, these tend to suffer from a short range of application. *Altruism* is limited to family, tribe or other close *affinity group*; *freedom* contradicted by the imposition of irrational *limits*; *responsibility* known to be rare among others. Too soon our nobility disappears in the sands of hypocrisy – that which we claim for ourselves we cannot extend to others and are unable to perceive in the world at large.

EMBRYONIC PRINCIPLES   This brief selection of embryonic principles is intended to illustrate the *potential* of much in *grey culture*. In weeding our present *cultural* garden we will discover possibilities which will repay care and attention for the *future growth* of *green culture*.

Democracy (details) *evolves* to *consensus* (principles).

Centralism (state, corporation) *devolves* to *federation* (world, region, area, *community*, organisation of *diverse cultures*).

Loyalty (to *institutions*) *evolves* to treachery (in favour of the *environment*); traitor evolves to traitist (sovereign individual).

REVERSED PRINCIPLES   Examples of principles which must be reversed are:

Linear processes be turned into *cyclic.*

Position rejected for *function.*

Exclusivity rejected for *inclusivity.*

Monoism rejected for *diversity.*

Hierarchies replaced by *matrices.*

Competition rejected in favour of *co-operation.*

These examples are not a comprehensive list. Reversal may be applied to any area of *terminal* human activity.

SPECIFIC PRINCIPLES   specific principles derived from *Deep Ecology* by Barry Commoner[1]:

Everything is connected to everything else. *Life* is a delicate, interwoven *web*; touch one thread and the *whole* vibrates (see **holism, Gaia, morphology**).

Everything must go somewhere. Nothing simply vanishes, and anything man-made can cause *pollution.* There is no *away* (see great **cycle** of **life**).

Nature knows best. When we toss chemicals into an organism, it is as though we were tossing a random assortment of nuts and bolts into the most delicate machinery ever made (see **anticipation, potential**).

Commoner's principles are encapsulated in the economists' cliché: 'There is no free lunch'; there is a price on everything we do against *nature.*

Sustainability requires the application of two general principles: a decrease in human population (see **numbers**); a radical *change* in the *means* of human fulfilment (see **economy**).

For all *processes* the guiding principle is that of maximum viability. This requires that the end of any *process*, or its incidental by-products, must incorporate the beginning of another. Any *process* involving *life* material should maintain that material at the highest level of viability, returning it to the *biosphere* with the minimum loss of *energy* and without disrupting the overall *balance* of assimilating *systems.*

Principles for *processes* involving inanimate materials or non-replaceable *energy* must be subject to the principle of maximum utility. This demands that things be made using the minimum of materials, while having maximum durability. The *energy* involved in any transformation should be subject to minimum use (maximum re-use) and maximum *efficiency*.

These considerations of *process* require that we adopt the principle of the best *quality* in things and *life*, rather than *quantity*. The core principles of *green culture* may be summarised thus:

1 Everything is connected to everything else.
2 There is no *away*.
3 We are an integral part of *nature*; *nature* must come first.
4 *Diversity* in *nature* is strength.
5 All *life* has *inherent value*.
6 All *life* has equal *rights*.
7 All *life* must be in *balance* within the *biosphere*.
8 All *life* has the *right* to fulfil its *potential*, providing this does not inhibit the fulfilment of other *life*.
9 Greater *consciousness* brings greater *responsibility*.

<u>Relationships</u> **philosophy, culture**.
<u>See also</u>   **politics, life structure**.
<u>References</u>
1 Barry Commoner, 1971, *The Closing Circle*, Jonathan Cape, London; see also Colin Johnson, 1991, *The Green Bible: Creating Sustainable Life on Earth*, Thorsons, London.

PROBLEM (see **global predicament**)   Doubtful or difficult question or task; thing hard to understand.
PROBLEM OF PROBLEMS   In seeking to solve one problem others may be *created* in the *future*. The problem of problems is a feature of *terminal culture* which came to notice with reliance on the technofix. It is a *symptom* of a *philosophy* which has no further *potential*, whose use has become misdirected. Answers sought within its *structure* simply produce other problems. For example, whereas *organic* agriculture is essential, to try to bolt it on to old ways can produce adverts for *organic* peat supplies at the same time as Friends of the Earth run a campaign to save the disappearing peat bogs.
PROBLEM TRANSFER   At best *grey culture* achieves problem transfer. *Institutions* maintain belief in continuity, in '*away*' and the possibility of 'more', while their mechanisms transfer deprivation and *pollution* to *institutionally* weaker areas, and remove resources to the stronger. This *process* has *limits*; we share one *earth*, one destiny, and there is a *limit* to the degree to which we

can sue the *future* to answer today's problems.

Problems of *terminality* can only be solved (along with all problems of *dynamic systems*) in terms of *models* which *anticipate* the possible problems of the proposed solution. Safe aeroplanes are designed, not by understanding how they fly, but by examining all the ways they may not.

The unattainable but essential *objective* of *green philosophy* is to develop the capacity to *anticipate* and avoid *future* problems, rather than, as at present, devoting resources to solutions of foreseeable *problems*. The best we may hope for is to minimise problems, rather than to magnify them (see **casualty problem**).

<u>Relationships</u>   **perspective, process, philosophy**.
<u>See also</u>   **anticipation, potential**.
<u>References</u>

1 See World Commission on Environment and Development, 1987, *Our Common Future*, Oxford University Press, Oxford, England:

> The present decade has been marked by a retreat from social concerns. Scientists bring to our attention urgent but complex problems bearing on our very survival: a warming globe, threats to the Earth's ozone layer, deserts consuming agricultural land. We respond by demanding more details, and by assigning the problems to institutions ill equipped to cope with them. (Gro Harlem Brundtland, Head of the Commission)

PROCESS   Course of action, proceeding, especially of series of operations in manufacture or production.

The meaning of process requires clarification and *extension*. Process is that which happens in any interaction; it can be a description of the *dynamics* of the interaction, as legal process or atomic fisson.

The word has been distorted in some *green* circles by using it as a description in itself, as a means of avoiding describing the *nature* of the process occurring. Thus group *dynamics* becomes 'group process', and problems within groups become 'bad process'.

For *greens* the importance of process is in its distinction from the *events* it may produce. *Grey culture* focuses on *events* – another new car, seal-skin gloves, a baby. *Greens* seek to understand the processes which produce *events*, their consequences and effects. 'The major advances in civilisation are processes that all but wreck the societies in which they occur.'[1]

<u>Relationships</u>   **limits, potential, system, structure**.
<u>See also</u>   **economy, politics, evolution**.
<u>References</u>

1 A.N. Whitehead (1861–1947), British mathematician and philosopher. In *Process and Reality: An Essay in Cosmology* (1929) he used a complex and specific

terminology to formulate a comprehensive 'philosophy of organism'; Whitehead did not believe that conventional categories of philosophy described the inter-connections among matter, time and space, nor allowed the statement of general metaphysical principles.

PROGRESS   Move forward, onward, further; advance or develop. It is usually implied that progress leads to something better, bigger or more, or to another state or form.

Progress, despite the claims made upon it, is a neutral term, best summarised as meaning the unfolding of *inherent* possibilities within the *dynamics* of *evolution.*

The progress of humanity occurs within the constraints of the *ethics* of a particular *culture. Terminal culture*, with its pursuit of the domination of *nature*, the *hidden agenda* of conversion of more of the *environment* into human replicas, specialises in removing constraints on the blind *progress* of the *genetic* imperative.

Grey progress, despite many worthwhile details, has had one undeniable, unavoidable result. The sum of human endeavour, with the *consumption* of *finite resources*, the destruction of *environment* and species, has resulted, not in the universal well-being of humanity, but simply in a gross increase in human *numbers.* More people have more than ever before; more people suffer malnutrition and die of starvation than at any other time. *Grey culture* congratulates itself, while the direction it has taken has brought it to the edge of *extinction.*

The *future* requires that we understand human (*life's*) *motivation* and learn to be selective, to choose the direction of progress. *Green* progress requires the *conscious evolution* of our species, the re-integration of humanity within the *limits* of the *biosphere* and *finite resources.* True progress is the *creation* of a *sustainable balanced life dynamic* for the rest of time.

Relationships   **mindset, evolution, potential**.
See also   **numbers, shift, sink.**

PROJECT (see **extension**)   Cast, throw, impel, extrapolate; cause to be visible, as light on a screen.

The concept is important in considering *socio-cultural change.* The *philosophy* of a society, together with other compatible areas of belief such as religion, *politics* and *economics*, projects its *culture.* People live in *symbiosis* with their *culture*; to *change* the *way of life* generated it is essential to *change* the *philosophical* projector (see **philosophy**).

PROVISION Provide for, against, anticipated *need* or circumstance.

Green thought addresses the *needs* of the *future*; what must be *created*, what rejected, and the provision which should be made from what may be selected from the *past*.

FUTURE PROVISION Securing that which will further the *objective* of *sustainability*.

Proposition: we need to ensure that we go into the *future* with all that is necessary or worthwhile from the *past*.

Grey culture tends to eliminate that which does not comply with its *terminal ethos*; there are areas of *knowledge*, *ideas* and beauty in the *past* which must be rescued for the *future*. Some essential strands are included in this dictionary, but the task requires many hands and *minds* for its success. People who believe in a *sustainable future* are needed to clear the decks for that *future*, to bring from the *past* that which is relevant but overlooked or hidden; the works of Blake, Rousseau and Jung spring to mind, but there is much more from all human *cultures* which should be built into the very foundation of a *sustainable future* as part of its mainstream of understanding.

The *need* is for an *elite* intellectual salvage crew to bring forward into new realisation of relevance gems from the *past*, before they are lost in the spread of illiteracy, trampled to dust by meaningless *numbers*, or become meaningless to *institutionally* anaesthetised brains.

The essence of the *process* is to distinguish the academic tail from the intellectual dog it immobilises; those countless thousands who, without a contribution of their own, endlessly write about what was written, then assess the writing about what was written, discuss its style, its shape, its meaning, its relevance, and so on, until the point, the essential point, of the original is finally lost. Part of the *hidden agenda* of academic *institutions*.

Future provision requires that we rediscover and refine, *synthesise*, all the strands of human *wisdom* which contribute to human *values* and to a *sustainable future*. The *terminal process* of defining, analysing, of reducing to *institutional*, numerical, *values* must be rejected.

Relationships **future, culture**.
See also **information, institution**.

PSYCHO- Of the mind and soul (*psyche*, from the Greek psukhe = breath, life, soul).

Prefix, as in -analysis, -dynamic, -therapy, etc.

PSYCHOSYNTHESIS (see **personal growth**) A comprehensive approach to self-realisation, a *system* for psychological and *spiritual growth*.

Psychosynthesis is one of the *holistic alternatives* to psychoanalysis, although it has its roots in the same tradition. Formulated by Italian psychiatrist Roberto Assagioli, psychosynthesis aims to free people from past conditioning (rather than focus and thus expand it, as in analysis), to assist the resolution of inner conflicts, to develop individual will and the capacity for *freedom*; generally to bring out the *creative potential* of the individual. The *process* is expressed as the exploration of the great inner journey; a quest for the (individual) meaning of *life*, exploration of the borderlands of *existence*.

Part of the *dynamic* of *personal growth* is to break the continuity of the *past*, to bring people from sheltering in the *morphology* of the recent *past*, where they have no influence on the course of *future events* (victims), to *life* in realisation of 'now', where the *future*, and the many paths it offers, is open (creator). The summary objective of psychosynthesis is for everyone to become *creative* in the cause of *life* and the *evolution* of the human species.

Relationships   **mindset, change, culture, future**.

See also   **morphology, evolution**.

References

See Piero Ferrucci, 1982, *What We May Be: The Vision and Techniques of Psychosynthesis*, Thorsons, London; also Arnold Mindell, 1985, *Working With the Dreaming Body*, Routledge & Kegan Paul, London.

PURISM (also **purist, purity, perfection, perfectionist**) Insistence on scrupulous, dogmatic, belief; behaviour resulting from such insistence.

Frequently a means of avoiding consideration of other possibilities, or of confronting the need to make *choices*. Also a refuge from reality.

The one-dimensional nature of perfection, as a *projection* of *ego* or a means of discounting *diversity* and *interrelationships*, runs counter to *green intuition*. The principles of uncertainty and *change*, both fundamental to *life*, make the concept of perfection untenable.

Purism should not be confused with *philosophical integrity*.

PURPOSE (see **question**)   Object to be attained, that which is intended; *function* designed to be fulfilled.

The purpose of *existence* can only be described in the widest terms. In a *universe* alive with its own logic the purpose is in *being*. The purpose of *life*, through *synergy*, is to seek immortality; *life* fulfils a *function* somewhere between *energy* seeking *entropy* and matter seeking *stability* (see **universe**).

Green purpose is to *create sustainable ways of life* which re-integrate humanity with the *great cycle of life* of the *Gaian whole*, human life as an indefinitely *sustainable* proposition.

<u>Relationships</u>   **existence, motivation, potential**.
<u>See also</u>   **life, morphology, evolution**.

QUALITY   Degree of excellence, relative nature, kind or character. That which is inherent.

Quality is largely meaningless in *grey culture*, unless it is acknowledged by others as a prop to status or *position*; the focus is on *quantity* in its obsession with 'more'. *Greens* believe *sustainability* requires focus on quality, in the sense of the highest degree of excellence possible in all things. Thus the maximum *utility* would be derived from long-lasting *energy-efficient artefacts*. The same requirement should be applied to everything in human affairs; high quality should take precedence over *quantity* (see **consumer**).

Within the human species the quality of *life* for each individual, for every *community*, must become a clearly established concept with agreed standards. High quality in *sustainable balance* with the *biosphere* will require a reduction in *quantity* (see **numbers**).

Within the *Gaian whole* humans should do nothing which degrades the quality of other *life forms* or their *environments*; we can only *extend* our *life-options* by enhancing the capacity and quality of all *life* (see **balance**).

<u>Relationships</u>   **principles, sustainability, art of living**.

<u>See also</u>   **numbers, terminal culture**.

QUANTITY   Property of something that may be determined by reference to a measurement. Usually the number, amount, size of, a thing (see **quality**).

QUESTION   Seek information of; cast doubt upon.

The most powerful question is Why? Why are things the way they are? Why can't we do it differently, etc.? It is important to keep asking the question Why?

'Why?' is the natural question; children ask it all the time. Most parents fail to answer, tell lies, or get angry with the child for asking. So the child is discouraged and eventually stops asking. Our *culture* thus suppresses our questioning nature, blunting inquisitiveness in favour of ignorance and conformity, because the previous generation was subjected to the same process (see **education**).

In *grey culture*, question everything.

For *green future culture* two questions are relevant. Is it *sustainable*? If not, think again. If it is, does it enhance *life*? If it does, proceed.

<u>Relationships</u>   **change**.

<u>See also</u>   **information**.

RADICAL Of the root(s); naturally inherent, essential, fundamental, basic; affecting the foundation, going to the root, starting
from basics.

Radical is a word whose meaning has split on the rock of *grey
culture stability*. It is used on the one hand to elicit approval for
apparent *change*; 'radical reform' is usually trivial, far from radical.
On the other it is used, in meaning unacceptable or extreme, as a
way of warning or frightening away from an *idea* or course of
action.

Greens need to use radical in its real sense of something
different, not a modification, development or PR presentation. A
radical proposition is something new, although not necessarily
entirely so, which addresses a *problem* or situation from basics.
Radical solutions tend to address the *future* with little regard for
the *past, position*, or vested interests.

<u>Relationships</u> **future, alternative**.
<u>See also</u> **change, assumption, expectation**.

RAINBOW Principal colours of spectrum produced in sky by
refraction of sunlight by raindrops.

A natural wonder, revealing *diversity* within *unity*.

RAINBOW ALLIANCE (aka RAINBOW COALITION)

> The 'alternative' movement or movements, so amorphous
> that one is at a loss to say where they begin or end, or when they
> first appeared on the scene, have shown an interest in out-
> rageous thoughts like 'producing for need', small is beautiful,
> growing one's own cabbage, and ideas that threaten the people
> who want to organise our lives for us. It could be that we are
> clutching at straws. A lot of these people are unbearably fey.
> They have premonitions and intimations and deep, deep feel-
> ings. Some of them are so spiritual that you could hit the spirit
> with a housebrick. But as they say in Gloucestershire, it don't
> make no difference.

They have made a paradigm shift that leaves the politicos shuffling and mumbling in their imaginative poverty. If we survive the next few decades, if one of the catastrophes being spawned by this crazy socio-economic system on an ever-closing frequency don't wipe us all out, it will be a rainbow coalition of all these daft buggers that will save us.[1]

RAINBOW ECONOMY   That diverse array of, usually *co-operative* sometimes *community* based, initiatives where people seek to do worthwhile things which fulfil *needs* and provide better ways of working, of doing things. A difficult area since any *green* enterprise inevitably interfaces with the *grey* world around it (see **co-operative**).

Some writers[2] have attempted to give the concept literal meaning by ascribing values to the colours of the rainbow and relating these values to economic activity:

Purple for spiritual values.
Dark blue for planetary values.
Pale blue for economic values.
Green for ecological values.
Yellow for values of personal creativity and fulfilment.
Orange for local community values.
Red for social values.

The concept may better be seen as a symbolic indication of the need for small-scale *diversity* and direct supply rather than as a rationally based intellectual proposition.

RAINBOW WARRIOR

When the earth has been ravaged and the animals are
dying a tribe of people from all races, creeds
and colours will put their faith in deeds not words
to make the land green again; They shall be known as
the Warriors of the Rainbow.
    Protectors of the Environment.[3]

Hopi Indian Prophecy

Relationships   **green movement, stewardship**.
See also   **shift, Earth First!, Greenpeace**.
References

1 Ken Smith, 'The End of Politics', in *Freedom*, Volume 51, Number 12, 16 June 1990. Freedom Press, Angel Alley, 84b Whitechapel High Street, London E1 7QX; see also Ken Smith, 1988, *Free is Cheaper*, John Ball Press, May Hill, Gloucester, England.

2 Guy Dauncey, 1988, *After The Crash: The Emergence of the Rainbow Economy*, Green Print, London.
3 Hopi Indian prophecy.

REAL   Actually existing as thing or occurring in fact.

REALITY   Property of being real; real existence; what is real, what underlies appearance; real nature of.

The *philosopher's* equivalent of the holy grail; as the preceding definitions show, it is difficult to get to grips with reality.

Given the *nature* of human *perception*, it is probably better not to try to pin down or fix reality. For practical purposes it is a relative concept. Reality is that which is agreed, best seen as a multidimensional and shifting interpretation of circumstances and *existence* (see **scientific objectivity**).

'Be realistic, demand the impossible!'[1]

<u>Relationships</u>   **perception, assumption, mindset, culture**.

<u>See also</u>   **institutional process, myth appropriation**.

<u>References</u>

1 1960s graffiti.

RECLAMATION   see **restoration**.

RECYCLE   Return to previous stage of *cyclic process*, especially to convert *waste* to reusable material.

Recycling has been grasped as an answer to many of the problems of *waste* and *pollution*. Although desirable, it is of *limited* applicability. While all *natural* substances can be recycled, *artificial* substances present problems, and *energy* is a one-way proposition. And too often '*recycling*' means using *nature* as a convenient dustbin.

Greens believe that things should either be part of, and contribute to, *natural cycles*, or should be made to last indefinitely. The order should be: re-use, repair, and finally recycle at the highest possible *energy* level. Among *natural cycles* being established to fulfil human need, many are not yet complete; *organic* farming is still part of a *flow system* as far as the *consumers* of its produce are concerned.

<u>Relationships</u>   **cyclic, utility, economics**.

<u>See also</u>   **energy, balance, limits**.

<u>References</u>

See Jonathon Porritt (ed.), 1987, 1990, *Friends of the Earth Handbook*, Macdonald Optima, London; also Sandy Irvine and Alec Pontin, 1988, *A Green Manifesto:*

Policies for a Green Future, Macdonald Optima, London; and John Elkington and Julia Hailes, 1988, *The Green Consumer Guide: From Shampoo to Champagne, High Street Shopping for a Better Environment*, Gollancz, London.

REDUCTIONISM (see **Cartesianism**)   Analysis of complex things into simple constituents; view that a *system* can be fully understood in terms of its isolated parts; an idea in terms of simple concepts.

Grey culture is founded on a reductionist *philosophy*. *Greens* reject this in favour of *holism* (see **holism**).

> Although the reductionist approach has been extremely successful in biology, culminating in the understanding of the chemical nature of genes, the basic units of heredity, and in the unravelling of the genetic code, it nevertheless has severe limitations ... The functions of a living organism that do not lend themselves to a reductionist description – those representing the organism's integrative activities and its interaction with the environment – are precisely the functions that are crucial for the organism's health.[1]

Relationships   **philosophy, culture**.
See also   **synthesis**.
References
1 Fritjof Capra, 1982, *The Turning Point: Science, Society and the Rising Culture*, Simon & Schuster, New York.

REFINE   Purify, clarify; make elegant or cultured, imbue with delicacy of feeling or taste.

Most refinement in the *processes* of *grey culture* amounts to *problem* improvement. The Clean Air Acts in Britain which removed the London smogs refined the *pollution* problem into *ozone* and *acid rain* (see **problem**).

The refinement of materials can *process* them out of *natural cycles* or the scope of *energy efficient recycling*. Hence the need to focus on basics, *utility* and the maximum use of artefacts.
Relationships   **process, cyclic**.
See also   **linear, finite resources**.

REFORM   Form again; the removal of abuse, complication, or drawbacks, from *system*, usually in *politics*.
REFORMISM   The belief that things are basically OK, and may continue with some fine tuning or minor adjustment. Reformism is

the means of *evolution* within *terminal culture*. It has the effect of *refining terminal progress* (see **radical**).

Relationships   **stability, mindset, terminal culture**.

See also   **revisionist, evolution**.

REGION   see **bioregion**.

RELATIONSHIP   The connection(s) between things.

Conventionally human concern is for relationships with other people; of kinship, affection, or *economics*. Such emotional parochialism needs to be *extended* to encompass our relationships with the rest of *life* and as much of *existence* as our *minds* can behold.

Holism, a principal component of *green philosophy*, is about the relationship between things, the connectedness of all things, the interrelationship of all *life* within the *Gaian whole*. Describing the *dynamics* of the relationships within the *web* of *life* is the *function* of *morphology* – to produce maps of the interactions of the many shapes of *existence*. It is only by understanding the *matrix* of *existence* that we can appreciate the effects of our actions or proposals upon the *environment* and all of its constituents.

Relationships   **holism, morphology**.

See also   **needs, community**.

RENEWABLE (also **replaceable**) Used to describe *cyclic resources*.

RENEWABLE RESOURCES (see **resource**) Things which are replaced by the *cycles* of *nature*.

There is a split between *green* and *grey* over renewable resources. While *greens* are in favour of the use of such resources as the only source of *sustainable ways of life*, they oppose the *grey* view of total *exploitation*, of world *diversity* reduced to *genetically* engineered biomass designer mono-cultures exclusively for human (*institutional*) *needs*. The use of renewable resources raises the question of the *rights* of the *life* forms which are being used (see **life contract**).

The *sustainable* use of renewable resources requires *restoration* of *balance* within the *biosphere* and the recognition by the human species of the *rights* of all other species (see **rights**).

Relationships   **sustainability, philosophy, limits**.

See also   **perspective, mindset**.

RESONANCE   see **morphic resonance**.

RESOURCE (see **finite resource, renewable resource**)   Means of supplying what is needed; stock that can be drawn upon. Skill, practical ingenuity, as in being resourceful.

In *grey culture* a resource is anything which may be *exploited*, usually profit being the only consideration (see **market**).

HUMAN RESOURCE   The energy and talent of people.

We must look to ourselves for the answers to the problems we generate.

The *green* view is that there is no option other than to accept positively the challenges involved in seeking *sustainable ways of living* within the *limits of nature* with confidence in our abilities. *Greys* believe the *green* view is impossible and prefer to continue towards *terminality*, meaning the *Impossible Party* of *consumption* and destruction. Ultimately, if there are survivors, they will have the challenge thrust upon them with the added burden of *survival* with a depleted, more damaged, resource base.

Relationships   **perspective, potential**.
See also   **sustainability, choice**.

RESPONSIBILITY (see **freedom**)   Accountability for actions, behaviour; capable of expression of rational conduct; liability for, accountability.

Responsibility *balances freedom*; it is the price paid for *freedom* taken. The concept implies a *social* mechanism whereby standards are declared and *limits* acknowledged. In general the greater the *freedom* the greater the responsibility, and vice versa.

In *grey institutional culture* individuals are progressively deprived of both responsibility and *freedom* as *institutions structure* the *life* and *choices* of populations. People are left with the responsibility of *consumers* and the *freedom* to select from endless junk placed before them by the *economic flow. Reality* is managed elsewhere and *life* expressed in emotional flushes stimulated by the telly soap industry, the *mass media* mental substitute for real living with responsibility and *freedom.* Most people still lead lives of quiet desperation,[1] but the proportion declines as the *institutional* cocoon closes.[2]

Responsibility involves *living* on our own account, not relying on *institutional* provision (see **institution**).

Relationships   **freedom, anarchy, community**.
See also   **choice, purpose, censorship**.

References
1 'The mass of men lead lives of quiet desperation', Henry David Thoreau (1817–62), 1985, *Walden, a Concordance*, Macmillan, London.
2 Erich Fromm (1900–80), 1942, 1960, *Fear of Freedom*, Routledge & Kegan Paul, London.

RESTORATION   Give back, (attempt to) bring back to original state, to former state or condition.

Along with a decline in human *numbers* and reduced demands on the *environment*, we should also have long-term plans for the restoration of the *environment*, the *Gaian cycles* which *sustain* it, and the *rights* of other species. Restoration involves the ideas of *balance* in the *biosphere*, the establishment of *sustainable ways of life*, understanding the *morphology* of the *Gaian whole*, and a willingness to allow *nature* to *exist* without the benefit of human interference in many parts of the *earth*. Implicit in the idea of *restoration* is the *assumption* that humanity is prepared to confront the *global predicament* and act positively to counter it (see **casualty problem**).

Philosophy is important because it will guide the many *processes* involved. All steps need to be taken at once; to restore our species to its own sovereignty, to move away from the trap of *institutional* provision and seek other *means* of fulfilment. We should also decrease *consumption* and *pollution*, go for *less* rather than more, accept *responsibility* for our actions, recreate *life in community*, renegotiate our *life contract*, restore human *life* to *human scale*.

Relationships   **choice, Fourth World, future, philosophy**.
See also   **renewable resources, rights**.

RETROSPECTIVE INNOVATION (see **future provision**)   The retrieval from the *past* of better ways of doing things, such as the use of *renewable resources, organic farming*, low-energy self-reliance, etc.

REVISIONIST (see **reform**)   Follower of policy of revision (reconsideration and correction or improvement on original) or modification, especially of Marxist–Leninist doctrine.

The *grey political* left equivalent of the *grey political* right *reformist*; working within the old *paradigm* rather than seeking a new one.

REVOLUTION (see **thematic compatibility**)   Motion in circular course or orbit.

Classically the overthrow of an established regime with force by a dissaffected section of society. The result of revolution is not fundamental *change*, but the takeover of existing *institutions* by different people (or at most the replacement of some *institutions* by others). The failure of revolutions can be seen as inevitable by understanding the *nature* of *institutions* (see **institution**).

Greens believe that *change* should be *evolutionary* rather than revolutionary. *Evolution*, in the *shift* to new *forms*, brings irrevocable change to new *states* of *existence*; revolution simply takes things round in circles within the same *paradigm*.

'Please don't sell me revolution when it's freedom I need.'[1]

<u>Relationships</u>   **stability, evolution, change.**

<u>See also</u>   **morphology, shift.**

<u>References</u>

1. Su Negrin, 1972, *Begin at Start*, Times Change Press, USA.

RIGHT(S)   That which is correct, true. A basis for just, fair, correct, treatment. Thing to which one is entitled.

When one form of *life* has developed the means to destroy all others without developing the *wisdom* of self-restraint to control its blind *progress*, the question of establishing rights becomes crucial.

Grey culture has an *inherent* resistance to the idea of rights. As part of its *hierarchical structure* and authoritarian *nature*, rights are denied wherever possible; *right(s)* is equated with might. Where the *idea* is accepted (forced upon) it is fragmented, perhaps under the influence of the concept of 'divide and rule', to avoid the consolidation of rights into a *system* of equality. Thus in *grey culture* rights are resisted under many headings – animal rights, civil rights, human rights, reproductive rights, property rights and so on.

Within *green philosophy* there is a need to develop the concept of universal rights; a concept which means exactly that, the rights *inherent* in *existence*. The theoretical concept of rights has more or less stalled since Tom Paine[1] and Rousseau.[2]

It is time for a *holistic*, less homocentric, approach. The past can offer, in paraphrase, a starting point:

When in the course of human events it becomes necessary for people to dissolve the cultural bonds which connect them with others, and to assume among the consciousness of the earth, the understanding and wisdom which the Laws of Nature and of Nature's God offer them, a decent respect to the opinions of humankind requires that they should declare the causes which impel them to the separation.

We hold these truths to be self-evident, that all life is created equal, that it is endowed in creation with certain unalienable Rights, that among these are Life, Liberty, and the Fulfilment of Potential – That to secure these rights wisdom must be instituted among humanity, deriving from human consciousness and knowledge and the consent of the biosphere – That wherever any form of consciousness or knowledge becomes destructive of these ends, it is the Duty of the People to alter or abolish it, and to institute New Forms, laying their foundation on such principles and organising its energy in such structures, as to them shall seem most likely to effect their Safety and Happiness.[3]

The inalienable rights of *life* can be described within parameters which are already established in *green philosophy*. Within the *life contract*, every *form* of *life* has the right to *genetic* integrity, to the conditions necessary for the maintenance of the *morphology* of its species, and the capacity for the fulfilment of its further *evolutionary* and other *potential*.

Such rights may be best clarified in terms of a system of rights, of one part of the *biosphere* in *relation* to others, and locally in terms of the *balance* within each particular *bio-region*. The *green objective* of an overall *balance* of *life* could thus be established in terms of rights, of rights to the physical *needs* of *life*, of amounts of natural *carbon-based* molecules, of space and association, of unpolluted land, sea, water, and air; of the right to comprehensive species and *environmental* integrity.

Such rights amount to a universal right to *freedom* from human interference for species and *environments*. The question of *food* and farming has to be confronted in *creating* the rights of a *sustainable biosphere*, as does the *grey* concept of the legitimate 'use' of other species. Outside the necessities of the *food net* (legitimacy which does not include suffering or distortion of *morphology*) there is very little such usage. Pets, companions, *symbiotic relationships* such as guide dogs and serf primates, require a code of mutuality. The *grey ethic* of conditioning scientists by animal experimentation must be completely rejected – there are other ways if the knowledge is *vital* (see **vital need**). *Tao* and *chi* indicate that the door of *knowledge* need not be battered open with the living bodies of other species; it can be given a gentle push that allows all through.

The question of human rights is complex. Where there are problems they are of human making. To generalise, they are problems of outdated *philosophy* and socio-*economic structures* blended with *hierarchical forms* of organisation and belief in *genetic elitism*. Alternatively, they are the result of the *compression* of *numbers* combined with the distortion of human affairs by the activities of *institutions*, for instance in equipping medieval fiefdoms with high-tech mass destruction weapons. The lack of human rights is a *symptom* both of out-of-*balance* traditional society and of the *terminal* path all traditional *cultures* follow.

What are human rights? The list claimed is long and endlessly varied; things some societies believe crucial, others discount as irrelevant. Basic rights may be to the *means* of *life*, to *life* in *community*, to expression of *potential* that does not restrict the *potential* of others, to the basics which Rousseau expounded in 1762 – to liberty, equality and fraternity. These are increasingly elusive in *grey culture*, which has concentrated its energies and provisions on establishing and protecting the rights of *institutions*.

There is also the question of *cultural rights*, the right of a people to *live* in a way they choose *free* from depredation by larger, more *institutionally* powerful *cultures*; the subtle but very real problem of *cultural* imperialism. In *Our Common Future*[4] (where the question of rights has two index entries), it is naively suggested that those small groups of *natural peoples* still living in *sustainable ways* should *create institutional structures* as a means of safeguarding their *cultural rights*.

Greens believe there will always be rights problems until a *culture* is *created* which is based upon *inherent* universal *rights*. Socio-*cultural structures* must be designed which require a *way of life* which expresses such rights as an *inherent* part of its *function*. Expecting people to operate the *community* of which they are a part, a right to privacy, to a non-public *life* containing voluntary expressions of behaviour between consenting adults, to the right of victimless behaviour, is equally important.

Perhaps the best way to think of human rights is in negative terms. Above some basic agreed foundation of rights, humans should be entitled to *extend* into the spaces not required by the rights of others less adaptable, less mobile and less imaginative than humans. In short, that the rights of *Gaia* and others must come *naturally* before those of humans.

<u>Relationships</u>   great **cycle** of **life**, **nature**, **numbers**, **universal credit economy**.

See also   **vital needs, life contract**.

References

1 Thomas Paine (1737–1809), 1791, *The Rights of Man*.

2 Jean Jacques Rousseau (1712–78), 1762, *Contrat Social*. For an overview of Rousseau's life and work see John Hope Mason, 1979, *The Indispensible Rousseau*, Quartet Books, London.

3 Based upon *The Declaration of Independence, In Congress, July 4, 1776, The unanimous Declaration of the thirteen United States of America*.

4 World Commission on Environment and Development, 1987, *Our Common Future*, Oxford University Press, Oxford, England: 'These groups' own institutions to regulate rights and obligations are crucial for maintaining the harmony with nature and the environmental awareness characteristic of the traditional way of life' (page 115). Tell that to the multinational logging/mining/beef ranching institution.

RUBBISH (see **waste**)   Waste material, debris, refuse, litter; worthless material or article, trash.

The *grey* definition of rubbish is itself an example of another meaning of the word: absurd idea or suggestion, nonsense. Nothing is worthless.

RULE   Principle to which action or procedure conforms or is bound or intended to conform; dominant custom, canon, test, standard; normal state of things.

Preference should be given to *tools* rather than rules. Rules are for *competitors* in someone else's *game*, for conformity to a *system*. They are a part of unquestioned *structures*, an essential part of its *stability*. This may be fine for football, but in social affairs they preserve *position* and the *status quo*. *Tools* enable *functions* to be fulfilled and *changes* made.

SCALE (see **human scale**)   Generally of position or relative dimensions.

Grey culture likes everything big, of the largest scale possible.

Greens believe in human scale; that when the whole of an undertaking cannot be understood by those involved it has passed a critical threshold of scale. This rejects the proposition of people as only cogs (only obeying orders) in vast institutional structures (see **Fourth World**).

SELF (selves)   Of individual person's essence or nature; individual as object of consideration, introspection, or action.

Self defines the end of one, and the beginning of others. Whether self as a concept, implying the possibility of isolation, is achievable is doubtful (see **holism**, **morphology**).

SELF-   Prefix expressing direct reflexive action.

SELF-ACCEPTANCE   Accepting ourselves for what we are; coming to terms with the extremes of our human nature and potential. It is difficult, some say impossible, to love another or others if you cannot love yourself.

SELF-MOTIVATION (see **need**)   The necessary inner turmoil. There is no final security, no way out of anxiety except purpose, no peace until everything is at peace. The problems of the human condition are motivational discomforts, part of life's drive towards immortality.

SELF-RELIANCE   Independence of spirit; confidence and ability in self. Necessary prerequisite for balanced mutual relationships between people, and of the human species within the biosphere.

Grey culture, with its ethic of passivity and mass consumption, encourages dependence; the hierarchical form demands compliance. Self-reliance requires that we de-couple from institutional provision and the economics of flow (see **economics**, **institution**).

The green model of self-reliance is based upon individuals in community, with the closed circuits of need fulfilment with

283

minimum outside inputs. Such *communities* would imitate *natural cycles*, with minimum-loss *ambient energy systems* and minimum *finite resource consumption*; they would produce zero *pollution* and minimum *waste*. The social *structures* would be characterised by optional *compression* without loss of *anticipatory* tension, by facilitation of *potential* within *natural limits*. Self-reliance requires that humanity lives within *human scale* without *consuming* the *environment* or other species.

SELF-SUFFICIENCY (see **retrospective innovation**)   The idea that people can/should attempt to meet all their needs by their own labours.

The idea was popularised by John and Sally Seymour with their bestselling books.[1] It remains a key *motivation* for rural resettlers, although the *reality* is a practical impossibility. Nevertheless, the aspiration to self-sufficiency, with its challenge of direct interaction with the *processes* of *life*, is a step in many right directions. Compatible social and *economic* infrastructures are developing to fulfil wider general *needs* and link various aspects of the self-sufficiency movement into *communities* (see **co-operative**).

<u>Relationships</u>   **personal growth, human resource, rights, community**.

<u>See also</u>   **psychosynthesis, evolution, limits**.

<u>References</u>

1 John and Sally Seymour, 1973, *Self Sufficiency*, also the coffee-table book, 1976, *The Complete Book of Self-Sufficiency*, both Faber & Faber, London; also John Seymour and Herbert Giradet, 1987, *Blueprint for a Green Planet*, Dorling Kindersley, London; see Sedley Sweeney, 1985, *The Challenge of Smallholding*, Oxford University Press, Oxford, England; and various 'backyard' titles by Prism Press, such as Ann Williams, 1978, *Backyard Farming*, Prism Press, Stable Court, Chalmington, Dorset DT2 0HB, England.

SEX   Being female or male; the distinguishing biological characteristics of female or male. Characteristics of sexual origin are classified as feminine or masculine.

The belief that sexual differentiation is simply biological, and almost entirely limited to reproductive organs and their supporting *systems*, is common to many standards of *grey* and *green* thought (see **sexual dimorphism**).

SEXISM (see **-ism**)   Prejudice or discrimination on the grounds of the sex of a person.

Generally used to describe the individual and *institutional* discrimination/oppression of women by men. Sexism may also be the expression of prejudice against sexual minorities, either on the grounds of blurred gender or sexual behaviour.

Sexism is also used in a reversed way by some *feminists* to repress males. Frequently this involves a battle over what is referred to as pornography.[1] This reversal produces a contrary effect, where those seeking liberation (feminists) align with the most censorious and repressive elements in society (see **censorship**). While acknowledging that *freedom* is/can rarely be given, liberation cannot be achieved by repression.

SEXUAL BEHAVIOUR   A vast range of human behaviour may be classed as sexual or sexually motivated, from the obviously physical to simply looking at other people, into the realms of advertising and to protective *altruism* for women and children.

Sexual behaviour usually means the physical expression of sexuality. Again there is a wide range; from the narcissistic and masturbatory to formation dancing (dancing, 'the vertical expression of a horizontal desire', George Bernard Shaw) to another wide range of copulatory behaviour involving stimulation to orgasm.

The *purposes* of human sexual behaviour are as *diverse* as its means of expression. *Grey culture* has official limits to its accepted sexual expression; having children and expressing *love* (frequently used as a synonym for sex) within marriage. Anything beyond this limit causes problems; the *culture* is loath to come to terms with human sexuality. It seeks to maintain control by *institutional* licence and denial of reality. This is a reflection of the prejudice within *cultures* for and against various forms of sexual behaviour. Concepts of normality are part of the assumptive base of each society and every *culture.* Our sexual behaviour, because its *motivation* is basic and deep, seems vulnerable to imprinting by a wide range of prejudices.

There seems to be no reason to accept restrictions on sexual behaviour, other than those which may be described as *natural limits*. These are primarily the *limit* of informed consent; participants in sexual behaviour must be capable of making an *informed choice* on *participation.* Ignorance of sexual matters and possibilities, whether among adults or children, only helps *create* victims. Secondary *limits* are a matter for individual *choice* and inclination and cannot be prescribed.

The final *limit,* that of disease, also hinges on *information.* In the age of AIDS there is only one safe *assumption* about other people, that they are infected. The HIV virus has been found in all bodily fluids except ear wax. This can make spontaneous expressions of sexual behaviour difficult, and ignorance in the heat of a particular moment *potentially* lethal. The fatal *nature* of AIDS makes it essential that everyone comes to terms with the *reality* of the risks of sexual behaviour.

SEXUAL DIMORPHISM (see **life dynamic**)   The difference in *morphology* between female and male, in this instance in humans.

Every individual has a blend of female and male characteristics in every dimension of their make-up. For most the deciding factor on whether they are male or female is their sexual organs. For a minority their inclination is contrary to their predominant physiology; some are neutral, and some oscillate. Human sexual roles are so complex that ultimately the *choice* of which one is under what circumstances is for the individual.

Our understanding of the differences between the sexes is far from complete. Unless we understand the *nature* of these differences it will be difficult to *create* satisfactory *cultural, social* or personal *relationships* in the *future.*

The *evolutionary* background reveals the human 'chicken or egg' conundrum; did tribal social *dynamics* produce differentiated characteristics and roles around sexual differences, or was the tribal *way of life* a *natural* result of these (*inherent*) differences?

It is accepted that for most of our *evolutionary* time as *homo sapiens* our species lived as gatherer-hunters, with the core group of females nurturing the young, old and injured as well as the social *knowledge* of the group.[2] The males formed a scattered perimeter for protection, warning, scavenging and hunting. The primary *functions* of each sex required each to have radically different sexual characteristics, and, under the influence of their social-tribal *functions,* to evolve subtly different physiologies. It is also believed that the *processes* of the *minds* of female and males not only have different priority influences, but are also different in their modes of *perception* and in the ways they deal with the same sensory input.[3]

We owe our primary sexual characteristics to our forest ape precursors. Around 17 million years ago there was a shake-out among the apes; *ecological* changes replaced much of the forest canopy with savannah – grass plains with intermittent tree cover. This led to our ancestors standing up and losing their fur. The effect was to initiate oscillations in *sexual/social dynamics* which continue to the present. By standing up, the male exposed his sexual organs, whereas the female hid hers; the excessive development of secondary sexual display characteristics, in the form of fat deposits on breasts and hips, may be seen as her counter to the male display. Standing up changed our hormone make-up and physical shape; in the long view of *evolution* it may be said to have initiated the population explosion by heightening human sexuality.

Other differences also became accentuated. The female body fuels itself differently to the male. Females, having lost their fur but being occupied in more static caring/gathering roles, replaced it with a subcutaneous layer of fat. This both insulates for warmth and provides a long lasting slow release source of *energy*. Body fat, burned with sugars from fruit, fit the female for endurance, for the long haul of childbirth or long distance movement.

The male, by contrast, has (should have) little body fat. He is designed for sprinting and final decisive bursts of high *energy* output. The male source of energy is the glycogen store in a relatively much larger liver. Under the influence of adrenaline this is released to produce explosive *energy*. It is because of the difference in liver size that men can drink more alcohol and generally metabolise more *toxic* substances than women. The differences in body fuelling systems are reflected in different input preferences; men are predominantly meat-eating feasters, after which they fall asleep to recharge their glycogen stores, whereas women are fruit, nut, and plant nibblers, an eating pattern which keeps their 'current account' energy systems and body fat constant.[4] All this explains why she prefers the candlelight while he eats the supper.

Although the idea of differences in brain, *mind* and mental *processes* may be resisted by those who believe in the equality of the sexes, research shows that they do *exist*. That is not to say that one sex is more intelligent than the other, but that their *processes* of intellect are different. (What is intelligence? If it is the ability to survive, even in *limited* tests or *problems*, then male and female form different, complementary parts of a *whole*.)

Males, as one would *anticipate* of hunters, are better at spatial co-ordination. Females, as befits gatherers, are better at pattern recognition. There are also differences in risk assessment and risk situation response. The John Wayne tomcat male rises to, goes towards, the challenge like the territorial animal he is, whereas the female retreats to shelter, to be sheltered by the gatherer core.

To over-simplify, the *perceptual* differences are analogous, for the female, to seeing things through a peg board. She is cautiously aware of the gaps in *knowledge/perception*, and behaves accordingly. The male sees the same points of light, but to him it is like a filament that penetrates to the very heart of every matter. He saw the movie, he can fly the 747. He acts on such flimsy *ego*-inspired belief despite (because of) the cautions of others.

Sexual dimorphism is expressed in different behaviour patterns and preferences, in different interests and preoccupations. Female and male *morphologies* may be seen as separate circles which include mutual points of interest but have widely varying degrees of overlap, with many areas which may be exclusive to one sex or the other.

Our sexual dimorphism has affected our *socio-cultural dynamic*. Dominance within our species has swung between the sexes with each major step in *socio-cultural evolution*. Human tribes began with core group gatherers and peripheral expendable hunters. Males became farmers, then aristocrats and city brokers, with females as nurtured *resources*. The male dominance of the present phase, and the threatened female dominance of the next, are equally untenable. Women are moving into *institutional structures created* by men; women seem better able to survive the internal stress. The male sprinter's heart cannot take the long haul, whereas the female is built for it.

Within *terminal culture* males and females seem to be moving further apart in the *evolutionary* dance. Paradoxically this seems to be the result of our separation from our fellows within the *social dynamic* of the *culture*. Males separated from fellows have the opportunity to become unrestrained tyrants, beating wives, abusing children. Tomcat youth groups with no peer group pressure to maturity/conformity go beyond the rebellion of youth into the permanent immaturity of a *structureless* nihilism. There is little to rebel against, only *terminal conflict* with *institutionalised* authority.

Severed from the *dynamics* of the group, females suffer the depression of settling in a suburban breeding box. Having failed to become a queen, she settles for rebuilding a tribe from her womb and the compensation of material *consumption*.

Both are deprived of a *life* with meaning; *terminal culture* has *created* an exclusive *spiritual* wasteland as part of its prelude. *Compression* within its *dynamic* produces the perpetual premature ageing struggle against *inherent* anxiety and insecurity. (And its reaction, in the pursuit of the 'youth culture'.)

For the *future* we need *models* of a *balanced* co-existence which bridges the sexual dimorphism of our species, a co-existence which amplifies the complementary *nature* of each to the disadvantage of neither. An essential part of *conscious* human *evolution* will be to *create ways of life* which allow for the different *morphologies* of male and female *existence*. *Greens* believe that *life* in a *coherent* and *co-operative* society, based on recognition of the *values* and *needs* of both sexes will satisfy human *need* and *potential* and be to the benefit of the world as a *whole.*

The present generation of parents has been brought up within the tradition of economic growth ... which has taught us to value the masculine elements of life (rational, demanding, competitive, aggressive, analytic) more highly than the feminine (intuitive, cooperative, responsive, synthesising). The terms masculine and feminine do not imply that members of each sex possess these characteristics exclusively; in many ways, the terminology is unfortunate. The Chinese talk about yin and yang, which is what is meant in the present context. Both elements are necessary in individuals and in the world for life to be balanced. However, in view of the historical imbalance in favour of the masculine characteristics, particularly in the last 250 years, accelerated by the onset of industrialisation, the feminine elements need to be powerfully reasserted in order that the balance be redressed.[5]

Relationships   **human nature**, **evolution**, **culture**.
See also   **life**, **morphology**.
References

1 See, for example, Andrea Dworkin, 1981, *Pornography: Men Possessing Women*, The Women's Press, London.
2 Richard Leakey and Roger Lewin, *People of the Lake*, Collins, London; and Richard Leakey, 1981, *The Making of Mankind*, Michael Joseph, London; see also Desmond Morris, 1967, *The Naked Ape*, Jonathan Cape, London.
3 See 'Profile: Vive La Différence', in *Scientific American*, October, 1990, on the work of Doreen Kimura, professor of psychology at the University of Western Ontario, London, Canada. Scientific American Inc, 415 Madison Avenue, New York, NY 10017, USA.
4 For those readers caught by the terminal culture preoccupation with body fat, see Suzie Orbach, 1979, *Fat is a Feminist Issue*, Hamlyn, London; for a more detailed explanation of the functions of fat see Arabella Melville and Colin Johnson, 1990, *Eat Yourself Thin: Lose Weight, Gain Energy*, Michael Joseph, London.
5 Juliet Solomon, 1990, *Green Parenting*, Macdonald Optima, London.

SHIFT (see **morphic shift**)   Change of position, form or character.

In this sense, of *evolutionary change*, the shift which occurs when a *genetic* formulation *changes* to produce a variation or new form. Also of *paradigm* shift, the *change* in *mindset* which may concern a particular *paradigm* or *model*, say of acceptable social behaviour, or a more general shift as in *perception* of *existence*.

A shift is one of three *evolutionary options*; under circumstances which provoke *change* things either shift to a new form or *sink* to a former or remnant state. In the absence of provocation, things tend to remain *stable.*

Greens seek to *create* a shift in human *consciousness* and *culture.* The means for achieving this shift is the spread of *green philosophy* and the *creation* of *sustainable ways of life.*

Relationships   **evolution, morphology, compression, rainbow alliance**.

See also   **stability, sink.**

SICKNESS   see **illness.**

SINK   Fall slowly downwards, disappear in part or wholly beneath surface; come to a lower level or pitch.

The concept which is important in a *social/evolutionary* context is that of the behavioural sink.

BEHAVIOURAL SINK   Term coined by Calhoun[1] in research into overcrowding in animals. Behavioural distortion of many forms is found when overcrowding becomes extreme, even when *food,* water and shelter are plentiful. Aberrant behaviours among rats include cannibalism, indiscriminate sexuality, random violence and loss of normal parenting behaviour. These distortions persist after the animals are moved to a less crowded *environment.*

The animals suffer a distortion of their *morphology.* Similar distortions have been observed in other species, including primates. The degree to which the phenomenon can be associated with human behaviour is a matter of conjecture, but there is no reason why it should not.

Relationships   **compression, morphology, evolution.**

See also   **stability, shift, terminal culture.**

References

1 J. Calhoun, 1983, *Environment and Population: Problems in Adaptation,* Praeger, New York, USA.

SLICE (at a time)   Thin piece cut from whole; part taken, allotted or gained.

Proposition: That people are unwilling or unable to take in *whole* concepts or large *ideas,* or to follow propositions to their logical conclusions. They can take things a slice at a time, with frequent pauses, and may eventually arrive at the *whole* loaf.

Also that although they may take all the slices, they cannot put them together (*synthesise*) and come up with the *whole* loaf.

An individual *mindset* will resist *change,* and even if willing to *change,* will be reluctant to junk old *ideas* until a better replacement is found. Resistance to total *change* is a means of protecting the integrity of the inner *whole; change* takes *time.*

Such resistance to *change* is also apparent in *cultures* and *institutions.* They will selectively absorb the parts they can digest and reject the rest. Thus the *nature* of the total proposition, or the logic of its fulfilment, is lost, and some pale shadow of the *vital* original is offered in its place. Examples, 'official' art or version, authorised editions, etc.

Relationships   **mindset, change, culture.**
See also   **evolution, meme.**

SMALL IS BEAUTIFUL   Catch-phrase, title of Fritz Schumacher's book.[1]

The belief that any enterprise is better if it is small. Not so much beautiful as essential (see **human scale**).

Relationships   **perspective, dynamics.**
References
1 Fritz Schumacher, 1974, *Small is Beautiful,* Abacus, London.

SOCIAL   Living in groups or organised *communities;* gregarious. Humans are social animals, not fitted for or practising solitary life; interdependent, co-operative, practising division of labour; existing as member of compound organism or *structure.*

SOCIAL CONTRACT   The idea that an individual has a negotiable contract within a particular social *structure.* The idea was developed by Rousseau[1] to succeed notions of divine rights and ordained social *position.*

The concept of the social contract requires updating. Starting with an understanding of the *life contract* implicit in the *food network,* it should be *extended* into the form of an inclusive *holistic Gaian* contract (see **Gaia**).

In the social context of *community,* each would have a contractual understanding of its place in the *bio-region* of which it was a part; each such arrangement would be part of the total contract between humanity and the *Gaian whole.*

In human social affairs a *diversity* of *communities* under the umbrella of a *green culture* would allow individuals to move between a variety of *communities* to find social arrangements which are mutually satisfactory.

SOCIAL ECOLOGY   see **ecology.**

SOCIAL WAGE (aka SOCIAL INCOME, GUARANTEED BASIC INCOME) The idea that people should be given the *means* of *living* as a *right* (see **universal credit economy**).

SOCIO-CULTURAL EXTENSIONS (see **extensions**) The extension of social forms of organisation; the expression of morpho-genetic *potential* in social or cultural forms of organisation, artefacts, or *structures*; the expression of a *way of life*.

The most significant forms of socio-cultural extension projected by humanity are its successional *institutional forms* (see **institutions**).

<u>Relationships</u>   **community, diversity, culture, morphology, evolution.**

<u>See also</u>   **philosophy, Gaia, structure.**

<u>References</u>

1 Jean Jacques Rousseau (1712–78), 1762, *Contrat Social*, described as his masterpiece, in which Rousseau set out to answer the proposition of its opening statement, 'Man is born free; and everywhere he is chains'. His answer was in terms of a social contract which would confer 'Liberty, equality and fraternity'.

SOLAR ENERGY   see **energy**.

SPIRIT   Animating or vital principle of person or animal; intelligent or immaterial part of person, soul. Rational or intelligent being not connected with material body. Person's character, mental or moral nature.

Energy of *life*; the *life force* (see **life**).

'Spirit' is sometimes used (by *vegetarians, vegans*) to differentiate between animals and plants. Thus plants have a *life force* and may be eaten, whereas animals have a spirit (soul) and should not.

Greens believe there is a spirit in all *existence*, an intelligent (or logical) immaterial part of every form. 'For everything that lives is holy, life delights in life.'[1]

SPIRITUAL, SPIRITUALITY   Of spirit, as opposed to matter; of the soul, especially acted upon by god; quality of person, thing in relation to church or other religious institution.

The concept in its current usage appears to be very plastic; spirituality is shaped to suit individual *needs* and circumstances. The amorphous nature of the concept is increased by the inclusion of god(s) in the property.

The *philosophy* of the West (*Cartesian* reductionism) has separated the spiritual from the material in an absolute way. The effect has been to remove moral influences from intellectual activity, and encourage the disposal of the *environment* and other species.

Basic *green* spirituality is seen in the connectedness of all things; in the *nature* of those connections, in the *unity* of all things. Beyond that the inclusion of other *values* or concepts are matters of individual choice.

Relationships   **holism, life, existence**.

See also   **intuition, institution**.

References

1 William Blake (1757–1827), *America*, 71; for matters of green spiritual concern, see *Resurgence*, Worthyvale Manor Farm, Camelford, Cornwall PL32 9TT, England.

SPONTANEOUS   Acting, done, occurring, without external cause.

That which emerges from within, *inherent*, instinctive or *intuitive*, without obvious motive.

SPONTANEOUS UNDERSTANDING (see **intuition**)   Property which flows from the unfolding of the *inherent potential* of things; the understanding of *relationships, processes*, and possibilities.

It is human *responsibility* to select from what is unfolded, from what emerges in the *evolution* of things. *Philosophy* and *morality* are essential in guiding our *choice*. *Grey culture* has relied upon divine providence and blind *progress* to avoid the pain of *choice*.

Green culture has to confront the *choices* before us. It has to seek actively the emerging, unfolding *morphology* of things, to *anticipate* possibilities before they become established by default. As Pasteur put it, 'chance favours the prepared mind'; the *green movement* is preparation of our *minds* for the *future*. We have to be aware of our *intuition*, of windows of spontaneous understanding which reveal the *inherent potential* of things.

Relationships   **perception, meme, evolution**.

See also   **morphic potential**.

STABLE   Fixed, established, balanced; not easily changed, removed, unbalanced or altered in values.

STABILITY   Stability has many faces: stability of opposition, *dynamic* stability, or inert, moribund, stability.

In human affairs the most important factor in stability is the *perception* of the property.

A constant, or constantly accelerating, rate of *change* can give the appearance of stability.[1] Thus *terminal culture*, with its requirement of constant (accelerating) *growth*, believes its *dynamic* is one which produces stability (see **exponential growth**). *Greens,* while appreciating this *process,* believe it is an illusory stability, in that it is not *sustainable,* and is approaching finite *limits.*

Within *life processes* there is the *dynamic (organic)* stability of *homoeostatic systems,* of self-regulating *balance,* which may involve *cycles* of *growth* and decline (see **balance, Gaia**). Stability should not be confused with stasis: 'The stability of self-organising systems is utterly dynamic and must not be confused with equilibrium. It consists in maintaining the same overall structure in spite of ongoing changes and replacements of its components.'[2]

Growth may be seen as stability with *change.* The problem in human affairs is to select directions of *growth* and *extension* which maintain stability both within the human species and of the *Gaian whole.*

In *evolution,* stability is that state of a species or *ecological system* where no *change* is provoked or emerges from within (see **potential**).

<u>Relationships</u>   **sustainability, evolution, Gaia.**
<u>See also</u>   **sink, shift.**
<u>References</u>
1 Albert Einstein (1879–1955), 1905, 1916, *Special and General Theories of Relativity*; see 1920, *Relativity: The Special and the General Theory – A Popular Exposition,* Methuen, London.
2 Fritjof Capra, 1982, *The Turning Point: Science, Society and the Rising Culture,* Simon & Schuster, New York.

STATUS QUO   Status = social position, rank relative to others; position of affairs; quo = in which, so unchanged, previous. 'The way things are.' The social *positions* and *dynamics* of *terminal culture.* The status quo embodies the *values* and mechanics of blind *progress* towards *terminality* (see **stability**).

STEWARDSHIP (see **rainbow warrior**)   Function of trust and care over property of others, as in a great house or estate.

Humans find themselves in circumstances where they either accept the *responsibilities* and *freedoms* of *global* stewardship, or fail by default, taking much with them (see **choice**).

Greens prefer the *option* of stewardship to ownership. This is increasingly expressed in *co-operative* ventures and in new forms of *living* and *relationships* with the land (see **commune, community**).
<u>Relationships</u>   **values, perspective, community.**
<u>See also</u>   **bioregion, philosophy.**

STOCK (see **economy**)   Available goods, resources, etc.

Central principle of *green economics*. The current *unsustainable system* is of *flow*; *greens* believe that *economics*, that is the use of *finite* and other *resources*, must be based upon minimum *consumption* and maximum *utility*. Thus in a stock *economy* things made from *finite resources* would be required to have indefinite *life* and maximum *utility*; they and their components should be capable of *re-use*, repair and, finally, *recycling*.

Resources taken from renewable stocks, *ambient energy* and the produce of other *life forms*, should be in amounts that are compatible with the *needs* of the *web of life* as a *whole* (see **balance**). In setting *limits* we need understanding of the interactions of the complete *web of life* (see **morph mapping**). When we have *knowledge* and experience of such *limits*, humans should work on the basis of minimum stock usage rather than the maximum provision that the *biosphere* is believed to be able to bear (see **numbers**).

Relationships   **economics, sustainability, finite resources.**
See also   **consumer, flow.**

STRESS   see **compression.**

STRUCTURAL INERTIA   Characteristic of bureaucratic, hierarchical *institutions*, wherein individuals are dominated by considerations of *position* rather than *function*.

The *hierarchical form* is *inherently stable* as a *whole*; those at the bottom have little influence on the top, but those at the top frequently have difficulty motivating those at the bottom (see **change**).

There are occasional signs of movement, despite *structure*. At a convention in Geneva on global warming, Margaret Thatcher (then British Prime Minister) said we cannot afford to wait for 'further research' – a primary fixing pin in the inertia game and the usual means of delaying acknowledgment of even the possibility of a *problem*. However, too much hope should not be derived from such statements while the underlying *structure*, the source of the original *problem*, remains intact.

STRUCTURALISM   Philosophical doctrine which holds that structure dominates function.

Based on the structure of language and linguistics, its basic proposition is supported by such phenomena as the lack of a language for *health* and many other positive concepts which are effectively denied in *terminal culture* because they are thought of in terms of their opposites.

Structuralism is an analytical *philosophy* which is in many ways contrary to the *reductionist* tradition, in that it looks at the effects of things as *wholes*, rather than analysing the parts of things:

> The relations which Structuralism seeks to identify are two-way and a properly Structuralist way of seeing causes and effects is as the two terms of a relation. We all agree that there can be no effect without a previous cause, but find it harder to grasp that there can be no cause without a subsequent effect, for the good reason that until the effect is present the cause has not acquired its causal status.[1]

From its base in linguistics, structuralism, which shares much common terminology and emphasis with *green philosophy*, has *extended* into every sphere of human activity: 'the function of the human mind is either to recognise structures in whatever it turns its attention to or else to project structures into whatever it attends to'.[1]

Structuralism is important to *greens* in both applications. In the inner sense of structured *perception*, our required act of *conscious evolution* requires that we not only *change* what we think, but the way in which we think. Thus *conscious evolution* means the *conscious* manipulation of the structure of our thought *processes*, *changing* their form to produce different *functions* in terms of *perception* of the world, *reality, existence*, and so on (see **matrix**).

Externally a structuralist view, in its anthropological and *cultural* analytical application,[2] allows us to appreciate the effects of structure on *social* phenomena, and the possibility of creating structures which produce different effects. 'So also the social phenomena which we observe in any human society are not the immediate result of the nature of individual human beings, but are the results of the social structures by which they are united.'[3]

STRUCTURE   Means by which a thing is formed; supporting framework of whole or essential components.

Form, *morphology*, produced by *interrelationship* of parts in a *whole*.

Structure dictates *function*: form and *function* are closely *interrelated*. In social structures many *functions* are *projected* by the form of the structure; they are *inherent* properties of the form. Thus a society organised around *hierarchical* structures will *func-*

tion in ways projected by that form of structure.

Greens believe that much of the *global predicament* is the result of the human *life dynamic projected* by our *forms* of *socio-cultural* structures. These are *hierarchical institutions,* characterised by *power relationships, competition,* and individual status according to *position* (see **institution**). These structures are an *extension* of the structured breeding prerogatives of primate groups.

The *future* requires more *organic* structures, *socio-cultural* forms which will *project sustainable functions* into the world, and which will be *inherently stable* within their *bio-regional* context. The preferred *green* structure is the *matrix* from which *networks* of *relationships* may be selected in a *dynamic* of constant *change* according to *need.*

It is sometimes held by *grey* detractors that *green* ideas would lead to '*anarchy* and *chaos*'. *Greys* believe that what they perceive as *chaos* is incoherent no-*system* living. This is not so; it is the reaction against proposals for different structures, different *systems*, different ways of seeing and doing things.

Relationships **philosophy, holism, anarchy, matrix, human evolution, process.**

See also **power, hierarchy, formative causation.**

References

1 See John Sturrock, 1986, *Structuralism,* Paladin, London; in addition to a wide overview, this book contains an extensive bibliography of the subject.

2 Claude Gustave Lévi-Strauss, French social anthropologist, widely accepted as the founder of structural anthropology; see, 1958, English translation 1963, *Structural Anthropology,* University of Chicago Press, Chicago, USA. In *The Savage Mind,* 1962/1966, University of Chicago Press, Chicago, USA, he elaborated the view of culture as a system of communication structured by the unconscious working of the mind.

3 A. Radcliffe-Brown, *Structure and Function in Primitive Society,* Cohen.

SUBVERSION, SUBVERSIVE Seeking to overturn, upset, destroy, overthrow, established order, *status quo.*

From the *perspective* of the subverter the intention is desirable *change. Change* is always seen as *subversive* by those resisting it.

Greens, green memes, ideas, thoughts and actions are *inherently* subversive to *grey culture.* The battle is for *survival* via the *minds* and hearts of our species. *Means* of subversion can be anything from thinking differently to writing letters encouraging the good and discouraging the bad. Don't buy, don't *consume,* step out of the *flow economic system* which is *consuming* the *environment* and converting it to *waste.*

The *objective* of subversive acts is to disrupt the *anticipation* of who/whatever the act is directed against (see **anticipation**).

A necessary skill in the *creation* of a *future*.

Relationships   **change, evolution**.

See also   **culture**.

SUCCESSION, SUCCESSIVE   Following in order without intervention; order of development of species or community.

Form which will follow; *evolution, morphology*.

Greens believe they have to intervene in the *natural* succession of *grey culture*, before it reaches its *terminal* conclusion (see **subversion**).

The task confronting us is the denial of the logic of *institutional* succession. In stepping back from the edge of global disaster we have to de-couple from the *institutional process*. The succession sought by *greens* is one of *human scale* and *values* within the *processes* of *nature* and the capacity of the *biosphere*. The *green* debate is about the *creation* of a different, consciously chosen, direction for human succession.

Relationships   **philosophy, culture**.

See also   **institutions, progress**.

SUFFICIENCY   see **self-sufficiency**.

SURVIVAL   Continuing to live or exist in spite of adverse circumstances. 'All life evolves by the differential survival of replicating entities'.[1]

In the *process* of surviving, or increasing survival chances, humans have over-*extended* their *numbers* and capacity at the expense of the rest of the *biosphere* (see **rights**).

The *future* dilemma is differentiation. The term 'survivor' is used in some *green* circles to distinguish its opposite, a *grey culture* victim, i.e. a non-survivor. Given there is no long-term *choice* other than to live within a *sustainable life-dynamic*, what happens to those segments of humanity who do not adapt? Is differential survival possible in terms of *green islands* amid accelerating *grey* disaster (see **casualty problem**)?

Gaia survives as a *whole* or not at all; the remaining *question*, whatever the fate of humanity, is of the composition of a viable *whole*. Has too much already gone, and too much more already been irreversibly set on a path to destruction? We simply do not know.

The survival *choice* is simple. We can prepare now by making *changes* and preparing *future provision* for the unavoidable *problems* – the high level survival *choice*. Or we can continue with *grey terminal* business as usual, until we experience a *catastrophic sink*, at best to some remnant – the low level survival *choice*. It is important to realise that *grey culture*, of its *nature*, cannot make the high level *choice*. It is fixed on the low level option. (If it were to *change* to take the high level option it would no longer be *grey* and *terminal*.) The survival *agenda* of *grey culture* is not directed at humanity; it is directed at the *needs* of *institutions*. This is the fundamental situation which must be addressed for survival in the *future* (see hidden **agenda**).

When the buffalo are all slaughtered, the wild horses are tamed, the secret corners of the forest heavy with the scent of many men, and the view of the hills blotted out by talking wires, where is the thicket? Gone. And where is the eagle? Gone. The end of living and the beginning of survival.[2]

Twenty-five per cent of the world's flora is threatened with *extinction*.

<u>Relationships</u>   **choice, life, evolution, sustainable**.
<u>See also</u>   **culture, institution**.
<u>References</u>
1 Richard Dawkins, 1976, *The Selfish Gene*, Oxford University Press, Oxford, England.
2 Chief Seattle, 1855.

SUSTAIN   Endure without giving way, stand, continue indefinitely.
SUSTAINABLE, SUSTAINABILITY   Able to continue indefinitely, the capacity to continue indefinitely.

Grey culture takes a short-term view of things. The immediate *event*, the next election, the current *problem*, an obvious benefit, apparent improvement. Such a fragmented view is an *inherent* product of *Cartesian reductionist philosophy*, and is a *structural* part of the *culture* it *projects*.

The *global predicament* is the result. In seeking to overcome *limits* within this short-term view, we have discovered the apparent benefits of *consuming* via *technology*. The *progress* of *grey* civilisation is marked by its progressive increase in *consuming* its *environment*. From *consuming* the *diversity* of *forests* by fire for *limited* agricultural use (still happening today), we progressed to *consuming* the *past* by burning *fossil fuels* and *creating* the *greenhouse effect*; in parallel we *consume* ever increasing amounts of other *finite resources*. At some point in the last hundred years or so we started to *consume* the *future*. Investments have to make a return; this either comes from increasing the *flow* of the *economic system*, with its *waste* and *pollution*, or by buying things for that *system* to *consume* in the *future*, thus ensuring that the rate of *flow* will have to increase to make a return on the investment.

Grey culture is becoming aware that there may be *limits*. Currently the focus is on '*environmental*' concerns, on *limits* to the amount of '*away*', to the amount of *pollution* which can simply be put in the *environment*. It has yet to question the amount that can be removed from the *environment*. The ethos of *growth*, of more of everything, still underwrites the *progress* of *grey culture* to *terminality*.

Greens believe that there is only one option for humanity. That is to devise sustainable *ways of life* within the capacity of the *biosphere*. It is essential to acknowledge that 'within' means within the *rights* and *needs* of all other elements of the *Gaian whole*. There is a *grey-green* school of persuasion which encourages the management doctrine; that if only we could learn to manage the planet's *resources* to our better advantage we could, more or less, continue as before (see **sustainable development**).

Greens see the rationalisation of *consumption*, moves towards maximum *utility* in *finite resources* use by means of *re-use*, *repair* and *recycling*, conservation and *ambient energy* measures, the purposeful reduction in human *numbers*, and so on, not as ends in themselves, but as necessary prerequisites to *create* a sustainable *future*.

Sustainability requires devising ways of life which are dependent upon the mutual interaction of humanity with the current account *renewable resources* of the *ecosystems* of the *biosphere*. The *choice* we have is either to accept the challenge of adopting sustainable *ways of living*, or to allow blind *progress* to carry us into predictable disaster.

General objectives for sustainability can be described. We need to design suitable *life structures* which *function* as self-sustaining *systems*, consciously connected to (homoeostatic) *Gaiaostatic feedback loops*, so that human activity contributes to the *dynamic balance* of the *whole* (see **morphology**).

The problem presented by sustainability is to get from here to eternity without denying human *potential*, while not inhibiting the expression of the *potential* of other *life forms* (see **rights**).

SUSTAINABLE DEVELOPMENT (see **development**)   Outside the *natural evolutionary process*, sustainable development is a contradiction in terms.

The concept arises in *grey culture* as part of its attempt to reconcile the *Impossible Party* of *consumption* with the *needs* of *Third World* populations. It is felt that the *First World* may continue as it is, or without major upheaval, if the aspirations of others can be met by providing them with ways to *exploit* their *environment* in ways which will not adversely affect us. Thus we devise schemes for sustainable *exploitation* of rainforests, rather than schemes to replace the temperate zone *forests* which we cut down in the past.

The concept sees the world in human terms; it is another aspect of the homocentric, world at humans' disposal, *mindset*.[1]

Relationships   **future, cycles, philosophy, culture, evolution**.

See also   **terminal, progress, numbers**.

References

1 See Michael Redcliff, 1987, *Sustainable Development: Exploring the Contradiction*, Methuen, London.

SYMBIOSIS   Association of two different organisms living attached or in close proximity to each other.

The classic example of symbiosis is that of lichen, where fungus and alga live in symbiosis; the fungus provides the *structure* and secretes acid which dissolves the substrate, the alga uses the products for its *life cycle* which feeds the fungus.

In the most fundamental sense all *life* is symbiotic. Humans are crucially dependent upon the fauna of bacteria which colonise their digestive tracts.

Symbiosis *extends* to dependence on the integrity of planetary *cycles* within the *Gaian whole*. The *nature* of this macro-symbiosis is not understood, although the disruption of these *cycles* by human activity is revealing some of the *systems* upon which *life* depends.

Humanity lives in close symbiosis with the various *cultural structures* its *philosophies* and dogmas *project* into the world. They may be thought of as sheltering us in the widest sense, while we, in a very direct sense, sustain them as part of our *life cycles. Creating a sustainable future* requires that we understand and redirect these processes. Our *future* symbiosis must be via a *green cultural* umbrella with the planet as a whole (see **Gaia**). 'The needs of the planet are the needs of the person ... the rights of the person are the rights of the planet.'[1]

Life itself is the product of symbiosis between matter and *energy* (see **life**).

<u>Relationships</u>   **life, Gaia, sustainability.**

<u>See also</u>   **synergy, cycles, linear.**

<u>References</u>

1 Theodore Roszak, 1981, *Person/Planet: The Creative Disintegration of Industrial Society*, Paladin, London.

SYMPTOM   Perceptible change in body or functions, usually indicating injury, disease, etc.

Now taken as any sign of disruption in *system* or *function.*

SYMPTOMATIC   Of symptom(s).

The analytical tradition of *grey culture* focuses upon symptoms rather than causes; it is concerned with symptomatic effects (*events*) rather than the *processes* which produce the effects.

In treating *illness*, symptoms are addressed rather than causes; it is estimated that around 80 per cent of the disease suffered is avoidable yet, because we address symptoms, we continue to suffer all the causes until some point of breakdown is reached. The same is true of symptoms of the *global predicament*. In *terminal culture* 'cleaner', more efficient, 'environmentally friendly' treatments (themselves symptomatic of the *terminal mindset*) are sought to apply to symptoms of the massive disruption of *global systems*.

Symptomatic relief usually only causes greater *problems* to emerge later (see **problem of problems**). Giving a heart transplant is a waste if the *way of life* which ruined the original remains unaltered (transplant patients have to *change* their *lifestyles*; paradoxically, if they had done so before the transplant became their only option, it frequently would not have been necessary). Symptomatic relief by feeding the starving of one generation means their children will have to be fed in their turn.

Because symptomatic relief is at best just relief, not an answer, it is rejected by *greens*. Green *'consumerism'*, the greening of business, *sustainable development*, conservation, even *recycling*, are all symptomatic approaches. In the absence of fundamental *structural change* to the *morphology* of human *life* they will at best serve to refine *problems*, at worst be pointless gestures which may enable people to avoid the *reality* of the *global* situation a little longer.

<u>Relationships</u>   **mindset, philosophy.**

<u>See also</u>   **health, perspective.**

SYNCHRONICITY   Synchronous = existing or occurring at the same time. Hence, synchronicity, the occurrences of things at the same time without apparent causal link.

Synchronicity has been described as the perfect writer's defence; things can be made to happen in whatever way the imagination requires for the story. It was described as such in the film *The Eagle Has Landed,* wherein Hitler makes a highly impractical request – 'Capture Churchill and bring him to Bavaria.' Enter synchronicity. Churchill obliges by going to a remote Norfolk village which has the benefit of an estuarial river and a German spy infrastructure. Synchronicity can be the essential facilitator of fantasy.

In *reality* we know that the most unlikely *events* do coincide. This can be attributed to fate, to serendipity, to the effects of random probability, or, in human affairs, to some *function* of our collective sub/*unconscious*. The emergence of *ideas* at the same time, of *processes* which produce synchronous *events*, may be explained by the *morphic resonance* of our species, or by the unfolding *morphology* of things.

<u>Relationships</u>   **potential, inherent, morphology**.

<u>See also</u>   **event, process**.

SYNERGISTIC   The ability of things to potentiate other things. Events, processes, are said to 'feed off each other'.

SYNERGY   From the Greek *synergos* = working together. The property that the combined effects of drugs, organs, parts, etc., display in exceeding the sum of their individual effects.

The effect of synergy is commonly expressed as the *whole* being greater than the sum of its parts.

Extended by Buckminster Fuller[1] to describe the general effect achieved by the combination of elements in compatible *systems*; the realisation that, because of their *nature*, many things work together to *potentiate* each other, e.g. in chemical reactions, alloys of metals, physical *structures*, living organisms and groups of organisms.

The *green* understanding of synergy is that it is the key property of *life*, that property of *existence* which seeks to overcome the *entropy* of *energy* and the *stability* of matter. The synergistic combination of both is *life*.

Greens believe humans can only extend themselves indefinitely in the *future* by *living* synergistically with the rest of *life* and the *environment*, by understanding the *relationships* which make up

the *Gaian* whole, rather than *progressing* in ignorance, destroying the *inherent* synergy of the planet, encouraging *waste* and *entropy*.
Relationships   **life, energy, existence**.
See also   **potential, anticipation, morphology**.
References

1 Richard Buckminster Fuller (1895–1983), 'explorer in comprehensive anticipation design'. Fuller sought futuristic solutions to contemporary problems. His 'Dymaxion' (dynamic + maximum efficiency) house was conceived in 1927. Holder of more than 2,000 patents, he is probably best known for his tensegrity (tension + integrity) dome structure at the 1967 Montreal Expo. See, 1963, Buckminster Fuller, ed. Robert W. Marks, *Ideas and Integrities: A Spontaneous Autobiographical Disclosure*, Collier Books, New York; see page 65, synergy; 'this omnioperative behaviour of (the) universe'.

SYNTHESIS Combination, composition, putting together; building up of separate elements, components, facts, propositions, etc., into a coherent whole, especially of theory or *system*. Opposite of analysis.

An essential element of *green* thought and *philosophy. Terminal culture, projected* by a *philosophy* reliant upon analysis, has taken things apart in its search for final truth. It is now taking the world apart as blind *progress leads* to its version of final *reality.*

The *creation* of a *sustainable future* requires synthesis to dominate our ways of thought. It is only by synthesising our *knowledge* that we may gain a true understanding of our predicament, predict the effects of *processes* and go on to produce a *balanced* picture of the *interrelationships* in *existence.* Synthesis is essential for a new science of *life* which will allow us to illuminate the *dynamics* and requirements of all elements of the *biosphere.*

Synthesis is essential to turn *information* into *knowledge,* which, blended with insight and experience, may produce the *wisdom* necessary for the *future.* Crucially, synthesis will speed up our response time. This is necessary if we are to regain control of *events* rather than remain as their victims. Our fate as victims of the effects we *create* is rooted in the analytical tradition; unless we seek to understand total *systems,* their synergy will constantly surprise us. It will emerge as a *hidden agenda* of unidentified *relationships,* expressing their *potential* in unforeseen effects and unpredictable disasters – the present *global predicament.*

Synthesis is essentially *creative*; it is necessary for our understanding of the *morphology* of *existence,* the *dynamics* of *wholes,* of the *nature* of *Gaian cycles* and *relationships*; eventually of the *nature* of *Gaia* itself and the human place in the *whole.*

The most hopeful aspect of our present situation is that many of the pieces required for the foundation of a *sustainable future* are already available; they simply need bringing together to *create* a coherent *whole*. The primary purpose of *green philosophy* is to facilitate the synthesis of a view of *existence*, a view which can cope with the *dynamic* properties of *life* and the *synergy* of the *inter-relationships* of its many forms. Since the factors we are dealing with have an almost infinite number of possible arrangements, the possible ways of synthesising them will also approach infinity. It is in confronting this apparently unmanageable proposition that we are forced to rely upon those *values* which humanity shares with the rest of the *biosphere*, those 'unscientific' responses rejected by the analytical tradition, which may be our only guide in confronting the possibilities posed by *life* in its entirety.

SYNTHETIC (see **artificial**)   Made by synthesis, usually to imitate a natural product.

Usually used to describe 'man-made' substance, commonly products of polymer chemistry (see **plastics**).

Synthetic substances generally become locked outside the *natural organic cycles* of the *biosphere*. Thus the end product of such *processes* may be *toxic pollution* or perpetual inert litter (see **waste**).

Relationships   **dynamic, balance, philosophy, existence**.
See also   **Cartesianism, terminal culture**.

SYSTEM(S) (see **structure**)   Complex whole, set of connected things or parts; organised body of things, material or other; the established *political, social, economic* order.

Things may appear to be connected in a random, incoherent way, but all *existence* is systematic. Systems *evolve* as a *symbiotic function* between the things involved and their *motivation* (see **existence**).

The essence of a system is that things are related by common *values*, such as purpose, *motivation, inherent* properties. Thus, a *cultural* system, a railway system, a molecular system.

In complex *social* systems the real purpose of the system may be obscured by the apparent virtues of more obvious parts of the *processes* involved (see hidden **agenda**). The larger the system, and the more involved its *processes*, the more difficult it may be to perceive its true purpose or final product (see **institutional process**).

Systems have *inherent stability*. They also interact with other compatible *systems* to reinforce their *stability*. The British *education* system is a prime example. That it is of little general interest shows how well the present system *functions* to perpetuate itself. Those to whom it is of interest are those whose *motivation* is derived from the British class system. Thus the *education* system is *structured* to produce *mass* failures, who have no interest in *education*, and an aspiring *elite* who will keep things the way they are. Many *social* systems work correctly when no one *questions* (or needs to *question*) the system.

The *green* approach to systems is derived from the *philosophical* context of *holism*. *Holism* is concerned with the *relationships* between things, with the way things form systems which can be appreciated as specific or having a particular purpose (see **motivation**). The *processes* of systems, and their products, are also of primary importance in understanding how/why things happen.

Our approach to systems (and *structures*) is crucial to the *future*. We have to re-integrate human systems with those of *nature*, and incorporate the purpose of *sustainability* into *future* systems. Hence the importance of the *matrix* (*matrices*) as a *structural model*, and of *consciously* constructed *networks* rather than primitive primate *hierarchies* and fixed *institutions*. *Network* systems are flexible and adaptable, whereas *institutions* become *successive* forms with their own purposes.

Relationships   existence, symbiosis, synergy, structure.
See also   institutional process, hierarchy, matrix.

TAO, TAOISM   Religious doctrine originally based on the writings of Chinese philosophy Lao-tzu ('Old Philosopher'), c. 600–500 BC. From Chinese 'tao', right way, path. Taoism shares the allegiance of the Chinese with Confucianism and Buddhism. The treatise *Tao Te Ching* is the sole record of Lao-tzu's teaching of the way in which things came into being, and by which the phenomena of *nature* continue quietly without striving.

The religion of Taoism is dated much later; it is notable for its lack of reference to any god. Taoism is a means for the individual to become one with the harmony of the *universe,* presenting an image of the organic self integrated with the *whole* of creation. It tells of a way of unfolding which is *inherent* in all things; for the Taoist spontaneity is not in *opposition* to order but identical with it because it flows from the unfolding of the *inherent* order. Thus people follow the flow of *universal energy,* but have the ability, the duty, of *choice* within that flow (see **consciousness**).

Taoism is interesting since 'the way' sought by Taoism may be equated with the *green* search for a *balanced sustainable way of life.* Also some elements of the Tao allow access to concepts of *spirituality* in things (and in nothing, in the concept of the void before all things, to avoid giving *spirituality* an *exclusive* context) without the need to resort to a deity or *institutional* organisation.
Relationships   **spirituality, inclusive**.
See also   **chi**.

TECHNOLOGY (Greek, tekhnologia = systematic study, application, of practical arts)   Technology, in the sense of ways of doing things, is a *natural extension* of human *potential.* Like many human *extensions*, technology lacks context. In *grey culture* technology is directed to increasing the *flow* of the *economic system,* with a particular focus on weaponry, so its applications become part of the *problems* associated with the *ethics* of that *culture.*

The focus is on *events* (the goods) produced by technology

which is served by science which has become directed to its ends. Both have become disconnected, in the *minds* of those who demand the goods, from the *philosophy* which *projects* them. Thus, even if there were a *limiting* context for technology in *grey philosophy*, it would be unable to establish it. The order of priorities in *terminal culture* is open-ended; almost all applications of technology/science are valid, whatever their final effects.

The lack of context, the de-coupling of technology and science from *philosophy* and, by implication, also from morality, has *extended* the *problems* of technology for *greens*. Hence the confusion in its application. In a very real way the *problem* of technology is a reflection of the *problem* of humanity; technology needs to be brought back into a suitable context, much as humanity needs to be brought back into the context of *nature*.

Valid use of 'the application of practical arts' can be given context by the *philosophy* which guides *culture*. Thus with a *green philosophy* directing science and providing *values* for the essence of technology – the use of *energy* and materials – *limits* on the application of technology would be *inherent*. These would be marked by the over-riding requirements of *sustainability* and the *rights* of *life*.

> Ecologists are not hostile to technology *per se*, and the use of advanced technologies of many kinds is essential to the development of an ecological society. It is a matter of choice whether technology works to the benefit of people or perpetuates certain problems, whether it provides greater equity and freedom of choice or merely intensifies the worst aspects of our industrial society.[1]

There are various approaches to suitable applications of technology.

ALTERNATIVE TECHNOLOGY   Principally concerned with *ambient energy* and *energy conservation*, but also other *means* of *need* fulfilment.

The Centre for Alternative Technology,[2] sited in a disused slate quarry in mid-Wales, is both a *community* and a working demonstration of many forms of alternative technology. It has a bookshop, a restaurant (terrible coffee), and a walk up from the car park. They are hoping to raise money to install a hydraulic balance lift for those unable to manage the walk.

(Money is being raised by issuing shares; they have turned themselves into a plc. It is odd, but often the case, that people intensively involved in one area of the *green* spectrum are blind to other parts of the same spectrum. Thus the Centre for Alternative Technology goes for the absolutely conventional *institutional grey culture* 'answer' to its *structure/*financial *problems* – see also **organic** and **slice**.)

APPROPRIATE TECHNOLOGY   'In each case a technology which was entirely appropriate to the task in hand.'[3]

Technology distinguished by *utility, function* and appropriate ends. General features of such technology are low cost, high *efficiency,* long-life easy maintenance *systems, functions* within the understanding of the user, based upon *community* need.[4] Wind driven water pumps are the classic example.

INTERMEDIATE TECHNOLOGY

> Cheaper than the sophisticated highly capital-intensive technology of modern industry ... The intermediate technology would also fit much more smoothly into the relatively unsophisticated environments in which it is to be utilised. The equipment would be fairly simple and therefore understandable, suitable for maintenance and repair on the spot.[3,5]

Relationships   **needs, cyclic, sustainability**.
See also   **linear, finite resources**.
References

1 Jonathon Porritt, quoted in John Button, 1990, *New Green Pages: A Directory of Natural Products, Services, Resources and Ideas*, Macdonald Optima, London.

2 Centre for Alternative Technology, Llwyngwern Quarry, Machynlleth, Powys, Wales. They produce a regular journal, *Clean Slate*, available from the above address.

3 Fritz Schumacher, 1974, *Small is Beautiful*, Abacus, London.

4 See Ken Darrow and Rick Pam, 1978. *Appropriate Technology Sourcebook*, Volunteers in Asia Press, Stanford, California, USA; also Marilyn Carr, 1985, *The AT Reader: Theory and Practice in Appropriate Technology*, IT Publications, see 5 below.

5 Intermediate Technology Development Group (ITDG), Railway Terrace, Rugby, Warwickshire CV21 3HT, England; also IT Publications, 103–105 Southampton Row, London WC1B 4HH; see also L.T.C. Rolt 1947, 1988, *High Horse Riderless*, Green Books, Ford House, Hartland, Bideford, Devon, England.

L.T.C. Rolt's great relevance to us today is that he was the first thinker – and remains practically the only one – to address himself to the problem of how we should use machinery sensibly. This problem has hardly been given any consideration although it is perhaps the most important immediately practical problem of our time. (John Seymour, Introduction)

TELEOLOGY, TELEOLOGICAL   Greek telos + logos, words about the end.

Doctrine of final causes, view that developments are due to the purpose or design that is served by them (see **system**).

Grey culture divides in two camps over the question of *purpose*. Some believe that there is *purpose*, usually divine, in everything; others believe that *purpose* can only be ascribed to very *limited* activities, and all else is chance.

Green views vary. There is *inherent purpose*, *motivation*, in many things and *structures*. The *systematic* organisation of the *universe* – what is, rather than what is meant to be – may also be described as the result of *inherent* logic of the forms involved.

TERMINAL   Of or forming a limit, bringing thing or body to its end.

TERMINAL CULTURE   'All is for the best in this best of all possible worlds.'[1]

The present global culture; inward looking, based upon *linear processes*, *flow economics*, *unlimited growth*, increasing *consumption*, population *growth*, *institutional* provision, *hierarchical organisation*, isolation, *exploitation*, impotence and extermination.

It is the culture that produces global warming, the *greenhouse effect*, the thinning of the *ozone* layer, contaminated air, seas, rivers and groundwater, *pollution* by ever larger amounts of increasingly *toxic* chemicals, the destruction of *forests*, the erosion, desertification and salination of agricultural *land*, the *extinction* of species of mammals, birds, reptiles, insects and plants, and the continued runaway *growth* in human *numbers*. If continued, the planet will simply become uninhabitable; we will have passed the unseen point of possible recovery into inviability. That is the *nature* and direction of terminal culture.

An essential part of terminal culture is that it blinds people to the *nature* of its *progress*, to its direction, to its terminus (see example, *education*, in **system**). Nurtured by terminal culture, few are willing to face its *reality*, to think about what is actually happening. Aristocrats of unreality dressed for the total kill at the *Impossible Party* of ever increasing *consumption* and never ending *waste*, of total *toxic* overload *pollution* – 'why fret about tomorrow if today be sweet?'[2]

The majority believe, as majorities always have, that their culture is not vulnerable to decline or fall. And to a degree they are right. Every culture, and every element of culture, has *systematic*, even systemic, self-perpetuating, mechanisms built into its *structure*. These elements of cultures *evolve* as co-adapted complexes with *inherent stability*. In terms of *genetic* biology, they *form evolutionary stable* sets. The cultural analogy is with the *memes* of culture:

> Has the god meme, say, become associated with any other particular memes, and does this association assist the survival of each of the participating memes? Perhaps we could regard an organised church, with its architecture, rituals, laws, music, art, and written tradition, as a co-adapted stable set of mutually-assisting memes.[3]

There is an in-built self-perpetuating *dynamic* in terminal culture. The paradox is that such self-perpetuation is obviously a terminal *process*.

> America is an extreme example of the entire Western process; it is a ferocious attack on the planet, its resources, our posterity and ourselves; it expresses all the symptoms of the excess of a deranged drunkard, driven by forces which have no conception or understanding of the consequences of what they are promoting and no capacity whatsoever to put a moral evaluation on their own actions as they blight nature, blight cities and blight human lives to a degree which can only result in the total collapse of all that human creative effort has sought to build down the centuries.[4]

One may say that it is all relative; that a person from India may see Europe in the same light; or someone from parts of Africa see India as an extreme attack on the planet. The point is that the vast majority of our species, no matter how deprived or frugal its *way of life*, has got it wrong. As part of the *dynamic* of terminality, the path the (relatively) poor wish to tread leads to the *Impossible Party* of planetary *consumption* (see **casualty problem**).

Underlying the *dynamics* of terminality is the *death*-orientation of many human cultures. Religions offer followers salvation which lies in 'another life'; by implication this *existence*, provided the *rules* are observed, may be discounted. As long as conformity has ensured the soul, everything else may be destroyed. The *whole* ethos is, in its final *institutional analysis*, anti-*life*, terminal.

Greens believe a *sustainable* culture can only be created from a reverence of *life*, from the realisation that if there is to be a heaven it will be here on earth in the brief interval in eternity we each share with each other, during which we can either contribute to the continuation of a *sustainable way of life*, or detract from the total *life process*. There are few in betweens; each of us is either part of the *problem* or part of the solution; there are no innocent bystanders. Terminality must be rejected by whatever means are possible, and *sustainability created* in its place.

Relationships   **philosophy, culture, mindset**.

See also   **dynamics, anticipation, institutions**.

References

1 François Marie Arouet de Voltaire (1694–1778), 1756, *Candide*, a novel attacking what Voltaire understood by the Leibniztian optimistic theology that 'all is for the best in this best of all possible worlds'. *Candide* concludes with the advice that we should all 'cultivate our gardens'.

2 *Rubaiyat* of Omar Khayyam Quatrain XXXVII.

3 Richard Dawkins, 1976, *The Selfish Gene*, Oxford University Press, Oxford, England.

4 John Papworth, 'Fourth World American Spectator', in *Fourth World Review*, Number 42, Autumn 1990, 24 Abercorn Place, London NW8 9XP.

THEMATIC COMPATIBILITY   'Come into my parlour, said the spider to the fly.'[1]

The compatibility, sameness, especially of apparent opposites, of things united by a structural or functional theme; the underlying commonality in things.

Thus all *life* has obvious thematic compatibility; all *energy*, matter, and so on.

The particular application of the concept in *green* thought is with opposites, *'alternatives'*, within the *dynamics* of *grey culture*. Thus *democratic systems* have Tweedledum and Tweedledee, Labour and Conservative, Republican and Democrat, etc.; the 'and' usually indicating the marriage of two compatible parts which, although outwardly in *opposition* to each other, actually form compatible parts of the same *system*. Each is essential to the other; each props up the other, like the sides of a letter 'A' with the bar the 'and' tying them together. Tweedledum and Tweedledee became indistinguishable, losing their identity in the fusion. The tedium of *structural inertia* results.

Opposition to the *system* encounters the thematic compatibility of the *whole*. For *greens* this may be becoming apparent; those who wish to propose *radical change* to the present *status quo* find the entire *system* against them. First there is the entry fee; *opposition* is expected to come from a group, association, corporate body, or preferably an *institution*, because individuals count for little in the present *system*. An *institution* gives a degree of thematic compatibility with the *status quo*; you are, as it were, wearing acceptable *socio-cultural* clothes. Next make your ideas known; in doing this it will be discovered that there are rules – *scientific objectivity*, accepted wisdom, social *assumptions*, the way things are done, and so on. Effectively you are being asked to play on their pitch, at times and dates they fix, with their ball, to their rules, with their score-keeper and under the watchful eye of their referee. It is all part of the self-perpetuating *structure* whose themes you are trying to change (see **terminal culture**).

If you succeed despite all, it will be because, in the *process*, you have become part of the *system*. Your *opposition* has proved its thematic compatibility; you are now part of the *problem* you set out to solve (see **structure**).

Struggle within is only valid if you agree with what is within and wish to control it (see **power**). The *process* of *opposition* only serves to refine *problems*, to reinforce existing *structures* (see **opposition**). Influence from without, via pressure groups, although essential to initiate *changes* in public/*political consciousness*, is only effective up to a point. Once such groups seek *power* to implement their views, the general mechanism of the *system*, the price to be paid for *power*, admits them to its corrupting embrace.

A warning from the *past* proved all too prophetic for those *greens* who devoted themselves to the dubious proposition of *political power* within *existing systems*:

It is necessary, I believe, for everyone in the ecology movement to make a crucial decision; will the eighties retain the visionary concept of an ecological future based on the libertarian (anarchist) commitment to decentralization, alternative technology and a libertarian practice based on affinity groups, direct democracy, and direct action? Or will the decade be marked by a dismal retreat into ideological obscurantism and a 'mainstream politics' that acquires 'power' and 'effectiveness' by following the very 'stream' it should be seeking to divert? Will it pursue fictitious 'mass constituencies' by initiating the very forms of mass manipulation, mass media, mass culture, it is committed to oppose? These two directions cannot be reconciled. Our use of 'media,' mobilisations, and actions must appeal to mind and to spirit, not to conditioned reflexes and shock tactics that leave no room for reason and humanity. In any case, the choice must be made now before the ecology movement becomes institutionalised into a mere appendage of the very system whose structure and methods it seeks to oppose. It must be made consciously and decisively – or the century itself, and not only the decade, will be lost to us forever.[2]

In 1985 Bill Devall and George Sessions could write[3]:

One hopeful political movement with deep ecology as a base is the West German Green political party. They have as their slogan, 'We are neither left nor right, we are in front.' Green politics in West Germany, and to some extent in Great Britain, Belgium and Australia in the 1980s, goes beyond the conventional, liberal definition of a party, combining personal work (that is, work on clarifying one's own character) and political activism. In West Germany, especially, the Green party has sought a coalition with antinuclear weapons protesters, feminists, human rights advocates and environmentalists concerned with acid rain and other pollution in Europe. Ecology is the first pillar of the German Greens' platform.

However, by 1990, Sarel Sarkar, writing in the *Ecologist*[4] reported:

The *Realo* or 'realist' faction, which probably represents around 40 per cent of Green Party members, has led the way in realigning the movement. Two *Realo* theoreticians have written that the Green Party should represent the interests of the 'new middle classes' to which about 40 per cent of voters belong.[5] In February 1988, with several theoreticians advocating an 'ecological market economy', one of the chief spokespersons of the *Realos* said that the goal of the Green Party should be 'ecological capitalism'.[6] A few months later the *Realos* presented a 'draft manifesto of Green Realpolitik' which declared that Green politics should be aimed at:

"... the urban, liberal, consumerist citizen, who is primarily orientated towards his individual plans for life, who, however, at the same time not only protests against atomic energy and ecological madness, but also feels solidarity with the minorities who are poor and excluded from society."[7]

Whereas in the second half of the 1970s the movement emphasized satisfying basic needs, since the middle of the 1980s the emphasis has shifted to overcoming the ecological crisis without having to reduce standards of living. Thus, Joschka Fischer, when Ecology Minister of Hessen, put an advertisement in a national daily in which he stated that opting out of atomic energy was possible 'without having to forgo the comforts one is used to.'[8] In the debates that took place after the Chernobyl disaster, speakers from the ecology movements sought to show that the total need for electricity in West Germany at that time could be covered even if all the atomic power plants were shut down – namely by using thermal power to full capacity. It was conveniently ignored that if this was done on a global scale it would increase air pollution and CO_2 emissions and inflate oil prices, thus adversely affecting Third World countries. Energy savings were discussed, but these were to be achieved, not by means of reducing consumption, but by a state subsidized programme of replacing old equipment with new, more energy efficient technologies. The final step in this process of accommodating industrialism was reached in a book by Joschka Fischer published in 1989 in which he argues that the West German economy must boom so that it can afford the gigantic sums of money necessary to pay for protecting the environment.[9]

Within thematic compatibility the only way to become '*green*' is to become even more *grey* – 'Come into my parlour'. Within the *structures* of the *existing system*, as the German *greens* have discovered, there is no room for *ecology* as a pillar of a *green* platform; indeed the present *system* cannot accommodate a *green* platform at all.

To believe that placing *green politicians* at the head of *grey institutions*, while leaving the *institutional structures*/logic intact, will bring fundamental *change* is just old-fashioned naiveté. It is *symptomatic* of old ways of thought, of the *mindset autopilot* re-exerting the old course. Similarly, to believe that achieving the commanding heights of *institutional* monoliths will enable them to be remade misunderstands the *nature* of the path to the top, that of the *structure* which it climbs, and the effect of ascending on those who climb.

Greens should beware of the illusion of *opposition* as a means of *change*, of the futility of struggle within, of the *waste* of fighting your corner in the wrong game. Instead we should echo the sentiment of Blake: 'I must Create a System, or be enslaved by another Man's: I will not Reason and Compare; my business is to create.'[10]

Greens have to create – new *structures*, new *means*, new ways of thought and ways of seeing things. *Create* and give away, or let them be stolen; leave the *grey* behind, invent new games with better rules, disappear innovating into the *future*. There is no *future* in the *past*, no answer in thematic compatibility to the *problem*.

Relationships **structure, politics, opposition.**

See also **create, choice, change.**

References

1 Traditional nursery rhyme.

2 Murray Bookchin, 1980, *An Open Letter to the Ecology Movement*, published in *Rain* and other American publications.

3 Bill Devall and George Sessions, 1985, *Deep Ecology*, Peregrine Smith Books, Salt Lake City, Utah, USA, page 9.

4 Sarel Sarkar, 'Accommodating Industrialism: A Third World View of the West Germany Ecological Movement', in *The Ecologist*, Volume 20, Number 4, July/August 1990; *The Ecologist*, Corner House, Station Road, Sturminster Newton, Dorset DT10 1BB, England.

5 T. Stryck, and H. Wiesenthal, 'Zwischen Identität und Modernität: Die Grünen in der Klemme', in *Kommune* 9, 1987, page 9.

6 Hubert Kleinert said this in an interview he gave to the weekly magazine *Stern*, quoted in Ebermann, T. and Trampert, R., 'Yuppie ayeah!', in *Konkret* 7, 1988.

7 Quoted in 6.

8 *Frankfurter Rundschau*, 24 May 1986.

9 Fischer, J., *Der Umbau der Industriegesellschaft*, Eichborn, Frankfurt, 1989, page 110.

10 William Blake (1757–1827), *Jerusalem*, f. 10, 20.

THERAPY see **illness, health.**

THERMODYNAMICS see **entropy.**

THERMONUCLEAR see **nuclear.**

THIRD WORLD The peoples, populations, nations, that are deprived of, lack, the basic *needs* of *life*.

See also **First World, Fourth World.**

TIDAL ENERGY see **energy.**

TIME Non-spatial continuum in which processes take place and events occur.

The product of motion in the *universe*.

Locally, time is running out for positive action for planet *earth*, especially its human and large mammalian, content.

See also **existence, universe.**

TOOL   Implement for working; means of *extension* of hand or other faculty.

Traditionally hand tools, used to make or operate things, tool has been *extended* to cover any means of manipulation (which has itself been *extended* to mean moving, modifying, or *creating change* in a medium).

Greens, while not discounting the value of hand tools, are concerned with mental tools, those *memes*, *ideas* and concepts which are necessary to build and *sustain* the *future*. The distinction is clearly made between tools and *rules*. *Grey culture* gives – 'hands down' – *rules* by which people should live and which have the effect of removing options and circumscribing *life*. Tools, by contrast, allow people to *create*, to make *choices*, and to make other tools for *future* situations.

Innumerable confusions and a profound feeling of despair invariably emerges in periods of great technological and cultural transitions. Our 'Age of Anxiety' is, in great part, the result of trying to do today's job with yesterday's tools – with yesterday's concepts.[1]

<u>Relationships</u>   **extension, meme, model, philosophy**.
<u>See also</u>   **perspective, mindset**.
<u>References</u>
1 Marshall Mcluhan and Quentin Fiore, *The Medium is the Massage*, Penguin Books, London.

TOXIC, TOXIN   Of poison, poisonous; poison especially of animal or plant origin, also of poison formed in body by pathogen.

Now any substance which acts as a poison.

The problem with defining toxins is that effects vary with quantity, and some substances may be toxic for some people under some circumstances but not for or under others (see **artificial**).

TTO (TOTAL TOXIC OVERLOAD) (see **pollution**)   State where the natural *life*-supporting *cycles* and processes of the planet can no longer function; where the *web* of *nature* which *creates* the *food network* has been taken apart and overloaded with poisons.

TOXIC WASTE   Artificial substance which is neither *bio-assimilable* nor totally inert (see **plastics**).

Grey culture defines levels of toxins in substances to discriminate between toxic waste (heavily *polluted*) and other waste (less heavily *polluted*) with reference to the *pollutant* measured. Toxic waste dumps are inevitable sources of *environmental* contamination, threatening water and air, since permanent containment is impossible (see **away, nuclear**).

Many whale corpses are now being classified as toxic waste because levels of PCBs in their flesh are so high.

Relationships   **pollution, balance, limits**.

See also   **waste, economics**.

TRANSCEND   Be beyond the range or realm or present understanding of human experience or belief.

TRANSCENDENTALISM   Transcendental *philosophy*; state of *spiritual* or visionary existence.

Best seen as occasional journeys ahead of *morphology* of *self*, species, *existence*.

Sometimes used as a form of fatalism, 'what will be will be'. Also more positively to experience the *events*, beauty, of *nature* as opposed to its *processes*.

Relationships   **spirituality, existence**.

See also   **morphology, evolution**.

TRANSPORT   Move things, goods, people, from one place to another; means of moving things.

Our *economic system* depends on the movement of goods and services; as individuals we are fascinated by the *extension* of our animate power by everything from horses to being beamed up by Scotty.[1]   *Questions* of transport are at the heart of a modern human enigma. We all want to be somewhere else much of the *time* (whether in *reality* or fantasy). The mass-produced car has become the repository of *ego*, status and virility, a means of expression, of social display and *environmental* destruction – 500 million-plus cars distort the *environment* and compete with *life* for space and air. We are so attached to our mobile exomorphic *structures* that many would die rather than give them up. Personal transport is the largest single area where we need to find new *means* of fulfilment. What is good for General Motors has become very bad for everything else.

Why do we always want to be somewhere else? Why are millions airborne every hour in search of dreams that are always somewhere else? The *life dynamic* we should aim for, whatever the *need*, is one of local satisfaction. Hypocrisy drives many to fulfil *needs* elsewhere that they deny at home. The desire for *change* should be fulfilled by moving to different climates and *cultures*, staying long enough to be assimilated and contribute before moving on. Tourism destroys that which it seeks; package holidays put everything in the same tacky package, destroying difference and delight. If you must go there, stay there. Become part of what attracts you, not the means of its destruction.

It is an illuminating comment on *grey economics* that the only people who can afford to walk are the very rich or the very poor. In *grey culture* few have the time for such *self*-indulgence, and many avoid it because of its association with poverty. Yet it remains the healthy long-term option for most of our needs. Many people have to build artificial sessions of exercise into their sedentary lives; the use of muscle power, both human and animal, would remove the artificiality and contribute to an *inherently healthy way of life.*

The ultimate *green* mobility machine is the bicycle (see **bicycle**). Since, in Britain at least, the average car journey lasts 6 minutes (which means many must cover only a mile or so), the sense of the bicycle is only denied by irrational considerations outside the sphere of transport and movement.

In the medium term we need to develop, or re-invent (see **retrospective innovation**), transport based on *ambient energy.* This is quite feasible if we remove the need to move instantly, and *extend* the idea of local *self-reliance.* The rich sail the oceans of the world, so could we all. We should also sail the skies; wind and sun carry *life* around the globe and have abundant *energy* for our *needs.* However, the guiding principle for goods should be that of the shortest possible line of supply, Schumacher's example of the lorries that pass on the M1 motorway is often quoted[2] – those heading north are carrying biscuits from London to Glasgow, those heading south are carrying biscuits from Glasgow to London. That this is feasible, profitable, and encouraged are all *symptoms* of the irrationality of *terminal culture. Consumer choice* is reduced to international world *consuming* and *polluting* mass movements of superficial 'necessities'.

In transition to *green culture*, transport policy should be quite simple. Within cities and between them priority of provision must be given to pedestrians and cyclists. In addition to this the most *energy/resource efficient* public transport should be free. *Energy consuming* private transport should be taxed not only to cover some notion of *environmental* damage and *resource* depletion, but also the cost of public transport. Priority provision should be made for human-powered mobility. The underlying change in *life style* required is that of living and working in the same locality; having to escape the industrial area to get away to somewhere tolerable to

sleep or weekend are *symptoms* of a disastrously wrong *way of life*.
<u>Relationships</u>   **needs, way of life, perspective**.
<u>See also</u>   **exponential growth, limits, pollution**.
<u>References</u>

1 See *Star Trek*, futurist time/space exploration TV series and films.
2 Fritz Schumacher, 1974, *Small is Beautiful*, Abacus, London.

TREES   A tree planted today will begin to absorb carbon tomorrow.
Trees should be planted in autumn or winter after the leaves
have fallen or in spring when the ground has dried out but before
the leaf buds open. Alternatively, gather seed in later summer and
plant in spring. You don't have to own *land* to do this.

TURNING POINT   The idea that a point of significant, fundamental, change can be identified. Frequently confused with the
effects of *processes* of *growth*. May be associated with *cyclic*
change, as in up-turn or down-turn, but more usually intended to
imply a new direction in things, affairs, etc.

> After a time of decay comes the turning point. The powerful
> light that has been banished returns. There is movement, but it
> is not brought about by force ... The movement is natural,
> arising spontaneously. For this reason the transformation of the
> old becomes easy. The old is discarded and the new is intro-
> duced. Both measures accord with the time; therefore no harm
> results.[1]

A turning point can be seen as the point at which a new form
begins to unfold, as a fold in the continuing emergence of the
morphology of a thing or *process*, as the point at which an
evolutionary shift or *sink* is initiated. A turning point could thus
lead to a new emerging state of *existence*, or over-the-edge into
nothing. The problem of any *process* of *change* is that of *perspective*. How is the current point to be seen in *relation* to the
preceding and following *process*? Or, put another way, what
happens if all the turning points are joined up?

At frequent points in history, circumstances lead to the *perception* of a turning point having been reached. This is usually a point
when the change produces apparent difference in *quality*. Such
points may mark the *change* from one sector of *morphology* to
another, the transition from one form of *existence* to the next.
Viewed from sufficient distance, turning points could be seen as
constant features of the total *system* of *existence*. From this distant

position the turning point as a constant feature of a *system* produces a wave, a circle *extended* through *time*. Viewed from a timeless position the *great cycle of life* is a circle, continually turning around the same centre. *Time extends* circular movement into a spiral. The total *process* of *life* becomes a macro *model* of the perpetual *genetic* spiral.[2]

Greens believe that within the macro *dynamics* of things which are beyond human influence, sufficient *choice* remains for us to direct the general parameters of our state of *existence* beyond the present *time* of decay. We can *anticipate*[3] the possibilities and *extend* our *potential* to master the paradox of a retreat from the edge of *terminality*, a step back in present *evolutionary progress*, and thence forward into a *sustainable way of life* within the *inherent limits of nature.*

Relationships   **change, evolution, morphology.**

See also   **perspective, limits.**

References

1 *I Ching*, quoted in Fritjof Capra, 1982, *The Turning Point: Science, Society and the Rising Culture*, Simon & Schuster, New York, USA.

2 Colin Johnson, 1991, *Green Bible: Creating Sustainable Life on Earth*, Thorsons, London.

3 See Turning Point network, initiated by author James Robertson (see 1978, 1983, *The Sane Alternative: A Choice of Futures*) in 1973. Details, and copies of book, from James Robertson, The Old Bakehouse, Cholsey, Wallingford, Oxon OX10 9NU, England.

UNCONSCIOUS   see **conscious**.

UNDERGROUND ECONOMY   see **economy**.

UNITY   Oneness, being *one*, singular or individual. Being of one mind or purpose; formed of parts, individuals, that constitute a coherent whole. Also expression of harmony, accord.

Should not be confused with uniformity, which is characterised by indistinguishability between the parts or individual constituents. Crystals are composed of identical molecules whose uniformity is expressed in regular geometric arrangements; rocks, by contrast, are an expression of the unity of the various substances combined in a particular yet irregular and *diverse* unity of *form*.

It is the combination of unity and *diversity* which is of interest to *greens*. Of the ability of essential expressions of individuality, of *diversity*, to *form coherent wholes*, unity, without the need to sacrifice that *diversity* in the *process*. Many *trees* make the *diversity* of the unified *forest*.

The frequent demand for conformity in *grey culture* human affairs is an expression of weakness, of insecurity in the *whole*, rather than an expression of the strength it is intended to illustrate. It is uniformity rather than unity.

Greens believe that humanity requires the unity of a global *green culture* which will express the *values* of *sustainability* in all human affairs and the enhancement of *life* in its interaction with the *biosphere*. Yet within that global *culture* there is room for infinite *diversity* of expression.

Relationships   **diversity, existence**.
See also   **dynamic, balance**.

UNIVERSAL CREDIT ECONOMY (UCE)   Means of providing livelihood within a *stock economy*.

UCE would *function* by giving everyone regular credit. This may be used to obtain the *means* of *existence* at an agreed subsistence level. Credit could be augmented by *work*; the amount of reward being related to both the necessity of the *function* and the contribution it makes to *sustainability*, contribution to *life*, etc. Those who are *self-sufficient*, using only local *renewable resources*, would tend to accumulate credit, whereas dependent *consumers* would not.

Such a *system* would have to relate to the *dynamics* of *life* within a *self-reliant community*, and would involve basic questions of the *numbers* of people a *community* could *sustain* and the overall long-term viability of the *community* as a *whole*. It would also require a global *system* of credit related to a universal constant asset value of the *sustainable resource* base available to humans (as human *numbers* decrease this resource base should also decrease, leaving more for other species).

UCE economics would thus involve many other aspects of a *sustainable way of life*; *morph-mapping*, a *balanced biosphere*, the establishment of *universal rights*, parameters of *sustainability*, fulfilment of *potential*. By these means the human *economy* would be brought within the *dynamics of life* and the global *environment*, rather than, as at present, *consuming* both. The human *way of life* would become *sustainable* rather than *terminal*.

Those who *consume* less would save more, and saving would mean saving the planet, not investing in *consuming* the *future*. Periodic adjustments of savings would allocate more space/*resources* to those who use least, such as *natural self-sustaining peoples*. Thus the meek would inherit the earth ...

Relationships   **economy, stock, sustainability.**
See also   **finite resources, balance, numbers.**

UNIVERSE   All existing things, the whole creation.

Cosmology is the science or theory of the universe, of its *nature*, origin and *dynamics*.

All *philosophies* produce a picture of *existence* in its most absolute obtainable *form* compatible with the tenets of the *philosophy*. Thus the more dogmatic the *philosophy* becomes, the more fixed its view of *creation*, *existence*, etc. Thus *greens* have no fixed views of a cosmology of the universe, but accept that its *nature* is subject to the general *principles* which are discerned in all things: a *cyclic dynamic, coherence, holism*, subject to *evolution* and the expression of *diverse morphologies*.

Any cosmology is an assessment of the universe which bears the marks of the age which produces it. Humanity has described the totality of *existence* in many ways: as divine *creation* with *earth* and humanity at its *centre*; as a vast machine subject to immutable laws; and as dancing quantum serendipity. *Green* cosmology will doubtless be subject to *shifts* as *knowledge* expands beyond current possibilities.

The universe is as large as your mind can make it. The observable universe is a roughly egg-shaped globe some 26,000 million light years in diameter. The *limits* to observation form our subjective *existence* horizon. This horizon poses a *philosophical* question: If we know there must be galaxies beyond the *limit* at which we can detect them, then in what sense do they *exist*, apart from in our *minds*?

What and where the universe is are *questions* for endless speculation. From the inside we are *limited* to describing the cosmos as a total *inclusive* phenomenon. The manifestations can be seen in a grain of sand – *energy*, matter, form and space.

Theories of the origin of thè universe fall into two camps – the big bang and steady state. The big bang requires a moment of *creation*, before which there was nothing, or more probably a point singularity of all matter surrounded by wave-form *energy* (the primal atom). Instability caused the primal atom to expand at an instant, eventually to form the universe we experience today. By contrast the steady state holds that matter and *energy* are in constant interaction everywhere, and that the universe we experience is more or less *stable* and indefinite.

The best explanation of observable phenomena combines elements of both theories. At the point of initiation of the present universe, many phenomena interacted. At inception *time* raced, like an instantly released spring, and an infinity of dimensions were brought into being. As matter and *energy* expanded the number of dimensions declined and *time* slowed to now, its pace fixed by the velocity of aggregates of matter in space. The speed of light became the summary expression of the mass/energy state of the universe. Throughout all its *dynamic progress* the total *energy* of the universe remains constant, at zero, as all *energy* and *energy*/mass equations *balance*.[1]

We still search for a theory which will unify macro and micro states of *existence*. The quantum interaction of *energy* and matter may be seen as a dimensional residue, as may other manifestations which tend to underwrite the steady state theory. As *time* slows down the rate at which it decays will also slow, so steady state phenomena will tend to persist, co-existing within the declining evidence of the big bang.

The further development of *models* of cosmology depend upon two further propositions; that of infinite space, or of space defined by matter/*energy*. If we follow infinite space, the logic is that the universe will simply continue to expand, slowing in *time* as it becomes more diffuse, eventually losing all dimensions and ceasing to *exist*. The concept of space defined by matter allows a preferable, although not logically more defensible, outcome. While relying on the concept of nothing beyond space, linking the *existence* of space to matter/*energy* produces a *cyclic model*.

At some point in dimensional/*time* decay, local superaggregates of matter/*energy* (black holes) form. Eventually these link up by mutual attraction and absorb all the matter in the universe, with free *energy* forming a surrounding wave-form horizon beyond which is nothing. *Time* and *existence* will have ceased, until some random instability between the point of dimensionless matter and *energy*, leading to the escape of a photon for instance, initiates another expansion, another universe.

Tomorrow this *model* may seem as quaint and ridiculous as that produced by ancient *philosophers*, of the world as a hemisphere supported on the backs of four enormous elephants, all standing on the back of an even more over-size turtle. For now we live in a universe alive with its own logic, moving inexorably in an endless song of praise for *existence*. Why not just enjoy the moment?

Relationships   **existence, holism.**

References

1 Stephen W. Hawkins, 1988, *A Brief History of Time: From the Big Bang to Black Holes*, Transworld, London.

UTILITY   Usefulness, made or serving practical purpose.

In *green* belief, all artefacts should be characterised by maximum utility. By this it is meant that they should fulfil the required *function* with the best *efficiency* possible, and the artefact should last indefinitely, so that the *function* may be fulfilled indefinitely.

That is not to say that things need be drab or boring; form and *function* can express an *inherent* beauty which may be further increased by individual expression. In *grey culture* form, in the appearance of things, has taken over from *function*. Thus many things are made with appearance in mind rather than *function*; because of their lack of utility this amounts to manufactured *waste*.

<u>Relationships</u> **resources, sustainability, function.**
<u>See also</u> **waste.**

UTOPIA Imaginary place with perfect *social* and *political system*; ideally perfect place or state of things.

The problem with utopias is that one person's perfection is another's unacceptable imposition. Best seen as *models* of possibility, as expressions of *potential.* There may be as many utopias as people who wish to design them.

<u>Relationships</u> **models, systems, future.**
<u>See also</u> **freedom, responsibility.**
<u>References</u>

For a critical overview of utopias, from Plato's *Republic* to Huxley's *Brave New World,* see Marie Louise Berneri (1918–1949), 1950, 1982, *Journey Through Utopia*; 1950, Routledge & Kegan Paul, London; 1982, Freedom Press, Angel Alley, 84b Whitechapel High Street, London E1 7QX.

VALUE Worth, desirability, *utility*, qualities on which these depend.

The *grey* meaning of value usually relates to worth in money terms. Because of the distortion of *flow economics*, as well as shifting concepts of desirability, value in this sense is relative to the values of the *economic system* on the one hand and individual whim on the other (see **market**).

Green value is centred on the *quality* of enhancement of *life*. That which enhances life as a *whole* is valued, that which does not is not.

VALUES Beliefs and opinions, assumed qualities, expected properties.

End expression of sequency of belief; *philosophy, principles,* practice based upon values derived. Expression of *inherent* belief. Everything has a value, or involves a value judgment, in/of its *relationship* with others.

Some believe that *change* will only occur with a *change* in human values. However, without a change in the foundation *philosophy* to fix those values they will simply float, be the subject of fashion or whim, the desirability of the moment, the flavour of the month. The *green* task does involve changing human values, but it involves changing *philosophy* and *principles* as well (the long front described by Arne Naess). All must form a compatible *whole* in a *synergistic relationship* (see **system, structure**).

Thus, because of their shared *philosophy, greens* (or *greys*) will express a *way of life* based upon values held in common.

Relationships   **quality, principle, philosophy**.
See also   **perspective, quantity**.

VEGAN (see **food**)   Person who eats no animal products whatever.

Extended to mean person who uses no animal products, such as leather.

A *way of life*, which, although understandable in view of the excesses of *exploitation* in *grey culture*, is nevertheless of itself outside many *cycles of life*, for example in relying on *plastics* for clothing.

VEGETARIAN (see **food**) Person who does not eat meat, poultry or fish. Many vegetarians do consume animal products, such as milk, eggs, cheese, honey.

The further humans move north/south from their sub-tropical proto-*environment*, the more dependent they become upon animal sources of *food*. In the temperate zones animal residues are necessary to maintain soil fertility.

VICTIM see **structure, institutional process**.

VISION Act or faculty of seeing, sight. Imaginative insight, fore-sight, sagacity.

VISION EXCHANGE (see **exchange**) Part of *green movement*, various *means* for exploring possibilities for the *future*. Models, theories, *means*, are discussed, developed, criticised, by publi-cation, graffiti, meetings, computer *networks*.

VISUALISATION Process of forming concept, *idea*, into imaginary form. *Means* of relating to thing or *need* by giving it an inner form.

Used as *means* of focusing on a desirable end, a development of positive thinking. If you visualise a successful outcome you will aid the *creation* of that outcome. Dubiously applied in various *thera-pies*, where the opposite, i.e. the disease agent (usually cancer) is *visualised* rather than a *healthy whole*.

It is necessary to visualise *models* of a *sustainable future*. The act of *creation* is first to see, to feel, *intuitively* to *know*, what is possible, what is compatible with what is desired and so to encourage its emergence into *reality*.

The first Rule of Bicycle Riding:
How to improve your chances of staying on your bike and getting to where you would like to be.
If you look at the hazards you will go towards them; unless they are in your path and absolutely unavoidable, ignore them, go round. Focus firmly on where you want to go, if the structure is appropriate and the process right the problems will be left behind.[1]

Relationships **intuition, anticipation, morphology**.
See also **utopia, creation, system**.

References

1 Colin Johnson, 1991, *The Green Bible: Creating Sustainable Life on Earth*, Thorsons, London.

VITAL   Of or concerned with or essential to *life*; essential to *existence* of a thing, or to the matter in hand. Also in negative sense; a vital wound, loss, etc., being fatal.

VITAL NEED(S)   Many things vital to *grey culture* and its *terminal progress* are vital losses to the *environment* and *biosphere*. Because this dichotomy of *dynamics* is *unsustainable*, humans have to redirect their *culture*. This is a vital need for the *future* of all *life*. Unless the vital needs of all species are expressed and fulfilled in concert, the *whole* will eventually fail. *Green philosophy*, thought and action are concerned with the expression of such vital needs.

At an individual level the expression of the vital need of one will amount to the denial of that vital need in others, simply by essential *participation* in the *food network* (see **food**).

The *balance* of *life* must be maintained in terms of species rather than individuals. The vital need for any species, or sub-species, is to *survive*. Human action is denying this *need* on an incomprehensible scale to unknown numbers of species as part of its *terminal progress*. Beyond this *basic need*, we come into the area of *rights* (see **rights**).

Within a *structure* of *universal rights* we encounter the ultimate dilemma of *stewardship*. How should the choice be made between species? Is it over-presumptuous to assume that the decision is ours? Humanity has so disrupted the *dynamics* of *natural processes* that it is unlikely we shall be able to avoid the *question* in *future*. What are the criteria for *survival*? That species thought to be of 'higher' intelligence, or that which is vital to more other species? More debate will be needed on such *problems*.

Relationships   **balance, rights, life, contract, Gaia.**

See also   **sustainable, numbers, morphology.**

WALDSTERBEN   (German = forest-death)

Since 1980, many forests in the eastern US and parts of Europe have suffered a loss of vitality – a loss that could not be linked to any of the familiar causes, such as insects, disease or direct poisoning by a specific air or water pollutant. The most dramatic reports have come from Germany, where scientists, stunned by the extent and speed of the decline, have called it Waldsterben.[1]

Thought to be the result of low level *ozone* poisoning which damages the needle-like leaves of coniferous trees. Combined with *acid rain* and acid winter mists, *ozone* poisoning is stripping the *forests* from much of the temperate zone of the planet (see **acid rain**).

When the *trees* are gone the soil will follow; deserts will spread as the climate changes and the water cycle speeds up; flash floods will change local *environments* and *ecosystems*; rising sea levels will add to the disruption. To save the planet, plant *trees* and cut down on people and *pollution*.

Relationships   **pollution, economy**.

See also   **forest**.

References

1 *Scientific American*, quoted in P.H. Collin, 1988, *Dictionary of Ecology and the Environment*, Peter Collin Publishing, Teddington, Middlesex, England.

WAR (see **peace**)   Armed conflict, usually between nation states, or factions fighting for control of state or other institution.

'Der Krieg ist nicht anderes als die Fortsetzung der Politik mit anderen Mitteln.' (War is nothing more than the continuation of politics by other means).[1]

Some believe that human aggressive patterns are part of the *genetic* programming of a naturally territorial, reproductively *hierarchical* animal.[2] War is an *extension* of this behaviour which became *institutionalised*[3] in human affairs under the dictum of Vegetius so dear to the hearts and *minds* of *grey culture politicians*: 'Qui desiderat pacem, praeparet bellum' (Let him who desires peace prepare for war).[4]

It cannot be denied that a significant part of individual human *nature* likes war, is excited by the concept and fascinated by the prospect and experience of the extremes that the situation of ultimate conflict produces. When this propensity is combined with *institutional* direction the mechanics of war become undeniable. Those who stand against the tide of conflict are a notable minority. *Anarchists* have always believed that war is a *structurally inherent* part of the nation state – 'War is the health of the state' – and many others have supported this view.[5]

In terms of historic and present human *culture* war may be seen as a local *socio-cultural sink*; a means of temporary relief from *compression*, of expressing a counterbalancing irresponsibility, of cleaning out the surplus people and materials which clog the *economic flow system* from time to time, of crude refinement by *waste* and attrition.

It is pointless being anti-war in *grey culture*. Pacifists are led into a *structured process* of *thematic compatibility* by the *culture* of which they and war are inseparable parts. The only answer is to be pro-some other *model* (*peace*, as the absence of war, is as illusory as *health* being the absence of disease), a *model* of *culture* which is *structured* for peace as a positive *dynamic* of behaviour. If you want *peace*, prepare for *peace*.

And yet, if Lorenz[2] is right and our fascination with war seems to confirm his analysis, there will be *limits* to the *socio-cultural* and *environmental* modification of a basic urge of human *nature*. Even if the 1960s prescription 'Make Love Not War' were carried to its logical and extreme conclusion, it may not still the insistence of the equally powerful and closely parallel internal wiring of the human brain where the sexual and aggressive *systems* are closely associated. We may have to make some rational provision for those driven to express this part of themselves.

Those with undeniable blends of John Wayne romanticism and tomcat urges, wishing to experience ultimate irresponsibility and personal jeopardy, could be sent to an isolated area, such as the Malvinas/Falkland Islands, landed on either East or West to fight against the other. Conditions equal to, say, the extremes and weaponry of the Boer wars could be provided. *Survivors* could be allowed to return to *community* or continue as desired.

Relationships   **nature, power, competition, hierarchy, institution**.

See also   **human scale, community**.

References

1 Carl Von Clausewitz (1780–1831), translated 1873, 1989 *Vom Kriege* (On War) Princeton University Press, Princeton, New Jersey, USA.

2 See Austrian zoologist Konrad Lorenz. Lorenz's later work dealt with the evolution or behavioural patterns that enable species to survive. In *On Aggression*, 1963, English translation 1966, Harcourt Brace Jovanovich, San Diego, California, USA: he argued that aggression is genetically programmed in humans, but may be environmentally modified.

3 St Augustine (354–430), *The City of God*:

The true believer must not condemn war but must look upon it as a necessary evil, as a punishment which God has imposed upon men. For war is, like pestilence and famine and all other evils only a visitation of God for the chastisement of men for their betterment, and to prepare them for salvation.

4 Flavius Vegetius Renatus, fourth century, AD, produced after 375 AD *Epitome Institutionum Rei Militaris*, mainly extracted from other works, which during the Middle Ages was the reference text on matters of warfare.

5 Charles, Baron de Montesquieu (1689–1755), *Considérations sur les causes de la grandeur des Romains et de leur décadence*, Chapter 8, 'An empire founded on war has to maintain itself by war'.

Also Guy de Maupassant (1850–93), French novelist, as quoted by Leo Tolstoy (Count Leo Nikolayevitch Tolstoi, 1828–1910), in *Bethink Yourselves*:

War is held in greater esteem than ever. A skilled proficient in this business, that murderer of genius, von Moltke, once replied to some peace delegates in the following terrible words:

'War is sacred, it is instituted by God, it is one of the divine laws of the world, it upholds in men all the great and noble sentiments – honour, self-sacrifice, virtue, and courage. It is war alone that saves men from falling into the grossest materialism.'

To assemble four hundred thousand men in herds, to march night and day without rest, with no time to think, read, or study, without being of the least use to anybody, wallowing in filth, sleeping in mud, living like animals in continual stupefaction, sacking towns, burning villages, ruining the whole population, and then meeting similar masses of human flesh and falling upon them, shedding rivers of blood, strewing the fields with mangled bodies mixed with mud and blood; losing arms and legs and having brains blown out for no benefit to anyone and dying somewhere on a field while your old parents and your wife and children are perishing of hunger – that is called saving men from falling into the grossest materialism!

WASTE   Expend or employ to no *purpose*, or for inadequate result; use extravagantly or ineffectually.

Waste is the unique human product.

There is no waste in *nature*; everything is part of some *cyclic process*, at some stage in the *energy*/matter transference of the *life* of the *whole*.

Human waste has many dimensions: the excessive, unnecessary *consumption* of the *Impossible Party,* supported by waste as a necessary, *inherent,* part of *flow economics*; as generalised effects of human *numbers* on the *biosphere*; in the locking of materials outside *life* and *utility cycles* as non-*bio-assimilable pollution.* Waste is the product of all human activity which diminishes the totality of *life* on the planet, the *consumption* of the *future* to no purpose other than to hasten *terminality.*

A *sustainable future* demands the elimination of waste. The products of one *process* must be incorporated into others, the end of one forming the beginning of others; all in a state of *balance* within the capacity of the *biosphere. Finite resources* must be used with maximum *utility*; such substances should be treated as if they had to last for ever.

Relationships   **pollution, rubbish, resources.**
See also   **balance, cycles, sustainability.**
References

For a thousand and one ways to help reduce waste, see Bernadette Vallely, 1990, *1001 Ways to Save The Planet*, Penguin, London.

WAVE ENERGY   see **energy.**

WEALTH   Riches, large possessions, opulence, being rich; abundance, profusion, great quantities.

Terminal culture equates wealth with possession of *resources* or material products, with the amount of *flow economic* products an individual can retain.

Humanity has yet to discover the real wealth of the world; to *evolve* our primitive behaviour from obsession with collecting the fabric of the planet and *consuming* it in excessive ways or locking it in vaults or *pollution.* The wealth of the planet is its *diversity* of *life*, its riches the continual interactions of its many expanding *cycles.* When humans discover the *ecstasy* of *ecology* and learn to live within the *limits* of the planet, wealth will be an *inherent* expression of existence rather than something to be acquired at the expense of others.

Relationships   **terminal culture, flow economics.**
See also   **ecology, finite resources, sustainability.**

WEB (see **network**)   Woven fabric, thing connected in two or three dimensions.

Useful metaphor for things, *ideas*, connected or forming a

coherent whole. 'Each link in a web is fragile, but woven together creates a strong and coherent whole. A web with few links is weak and can be broken, but the more threads it is composed of, the greater its strength'[1] (see **diversity**).

WEB OF LIFE   Used to describe the living content of the *Gaian whole.*

Relationships   **life, Gaia, matrix, network.**

See also   **synergy, symbiosis.**

References

1 Alice Cook and Gwyn Kirk, 1983, *Greenham Women Everywhere.*

WEED   'What is a weed? A plant whose virtues have not been discovered.'[1]

References

1 Ralph Waldo Emerson (1803–82), *Fortune of the Republic.*

WHOLE   see **holism.**

WHOLEFOODS (see **food**)   Whole, unadulterated, although not necessarily *organic*, staple, unrefined and minimally processed foods.

WILDERNESS   Area of planet without human influence.

There is no pure wilderness; human activity has spread *pollution* to every part of the planet (see **restoration**).

WIND ENERGY   see **energy.**

WISDOM   Being wise; possession of experience and *knowledge*, together with the power of critical or practical application.

The capacity for integration with the logic of *existence*; its understanding, interpretation, and *anticipation.* The ability to perceive possibilities and *limits* (see **ethics, choice**).

EARTH WISDOM   The *inherent* capacity of *nature*, and the *Gaian whole*, to self-regulate and fulfil its *potential.*

We may not need something new, but need to reawaken something very old, to reawaken our understanding of Earth Wisdom. In the broadest sense, we need to accept the invitation to the dance – the dance of unity of humans, plants, animals, the Earth.[1]

Relationships   **inherent.**

References

1 Bill Devall and George Sessions, 1985, *Deep Ecology: Living as if Nature Mattered*, Peregrine Smith Books, Salt Lake City, Utah, USA.

WORDS   'Ready for our escape, we created a kingdom of free words' (East European poet, speaking in late 1990).

WORK   Expenditure of energy, striving, application of effort or exertion to a *purpose*.

Within *grey culture* work has come to mean paid employment, regardless of point or *purpose*. Unpaid work, no matter how essential, is discounted.

Work, in the sense of the *creative* expenditure of *energy* in excess of that required to maintain *life*, is essential to humans. It is an *extension* of play in recreation seen in many species.

WORKER CO-OPERATIVE   see **co-operative**.

REAL WORK   The focus of effort on those things essential for the *future* (see **future provision**).

For *greens* this means the work of really looking at ourselves, of becoming more *real*; and *extending* ourselves for the *future* by the work of *conscious evolution*. 'The real work is what we have to do, knowing that we are real, and that the world is real, then it becomes right. And that's the real work: to make the world as real as it is and to find ourselves as real as we are within it.'[1]

But we must also beware of the over-simplification of human *nature*. We are star-stuff and butterflies, eagles and mice, quiet and tumultuous, *inherently* as paradoxical as *life*. And we must live within *reality* and have intimate understanding of all its *processes*, but if we are tied to it our *minds* will die and our *spirit* have no expression.

Relationships   **create, spirituality, potential**.

See also   **exploitation, limits**.

References

1 Gary Snyder, 1980, 'The Real Work', in *New Directions*, New York, USA.

XENOBIOTIC (foreign to life) *Artificial* substances, especially those which *pollute*, or distort, *life* structures.
<u>Relationships</u> **pollution, artificial**.

YIN/YANG Female (yin) and male (yang) – *principles* of Chinese *philosophy* which are held to permeate all of *nature*. According to Chinese *philosophy*, yin and yang must be maintained in *balance*. Yin is the passive female *principle* of the *universe*; yang is the active male *principle*.

As an expression of *natural* duality (or paradox) it is sometimes used to support the duality of the *reductionism* of the West (see **Cartesianism**). In Chinese *philosophy* yin and yang were not seen as divisive, but as complementary parts of the *whole*.

Relationships   **philosophy, holism**.

See also   **sexual dimorphism**.

ZEN Zen is as near as English can get to a transliteration of 'a Japanese translation of a Chinese translation (ch'an) of the Sanskrit word (dhyana) for meditation'.[1]

A form of Buddhism emphasising the *value* of meditation and *intuitive* insight.

Known in the West for the *creative* use of paradox, e.g. 'An independent reality in the ordinary sense can neither be ascribed to the phenomenon nor to the agencies of observations.'[2] Or 'As far as the laws of mathematics refer to reality, they are not certain; as far as they are certain, they do not refer to reality.'[3] And the more traditional, 'It does not matter how slowly you go so long as you do not stop.'[4]

Zen insights may be seen as a modern counterpart of the Tao. And, to my *mind*, as an expression of the *spirituality* of the *mind*.

References

1 From Jon Winokur, 1989, *Zen to Go*, Plume Books, New American Library, Penguin Books, New York.
2 Niels Henrik David Bohr (1885–1962), Danish physicist, quoted in 1.
3 Albert Einstein (1879–1955), German mathematician and physicist, quoted in 1.
4 Confucius (K'ung Fu-tse) (551–479 BC), Chinese philosopher.

  See Byron Kennard on the Zen of social activism, *Nothing Can Be Done, Everything is Possible*; also the recently popular book, Robert Pirsig, 1974, *Zen and the Art of Motorcycle Maintenance*, Bodley Head, London, in some ways a processed derivation of the previous generations' source of insight, Eugen Herrigel, *Zen in the Art of Archery*, Arkana, London.

ZERO POPULATION GROWTH (ZPG) (see **numbers**) The idea that human population must be stabilised.

If the human population is not contained and returned to *sustainable* levels, as far as any worthwhile *future* is concerned it will simply be the end.

LIST OF ENTRIES